A Java GUI Programmer's Primer

Fintan Culwin
South Bank University, London

An Alan R. Apt Book

Prentice Hall
Upper Saddle River, New Jersey 07458

Library of Congress Cataloging-in-Publication Data

Culwin, Fintan
    A Java GUI Programmer's Primer,
Fintan Culwin.
        p. cm.
    Includes bibliographical references and index.
    ISBN: 0-13-908849-0
    CIP DATA AVAILABLE

Publisher: **ALAN APT**
Acquisitions editor: **LAURA STEELE**
Editor-in-chief: **MARCIA HORTON**
Production editor: **IRWIN ZUCKER**
Managing editor: **BAYANI MENDOZA DE LEON**
Copy editor: **SHARYN VITRANO**
Director of production and manufacturing: **DAVID W. RICCARDI**
Cover director: **JAYNE CONTE**
Manufacturing buyer: **PAT BROWN**
Editorial assistant: **TONI HOLM**
Cover illustration: A Courtesan Dreaming of Her Wedding by Kitagawa Utamoro
(British Museum, London/ Bridgeman Art Library, London/Superstock)

©1998 by Prentice-Hall, Inc.
 Simon & Schuster / A Viacom Company
Upper Saddle River, New Jersey 07458

Printed in the United States of America

10 9 8 7 6 5 4 3 2 1

ISBN   0-13-908849-0

Prentice-Hall International (UK) Limited, London
Prentice-Hall of Australia Pty. Limited, Sydney
Prentice-Hall Canada Inc., Toronto
Prentice-Hall Hispanoamericana, S.A., Mexico
Prentice-Hall of India Private Limited, New Delhi
Prentice-Hall of Japan, Inc., Tokyo
Simon & Schuster Asia Pte. Ltd., Singapore
Editora Prentice-Hall do Brasil, Ltda., Rio de Janeiro

**. . . In memory of
Maria's drawers. . . .**

this book makes much more modest claims about what it might be able to do for the

Preface

The digital Webster dictionary application running on my workstation defines *primer* as

> ... a small introductory book ...

Alongside my workstation there is a collection of Java reference books. A quick Web search reveals that, despite Java being less than two years old, there are already well over one hundred books about Java published. I feel that I should justify adding further to this plethora which already includes other introductory books.

This book is described as a *primer* in contrast with the many *tome*s some of which contain well over a thousand pages and promise on the cover to teach the reader everything they need to know about Java programming in a frighteningly short period of time. I have been involved with teaching Software Engineering and Software Development for over two decades and my minimum estimate for the transition from novice developer to an initial competence would, for an exceptional student, be in the order of two years. For an experienced developer, without experience of GUI design and development, a shorter period of time might be required by many new concepts and considerations would have to be assimilated and new skills practiced. Consequently this book makes much more modest claims about what it might be able to do for the reader.

AWT and GUIs

This book assumes that the reader is already minimally competent in Object-Oriented Software Development and has some experience of implementation using C++ or Java. (If you are reading this preface with a view to starting to learn Software Development, and Java, from scratch, you should be reading the preface of my *Java: An Object First Approach* book instead.) This book is intended to allow readers with this minimal competence to obtain an initial competence in the skills involved in using the Java Abstract Windowing Toolkit (AWT) to develop applets and applications which have a Graphical User Interface (GUI).

The development of GUIs adds a further layer of considerations, and complications, to those already involved in the development of general purpose software artifacts. The first of these considerations is that such interfaces must have usability engineered into them from the outset. In the recent history of computing there have been two products, Apple's Hypercard and Microsoft's Visual Basic, which have given developers both an environment and a platform to produce highly interactive graphical artifacts. Despite some excellent applications produced using these tools the average quality of products developed with them has been abysmal.

The reason for this is that, in some senses, they have been too easy to use allowing unskilled and untrained programmers to produce GUIs which do not embody any consideration of the user. Some years ago an educator in California asked on the Usenet comp.lang.visualbasic newsgroup if anyone could advise her on design techniques which she could introduce to her students. There was absolutely no reply from the global community of Visual Basic developers. Concerned about this she asked again, more insistently, and received a single reply. The author of the reply admitted that they too did not know how to design Visual Basic applications but recommended my book on X/ Motif as a good place to start.

User Interface Models

It is against this background that I prepared this book. Like the X/ Motif book the central consideration is the modeling of a user interface in the form of State Transition Diagrams (STDs). From these it is possible to divide the application and its interface into three areas of concern: the visible part of the interface, the program logic which controls it and communicates with the third part which provides the application's functionality. This concern with usability from the outset of the design and production process attempts to ensure that the artifacts produced have a high level of both software engineering quality and usability.

Key Features

- Unified Modeling Language design notation consistently used and emphasized.

- Exclusive use of release 1.1 of Java and its AWT.

- Interface usability modeled using State Transition Diagrams (STDs).

- Software design by consistent use of class and instance diagrams.

- An example of every 1.1 AWT component included.

- A case study illustrating different user interface styles.

- Internationalization and localization techniques.

- Production of specialized components covered.

Overview

The book starts in Chapter 1 with an overview of the developmental process where an initial artifact is designed and produced. Chapter 2 then briefly introduces each of the components which the AWT supplies. Chapter 3 starts the process of illustrating how the existing components can be extended by the developer to satisfy particular requirements. This is considerably easier in Java than in any other common GUI development environment and is central to the production of high quality interfaces.

Interface Styles

Chapters 4, 5, 6, and 7 can be thought of as a case study where four different styles of interface are provided for a single application. The application chosen is a Logo style turtle graphics environment known as the tuttle. Some of the interface styles presented are dramatically unsuitable for the controlling of a tuttle. However the intention is that these techniques for the construction of these styles of interface can be applied where the style would be more appropriate. The first of these chapters, introducing the tuttle, also provides an introduction to Java's general purpose graphical and image processing capability.

Internationalization

Chapter 8 extends the functionality of the tuttle, and of its interfaces to encompass undo, save and load capabilities. The final chapter, Chapter 9, introduces Java's facilities for customization, localization, and internationalization. The importance of these considerations belies their location in the sequence; however it would not be possible to introduce these techniques before Chapter 3. Consequently Chapter 9 could be read following Chapter 3, before the tuttles are considered.

UML

Appendix A supplies information concerning other resources which might prove useful. Appendix B contains the source code for some of the classes which do not seem important enough to be included in their corresponding chapters. Appendix C discusses the terminology used in this book compared with the terminology used in other resources. This appendix also provides a reference to those parts of the Unified Modeling Language (UML) notation which is used to express the STDs, class, and instance diagrams.

Java Standards

At the time of completing this book, version *1.1.5* of Java, and of its AWT, had just been released. (Details of how to obtain it are contained in Appendix A.) All of the source code in this book has been compiled with the *-deprecation* flag against Sun's 1.1.5 *javac* compiler. During this process I noticed that several constructs which should have caused a deprecation warning to be issued, indicating that they should only be used with the 1.0 Java version, were compiled without comment.

Website

Consequently, although I think that the book is fully compliant with the 1.1 specification, and makes no use of 1.0 constructs which should not be used, I cannot be certain of this. Likewise although I have carefully engineered all the examples used in the book, and tested them on Windows 95, Unix and, partially, on Macintosh platforms, I cannot be certain that there are not any remaining bugs. All I can do is ask that if a reader finds any use of 1.0 facilities, or uncovers any bugs, they should e-mail me the details and I will maintain a list of problems on the Web site associated with my Java books. The URL of this site is given at the end of the preface.

Typography

The typographic convention adopted is to use *normal italic text* whenever a new technical term is introduced, or its meaning significantly elaborated. Helvetica is used for any Java terms used with **bold Helvetica** for reserved words and *italic Helvetica* for developer decided terms. Program listings are in `small courier` with preceding four digit line numbers. Phrases from design schematics which do not directly translate into program terms are also presented in *normal italic*.

This is the fifth book I have written in the last six years and I have promised my family after completing each that that I would not start another one, at least for some time. They have accepted this promise with more than a pinch of salt and have not complained (too much) about my self-imposed incarceration in my office at times when I should have spent more time with them. Although they are getting rather passé about seeing their names in print; Maria, Leah, and Seana are still providing plenty of hot coffee and patience.

Peter Chalk again took it upon himself to critique each chapter in detail at various stages in its production. This was twice the task associated with previous books and he did not complain when the 1.0 draft was rewritten to 1.1. standards. Jackie Harbor was again consistently supportive and made herself immediately available when consultations about the book's production were required. The proximity of the best pizza restaurant in London (the Castillo at the Elephant and Castle) had very little to do with this. Derek Mosely and Alison Stanford provided efficient and effective support to Jackie at Prentice Hall. A selection of students at South Bank had, for them, the rather un-unique experience of allowing themselves to be guinea pigs for yet another of my books. Their experiences with the tuttles chapters in particular revealed several obscure and subtle faults.

I would also like to thank Robert Hermann of Sun Microsystems and Jack Hodges of San Francisco State University, who reviewed the manuscript.

Fintan Culwin
South Bank University: London
fintan@sbu.ac.uk
http:\\www.sbu.ac.uk\jfl

Contents

CHAPTER 1

An Introduction to Java and STD Design

This book contains an introduction to the systematic development of Graphical User Interfaces (GUIs) using the Java environment. It does not attempt to introduce the Java language and it is assumed that the reader has some familiarity with Object Oriented Development (OOD) and its practical expression in Java. Suitable resources to assist with obtaining this knowledge are given in Appendix A. However, a brief explanation of some aspects of Java will be presented where appropriate, particularly where the aspect differs significantly from C++.

The Java Development Kit (*JDK*), also known as the Java environment, consists of a Java compiler producing Java bytecode which can be interpreted by a run time engine, for example Sun's *appletviewer*, to run Java programs. However the substantive part of the environment consists of the extensive collection of **package**s, **class**es and **interface**s collectively known as the Java Application Programmer Interface (*API*). The most important part of the API, so far as this book is concerned, is the Abstract Windowing Toolkit (*AWT*) containing the user interface *components* from which GUIs are constructed.

In this book whenever a Java reserved word is used this **bold alternative** font will be used. The alternative font by itself will indicate the use of an API resource and an *italic alternative font* for developer supplied Java resources. The *italicised normal font* will be used when a new technical term is introduced for the first time or when its meaning is significantly extended. This *italicised font* is also used when a design fragment is referred to which cannot be identified by a corresponding Java term. A similar convention is used in program listings where `this bold font` indicates Java's reserved words, `italic  font` indicates developer supplied resources and `normal font` Java API resources.

This first, introductory, chapter introduces the systematic development of Graphical User Interfaces which a user can interact with in order to control an underlying application. This is done by the exposition of the development process involved in the construction of a relatively trivial application. The considerations, stages, and proce-

1

dures involved may seem to be far too complex for this application's requirements. However, the processes presented in this chapter are essential for the successful development of more complex GUIs and it is only by practicing and perfecting these skills on relatively simple applications that they can be successfully applied to more complex ones.

1.1 The *ClickCounter* Application Class

This book is concerned with the development of user interfaces, not with the production of the applications to which the interfaces provide access. One of the most basic software engineering principles is to divide a specification into separate concerns and to implement each concern as an independent program module. For specifications which include a graphical user interface, this would imply that the application and its interface should be developed independently. This design principle has the consequence of allowing the application modules to be reused with differing styles of user interface, or even used in embedded applications that do not have any direct interaction with a user.

Design Advice

Keep the application and interface functionality clearly separated in the design and consequently in the implementation.

In order to concentrate on user interfaces, the detailed design and implementation of the application-level classes will not be presented in the text. Appendix B includes the source code of some of the application classes which are used throughout the book.

For this initial example, an application known as a *ClickCounter* will be developed. It is based upon the small mechanical devices which are sometimes used to count people as they enter a room. The device consists of a counting button and a numeric display; every time the counting button is pressed, the value on the display is incremented by one. A second button is used to reset the display to zero.

The application-level object which implements this requirement has had its functionality extended beyond this minimal requirement, for reasons which will be described later. The class diagram of the *ClickCounter* class is shown in Figure 1.1.

A class diagram illustrates the resources which instances of a class will supply, details of the class diagram notation used in this book are given in Appendix C. This diagram indicates, at the top, that the *ClickCounter* class is an extension of the pre-supplied Java Object class. Each instance of the class contains three encapsulated *data attributes*[1]: *minimumCount*, *maximumCount*, and *clicksCounted*. As encapsulated resources they are totally **private** to the class and cannot be seen or referenced from anything outside the class.

---

[1]The term *data attribute* is used in the description of the Unified Modeling Language design notation. The Java White paper, which describes the Java language, would use the term *field*. A discussion of the terms used in this book and the terms used in other documents and environment is contained in Appendix C.

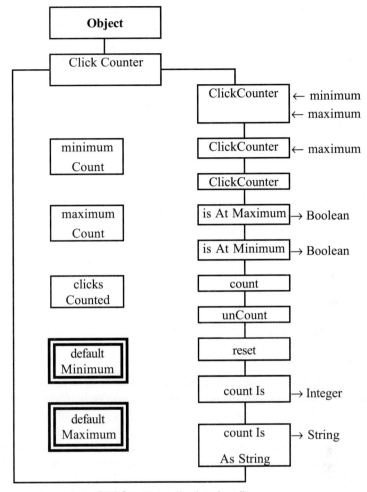

Figure 1.1   *ClickCounter* application class diagram.

The *minimumCount* and *maximumCount* attributes delineate the range of values which the *ClickCounter* will count through, and the *clicksCounted* attribute is the current number of occurrences counted. The class also contains two **private** *class wide* constant attributes for the *DEFAULT_MINIMUM* and *DEFAULT_MAXIMUM* of the range; in this implementation they are set to 0 and 999.

Resources shown crossing the right side of a class diagram are fully **public** and so are totally visible outside the class. The first three of these resources have the same name as the class and so are *constructors*. The purpose of a constructor is to create an instance of the class and place it into a well-defined initial state.

The first constructor has two arguments, shown as incoming data flows labeled *minimum* and *maximum*, which allow the range of values to be counted between to be fully specified. The second constructor requires only the *maximum* value to be specified using *DEFAULT_MINIMUM* for the *minimum* value. The last constructor uses the defaults for the *minimum* and *maximum* values.

The next two **public** resources are *inquiry methods,* which can be used to determine the state of the **private** resources. These two methods both return a **boolean** value, as shown on the outgoing data flow. The first of these methods is called *isAtMaximum()* and will return **true** if the value of *clicksCounted* is equal to the value of *maximumCount,* and **false** otherwise. The *isAtMinimum()* method is similar but compares the values of *clicksCounted* and *minimumCount.*

The following three methods embody the essential functionality of the click counter. The *count()* method will increment the value of *clicksCounted* unless it is at its maximum value, in which case the value will not be changed. The *unCount()* method will likewise decrement the value of *clicksCounted* unless it is at its minimum. The *reset()* method will reset the value of *clicksCounted* to the minimum value as established upon construction. The final two resources are inquiry methods which return the value of the *ClickCounter* as an **int**eger and as a three-character String formatted with leading zeros.

One difference between the functionality of the mechanical click counter and of this software model concerns its behavior at the maximum limit of its range. If a mechanical click counter is at the maximum of its range, a press of its counting button will cause its value to change to the minimum of the range. This software model will not do this and will not even give any warning if the *count()* method is called when it is at its maximum. The consequences of this consideration will be explored later.

1.2 The *ClickCounter* Behavioral Design

State Transition Diagrams (STDs) are used to design the interaction which the user will have with the application, and from   this the behavior of the user interface. Using the behavior of the mechanical click counter as a starting point, the first version of a possible STD design for the artifact is given in Figure 1.2.

A STD consists of one or more states, shown as rectangular boxes, connected by transitions shown as arrows. The state boxes can also be used to give an indication of

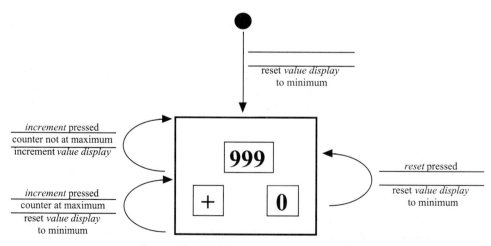

Figure 1.2 *ClickCounter*— mechanical STD.

the appearance of the interface while in that state. A solid circle indicates the start of a STD and is associated with an initial transition leading to the initial state of the interface. Transition arrows can have three labels associated with them: the first label is the event which must occur for the transition to be considered; the second label is the precondition which must be true for the transition to be followed; and the last label indicates the consequences of taking the transition.

It is possible for the event label to be blank, in which case the transition will be considered as soon as the interface arrives in the state. The precondition will be continually tested and the transition will be taken as soon as it evaluates true. It is also possible for the precondition label to be blank, in which case the transition will be taken as soon as the event occurs. It is also possible for the consequences label to be blank, in which case only a state change occurs when the transition is followed.

There is no terminal transition in this design, which would be shown as a transition leading to a bulls-eyed circle. Consequently, this artifact will continue interacting with the user until it is destroyed using operating system facilities.

A STD design provides an objective model of the state changes taking place as the user interacts with the interface. As such, it describes the behavior of an application and its interface. Further details of STD notation can be found in Appendix C.

The initial transition at the top of this design indicates that the minimum value is always displayed when the click counter user interface is first shown to the user. The main part of the diagram indicates that this design has a single state to which all transactions return. The significant parts of the *clickCounter* interface are illustrated within the state box. These are: the *value display*, shown as **999,** the *increment button*, shown as **"+"** and the *reset button*, shown as **"0"**. Illustrating the contents of the *value display* as **999** indicates that it can display any three digits between 000 and 999.

The single state has three possible transitions, all of which lead back to itself. The simplest transition is shown on the right of the diagram and is associated with a press of the *reset button*. The absence of a *precondition* indicates that this transition will always be followed when the *reset button* is pressed. The *consequence* of this transition is to reset the *value display* to its minimum value. One consideration here might be that the *reset button* can be pressed while the counter is at its minimum value, causing it to be reset to its minimum value. The alternative possibility, stating the *precondition* that *value display* should not be at its minimum value for the transition to be followed, seems to add complexity for no particular benefit.

The other two transitions are associated with the pressing of the *increment button*. The transition at the top is taken when the *value display* is not at its maximum value and results in the *value display* being incremented. The third transition, at the bottom, is followed when the *increment button* is pressed and the *value display* is at its maximum. This transition results in the *value display* being reset to its minimum value.

This STD design describes the interface designer's cognitive model of a simple mechanical click counter, and can form the basis of the design of the user interface which will be provided for this application. However, the provision of a software artifact which models a real world object need not be limited to the behavior in the real-world. It is possible, and in most cases desirable, for the software model to extend or augment real-world behavior.

The first change from the mechanical click counter's real-world appearance and behavior is to consider the provision of a *decrement button* (**-**), which can be used to un-count an occurrence. This change will add functionality to the software application which is not present in the physical artifact, in order to make it more useful.

The second change is to modify the behavior of the counter so that it cannot be incremented beyond the maximum of its range or decrement below the minimum of its range. This change is somewhat arbitrary and has been made in order to introduce some usability considerations in the designs which follow. The first possible STD design for this extended artifact is shown in Figure 1.3.

In this design, the *increment* and *decrement* buttons have appropriate *preconditions* which prevent their transitions being followed if the *value display* is showing its maximum or minimum value, respectively. One consequence of this design refinement is that if the counter is at its maximal state the user may press the increment button with nothing apparently happening. If the user is not paying too close attention to the application while this happens, they may be unaware that their clicks are not being counted. There is a corresponding problem when the counter is at the minimum of its range. One possible solution to this problem is shown in a second design refinement, given in Figure 1.4.

This design alerts the user to the unavailability of the counting functionality at the limits of its range by *posting* a *modal* error *dialog* if the appropriate button is pressed. These dialogs should contain an appropriate message explaining to the user why the application is unable to perform the action they have requested. A *modal* dialog will allow no interaction with the application it is posted from, until the dialog is attended to and *dismissed*. This is accomplished, in this design, by pressing the *OK button*, which causes the transition back to the counting state to be followed.

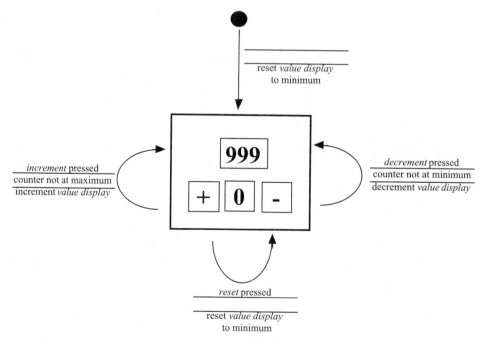

Figure 1.3 Extended *ClickCounter*, first STD design.

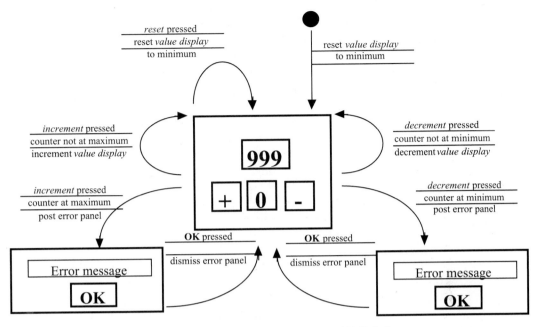

Figure 1.4   Extended *ClickCounter*, second STD design.

The problem with this design is that it allows the user to request an action which the application is unable to fulfill. On the basis that prevention is better than cure, the third (and final) design refinement for the *clickCounter* application interface is given in Figure 1.5.

This design has refined the *ClickCounter* into three distinct states: the *minimal state* when the *value display* is at its minimum, the *maximal state* when the *value display* is at its maximum, and the *counting state* in all other cases. When the application is launched the application is placed in the *minimal state*, in this state the *decrement* and *reset* buttons are *desensitized*. A desensitized button, or any other interface component, is presented to the user in a greyed-out state and is not responsive to the users actions; i.e., for a button it cannot be pushed.

In the *minimal state* only the *increment* button is sensitive, and pressing this button causes the transition to the *counting state* to be followed. The *consequence* of this transition is to increment the *valueDisplay* and to sensitize the *decrement* and *reset* buttons. From the *counting state* further presses of the *increment* button will increment the *valueDisplay* until the *penultimate* value is reached, at which point a further press will cause the transition to the *maximal state*. In the *maximal state* the *increment* button is desensitized, preventing the user from attempting to increment beyond its maximum value.

A similar pattern of events using the *decrement* button from the *maximal state*, through the *counting state*, and back to the *minimal state* can be followed on the STD.

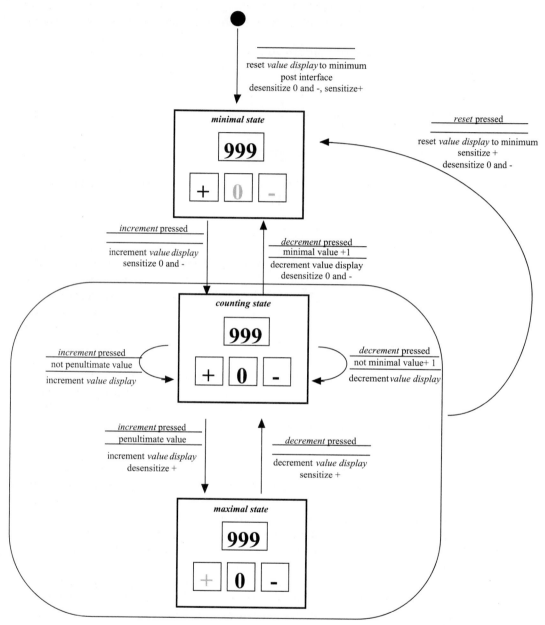

Figure 1.5 Extended *ClickCounter*, third STD design.

The *counting* and *maximal* states are grouped together on the STD to share a single transition associated with the *reset* button. This is interpreted to mean that when the *reset* button is pressed, in either the *counting* or *maximal* state, the transition which returns the application to the *minimal* state is followed.

This design prevents the user from requesting an action the application is unable to provide by dividing the behavioral space of the application into three distinct states.

A ***state*** in a ***State Transition Diagram*** is defined as a place in the behavioral space of the application which is functionally ***and*** visually distinct from all other places.

This final refinement of the design also illustrates another fundamental design principle.

Design Advice

It is better to prevent the user from making 'errors' than to allow them to make the 'error' and have to explain it to them.

The final STD is an explicit specification of the interface which is to be built. It can also be used as the basis of the software design and, once the interface has been constructed, be used to verify that the product implements its specification. It also focuses the developer's attention upon the usability of the product from the outset of the design process and thus hopefully ensures that usable interfaces are constructed. It cannot be guaranteed that interfaces constructed from STDs will be found acceptable by all eventual end users, but it is more likely that an interface with a formal usability design will be found so.

As with all design processes, the design notation should be used to explore different possibilities. In this example, three different STD designs for the interface were considered. It is clearly preferable for the implications and consequences of different behaviors to be explored at this stage, with pencil and paper, than to construct an interface and discover it to be inadequate or inappropriate.

1.3 Application, Presentation, and Translation Implementation

The essence of almost all software engineering approaches to implementation involve the partition of the specification into separate areas of concern and their subsequent implementation as distinct modules. It has already been emphasized that the application functionality should be implemented separately from the interface, what is not so obvious is that the interface module should itself be divided into two areas of concern. This is illustrated in Figure 1.6, which presents an application and its interface as if it were an iceberg.

As with an iceberg floating in the sea, the visible part of a graphical user interface represents only a small part of the interface as a whole. The majority of the interface, which cannot be seen, implements the behavior of the interface and is considerably more complex than that part which can be seen. Accordingly the interface should be implemented in two parts: the *presentation* aspects which will be seen by the user, and the *translation* aspects which supply the behavior. The iceberg diagram also indicates the *application* part of the artifact, which may be a relatively small component (if the iceberg if floating in shallow water) or may be immensely larger than the other two parts (if the iceberg is floating in deep water).

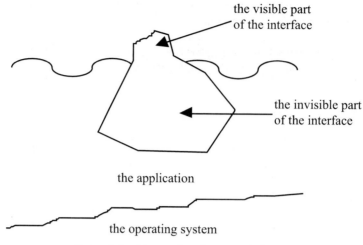

the visible part
of the interface

the invisible part
of the interface

the application

the operating system

Figure 1.6   The user interface as an iceberg.

Design Advice

Implement the graphical user interface as a *presentation* module, containing the visible parts, and a *translation* module, containing the behavior of the interface.

Before presenting the design and implementation of the interface for the *Click-Counter,* an overview of the ways in which *events* are created and transmitted in a Java artifact, and how this is used to implement an interface's behavior, will be presented. The mechanism is illustrated in Figure 1.7.

When the user interacts in some way with an interactive component of the *presentation* module, for example pushing a button, an *event* is generated by the AWT. The event is then sent to the *translation* module, which has been registered with the button as its *listener.* The translation module then communicates with the *application* module, which performs the processing associated with the button which was pressed. When the application module has completed its processing, the translation module calls methods in the *presentation* module to change its appearance. The user thus has a visual feedback of the consequences of their action, *closing* the cycle.

For example, in the *ClickCounter* application the user might press the *increment* button while the interface is in its *minimal* state. This will cause an event to be dispatched to the button's listener. The listener object will call the counting object to count the occurrence and then ask the counting object for its current value. The listener object will then pass the current value to the *value display*, to be shown to the user, and also set the sensitivities of the three buttons to that appropriate for the *counting* state.

Each part of this design approach: (*presentation, translation* and *application)* will be implemented as a distinct class. An instance of the *ClickCounter* class, which has already been presented, will provide the *application* part. An instance of the *Click-CounterPresentation* class, which will be described later, will provide the *presentation*

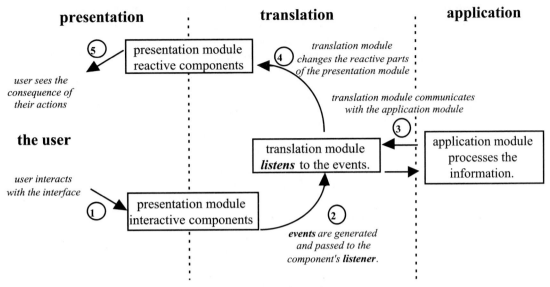

Figure 1.7   Event generation and consequences.

part and an instance of the *ClickCounterTranslation* class, which will also be described later, will provide the *translation* part.

The *ClickCounterTranslation* class will extend the **Applet** class and so have the responsibility for initializing *theApplet*, constructing the other two parts, and starting the application. An *instance diagram* for this application is given in Figure 1.8.

An instance diagram is used to indicate which instances of which classes, and the relationships which exist between them, are required for the implementation of a particular artifact. The instances are all ***instances of*** some class and the parent–child rela-

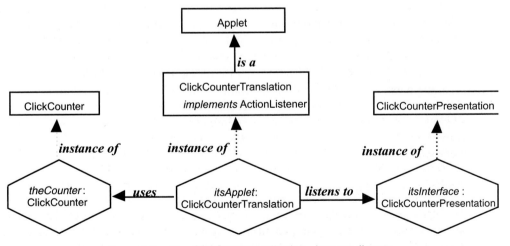

Figure 1.8   The *ClickCounter* application—instance diagram.

tionships between the classes can also be shown on the diagram. Full details of instance diagram notation can be found in Appendix C.

In this diagram its*Applet* is an instance of the *ClickCounterTranslation* class, which itself *is a*n extension of the AWT Applet class. The *ClickCounterTranslation* class is also shown as implementing the Java ActionListener **interface** in order for its instances to be able to *listen to* the events generated by the presentation object. As an extended Applet, the *ClickCounterTranslation* class inherits all the methods required for the application to initialize itself, post itself onto the screen, and interact with the keyboard, mouse and screen.

The object which *theApplet* is *listening to* is shown as an instance of the *Click-CounterPresentation* class called *itsInterface.* This instance contains the visible components of the interface, the *valueDisplay,* and the three buttons. The instance diagram also shows that *theApplet uses* an instance of the *ClickCounter* class called *theCounter* to actually do the counting.

1.4 The *ClickCounterPresentation* Class

The most obvious of the three classes is the *ClickCounterPresentation* class and so will be described first. The class diagram of the *ClickCounterPresentation* class is given in Figure 1.9.

The diagram indicates that the class encapsulates the four visual components illustrated on the state transition diagram in Figure 1.5: the *valueDisplay,* the *incrementButton,* the *resetButton,* and the *decrementButton.* The *ClickCounterPresentation* constructor is responsible for creating these components and mounting them within the *ClickCounterTranslation* instance's window, identified as *itsApplet,* passed as an argument. The *setValueDisplay()* method will change the value shown in the *valueDisplay* to that passed in its *setTo* argument. The three remaining methods: *setMaximumState(), setCountingState(),* and *setMinimumState()* are all concerned with setting the sensitivities of the three buttons as required by the STD.

In order for the constructor to be implemented, the detailed visual design of the application's interface has to be produced. The visual appearance of the *ClickCounter* interface, identifying the names of the components, is illustrated in Figure 1.10.

This diagram indicates that the interface will require four obvious components: the three Buttons at the bottom and the *valueDisplay* at the top. What is not so obvious is that there is also an area upon which these components are mounted, the Applet's area. Even less obviously the buttons will have to be mounted upon their own area and the *valueDisplay* upon its own area, both of which are subsequently mounted on the Applet's area. The reasons for these seemingly convoluted considerations are concerned with controlling the layout of the application, and a full explanation will be given in Chapter 3.

In Chapter 2 a description and an illustration of every simple user interface component which is supplied by Java will be given. For the time being, the reasons why some of the following decisions have been made will have to be taken largely on trust.

The area upon which all other components are mounted will be the application object itself, which is an extended Applet component. The two areas upon which the *valueDisplay* and the buttons are mounted will be Panel objects. The *valueDisplay* will

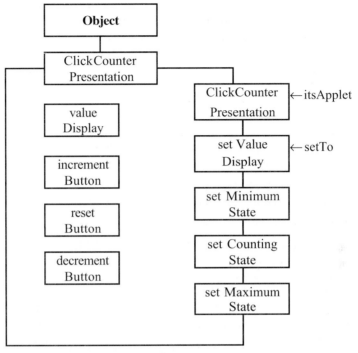

Figure 1.9   *ClickCounterPresentation* class diagram.

be implemented as a Label object and the three buttons Button objects. The relationships between these components are given in Figure 1.11.

A diagram such as this, which illustrates the *parent–child* relationships of the component instances required to construct an interface, is known as an *instance component hierarchy*. When the application is constructed, it will have to create each of the components and connect them together using the relationships shown.

The root of the hierarchy, at the top of the diagram, is identified as *itsApplet* and is shown to be an instance of the *ClickCounterTranslation* class, passed to the *ClickCounterPresentation* constructor as an argument. The implementation of the *ClickCounterPresentation* class, as far as the start of the constructor, is as follows.

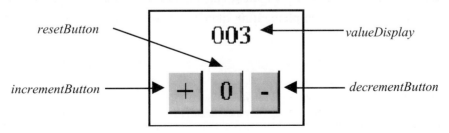

Figure 1.10   The *ClickCounter* interface—physical appearance.

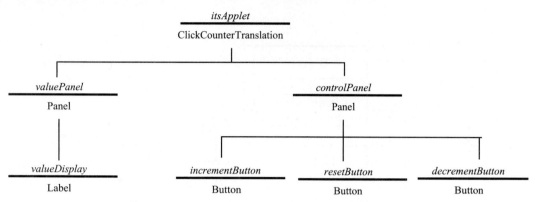

Figure 1.11   The application instance component hierarchy.

```
0001   // Filename ClickCounterPresentation.java.
0002   // Provides an interactive interface for the ClickCounter
0003   // class. Written for the Java Interface book Chapter 1.
0004   //
0005   // Fintan Culwin, v 2.0, August 1997.
0006
0007   import java.awt.*;
0008   import java.applet.*;
0009   import java.awt.event.*;
0010
0011
0012   public class ClickCounterPresentation extends Object {
0013
0014   private Button   incrementButton;
0015   private Button   resetButton;
0016   private Button   decrementButton;
0017   private Label    valueDisplay;
```

The classes **import**ed on lines 0007 to 0009 are required to provide easy access to the AWT, Applet, and event facilities, respectively. On lines 0014 to 0017 the four interface objects identified from the instance hierarchy in Figure 1.11 are declared, but not constructed. As indicated in Figure 1.7, the interactive interface components, in this interface the three Buttons, need to know the identity of the object which will listen to the events they generate. In this implementation this will be the client program object which, as noted in Figure 1.8, implements the ActionListener interface to allow it to do this. The source code implementing the *ClickCounterPresentation* continues with the constructor, as follows.

```
0022       public ClickCounterPresentation( ClickCounterTranslation itsApplet) {
0023
0024       Panel valuePanel   = new Panel();
0025       Panel controlPanel = new Panel();
0026
0027           itsApplet.setLayout( new GridLayout(2, 1, 10, 10));
```

```
0028
0029          valueDisplay = new Label();
0030          valuePanel.add( valueDisplay);
0031          itsApplet.add( valuePanel);
0032
0033          incrementButton = new Button( "+");
0034          incrementButton.setActionCommand( "increment");
0035          incrementButton.addActionListener( itsApplet);
0036
0037          resetButton = new Button( "0");
0038          resetButton.setActionCommand( "reset");
0039          resetButton.addActionListener( itsApplet);
0040
0041          decrementButton = new Button( "-");
0042          decrementButton.setActionCommand( "decrement");
0043          decrementButton.addActionListener( itsApplet);
0044
0045          controlPanel.add( incrementButton);
0046          controlPanel.add( resetButton);
0047          controlPanel.add( decrementButton);
0048          itsApplet.add( controlPanel);
0049      } // End ClickCounterPresentation constructor.
```

The two remaining components from the instance diagram in Figure 1.11, the *valuePanel* and the *controlPanel*, are declared and constructed on lines 0023 and 0025. Knowledge of these components is only required as the interface is constructed and so, in accordance with the principle of keeping declarations as limited as possible, they are provided as local declarations of the constructor. Although these variables will be destroyed when the call of the constructor finishes, the Panels which they reference will continue to exist within the application's interface until it is destroyed, when the applet is destroyed.

The Applet class is an extension of the Panel class, and the Panel class is an extension of the Container class. The Container class introduces the capability to control the layout of its instance children into the AWT hierarchy. Thus, Panel and Applet instances are extended Container instances and so inherit the capability to position their children. The relationships between the components in the AWT hierarchy, and their capabilities, will be explained in detail in the two following chapters.

There are several different possible policies for controlling the positioning of a Container's children, and the Container.setLayout() method can be used to indicate which style of *layout control* is to be used. On line 0027 the setLayout() method of the extended Applet instance, passed as an argument to the constructor, is specified as a GridLayout. The arguments to the GridLayout constructor indicate that it can contain two children in a 2 row by 1 column pattern, each separated from each other by 10 pixels in the horizontal and vertical directions.

The default layout for a Panel is a FlowLayout, where the child components are laid out from left to right in the order in which they are added to the parent and centered within the available space. As this layout is suitable for the *valueDisplay* and for the three buttons, the setLayout() method of the *valuePanel* and *controlPanel* Panels need not be called.

On line 0029 an instance of the AWT Label class is constructed and assigned to the instance attribute *valueDisplay*. The constructor does not specify the text which it is to display although an initial text will be supplied before it becomes visible, as will be explained later. On line 0030 the *valueDisplay* Label is added to the *valuePanel* using its *add()* method, establishing the parent–child relationship shown on the instance hierarchy in Figure 1.11. Once this has been accomplished, the *valuePanel* is added to *itsApplet* parent to establish the relationship between the *valuePanel* and *itsApplet* also shown on the instance hierarchy diagram. The children of a Container which has a GridLayout style are positioned in a left–right, top–down manner in the sequence in which they are added. Thus, the *valuePanel* will be placed at the top of the *itsApplet*s window as required by the visual design shown in Figure 1.10.

On line 0033 the *incrementButton* is constructed, the argument to the Button constructor specifying the text ("+") which it is to display. Once constructed, on line 0034, the actionCommand resource of this Button instance is specified as "*increment*" and on line 0035 the actionListener resource is specified as *itsApplet*. The actionListener resource, specified by using the *addActionListener()* method, determines which object events generated by the Button will be sent to. As all three of the buttons in this example will be using the same ActionListener destination, the actionCommand resource (specified by using the setActionCommand() method) is required to indicate exactly which of the buttons was pressed.

On lines 0037 to 0039 a similar sequence of steps constructs and configures the *resetButton,* and on lines 0041 to 0043 the same is done for the *decrementButton*. Having constructed all three buttons, they are added to the *controlPanel* on lines 0045 to 0047. A Panel has by default a FlowLayout layout policy which will position its children centrally from left to right in the sequence in which they are added. Finally, on line 0048 the *controlPanel* is then added to the *itsApplet* taking up the second cell below the *valuePanel,* which has already been added. These layout relationships are illustrated in Figure 1.12.

The remaining methods of the *ClickCounterPresentation* class are concerned with changing the appearance of the interface in response to the user's actions, and as it moves between states. The implementation of these methods is as follows.

```
0056      public void setValueDisplay( String setTo) {
0057          valueDisplay.setText( setTo);
0058      } // End setValueDisplay.
0059
0060
0061      public void setMinimumState() {
0062          incrementButton.setEnabled( true);
0063          resetButton.setEnabled( false);
0064          decrementButton.setEnabled( false);
0065      } // End setMinimumState.
0066
0067      public void setCountingState() {
0068          incrementButton.setEnabled( true);
```

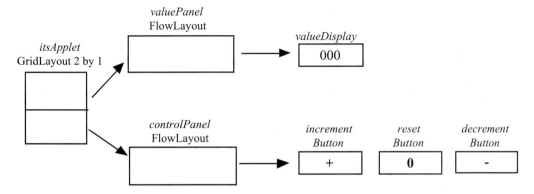

Figure 1.12   Layout management of the *ClickCounter* application.

```
0069          resetButton.setEnabled( true);
0070          decrementButton.setEnabled( true);
0071      } // End setCountingState.
0072
0073      public void setMaximumState() {
0074          incrementButton.setEnabled( false);
0075          resetButton.setEnabled( true);
0076          decrementButton.setEnabled( true);
0077      } // End setMaximumState.
0078
0079  } // End class ClickCounterPresentation.
```

The *setValueDisplay()* method uses the *valueDisplay* setText() method to set the text displayed by the Label to that supplied in the *setTo* argument. The three remaining methods use the *setEnabled()* method of each Button instance to ensure that the button is enabled **(true)** or disabled **(false)** as required by the state transition diagram in Figure 1.5.

1.5 The *ClickCounterTranslation* class

As shown in the instance diagram in Figure 1.8, the *ClickCounterTranslation* class provides *theApplet* which implements the application. Its responsibility is to construct an instance of the *ClickCounter* class, called *theCounter*, and an instance of the *ClickCounterPresentation* class, called *itsInterface*; and to place the application into its initial state. It also has the responsibility of listening to the events generated from the interface, calling methods of the application module, and instructing the visible part of the application how to change itself in response. The class diagram of the *ClickCounterTranslation* class is given in Figure 1.13.

The *init()* method will be automatically called after the inherited (Applet) constructor method has been called and before the Applet is posted to the display. It will be used to create the instances used by this interface, as shown in Figure 1.8, and to

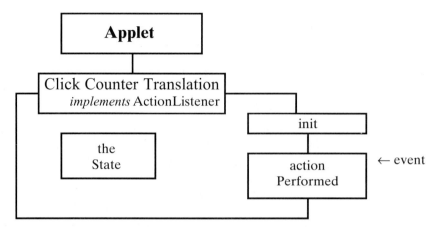

Figure 1.13   *ClickCounterTranslation* class diagram.

place them, and itself, into a well-defined initial state. The only other method is *action-Performed()*, so called as it is the method performed when an event is dispatched to it from any AWT components which have registered it as their action listener. This is the only method which this class must supply in order for it to implement the **ActionListener** interface. The implementation of this class, as far as the end of the *init()* method, is as follows.

```
0001   // Filename ClickCounterTranslation.java.
0002   // Provides the behaviour for the interactive ClickCounter.
0003   // Written for the Java Interface book Chapter 1.
0004   //
0005   // Fintan Culwin, v 2.0, August 1997.
0006
0007   import java.awt.*;
0008   import java.awt.event.*;
0009   import java.applet.Applet;
0010
0011   import ClickCounter;
0012   import ClickCounterPresentation;
0013
0014   public class ClickCounterTranslation extends    Applet
0015                                        implements ActionListener {
0016
0017   private final int INITIAL_STATE  = 0;
0018   private final int MINIMUM_STATE  = 1;
0019   private final int COUNTING_STATE = 2;
0020   private final int MAXIMUM_STATE  = 3;
0021   private       int theState       = INITIAL_STATE;
0022
0023   private ClickCounter          theCounter;
```

```
0024    private ClickCounterPresentation itsInterface;
0025
0026
0027       public void init() {
0028          theCounter   = new ClickCounter( 0, 5);
0029          itsInterface = new ClickCounterPresentation( this);
0030          itsInterface.setValueDisplay( theCounter.countIsAsString());
0031          itsInterface.setMinimumState();
0032          theState = MINIMUM_STATE;
0033       } // End init.
```

The import statements on lines 0007 to 0009 provide access to the Java API resources required by this class, and on line 0011 and 0012 to the *ClickCounter* class which provides the application part and to the *ClickCounterPresentation* class providing the presentation part. These two **import**ations are not strictly required, however, they document the dependencies between this source code file and the other two source code files in the application, as such, they should be used even though they are technically not required by Java in this case.

On lines 0017 to 0020 four manifest class-wide constants which are used to represent the states of the interface are declared, and on line 0021 an **int**eger instance variable, called *theState*, is declared and initialized to the manifest value *INITIAL_STATE*. The intention is that the value of this variable will always record the current state of the application and its interface.

On line 0023 an instance of the *ClickCounter* class, called *theCounter*, is declared and on line 0024 an instance of the *ClickCounterPresentation* class, called *itsInterface* is also declared. These two instances provide the two objects which are used by the application, as shown in Figure 1.8.

The first step of the *init()* method, on line 0028, is to construct the *ClickCounter* instance; the arguments to the constructor, 0 and 5, delimit a very small range of values which it can count between in order to allow the interface to be easily demonstrated and tested. On line 0029 *itsInterface* is constructed, passing as an argument the identity of the *ClickCounterInstance* which is currently being initialized (**this**) As explained, this will cause the interface components to be created and mounted onto **this** Applet's Panel and will also cause **this** instance to become the ActionListener of the buttons on the interface.

Once constructed, the *setValueDisplay()* method of the *itsInterface* instance is called passing as an argument the String obtained from the *theCounter*'s *countIsAsString()* method. This will cause the *valueDisplay* component of the interface to display the initial value of *theCounter* when it subsequently first becomes visible. The final initialization steps are to call the *itsInterface setMinimumState()* method to effect the transition from the initial to the minimum states, as required by the state transition diagram, and the value of *theState* is set to reflect this. When the *init()* method concludes, the applet will show itself to the user on the desktop and, as the *ClickCounterPresentation* instance has constructed the interface within the applet's window, this will cause the interface to become visible to the user.

The *actionPerformed()* method will be called every time the user presses one of the buttons on the interface; the ActionEvent, which is generated in response to the press, being passed as an argument to the method. The implementation of this method is as follows.

```
0036    public void actionPerformed( ActionEvent event) {
0037
0038    String buttonPressed = event.getActionCommand();
0039
0040        if ( buttonPressed.equals( "increment")) {
0041            if ( theState == MINIMUM_STATE) {
0042                itsInterface.setCountingState();
0043                theState = COUNTING_STATE;
0044            } // End if.
0045            theCounter.count();
0046            if ( theCounter.isAtMaximum()) {
0047                itsInterface.setMaximumState();
0048                theState = MAXIMUM_STATE;
0049            } // End if.
0050
0051        } else if ( buttonPressed.equals( "reset")) {
0052
0053            theCounter.reset();
0054            itsInterface.setMinimumState();
0055            theState = MINIMUM_STATE;
0056
0057        } else if ( buttonPressed.equals( "decrement")) {
0058
0059            if ( theCounter.isAtMaximum()) {
0060                itsInterface.setCountingState();
0061                theState = COUNTING_STATE;
0062            } // End if.
0063            theCounter.unCount();
0064            if ( theCounter.isAtMinimum()) {
0065                itsInterface.setMinimumState();
0066                theState = MINIMUM_STATE;
0067            } // End if.
0068        } // End if.
0069
0070        itsInterface.setValueDisplay( theCounter.countIsAsString() );
0071    } // End actionPerformed.
0072
0073 } // End class ClickCounterTranslation.
```

This method will be called whichever button is pressed, and the *event* instance will contain a copy of the *actionCommand* attribute of the button which caused it to be generated. The *actionPerformed()* method commences, on line 0038, by retrieving this attribute from the *event* by using its getActionCommand() method. The remainder of the method is a three-way selection which contains a branch for each button.

Lines 0041 to 0049 contain the steps required to respond to a press of the *incrementButton*, and starts by effecting the transition from the *MINIMUM_STATE* to the

COUNTING_STATE if the value of the *theState* attribute indicates that it should be taken. This is accomplished by calling the *itsInterface*'s *setCountingState()* method and updating the value of *theState* to reflect this. Following this, on line 0045 the *count()* method of *theCounter* instance is called to record the occurrence and finally, on lines 0046 to 0049, the transition to the *MAXIMUM_STATE* is taken if appropriate.

On lines 0053 to 0055 a press of the *resetButton* is handled by resetting *theCounter*, setting the *itsInterface* to its minimum state, and recording this in *theState*. Lines 0059 to 0067 handle a press of the *decrementButton* in a manner comparable to the way in which a press of the *incrementButton* was handled. The last step of the *actionPerformed()* method is to update the *valueDisplay* component on the interface by passing to its *setValueDisplay()* method the value obtained from *theCounter*'s *countIsAsString()* method.

Referring back to Figure 1.7, the identity of the *ClickCounterTranslation* instance is registered with the three buttons on the interface as their listener when they are constructed. Subsequently, when the user presses one of the buttons an *ActionEvent*, containing an **actionCommand** attribute to identify which button, is dispatched to its listener. When the event is received by the *ClickCounterTranslation* instance, its *actionPerformed()* method is called passing as an argument the *ActionEvent* instance received. Within the *actionPerformed()* method, public methods of the *ClickCounter* instance *theCounter* are called to perform the appropriate application functionality. Public methods of the *ClickCounterPresentation* instance, *itsInterface*, are also called to change the appearance of the interface to provide feedback to the user.

1.6 *ClickCounter*—Executing the Applet in a Browser

In its current state of development the *ClickCounter* can only be executed as an applet. In order for this to happen, it will have to be hyperlinked within a HTML document accessed from a Java-enabled browser or an appletviewer utility. A very minimal HTML file to accomplish this might be as follows.

```
<HTML>
<HEAD>
<!- Minimal HTML document to execute the              ->
<!- ClickCounterTranslation applet. Written for the Java ->
<!- interface book Chapter 1 - see text.              ->
<!- Fintan Culwin, v 0.2, August 1997.                ->
<TITLE>Click Counter test</TITLE>
</HEAD>
<BODY>
<CENTER>
<H1>
The Java Click Counter Applet
</H1>
<P>
<HR>
<APPLET CODE="ClickCounterTranslation.class"
        WIDTH  = 400
```

```
            HEIGHT = 250
</APPLET>
<HR>
<P>
<I>fintan@sbu.ac.uk</I>
</CENTER>
</BODY>
</HTML>
```

The <APPLET> tag in a HTML document indicates that a Java applet is to be retrieved from the server which supplied the document and executed. The CODE parameter to the <APPLET> tag identifies the applet, which in this simple example is assumed to be present in the same directory on the server as the HTML document. More details of HTML authoring and the use of the <APPLET> tag can be found in the references in Appendix A. The appearance of the *ClickCounter* applet when it is being executed by *Microsoft's Internet Explorer* is illustrated in Figure 1.14.

1.7 *ClickCounter*—Producing an Executable

In addition to constructing the *ClickCounter* so that it can be executed by a Web browser, it is also possible to include a *main()* method in the *ClickCounterTranslation* class declaration which allows it to be run as a stand-alone application. A minimal *main()* method is as follows.

```
0120    public static void main( String args[]) {
0121
0122        Frame           frame        = new Frame("Click Counter Demo");
0123        ClickCounterTranslation theInterface
0124                              = new ClickCounterTranslation();
0125
0126        theInterface.init();
0127        frame.add( theInterface, "Center");
0128
0129        frame.setVisible( true);
0130        frame.setSize( frame.getPreferredSize());
0131    } // End main.
0132
0133 } // End class ClickCounterTranslation.
```

The prototype of the *main()* method, as given on line 0120, has to be strictly adhered to in order for the Java run-time system to find and execute it. When the *ClickCounter* was run as an applet it was executed within a browser, which isolated it from the host's windowing system. When it is run as a stand-alone application, it needs to be able to interact with the host windowing system directly. To allow this to happen, a *ClickCounterTranslation* instance has to be installed within a Frame component.

The implementation of the *main()* method declares and initializes an instance of the Frame class called *frame* and an instance of the *ClickCounterTranslation* class

Figure 1.14   The *ClickCounter* applet executing within Internet Explorer.

called *theInterface*. The *init()* method, which was called automatically by the browser when it was run as an applet, now has to be called explicitly from the *main()* method to initialize the interface.

The default layout style of the Frame class is BorderLayout, as will be explained in Chapter 2, and *theInterface* is added to its "*Center*" location before the *frame*.setVisible() method is called to post the application to the display. Once posted the *frame*.setSize() method must be called to specify the frame's preferred size, as advised by the *frame*.getPreferredSize() method, in order for the window to be guaranteed just large enough to display the application. Figure 1.15 shows the *ClickCounterTranslation* running as a stand-alone applet with window borders and controls supplied by its Frame.

Figure 1.15   *ClickCounter* applet in minimal, counting, and maximal states, running under Windows '95.

Chapter Summary

- An application containing a Graphical User Interface (GUI) should be divided into *application*, *translation,* and *presentation* parts.

- A State Transition Diagram (STD) contains an explicit specification of the interface which is to be constructed.

- The physical appearance of an interface can be used to produce an application instance hierarchy which identifies the components required.

- An applet is constructed by extending the Applet class and its interface can be constructed by overriding the Applet init() method.

- Container classes, which include Panels, Frames and Applets, control the layout of their instance children using a layout policy.

- The *translation* class has to implement a suitable Listener interface and be registered with an interactive component as its listener in order for it to respond to the user's actions.

- The STD should be modeled in the *translation* class and call state-changing methods in the *presentation* class as appropriate.

- An applet can be executed in a browser without a main() method, but a main() method must be supplied for it to be run as a stand-alone application.

Exercises

1.1   Redesign the final STD so that pressing the *increment* button when the counter is displaying its maximum value will cause it to display its minimum value and likewise pressing the *decrement* button at the minimum value will result in the maximum. Hint: What will this change do to the number of states?

1.2   Implement the design from Exercise 1.1.

1.3   How can the *ClickCounter* applet, as developed in the chapter, be shown to be correct? Hint: You do not want to have to press the *increment* button one thousand times.

1.4   How could you determine which of the three possible implementations, that presented in the chapter, that developed in Exercise 1.3, and that suggested in Figure 1.4, would present the least number of usability problems to a user?

1.5   A *VehicleCounter* application is required. In this application, two click counter instances are required: one to be used to count cars as they pass the counter and one to count all other vehicles. A third numeric display is provided to show the total of the two counters. Produce a state transition diagram for this application and implement the resulting design.

1.6   Design and implement an application which will either display the date or the time. The application class should provide *dateIs()* and *timeIs()* methods, and this can be simulated for this exercise by returning constant strings. The interface should present a display area at the top and two buttons, a date button and a time button, at the bottom. The date button should be insensitive when the time is displayed and vice versa; pressing a button should have the expected effect.

A Whistle Stop Tour of the Abstract Windowing Toolkit (AWT)

In this chapter, a selection of the simpler user interface components supplied by the Java AWT will be presented. Each will have its methods and other resources described, and either a trivial *init()* method to illustrate its typical use and appearance or a demonstration applet will be given. The full implementation of GUIs as application presentation, and translation classes will not be presented in the interests of manageable simplicity. During this tour many of the ideas from the previous chapter, in particular layout managers, will be re-presented, consolidated, and augmented.

As well as providing an introduction to using existing Java components, an introduction to extending them will also be presented. It is often the case that a particular requirement is not satisfied by any existing component, and in these circumstances a specialized component has to be produced. In keeping with Java's Object Oriented philosophy, this is best accomplished by the extension of an existing component rather than the construction of a component from scratch.

The chapter ends with a number of practical exercises concerned with the design and construction of applets. These exercises should be conscientiously attempted, as the only sure way to assimilate the contents of the first two introductory chapters is to struggle with the software.

2.1 The Abstract Windows Toolkit

The *ClickCounter* interface from the previous chapter made use of the Button and Label components from the Java *A*bstract *W*indowing *T*oolkit (*AWT*) package. This toolkit supplies a number of classes, each providing an interface component which can be combined with other components to build a complete

Graphical User Interface. To produce interfaces which are more complex than those introduced in Chapter 1, the classes which comprise the AWT have to be understood and used. This chapter will present each of the major classes from the toolkit in turn and indicate how it could be used within a GUI. This will necessarily be only an initial introduction to each of the classes, and more details of most of the classes will be given in the following chapters.

The AWT is named as an *abstract* toolkit as it provides only the essential components and functionality which are common to all major windowing systems. For example the Microsoft Windows environment, the Apple Macintosh environment, and the various X Windows environments all supply a push button component. However the physical appearance of the button, precise behavior and API differ significantly between all three environments. Java abstracts the essential behavior of a push button and provides an API which is presented to the developer in the AWT. When an instance of the Java Button class is realized, the actual button which is presented to the user is obtained from the native environment.

Figure 2.1 presents the *ClickCounter* interface from Chapter 1 when it is realized in each of the three environments previously listed. In each case, exactly the same Java source code is used and the user can interact with the application in exactly the same way. However, the precise physical appearance is determined by the native windowing environment. All of the components of each of the implementations, and the three Buttons, the Label, and the Panels which they are mounted upon, are supplied by *peer components* from the native windowing toolkit.

2.2 The AWT Class Hierarchy

A simplified class hierarchy diagram of the Java AWT is shown in Figure 2.2. The missing classes are mainly concerned with *layout management* and *menus*; these parts of the hierarchy will be introduced later in this and subsequent chapters. The Object class, shown on the left as the root of the hierarchy, is not a part of the AWT; however, all Java classes, including the AWT classes, are descended from the Object class and so it is shown on this diagram.

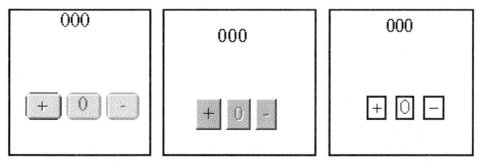

FIGURE 2.1   The *ClickCounterInterface* applet in the Windows 95, Macintosh, and X Windows environments.

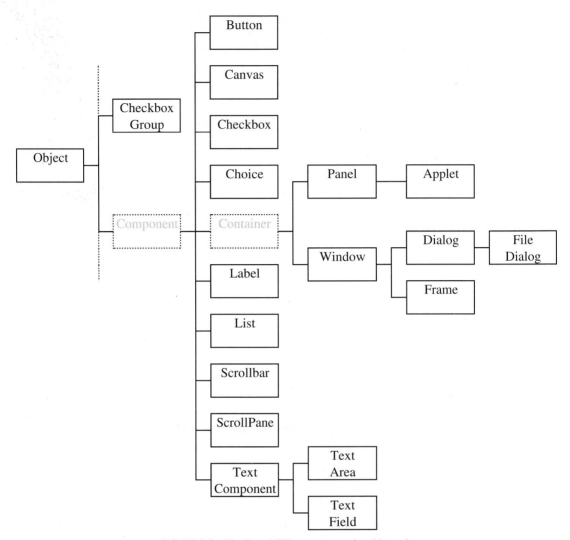

FIGURE 2.2 The Java AWT component class hierarchy.

2.3 The Label Class

An instance of the Java Label class was used in the previous chapter to provide the area upon which the value of a *ClickCounter* was displayed. This is a relatively simple class and provides a convenient point to start the tour. Table 2.1 lists the major methods and other resources of the class.

The data attributes of a Label instance are the text which it will display and the alignment of the text. The possible alignments for the text are enumerated by the three Label class-wide constants CENTER, LEFT and RIGHT, with a default of LEFT when it is not explicitly specified otherwise. The four public methods provide inquiry and modification methods for these two data attributes, allowing the value of each of the attrib-

constructors	
public Label()	
public Label(String *aString*)	Constructs a Label displaying *aString* with the *alignment*, which can be one of CENTER, LEFT or RIGHT, as specified.
public Label(String *aString*, **int** *alignment*)	

instance methods	
public **void** setText(String *newString*)	
public **String** getText()	Sets or obtains the text displayed by the Label.
public **void** setAlignment(**int** *newAlignment*)	Sets or obtains the alignment of the Label to *newAlignment*. Will throw an IllegalArgumentException if *newAlignment* is not one of the three manifest values.
public **int** getAlignment()	

TABLE 2.1   Major resources of the Label class.

utes to be retrieved from the object or a new value to be specified. The setText() method was used in the previous chapter whenever the value of the *ClickCounter* changed, in order to display the new value. This class does not have to explicitly provide attributes for resources such as the foreground and background colors or the font to be used because these are inherited from the Component class, as will be explained.

The following code fragment, showing the *init()* method of a class called *LabelExample* which extends the Applet class, creates three Label instances that illustrate each of the possible alignments.

```
0020        public void init() {
0021
0022        Label   leftLabel    = new Label( "Alignment left",   Label.LEFT);
0023        Label   centerLabel  = new Label( "Alignment center", Label.CENTER);
0024        Label   rightLabel   = new Label( "Alignment right",  Label.RIGHT);
0025
0026           this.setLayout( new GridLayout( 3, 1, 0, 10));
0027
0028           this.add( leftLabel);
0029           this.add( centerLabel);
0030           this.add( rightLabel);
0031        } // End init.
```

The layout policy of the *LabelExample* Panel is specified as a 3 row by 1 column GridLayout so the three Labels are maintained in single column, from top to bottom in the sequence in which they were added, thus producing the appearance shown in Figure 2.3

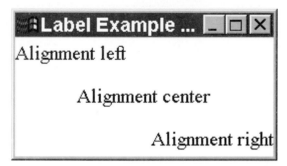

FIGURE 2.3 Three *Label* instances illustrating different alignments.

2.4 The Component Class

The Component class is the root class for almost all the interface components in the AWT. It is a complex class containing more than 20 data attributes and 130 methods, all of which are inherited by all the classes below it in the class hierarchy shown in Figure 2.2. This may seem an intimidating amount of detail to have to assimilate, however the attributes can be grouped according to the functionality which they provide and, in practice, only a small proportion of them need be used. As the Component class is so complex, many of the classes derived from it are comparatively simple as they inherit much of their functionality from Component.

Only an initial introduction to the major resources of the class, involving grouping and naming of various methods with a brief indication of their function, will be given here. Additional details of some, but not all, of the remaining attributes and methods will be given throughout the rest of this chapter and the book. The first group of methods to be considered are those concerned with the lifecyle of a component and are listed in Table 2.2.

A Component once constructed will create its *peer* in the native windowing environment, calling the addNotify() method once it is created and then waiting to become validated during layout negotiations (at which time it becomes visible but will only be shown when its instance parents are shown). The next group of methods, shown in Table 2.3, are concerned with the Component's physical appearance.

The foreground, background, and font resources will be described in the next chapter and the locale resource in Chapter 9. The following *init()* method of a class called *CursorExample* creates fourteen instances of the Label class, each bearing a text label describing the Cursor associated with it, and installs them within a 2 column by 7 row GridLayout layout policy.

```
0014    public void init() {
0015
0016    int     maxCursors    = Cursor.MOVE_CURSOR +1;
0017
0019    Label  cursorLabels[] = new Label[ maxCursors];
0020    String cursorNames[]  = { "Default",    "Cross Hair", "Text",
0021                                "Wait",      "South West", "South East",
```

protected Component()	Constructor, will be overridden in all child classes.
public void addNotify()	Called when the *peer* is created, allowing the physical characteristics of the component to be manipulated.
public boolean isValid() **public void** validate() **public void** invalidate()	A component is initially invalid and becomes valid when it has been laid out and can then become visible.
public void setVisible(**boolean** *flag*) **public boolean** isVisible()	A visible component may not yet be showing on the screen, but will take part in layout negotiations.
public boolean isShowing()	A component is shown when it is visible and its Container parent is visible and showing .
public void setEnabled(**boolean** *flag*) **public boolean** isEnabled()	A disabled component is shown in a greyed state and cannot be interacted with.
protected void finalize() **throws** Throwable	Supplied by Object, this method will be called just before the component is garbage collected.

TABLE 2.2   Lifecycle resources of the Component class.

public Color getForeground() **public void** setForeground(Color *fore*) **public** Color getBackground() **public void** setBackground(Color *back*)	The foreground and background colors of the component specified or inherited as an instance of the Color class, which will be described in Chapter 4.

public synchronized void
                    setFont(Font *setTo*)
public Font getFont()
public FontMetrics
         getFontMetrics(Font *forThis*)
	Sets the Font to be used for any text shown in the component, inherited from its instance parent if not explicitly specified. FontMetrics allow the sizes of the glyphs from the Font to be queried. An example will be given in Chapter 3.

public Cursor getCursor() **public synchronized void** setCursor(Cursor *setTo*)	Establishes the cursor to be shown when the mouse is traversing the component. The Cursor class contains pre-defined cursors.
public Locale getLocale() **public void** setLocale(Locale *toHere*)	Establishes the international and cultural Locale, allowing customization and internationalization. Described in Chapter 9.

TABLE 2.3   Physical appearance resources of the Component class.

```
0022                                    "North West", "North East", "North",
0023                                    "South",       "West",        "East",
0024                                    "Hand",        "Move"};
0025
0029        this.setLayout( new GridLayout( 7, 2, 0, 10));
0030
0031        for ( int index =0; index < maxCursors; index++ ) {
0032            cursorLabels[ index] = new Label( cursorNames[ index]);
0033            cursorLabels[ index].setCursor( new Cursor( index));
0034            this.add( cursorLabels[ index]);
0035        } // End for.
0036    } // End init.
```

The Cursor class declares fourteen class-wide manifest constants, identifying all the cursor images which it supplies. The last of these manifest values is MOVE_CUR-SOR and, on line 0016, this value is used to initialize the value of the local **int** variable *maxCursors*. This value is then used on line 0019 to define the size of an array of Label instances called *cursorLabels*. Lines 0020 to 0024 then declare and initialize an array of Strings called *cursorNames*. The steps of the *init()* method commence with the establishment of a 7 by 2 GridLayout policy for the applet. The loop between lines 0031 and 0035 constructs each Label in turn, specifying a String from the *cursorNames* array as an argument to its constructor. Before the Label is added to the applet on line 0034, its setCursor() method is called, specifying a **new** Cursor instance whose argument identifies in turn each possible cursor.

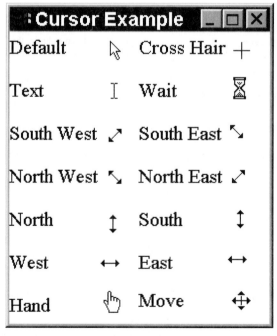

FIGURE 2.4   The fourteen Java cursors under Windows '95.

DEFAULT_CURSOR	CROSSHAIR_CURSOR	TEXT_CURSOR	WAIT_CURSOR
SW_RESIZE_CURSOR	SE_RESIZE_CURSOR	NW_RESIZE_CURSOR	NE_RESIZE_CURSOR
N_RESIZE_CURSOR	S_RESIZE_CURSOR	W_RESIZE_CURSOR	E_RESIZE_CURSOR
HAND_CURSOR		MOVE_CURSOR	

TABLE 2.4   The manifest cursor names supplied by the Cursor class..

Figure 2.4 illustrates the appearance of this applet; as the mouse pointer moves into each Label, the appearance of the cursor will change to that shown alongside its name. Table 2.4 lists the manifest names of the fourteen cursors supplied by the Cursor class; unfortunately there is no mechanism for preparing a cursor from a developer-supplied image.

Table 2.5 contains the methods associated with the Component's size and location.

public void setBounds(Rectangle *rect*) **public void** setBounds(**int** *x*, **int** *y*, **int** *width*, **int** *height*) **public** Rectangle getBounds() **public void** setLocation(Point *here*) **public void** setLocation(**int** *x*, **int** *y*) **public** Point getLocation()	A variety of methods concerned with the location and size of the component All x and y locations (apart from getLocationOnScreen()) are in relation to the instance parent's co-ordinate space.
public Dimension getSize() **public void** setSize(Dimension *size*) **public void** setSize(int *width*, int *height*) **public** Point getLocationOnScreen()	The Point class encapsulates an x and y co-ordinate, the Dimension class a width and height, and the Rectangle class, x, y , width and height.
public Dimension getMinimumSize() **public** Dimension getMaximumSize() **public** Dimension getPreferredSize()	These methods are used during layout negotiations and should be overridden in extended components. Details are given in Chapter 3
public float getAlignmentX() **public float** getAlignmentY()	Informs the component's container where it would like to be located between 0.0 and 1.0.
public boolean contains(Point *here*) **public boolean** contains(**int** *x*, **int** *y*)	Determines if the specified Point in the component's co-ordinate space is, or is not, within its bounds.

public Component getComponentAt(
              Point *thisPoint*)
public Component getComponentAt(**int** *x*,
              int *y*)
	Returns the identity of the component, if any, at the location specified.

TABLE 2.5   Size and location resources of the Component class.

`protected final void enableEvents(` `        long eventsToEnable)` `protected final void disableEvents(` `        long eventsToDisable)`	Only events which have been enabled on a component will be dispatched to their registered listeners. Adding a Listener automatically enables the associated event class.
`public synchronized void` `    addKeyListener( KeyListener listener)` `public synchronized void` `removeKeyListener( KeyListener listener)`	The Listener object is established, or removed, by these methods. More than one listener can be added but there is no guarantee about the sequence which they will be called.
`protected void processEvent(` `                AWTEvent event)`	All events received by the component are first passed to processEvent(), which indirects to the specialized process*Whatever*Event() method.
`protected void processKeyEvent(` `            KeyEvent event)`	The specialized method for handling KeyEvents.

TABLE 2.6   Event handling resources of the Component class.

Table 2.6 contains the methods associated with events. Only the details of the KeyEvent class are shown. There are a similar set of methods for the Component-Event, InputEvent, and MouseEvent classes. Further details of these and other event classes, such as the ActionEvent introduced in Chapter 1, will be given throughout the rest of this chapter.

The usual technique for handling events is to register a Listener object with the Component using the appropriate add*Whatever*Listener() method, for example addActionListener(). This will automatically enable the appropriate class of events on the Component and dispatch them to the actionPerformed(), or equivalent, method of the Listener. However when components are extended, as opposed to simply being used, the appropriate event classes will have to be explicitly enabled, using enableEvents(). Events generated by the Component will then be passed to the it's processEvent() method which, unless overridden, will indirect to the appropriate process*Whatever*Event() method. Introductory examples of extending components will be given later in this chapter and more extensive examples in Chapter 3.

The next table, Table 2.7, lists the methods associated with painting a component. The paint() method is actually responsible for drawing the component onto the screen, but should never be called directly. Instead one of the repaint() methods should be called, which will schedule a call of paint() in due course. Before paint() is called update() will be called to clear the area to be repainted to the background color, so paint() need not do this. All AWT components, apart from Canvas, take responsibility for painting themselves, but extended components may have to override paint() to draw themselves onto the screen. The Graphics class is required to draw onto the screen and will be explained when the Canvas class is introduced.

To complete this introduction to the Component class, Table 2.8 contains miscellaneous methods which do not belong to any of the previously mentioned groups.

`public void paint( Graphics context)`	Draws the component, and all its instance children, onto the screen.
`public void paintAll( Graphics context)`	
`public void update(Graphics context)`	Clears the area defined within Graphics to the background color and calls Paint().
`public void repaint()` `public void repaint( long within)`	
`public void repaint( int x, int y,` `                     int width, int height)`	Schedules a call of update() as soon as possible, or *within* the time (in milliseconds) specified.

`public void repaint( long within,`
`                     int x, int y,`
`                     int width,  int height)`
	Draws the entire screen or just the area defined by x, y, width, and height

`public Graphics getGraphics()`	Obtains the Graphics context for this component.

TABLE 2.7   Painting resources of the Component class.

2.5 The Button Class

The use of Buttons has already been introduced in Chapter 1. The major resources of the Button class are given in Table 2.9.

The second constructor was used in Chapter 1. The first, default, constructor will create a Button without a label. The first two methods allow the Button's label to be changed or obtained. The remaining methods are concerned with the Button's listener and the *command* string sent to it, as described in Chapter 1. The major resources of the ActionEvent class, an extension of the AWTEvent class itself an extension of the EventObject class, are listed in Table 2.10.

An example of detecting multiple mouse clicks is given later in this chapter, in Section 2.12. Details of how to determine which, if any, key was held down while the Button was clicked can be found in Chapter 8, Section 8.7. A Java program, which is intended to be used on any platform, should assume that the mouse has only one button, so as to work on Macintosh platforms. However there is a technique for determining which of the mouse buttons was used, using the same technique for determining which key was held down.

`public String getName()` `public void setName( String name)`	Establishes a *name* for the component which can be used to identify it within program code.
`public Container getParent()`	Obtains the Container of this component.
`public String toString()`	Obtains a String describing the component.

TABLE 2.8   Miscellaneous methods of the Component class.

constructors

public Button() **public** Button(String *aString*)	Constructs a Button without a label, or with *aString* as its label.

instance methods

public void setLabel(String *newLabel*) **public String** getLabel()	Sets and obtains the label displayed by the Button.

public void addActionListener(
              ActionListener *listener*)
public void removeActionListener(
              ActionListener *listener*)
	Registers or removes a listener for the ActionEvents generated by the button. More than one listener can be registered, but there is no guarantee on the sequence they will be called.

public void setActionCommand(String *command*) **public** String getActionCommand()	Associates a command string with the button which will be sent with the ActionEvent.

TABLE 2.9   Major resources of the Button class.

class-wide constant attributes

SHIFT_MASK CTRL_MASK META_MASK ALT_MASK BUTTON1_MASK, BUTTON2_MASK, BUTTON3_MASK,	Masks to be used to determine which keys were pressed as the button was pressed or which button on a multi-button mouse was pressed. (InputEvent).
ACTION_PERFORMED	Manifest ID of the event generated.

instance methods

public Object getSource()	Obtains the identity of the Object which generated the event (EventObject).
public int getID()	Obtains the ID of the event (AWTEvent).
protected boolean isConsumed() **protected void** consume()	A consumed event is not forwarded to the peer, used when extending (AWTEvent).
public String getActionCommand()	The command string of the source component.
public int getModifiers()	Keys held down when the event was generated.

TABLE 2.10   Major resources of the ActionEvent class (inherited resources as indicated).

2.6 The Checkbox and CheckboxGroup Classes

The Checkbox class provides a text label and an associated *on/off* state indicator. It is used to implement *check buttons* and, in conjunction with the CheckboxGroup class, *radio buttons*. The major resources of this class are presented in Table 2.11.

A Checkbox instance has three data attributes: the *label* which it will display, the CheckboxGroup to which it might belong, and the *state* (on or off) of its indicator. If a Checkbox instance is not a member of a CheckboxGroup, it will behave as a *check button* and its state can be set or unset independently of all other Checkbox buttons. If a Checkbox instance is a member of a CheckboxGroup it will behave as a *radio button*, where only one member of the group can be checked at any one instant and checking one of the buttons in the group will automatically unset all other buttons.

The first two constructors are comparable to the first two constructors of the Button class just given. The third constructor specifies its initial state, the last the initial state and the CheckboxGroup to which it belongs. The first six methods allow each of

constructors	
public Checkbox()	
public Checkbox(String *aLabel*)	Constructs a Checkbox with no label, or as specified by *aLabel*, with *itsState* on (**true**) or off (**false**) and as a member of *itsGroup* if specified.
public Checkbox(String *aLabel,* **boolean** *itsState*)	
public Checkbox(String *aLabel,* **boolean** *itsState,* CheckboxGroup *itsGroup*)	

instance methods	
public void setLabel(String *newLabel*) **public String** getLabel()	Sets or obtains the label to be displayed by the Checkbox.
public void setState(**boolean** *newState*) **public Boolean** getState()	Sets, or obtains, the state of the indicator, resetting the states of other members of the group if required.
public void setCheckboxGroup(CheckboxGroup *itsGroup*) **public** CheckboxGroup getCheckboxGroup()	Sets or obtains the group, if any, of the Checkbox.
public void addItemListener(ItemListener *listener*) **public void** removeItemListener(ItemListener *listener*)	Registers or removes a listener for the ItemEvents generated by the button. More than one listener can be registered, but there is no guarantee of the sequence in which they will be called.

TABLE 2.11   Major resources of the Checkbox class.

the three data attributes to be queried or set. The last two register and remove the Checkboxes' listener object.

Whenever the state of the Checkbox is changed, it will generate a ItemEvent instance which is dispatched to its registered listeners. The ItemEvent class is used by a number of different AWT Components and its major resources are listed in Table 2.12. For an ItemEvent generated by a Checkbox instance, the getItemSelectable() method returns the identity of the instance which generated it and the getItem() method will return its label.

The following header and *init()* method, from a class called *CheckExample* that extends *Applet*, creates four Checkbox components configured as check buttons, which might be a part of an interface that selects the formatting options for a font. The *CheckExample* class also implements the ItemListener interface, allowing it to be registered with each of the Checkboxes (**this**) as the destination of the ItemEvents generated when they are checked or unchecked.

```
0001   // Filename CheckExample.java.
0002   // Provides an example of the AWT Checkbox class,
0003   // configured as a check box buttons.
0004   // Written for the Java interface book Chapter 2 - see text.
0005   //
0006   // Fintan Culwin, v 0.2, August 1997.
0007
0008   import java.awt.*;
0009   import java.applet.*;
0010   import java.awt.event.*;
0011
0012
0013   public class CheckExample extends    Applet
0014                             implements ItemListener {
```

class-wide constant attributes	
SELECTED DESELECTED	Manifest value to determine what caused the event to be generated.
ITEM_STATE_CHANGED	Manifest value for the ID of the event generated.

instance methods	
public Object getItem()	Obtains the identity of the Item which generated the event.
public int getStateChange()	Returns SELECTED or DESELECTED
public ItemSelectable getItemSelectable()	Obtains the identity of the ItemSelectable which generated the event.

TABLE 2.12   Major resources of the ItemEvent class.

```
0015
0016  private Checkbox  boldButton;
0017  private Checkbox  italicButton;
0018  private Checkbox  underlineButton;
0019  private Checkbox  smallcapsButton;
0020
0021     public void init() {
0022         this.setLayout( new GridLayout( 2, 2, 5, 5));
0023
0024         boldButton = new Checkbox( "Bold");
0025         boldButton.addItemListener( this);
0026         this.add( boldButton);
0027
0028         italicButton = new Checkbox( "Italic");
0029         italicButton.addItemListener( this);
0030         this.add( italicButton);
0031
0032         underlineButton = new Checkbox( "Underline");
0033         underlineButton.addItemListener( this);
0034         this.add( underlineButton);
0035
0036         smallcapsButton = new Checkbox( "Small Capitals");
0037         smallcapsButton.addItemListener( this);
0038         this.add( smallcapsButton);
0039     } // End init.
```

The appearance of the interface produced by this code is shown in Figure 2.5 and shows that both the *Italic* and *Underline* Checkboxes have been selected by the user. A two by two GridLayout layout manager is installed into the Applet Panel in order to obtain the required visual appearance. From a consideration of the code and the image, it can be seen that components are added in a left right/ top down manner.

In order to implement the ItemListener interface, the CheckExample class must declare an *itemStateChanged()* method as follows.

```
0042  public void itemStateChanged( ItemEvent event) {
0043    System.out.print( "Item Selectable is ");
0044    if ( event.getItemSelectable() == boldButton) {
0045      System.out.println( "bold Button");
0046    } else if ( event.getItemSelectable() == italicButton) {
0047      System.out.println( "italic Button");
```

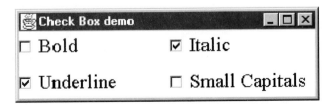

FIGURE 2.5   Checkbox example configured as check buttons.

```
0048          } else if ( event.getItemSelectable() == underlineButton) {
0049              System.out.println( "underline Button");
0050          } else if ( event.getItemSelectable() == smallcapsButton) {
0051              System.out.println( "small caps Button");
0052          } // End if.
0053
0054          System.out.println( "Item is " + event.getItem());
0055
0056          System.out.print( "State Change is ... ");
0057          if ( event.getStateChange() == ItemEvent.SELECTED) {
0058              System.out.println( "Selected");
0059          } else {
0060              System.out.println( "Deselected");
0061          } // End if.
0062
0063          if ( event.getID() == ItemEvent.ITEM_STATE_CHANGED ) {
0064              System.out.println( "ID is ITEM_STATE_CHANGED.");
0065          } // End if.
0066          System.out.println( "\n");
0066      } // End itemStateChanged.
```

The **CheckExample** class also declares a *main()* method, which does not differ significantly from the *ClickCounterTranslation main()* method of Chapter 1. When the application was launched and the *Italic* **Checkbox** selected and immediately deselected, the output produced was as follows.

```
Item Selectable is italic Button
Item is Italic
State Change is Selected
ID is ITEM_STATE_CHANGED.

Item Selectable is italic Button
Item is Italic
State Change is Deselected
ID is ITEM_STATE_CHANGED.
```

---

constructor

public CheckboxGroup()	Constructs a new **CheckboxGroup**.

---

instance methods

public void setSelectedCurrent(Checkbox *toSet*) **public** Checkbox getSelectedCheckbox()	Sets or obtains the currently selected member of the group.

TABLE 2.13 Major resources of the **CheckboxGroup** class.

The first line of each output is produced by lines 0043 to 0052 and shows that the getItemSelectable() method returns the identity of the Checkbox used. The second line is produced by line 0054 and shows that the getItem() returns the Checkbox's label. The third line differs between the two outputs and shows the use of the getState-Change() method on line 0057. Finally the only ID value which will be returned from a Checkbox is ITEM_STATE_CHANGE, used on line 0063.

In order to configure Checkbox instances as *radio buttons,* an instance of the CheckboxGroup class has to be created and specified as the group attribute of the set of buttons. The major resources of the CheckboxGroup class are given in Table 2.13.

The CheckboxGroup class encapsulates the identities of the Checkboxes which comprise its group and maintains knowledge of which one is currently selected. It has a single default constructor, an inquiry, and a modifier method for the currently selected component. The following *init()* method, from a class called *RadioExample*, creates four Checkbox components configured as radio buttons which might be a part of an interface that selects the formatting options for a paragraph.

```
0013   public class RadioExample extends    Applet
0014                          implements ItemListener {
0015
0016   private Checkbox   leftButton;
0017   private Checkbox   rightButton;
0018   private Checkbox   justifyButton;
0019   private Checkbox   centerButton;
0020
0021     public void init() {
0022
0023     CheckboxGroup theGroup  = new CheckboxGroup();
0024
0025        this.setLayout( new GridLayout( 2, 2, 5, 5));
0026
0027        leftButton = new Checkbox( "Left", false, theGroup);
0028        leftButton.addItemListener( this);
0029        this.add( leftButton);
0030
0031        rightButton  = new Checkbox( "Right", false, theGroup);
0032        rightButton.addItemListener( this);
0033        this.add( rightButton);
0034
0035        justifyButton = new Checkbox( "Justify", true, theGroup);
0036        justifyButton.addItemListener( this);
0037        this.add( justifyButton);
0038
0039        centerButton  = new Checkbox( "Centre", false, theGroup);
0040        centerButton.addItemListener( this);
0041        this.add( centerButton);
0042     } // End init.
```

Because all four Checkbox buttons have the same CheckboxGroup specified in their constructor, they will behave as a single group of radio buttons, and because the

Justify button has been constructed with its state specified **true,** it will be initially shown as selected. The appearance of the interface produced by the code, using a two by two GridLayout and with the *Right* radio button selected, is shown in Figure 2.6.

The examples in Figures 2.5 and 2.6 were realized in a Windows 95 environment and the use of a square marker for check box buttons and round markers for radio buttons is a property of the *peer* environment, not of Java.

Design Advice

A collection of mutually exclusive radio buttons should always be grouped closely together on an interface and made distinct from other groups of components.

The *itemStateChanged()* method included in the *RadioExample* class is exactly the same as that included in the *CheckExample* class. When the *Centre* button was pressed the output produced was as follows, showing that only the selection of the *Centre* button and not the deselection of the previously selected button generates an ItemEvent.

```
Item Selectable is centre Button
Item is Centre
State Change is Selected
ID is ITEM_STATE_CHANGED.
```

2.7 The Choice Class

The Choice class provides an *option menu,* which allows the user to select a single option from a list of choices. The major resources of this class are given in Table 2.14.

An instance of the Choice class encapsulates the list of Strings, known as *items,* which will be presented to the user on the option menu. These are added to the list using the add() or insert() method after the instance has been constructed, and can be removed using one of the remove() methods or the removeAll() method. If one of the select() methods is not used to indicate which item should be initially selected, the first item added is selected by default. The countItems() method will determine how many items are in the list, getItem() will obtain an item given its index, and the currently selected item can be obtained as an **int**eger value with getSelectedIndex() or as a String with getSelectedItem().

When an item in the list is selected, an ItemEvent instance is generated and passed as an argument to each of the *itemStateChanged()* methods of the Listener objects registered with addItemListener().

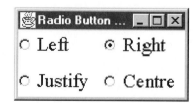

FIGURE 2.6   Checkbox example
configured as radio buttons.

constructor	
public Choice()	Constructs a new Choice instance.

instance methods	

public synchronized void addItem(
                    String *item*)
public synchronized void insert(
                    String *item*,
                    int   *here*)
	Adds *item* at the end of the list of options or at the location *here*, counting from 0.

public synchronized void remove(
                    int *fromHere*)
public synchronized void remove(
                    String *item*)
public synchronized void removeAll()
	Removes the *item* specified, the item at index location *fromHere*, or all items in the list. May throw *IllegalArgumentException*.

public void select(String *item*) **public synchronized void** select(**int** *toSelect*)	Selects the *item* specified, or the item at *toSelect*. May throw *IllegalArgumentException*.
public String getSelectedItem() **public int** getSelectedIndex()	Gets the *item* String, or position, of the currently selected item.
public String getItem(**int** *index*)	Gets the *item* at the position specified.
public int getItemCount()	Obtains the number of items in the list.

public void addItemListener(
                    ItemListener *listener*)
public void removeItemListener(
                    ItemListener *listener*)
	Registers or removes a listener for the ItemEvents generated by the button. More than one listener can be registered, but there is no guarantee on the sequence in which they will be called.

TABLE 2.14   Major resources of the Choice class.

The following *init()* method, from a class called *ChoiceExample,* creates a Choice instance and adds seven items enumerating the days of the week. It is preceded by a Label providing a prompt for the options.

```
0018    private Choice dayChoice;
0019
0020    public void init() {
0021
0022    Label promptLabel;
0023
0024        dayChoice = new Choice();
0025        dayChoice.addItemListener( this);
0026
0027        dayChoice.addItem( "Sunday");
0028        dayChoice.addItem( "Monday");
```

```
0029        dayChoice.addItem( "Tuesday");
0030        dayChoice.addItem( "Wednesday");
0031        dayChoice.addItem( "Thursday");
0032        dayChoice.addItem( "Friday");
0033        dayChoice.addItem( "Saturday");
0034
0035        promptLabel = new Label( "Today is ", Label.RIGHT);
0036
0037        this.add( promptLabel);
0038        this.add( dayChoice);
0039      } // End init.
```

This fragment need not specify a LayoutManager explicitly because the default FlowLayout is appropriate. The appearance of this interface is shown in Figure 2.7

A minor change was made to the *itemStateChanged()* method, as follows, to allow for the consideration that the only possible ItemSource for the event must be the *dayChoice* instance.

```
0042    public void itemStateChanged( ItemEvent event) {
0043
0044        if ( event.getItemSelectable() == dayChoice) {
0045            System.out.println( "Item Selectable is dayChoice.");
0046        } // End if.
```

The output produced when "Friday" was selected was as follows and is comparable with the previous outputs.

```
Item Selectable is dayChoice.
Item is Friday
State Change is Selected
ID is ITEM_STATE_CHANGED.
```

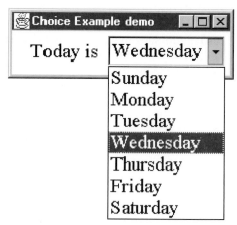

FIGURE 2.7   Choice example showing the days of the week.

This illustrates the distinction between the item and itemSelectable attributes of an ItemEvent instance which might not have been obvious from the previous examples. The itemSelectable attribute always identifies the Component which generated the event, and the item attribute the precise part of the Component which was selected; for CheckBoxes this was always the label which they were displaying, but for Choice components it can be any of the items on its list.

Design Advice

An option menu must always have one item selected. A set of radio buttons can have zero items selected, but this should be avoided as it would confuse the user. Radio buttons should be avoided when there are more than about five alternatives or when screen space is tight.

2.8 The List Class

The List class provides a (possibly scrolling) list box which allows the user to select one option, or a number of options, from a list of choices. The major resources of this class are given in Table 2.15.

An instance of the List class encapsulates a list of Strings, known as *items*, which represent the choices to be presented to the user. It also knows if it is available for single or multiple selections and the number of items in the list (*rows*) which are to be visible. If the number of rows is less than the number of items in the list, then the List will automatically supply a vertical Scrollbar to navigate the list.

The third constructor requires the number of rows to be specified and a **boolean** value to indicate if multiple selections are to be allowed. The two add() methods allow a single item to be added to the end of the list or to be added at a specific location within the list. The two remove() methods allow a single item or a continuous range of items to be deleted and removeAll() clears the list. The getItemCount() method indicates the number of items in the list.

The two methods, setMultipleMode() and isMultipleMode(), allow the multiple selection state of the list to be set or queried. The select() and deSelect() methods are supplied to allow items within the list to be selected, and the isSelected() **boolean** inquiry method will indicate the state of an individual item.

The getRows() and getVisibleIndex() methods indicate the number of visible items and the first item which is visible. The makeVisible() method makes sure that the specified item is visible somewhere within the list's window.

The getSelectedIndex() should only be used if the List is in single selection mode and returns the index of the currently selected item or -1 if none are selected. If the list

---

constructors	
`public` List() `public` List(**int** *numberVisisble*) `public` List(**int** *numberVisisble*, **boolean** *multipleAllowed*)	Constructs a new empty List with the default number of items visible or *numberVisible*, and allowing (**true**) or denying (**false**) multiple selections.

TABLE 2.15   Major resources of the List class.

TABLE 2.15 (continued)

---

instance methods

`public synchronized void addItem(`
`                String toAdd)`
`public synchronized void addItem(`
`                String toAdd,`
`                int    addhere)`
	Adds *toAdd* to the end of the list of options or at the location *addHere,* counting from 0.

`public synchronized void replaceItem(`
`                String replaceWith,`
`                int replacehere)`
	Replaces the String at the location *replaceHere* specified with *replaceWith.*

`public synchronized void remove(`
`                int fromHere)`
`public synchronized void remove(`
`                String item)`
`public synchronized void removeAll()`
	Removes the *item* specified, the item at index location *fromHere,* or all items in the list. May throw *IllegalArgumentException.*

`public synchronized void select(`
`                int toSelect)`
`public synchronized void deselect(`
`                int toDeselect)`
`public boolean isIndexSelected(`
`                int thisOne)`
	Selects the item at the index specified. Deselects the item at the index specified. Determines if the item at the index specified is selected.

`public synchronized String`
`                getSelectedItem()`
 	
`public synchronized int`
`                getSelectedIndex()`
	Gets the *item* String or the location of the currently selected item: **null** or -1 if none is selected.

`public synchronized String[]`
`                getSelectedItems()`
 	
`public synchronized int[]`
`                getSelectedIndexes()`
	Gets the *item* Strings, the locations of the currently selected items, or an empty array if none are currently selected.

`public String getItem( int index)` `public synchronized String[] getItems()`	Gets the *item* at the position specified or all *items* in the list.
`public int getItemCount()` `public int getRows()`	Obtains the number of options in the list. Obtains the number of currently visible items.

`public synchronized void`
`        setMultipleMode( boolean mode)`
`public boolean isMultipleMode()`
	Sets (**true**) or resets (**false**) multiple selections. Determines if the list is in multiple mode.

`public void makeVisible( int thisOne)`	Ensures that *thisOne* is visible, somewhere within the scrolling window.

`public void addItemListener(`
`                ItemListener listener)`
`public void removeItemListener(`
`                ItemListener listener)`
	Registers or removes a listener for the ItemEvents generated by the button. More than one listener can be registered, but there is no guarantee on the sequence they will be called.

is in multiple selection mode, the getSelectedIndexes() method will return an array of the indexes of the currently selected items. This will be empty (i.e., its length attribute will be 0) if none are selected. The getSelectedItem() and getSelectedItems() methods return a String or an array of Strings in a similar manner.

The following *init()* method, from a class called *SingleListExample*, creates a List instance and adds seven items naming European capital cities, accompanied by a Label providing a prompt for the choices.

```
0014   public class SingleListExample extends      Applet
0015                                 implements ItemListener {
0016
0017
0018      public void init() {
0019
0020      List    cityList;
0021      Label   promptLabel;
0022
0023        this.setLayout( new BorderLayout());
0024
0025        cityList = new List( 7, false);
0026        cityList.addItemListener( this);
0027
0028        cityList.addItem( "London");
0029        cityList.addItem( "Paris");
0030        cityList.addItem( "Barcelona");
0031        cityList.addItem( "Athens");
0032        cityList.addItem( "Rome");
0033        cityList.addItem( "Istanbul");
0034        cityList.addItem( "Berlin");
0035
0036        promptLabel = new Label( "Which city have you visited?");
0037
0038        this.add( promptLabel, "North");
0039        this.add( cityList,    "Center");
0040      } // End init.
```

A BorderLayout manager is required for this example because a GridLayout allocates identical amounts of space for all of its children and this would not be appropriate for this interface. A Container with a BorderLayout policy has a maximum of five children can be placed into its *"North," "South," "East," "West,"* and *"Center"* locations as shown in Figure 2.8. Unlike the GridLayout and FlowLayout managers, which have been used so far, this manager does not force all the children to be the same size. The location of a child within a BorderLayout policy is specified by a second String argument to the Container's add() method, as shown on lines 0038 and 0039.

The appearance of the *ListExample* is shown in Figure 2.9. The start of the *itemStateChanged()* method for this class is as follows. It differs from the previous versions by explicitly retrieving the identity of the ItemSelectable component from the ListEvent and, using a cast, storing it in the local variable *theList.* This allows the List getSelectedIndex()

North		
W e s t	Center	E a s t
South		

FIGURE 2.8   BorderLayout policy management.

and getSelectedItem() methods to be demonstrated on lines 0051 and 0052. The remainder of the method is as in the previous examples.

```
0043    public void itemStateChanged( ItemEvent event) {
0044
0045    List theList = (List) event.getItemSelectable();
0046
0047       if ( theList == cityList) {
0048          System.out.println( "Item Selectable is cityList.");
0049       } // End if.
0050
0051       System.out.println( "Item index  is " +
0052                            theList.getSelectedIndex());
0053       System.out.println( "Item string is " +
0054                            theList.getSelectedItem());
——          // Remainder as before!
```

The output produced by this method when "*Barcelona*" was selected is as follows.

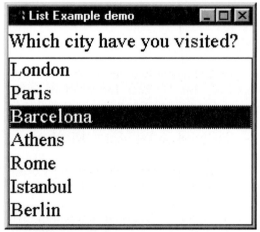

Figure 2.9   List instance in single selection mode
without a Scrollbar.

```
Item Selectable is cityList.
Item index is 2
Item string is Barcelona
State Change is Selected
ID is ITEM_STATE_CHANGED.
```

A small change to the *init()* method, in a class called *MutipleListExample*, will demonstrate the appearance of a List when a ScrollBar is required and when multiple selections are allowed. Both changes can be effected on line 0025 as follows. The appearance of this example is shown in Figure 2.10.

```
0025        cityList = new List( 4, true);
```

Figure 2.10 shows that only four of the seven items on the list are visible, the non-visible items can be made visible by using the scroll bar at the right of the list. It also shows, by the selection of "*Barcelona*" and "*Rome*", that multiple selection is allowed. The *itemStateChanged()* method for this class is as follows and outputs a list of all the items which are selected every time an item is selected or deselected.

```
0043    public void itemStateChanged( ItemEvent event) {
0044
0045    List    theList    = (List) event.getItemSelectable();
0046    String visited[]  = theList.getSelectedItems();
0047
0048        if ( visited.length == 0) {
0049            System.out.println( "No items are now selected!");
0050        } else {
0051            for ( int index = 0; index < visited.length; index++) {
0052                System.out.print( visited[ index] + " ");
0053            } // End for.
0054            System.out.println();
0055        } // End if.
0056    } // End itemStateChanged.
```

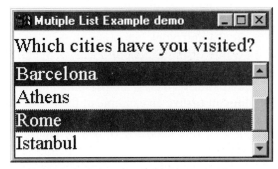

FIGURE 2.10   List instance in multiple selection mode with a Scrollbar.

On line 0045 the identity of the List is retrieved, as before, and on line 0046 the array of Strings containing the selected items is obtained using its getSelectedItems() method. If the list is empty, a message stating this is output on line 0049, otherwise, a **for** loop outputs all the items in the list on lines 0051 to 0055. The output produced by this method when the cities "*Barcelona,*" "*Istanbul,*" and "*Athens*" were first selected and then deselected is as follows.

```
Barcelona
Barcelona Istanbul
Barcelona Athens Istanbul
Barcelona Istanbul
Barcelona
No items are now selected!
```

Design Advice

Use a *list box* instead of an *option menu* when there are multiple items which have to be selected, when there is a large number of items to be selected from, or when the number of items in the list might change.

2.9 The Scrollbar Class

The Scrollbar class provides an area containing a *slider,* which can be dragged from one end of the bar to the other to indicate a quantitative value, and *arrow icons* at each end which can be used for fine adjustment of the slider. The major resources of this class are presented in Table 2.16.

A Scrollbar's orientation attribute determines if it is presented to the user in a HORIZONTAL or VERTICAL direction. The minimum and maximum attributes determine the value of the left (or top) and right (or bottom) of the Scrollbar and the value is determined by the location of the *slider,* whose size is controlled by the visible attribute. Clicking either of the arrow icons at the ends of the bar will adjust the value by the unit attribute, and clicking on the scroll bar outside the extent of the *slider* will adjust the value by the block attribute.

If no explicit values are established for these attributes then the default orientation is VERTICAL, minimum is 0, maximum is 100, value is 0, and visible is 10. Unit increment will default to 1 and block increment to the visible value.

Whenever the value of the Scrollbar is changed, an AdjustmentEvent is generated and dispatched to any AdjustmentListener objects registered with it. The major resources of the AdjustmentEvent class are presented in Table 2.17.

Because it is difficult to give an example of the use of a Scrollbar without embedding it in an applet, the example in this section will implement a *DecimalToHex* converter. The appearance of this applet is shown in Figure 2.11. It is used to convert between decimal and hexadecimal values in the (decimal) range 0 to 255.

The State Transition Diagram for this applet is given in Figure 2.12. It shows that there is a single state with five transitions, one for each possible user action. The single state and small number of transitions, all without preconditions, suggest that the applet should be simple and intuitive to use.

constructors

`public Scrollbar()`
`public Scrollbar( int orientation)`
`public Scrollbar( int orientation,`
`                int initialValue`
`                int pageSize`
`                int minimum`
`                int maximum)`
	Creates a new Scrollbar with all default values, or with *orientation* and other attributes as specified. The *orientation* attribute can be one of the values VERTICAL or HORIZONTAL.

instance methods

`public synchronized void`
`       setOrientation( int orientation)`
`public int getOrientation()`
	Sets or obtains the orientation of the Scrollbar.

`public void setValue( int newValue)` `public int getValue()`	Sets or obtains the value of the Scrollbar, between its minimum and maximum values.

`public synchronized void`
`            setMinimum( int newMinimum)`
`public int getMinimum()`	

`public synchronized void`
`            setMaximum( int newMaximum)`
`public int getMaximum()`
	Sets or obtains the minimum and maximum attributes.

`public synchronized void`
`       setUnitIncrement( int unitValue)`
`public int getUnitIncrement()`	

`public synchronized void`
`       setBlockIncrement( int blockValue)`
`public int getBlockIncrement()`
	Sets or obtains the unit and block attributes.

`public synchronized void`
`     setVisibleAmount( int visibleValue)`
`public int getVisibleAmount()`
	Sets or obtains the visible attribute.

`public void setValues(int newValue,`
`                int newVisible,`
`                int newMinimum,`
`                int newMaximum);`
	Sets the specified attributes of the Scrollbar.

`public void addAdjustmentListener(`
`            ItemListener listener)`
`public void removeAdjustmentListener(`
`            ItemListener listener)`
	Registers or removes a listener for the AdjustmentEvents generated by the Scrollbar. More than one listener can be registered, but there is no guarantee on the sequence in which they will be called.

TABLE 2.16   Major resources of the Scrollbar class.

class-wide constant attributes

UNIT_INCREMENT UNIT_DECREMENT BLOCK_INCREMENT BLOCK_DECREMENT TRACK	Manifest values to indicate exactly how the value was changed.
ADJUSTMENT_VALUE_CHANGED	Manifest value for the ID of the event generated.

instance methods

public Adjustable getAdjustable ()	Obtains the identity of the Adjustable object which generated the event.
public int getAdjustmentType()	Obtains the exact reason why the value changed.
public int getValue()	Obtains the adjusted value of the Adjustable.

TABLE 2.17　Major resources of the AdjustableEvent class.

The *init()* method of the *DecimalToHex* class creates the interface which consists of two Labels and a Scrollbar mounted on the applet's Panel in a three by one GridLayout.

```
0001   // Filename DecimalToHex.java.
0002   // Provides an example of the AWT Scrollbar class.
0003   // Written for the Java interface book Chapter 2 - see text.
0004   //
0005   // Fintan Culwin, v 0.2, August 1997.
0006
0007   import java.awt.*;
0008   import java.awt.event.*;
0009   import java.applet.*;
0010
0011
0012   public class DecimalToHex extends      Applet
0013                             implements AdjustmentListener {
0014
0015   private Scrollbar scroller;
0016   private Label     decimalLabel;
```

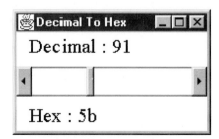

FIGURE 2.11　A Scrollbar-based *DecimalToHex* applet.

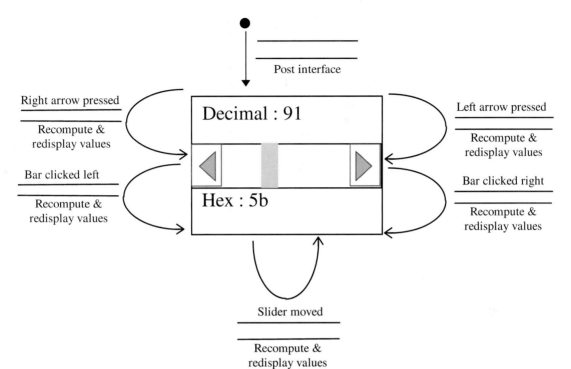

FIGURE 2.12   The *DecimaltoHex* applet's STD.

```
0017    private Label      hexLabel;
0018
0019    public void init() {
0020
0021        this.setLayout( new GridLayout( 3, 1, 5, 5));
0022
0023        scroller = new Scrollbar( Scrollbar.HORIZONTAL, 0, 1, 0, 255);
0024        scroller.setBlockIncrement( 10);
0025        scroller.addAdjustmentListener( this);
0026
0027        decimalLabel = new Label();
0028        hexLabel     = new Label();
0029
0030        this.add( decimalLabel);
0031        this.add( scroller);
0032        this.add( hexLabel);
0033
0034        this.update();
0035    } // End init.
```

The identities of the three components will be required by other methods within the class, so they are declared as **private** data attributes outside the scope of any method on lines 0015, 0016, and 0017. The *init()* method is comparable to the other *init()* methods previously presented in this chapter. The Scrollbar constructor on line

0023 creates a horizontal Scrollbar instance with an initial value of 0, a visible size of 1, a minimum of 0, and a maximum of 255. The *unit* increment defaults to 1, and on line 0024 the *block* increment is set to 10. On line 0025 the AdjustmentListener is specified as **this**, which requires the DecimalToHex class to implement the AdjustmentListener interface, as stated on line 0013.

A 3 row by 1 column GridLayout is specified on line 0021 to produce the required relationship between the three components, which are added in the appropriate sequence on lines 0030 to 0032. No explicit value is specified for either of the Label components because the call to the *update()* method on line 0033 will supply them.

In order to implement the AdjustmentListener interface, the *DecimalToHex* class has to declare an *adjustmentValueChanged()* method as follows. This method indirects to the *update*() method, causing the values shown on the two Labels to change, in order to reflect the new value of the Scrollbar.

```
0038    public void adjustmentValueChanged() AdjustmentEvent event) {
0039        this.update();
0040    } // End adjustmentValueChanged.
0041
0042
0043    protected void update() {
0044
0045    int     theValue    = scroller.getValue();
0046    String  decimalValue = new String( Integer.toString( theValue, 10));
0047    String  hexValue    = new String( Integer.toString( theValue, 16));
0048
0049    String  decimalString = new String( "Decimal : " +  decimalValue);
0050    String  hexString    = new String( "Hex : " +  hexValue);
0051
0052        decimalLabel.setText(  decimalString);
0053        hexLabel.setText(      hexString);
0054    } // End update.
```

The purpose of this method is to obtain the value of the slider, format it as a decimal and hexadecimal string, and then install the Strings into the two Labels. The precise details of this process are not relevant to the consideration of the user interface construction. Briefly the value is retrieved as an **int** on line 0045, formatted on lines 0046 and 0047, catenated with the prompts on lines 0049 and 0050, and installed into the Labels on lines 0052 and 0053.

The user can interact with this interface by dragging the slider and having the values continually updated. Alternatively they could click on one of the arrows to increment or decrement the value by 1, or click on the scrollBar outside the slider to increment or decrement the value by 10.

Design Advice

Use a *ScrollBar* for the input of quantitative data only when the range is relatively small; otherwise consider using a *TextField*.

2.10 The Canvas Class

The Canvas class supplies a screen area upon which graphical output can be produced, or which can be extended to provide a specialized user interface component. The major resources of this class are presented in Table 2.18.

The Canvas constructor takes no arguments and creates an empty drawing area. The only method declared by the class is paint(), which overrides the Component paint() method. The argument to this method is a Graphics *context* whose construction, meaning, and use will be explained later in this chapter and in following chapters.

To illustrate the Canvas class a *Doodle* applet will be constructed. This applet supplies a small drawing area upon which doodles can be produced by dragging the mouse pointer. The appearance of this applet is given in Figure 2.13 and its STD in Figure 2.14.

As with the *DecimalToHex* applet, the simplicity of this STD and the absence of any preconditions indicates that it should be very intuitive to the user. However, in order to implement this design the Canvas class will have to be extended to produce the *Doodle* class. The reason for this is concerned with the need for the *Doodle* instance to handle its own events and not to have them handled on its behalf by a listener object. This will require the *Doodle* instance handling its own events via the event-dispatching mechanism and, unlike all the examples which have been introduced so far, not relying upon the registration of listeners.

As an extension of the Canvas class, the *Doodle* class should be completely self-contained so that other clients could use a *Doodle* instance simply by **import**ing the class and not by having to both **import** the class and provide a listener.

In order for the Doodle class to encapsulate its own event-processing functionality, it will have to enable the appropriate events upon itself by using the Component enableEvents() method and overriding the appropriate process*Whatever*Event() methods. Specifically, from the STD, it will have to enable MOUSE_MOTION events and MOUSE_EVENT (mouse button) events, and override the processMouseEvent() and processMouseMotionEvent() methods. The first part of the implementation of the Doodle class is as follows.

```
0038   class Doodle extends Canvas {
0039
0040   private  int      lastX;
```

constructor	
public Canvas()	Creates a new Canvas.

instance methods	
public int paint(Graphics *context*)	Override to display the contents of the Canvas.

TABLE 2.18   Major resources of the Canvas class.

FIGURE 2.13 A Canvas-based *Doodle* applet.

```
0041   private  int        lastY;
0042   private  Graphics context;
0043
0044      protected Doodle( int width, int height) {
0045         super();
0046         this.setSize( width, height);
0047         this.enableEvents( AWTEvent.MOUSE_MOTION_EVENT_MASK |
0048                            AWTEvent.MOUSE_EVENT_MASK);
0049      } // End Doodle constructor.
0050
0051
0052      public void addNotify() {
0053         super.addNotify();
0054         context = this.getGraphics().create();
0055      } // End addNotify.
```

This class is not declared **public** as it is contained, for convenience, within the *CanvasExample* class file. This restricts its visibility to the *CanvasExample* class, pre-

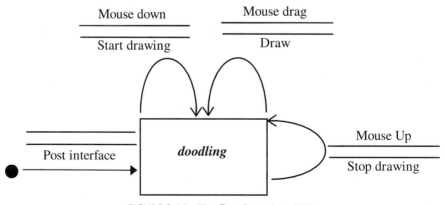

FIGURE 2.14 The *Doodle* applet's STD.

venting it from being seen or used outside that class. For this reason, its constructor is declared without **public** visibility on line 0044.

The first two **private** data attributes, *lastX* and *lastY*, declared on lines 0040 and 0041 are used to record the last known location of the mouse pointer. The third attribute, an instance of the Graphics class called *context*, is required to draw on the *Doodle*'s window as will be explained briefly now and in detail in following chapters.

The constructor commences by calling its parent (Canvas) constructor and then setting its size to that indicated by its two arguments. On lines 0047 and 0048 the two masks, MOUSE_MOTION_EVENT_MASK and MOUSE_EVENT_MASK, declared in the AWTEvent class, are *or*ed (I) together and the resulting value passed as an argument to the *Doodle*'s enableEvents() method. The consequence of this is that events generated by moving the mouse or pressing its buttons will be dispatched directly to the *Doodle* instance and not to any registered listener objects. In order for the instance to be able to respond to these events, its processMouseEvent() and processMouse-MotionEvent() methods will have to be overridden as shown later.

The *Doodle*'s addNotify() method also needs to be overridden in order to initialize the *Graphics context* instance. This method will be called when the peer component is created and it is only at this stage, when the physical properties of the component's window are known, that its Graphics attribute can be obtained and copied, as on line 0054.

```
0058      protected void processMouseEvent( MouseEvent event) {
0059
0060          if ( event.getID() == MouseEvent.MOUSE_PRESSED) {
0061              lastX = event.getX();
0062              lastY = event.getY();
0063          } // End if.
0064      } // End processMouseEvent.
0065
0066
0068      protected void processMouseMotionEvent( MouseEvent event) {
0069
0070          if ( event.getID() == MouseEvent.MOUSE_DRAGGED) {
0071          int currentX = event.getX();
0072          int currentY = event.getY();
0073
0074              context.drawLine( lastX, lastY, currentX, currentY);
0075              lastX = currentX;
0076              lastY = currentY;
0077          } // End if.
0078      } // End processMouseMotionEvent.
0079
0080  } // End class Doodle.
```

The *processMouseEvent()* method will be called every time a mouse button is pressed or released and, as this class is only interested in mouse press events, line 0060 uses the MouseEvent's getID() method to determine if the event was generated by a mouse press. If so, the getX() and getY() methods are called to obtain and store the current location of the mouse pointer in the classes' instance attributes, *lastX* and *lastY*.

The *processMouseMotionEvent()* method contains a similar guard and responds only to mouse drag events, drawing a line from the last known mouse location to the current location. As the current location will be the last known location for the next mouse drag event, the values of the instance attributes are updated before the method finishes. A Graphics instance encapsulates within itself all the knowledge required to draw onto a particular window; its drawLine() method, as used on line 0074, will draw a line from the position specified by its first two arguments to that specified by its last two arguments.

The effect of these two methods is that when a mouse down event occurs, the *Doodle* instance gets ready to draw by storing the location where the event occurred. A succession of mouse drag events may then occur, the first of which will cause a line to be drawn from the location of the mouse press to the current location of the mouse, and subsequently from where the last line ended to the current location. When the mouse button is released mouse drag events will stop being dispatched and the mouse can be moved, without drawing, until the button is pressed again, repeating the sequence.

The *processMouseEvent()* and *processMouseMotionEvent()* methods are both declared with **protected** visibility as they are called indirectly from the processEvent() method, inherited from the Component class as a consequence of the events being enabled upon the component by the enableEvent() method called on line 0047. This is unlike the declaration of methods by listener interfaces, such as actionPerformed(), which must be declared with **public** visibility.

As the *Doodle* class encapsulates all the drawing functionality, the *CanvasExample* class need only declare an instance of the class and install it, as follows, to provide the demonstration client. Any other client which requires a doodling area could likewise import the *Doodle* class, assuming it were stored in its own file, and create and install an instance into its interface.

```
0001   // Filename CanvasExample.java.
0002   // Provides an initial example of extending the AWT canvas class.
0003   // Written for the Java interface book Chapter 2 - see text.
0004   //
0005   // Fintan Culwin, v 0.2, August 1997.
0006
0007   import java.awt.*;
0008   import java.awt.event.*;
0009   import java.applet.*;
0010
0011
0012   public class CanvasExample extends Applet {
0013
0014   private Doodle aDoodlingArea;
0015
0016      public void init() {
0017         aDoodlingArea = new Doodle( 200, 150);
```

```
0018          this.add( aDoodlingArea);
0019        } // End init.
0020
0021
0022      public static void main( String args[]) {
—       // Details of main() omitted,
0032
0033        } // End main.
0034   } // End class CanvasExample.
```

This event-handling technique, enabling events on the component and overriding the methods which process the events enabled, should only be used when a Component is having its functionality extended. Where an established Component, either pre-supplied or extended, is being used in an interface then the alternative technique, of registering listeners with it, should be used. The Doodle component is totally self-contained and does not generate any events which have to be listened to, which may be required if it is to be re-used as a part of a more complex interface. The techniques to introduce this capability will be introduced when more complex extended components are introduced in the next chapter.

2.11 The TextComponent, TextArea, and TextField Classes

These three classes supply facilitates for the input, and output, of text information. The TextComponent class is not intended to be instantiated, although it is not declared **abstract**, and provides common behavior for the single-line TextField and multiple-line TextArea classes. This section will only introduce the TextField class, the TextArea class will be introduced in Chapter 5. The major resources of the TextComponent class are presented in Table 2.19.

There is no constructor for this class as it is only intended that instances of the TextField or TextArea classes be created. The major resources added by the TextField class are presented in Table 2.20.

The constructors allow various combinations of the String to be initially displayed and the number of columns to be specified. The number of columns defaults to the number of characters in the String for the second constructor and zero for the default constructor. The String contained within the TextField can be longer than the number of columns, in which case it can be scrolled to the left and right by the user's actions. If the echoChar attribute is set, then the specified character will be used to give the user feedback as they type in the field, as will be demonstrated. An Action-Event is generated whenever the user activates the text in the component, usually by pressing the <ENTER> key. The ActionEvent generated will contain the contents of the TextField as its actionCommand attribute. For single-line text, it is more convenient to handle ActionEvents than to handle the TextEvents which are generated every time the text in the component changes.

To illustrate the use of TextField components, a *PasswordEntry* applet will be produced. This applet will start by inviting the user to "Please enter the magic word" in a non-editable TextField. A second editable text field with the echo character set to an

instance methods	
public **void** setText(String setTo) **public** String getText()	Sets, or obtains, the text shown in the component.

public String getSelectedText()
public **void** selectAll()
 	
public **void** select(**int** *fromhere*
                    int *tohere*)
 	
public **void** setSelectionStart(
                        int *startHere*)
 	
public **int** getSelectionStart()
 	
Public **void** setSelectionEnd(
                        int *endHere*)
 	
public **int** getSelectionEnd()
	Obtains the selected text, or obtains or sets its location within the TextComponent. The extent of the selection may also be set by the users' interactions with the peer.

public **void** setCaretPosition(**int** *toHere*) **public** **int** getCaretPosition()	Sets, or obtains, the location of the insertion point (conventionally shown as a caret glyph).
public **void** setEditable(**boolean** *editable*) **public** **boolean** isEditable()	Allows the contents of the component to be changed (**true**) or not (**false**) by the user or obtains the value of the attribute.

public **void** addTextListener(
                    ItemListener *listener*)
 	
public **void** removeTextListener(
                    ItemListener *listener*)
	Registers or removes a listener for the TextEvents generated by the TextComponent. More than one listener can be registered, but there is no guarantee of the sequence in which they are called.

TABLE 2.19   Major resources of the TextComponent class.

asterisk (*) will allow the user to type in an attempt. When the user presses the
<ENTER> key the attempt will be checked, and if it is incorrect the password entry
field will be cleared so that the user can try again. When the user inputs the correct
password the password entry field will be removed from the interface, and the prompt
field will display "Welcome to the magic garden." The appearance of the two states of
the applet are shown in Figure 2.15.

The state transition diagram for this applet is given in Figure 2.16.

The implementation of this class, as far as the end of its constructor, is as follows.

```
0001   // Filename PasswordEntry.java.
0002   // Provides an initial example of the AWT TextField class.
0003   // Written for the Java interface book Chapter 2 - see text.
0004   //
0005   // Fintan Culwin, v 0.2, August 1997.
0006
0007   import java.awt.*;
0008   import java.awt.event.*;
```

constructors

public TextField()	
public TextField(String *contents*)	Creates a new empty TextField, or one with contents and number of columns, or default number of columns, as specified
public TextField(String *contents* **int** *columns*)	

instance methods

public void setColumns(**int** *thisMany*) **public int** getColumns()	Sets, or obtains, the number of columns visible.
public void setEchoChar(**char** *setTo*) **public boolean** echoCharIsSet() **public int** getEchoChar()	Sets, obtains, or determines if an echo character is set. If an echo character is set, then all input by the user will then be confirmed using this character.

public void addActionListener(
             ItemListener *listener*)
 	
public void removeActionListener(
             ActionListener *listener*)
	Registers or removes a listener for the ActionEvents generated by the TextField. More than one listener can be registered, but there is no guarantee of the sequence in which they will be called.

TABLE 2.20   Major resources of the TextField class.

```
0009   import java.applet.Applet;
0010
0011
0012   public class PasswordEntry extends    Applet
0013                            implements ActionListener {
0014
0015   private TextField passwordField;
0016   private TextField promptField;
0017
0018      public void init() {
0019
0020        passwordField = new TextField( 8);
0021        passwordField.setEchoChar( '*');
```

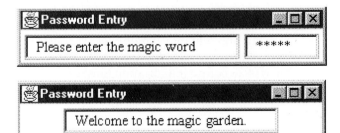

FIGURE 2.15   The two states of the *PasswordEntry* applet.

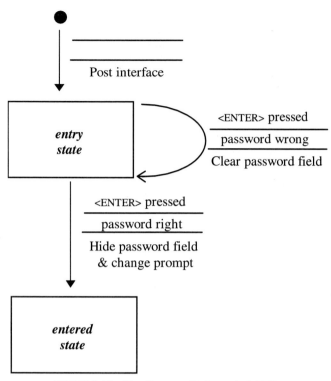

FIGURE 2.16 The *PasswordEntry* applet's STD.

```
0022          passwordField.addActionListener( this);
0023
0024          promptField = new TextField( "Please enter the magic word ");
0025          promptField.setEditable( false);
0026
0027          this.add( promptField);
0028          this.add( passwordField);
0029      } // End init.
```

On lines 0015 and 0016 two instance attributes of the TextField class are declared: the *promptField* to be used for the prompt, (shown on the left of Figure 2.15) and the *passwordField* used to collect the user's input (shown on the right). On lines 0020 to 0022 the *passwordField* is constructed as an eight-column empty TextField component, with its echo character set to an asterisk and its ActionListener set to itself. On lines 0024 and 0025 the non-editable *promptField* is constructed containing the text specified. The two TextFields are added to the applet Panel, using its default FlowLayout, on lines 0027 and 0028 before initialization finishes.

In order for this class to satisfy the requirement of the ActionListener interface, it must supply an *actionPerformed()* method as follows.

```
0032      public void actionPerformed( ActionEvent event){
0033
0034      String attempt = new String( passwordField.getText());
```

```
0035
0036            if ( attempt.equals( "fintan")) {
0037                promptField.setText( "Welcome to the magic garden.");
0038                passwordField.setVisible( false);
0039                promptField.getParent().doLayout();
0040            } else {
0041                passwordField.setText("");
0042            } // End if.
0043        } // End actionPerformed.
```

This method will be called every time the user presses the <ENTER> key and its first step, on line 0034, is to obtain the text which the user has input using the *passwordField* getText() method. The String obtained is then tested to see if it is the magic word, and if not the event handler will finish after the *passwordField* setText() method has cleared the password field, on line 0041.

If the user does enter the magic word the sequence of steps is first, on lines 0037 and 0038, to change the text in the *promptField* and to make the *passwordField* invisible. The doLayout() method of the *promptField*'s Panel parent is then called to cause the *promptField* to be centered within the available space, rather than to remain offset to the left after the *passwordField* disappears.

> ### Design Advice
>
> A non-editable TextField should only be used for a prompt when it accompanies another TextField, in order that the appearance of the two components will be compatible. Otherwise a Label should be used as a prompt.

An extensive example of the use of the TextArea class is included in Chapter 7 and a brief example in the next chapter.

2.12 PopUp Menus

The AWT menu classes form a separate hierarchy from the Component hierarchy used so far; its class hierarchy diagram is shown in Figure 2.17. This section will provide a brief introduction to implementing a popup menu; a more detailed introduction to menus in general will be given in Chapter 6.

The state transition diagram for this interface is given in Figure 2.18. It is based upon that for the *CanvasExample* given previously. A mouse down event will still cause drawing to start, but a double mouse click will post the popup menu offering the user two options of clearing the drawing or inverting the drawing colors. It is also possible that the user will unpost the menu by clicking with the mouse outside the extent of the popup menu.

The appearance of this applet showing the popup menu in the default (black on white) and inverted (white on black) modes is shown in Figure 2.19.

The popup menu is provided by an instance of the PopupMenu class upon which is mounted two instances of the MenuItem class, providing the two items labeled "*Clear*" and "*Invert.*" When the MenuItem buttons are pressed, an ActionEvent is generated which can be responded to by a registered ActionListener object. The *Doodle*

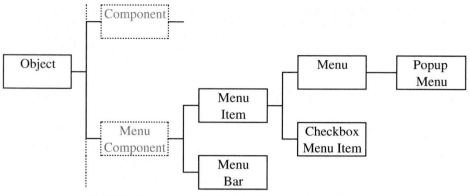

FIGURE 2.17   The Java AWT *MenuComponent* class hierarchy.

class, as just described, is the basis of the *PoppingDoodle* class whose implementation, as far as the end of its constructor, is as follows.

```
0041   class PoppingDoodle extends    Canvas
0042                      implements ActionListener {
0043
```

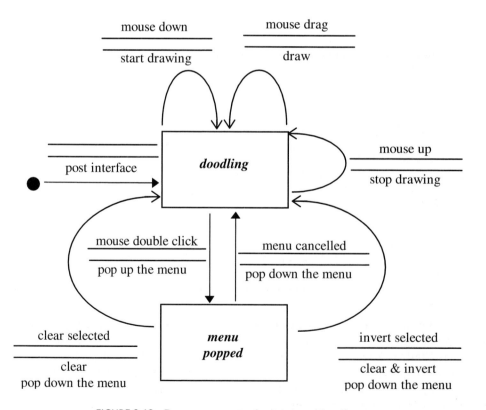

FIGURE 2.18   Popup menu example, state transition diagram.

FIGURE 2.19   Popup menu example in normal and inverted modes.

```
0044   private int        lastX;
0045   private int        lastY;
0046   private Graphics    context;
0047   private PopupMenu   popup;
0048   private MenuItem    clearItem;
0049   private MenuItem    invertItem;
0050
0051      protected PoppingDoodle( int width, int height) {
0052         super();
0053         this.setSize( width, height);
0054         this. enableEvents( AWTEvent.MOUSE_MOTION_EVENT_MASK |
0055                             AWTEvent.MOUSE_EVENT_MASK        |
0056                             AWTEvent.ACTION_EVENT_MASK         );
0057
0058         popup = new PopupMenu();
0059         this.add( popup);
0060
0061         clearItem = new MenuItem(   "Clear");
0062         clearItem.setActionCommand( "Clear");
0063         clearItem.addActionListener( this);
0064         popup.add( clearItem);
0065
0066         invertItem = new MenuItem(   "Invert");
0067         invertItem.setActionCommand( "Invert");
0068         invertItem.addActionListener( this);
0069         popup.add( invertItem);
0070      } // End PoppingDoodle constructor.
```

This class is not declared with **public** visibility for the same reasons as explained for the *Doodle* class. The first part of the constructor, as far as the call of *enableEvents()* starting on line 0054, is identical to that of the *Doodle* class. The argument to *enableEvents()* differs only, on line by 0056, by enabling ActionEvents in order to allow instances of the *PoppingDodle* class to respond to such events generated by the MenuItems contained within it.

The remaining parts of the constructor are concerned with constructing the popup menu and commence, on lines 0058 and 0059, with the construction of a Popup-Menu instance called *popup* and **add**ing it to the *PoppingDoodle* instance being constructed. On lines 0061 to 0063 the first MenuItem instance, called *clearItem*, is first constructed with its label set to "*Clear,*" has its actionCommand attribute set to "*Clear,*" has its actionListener attribute set to the current instance (**this**), and is finally **add**ed to the PopupMenu *popup.* The constructor concludes, on lines 0066 to 0069, by adding the *invertItem* MenuItem to the *popup* menu using the same techniques.

The *processMouseEvent()* method differs from that presented in the Doodle class as it now has to respond both to a single mouse press and a double mouse click. Its implementation, using the MouseEvent getClicksCounted() method, is as follows.

```
0098      protected void processMouseEvent( MouseEvent event) {
0099
0100          if ( event.getId() == MouseEvent.MOUSE_PRESSED) {
0101              if ( event.getClickCount() == 2) {
0102                  popup.show( this.getParent(), event.getX(), event.getY());
0103              } else {
0104                  lastX = event.getX();
0105                  lastY = event.getY();
0106              } // End if.
0107          } // End if.
0108      } // End processMouseEvent.
```

As with the Doodle processMouseEvent() method, this is only concerned with responding to mouse down occurrences. Line 0100 determines if this is the case and, on line 0101 the MouseEvent getClickCount() method is used to determine if a double mouse click occurred. If so, line 0102 pops-up the *popup* menu by calling its show() method passing as arguments the Component which it is to popup from and the location where it is to popup. Otherwise the steps taken for a single click, on lines 0104 and 0105, are the same as in the *Doodle* class.

The *processMouseMotion()* method and the *addNotify()* method do not differ from those of the *Doodle* class but a new method, *actionPerformed()*, has to be supplied in order for this class to conform to the ActionListener interface, as stated on line 0042. This method will be called whenever one of the MenuItems on the *popup* menu is activated and is implemented as follows.

```
0080      public void actionPerformed( ActionEvent event) {
0081
0082          String command = new String( event.getActionCommand());
0083          Color  hold;
0084
0085          if ( command.equals( "Clear")) {
0086              this.repaint();
0087          } else if ( command.equals( "Invert")) {
0088              hold = this.getBackground();
0089              this.setBackground( this.getForeground());
0090              this.setForeground( hold);
```

```
0091            context.setColor( hold);
0092            this.repaint();
0093         } // End if.
0094     } // End actionPerformed.
```

On line 0082 the actionCommand String is extracted from the *event* instance passed as an argument to the method and used on line 0085 to decide if the *Clear* menu item was pressed. If so then the repaint() method of the *PoppingDoodle* instance (**this**) is called, which will clear its window. Otherwise, on line 0087 the actionCommand is tested to see if it indicates that the *Invert* button was pressed and, if so, on lines 0088 to 0090 the Colors stored in the *PoppingDoodle*'s *foreground* and *background* attributes are swapped. Following this, line 0091 installs the new foreground Color into the Graphics *context* before *repaint()* is called. The effect of these steps is to invert the colors so, assuming that it is currently drawing in black on a white background, it will clear the window to a solid black background and prepare for drawing in white (or vice versa if it has already been inverted and is drawing in white on a black background).

Design Advice

A popup menu can save on screen space but gives no obvious clue of its existence, so it is difficult for a user to discover and is only suitable for experienced users.

2.13 The ScrollPane Class

The final Component to be introduced in this chapter is the ScrollPane class, which is a composite component supplying a window onto a larger child component and whose view of its single child component can be controlled by using its associated vertical and horizontal Scrollbars. The major resources of the ScrollPane class are given in Table 2.21.

constructors	
public ScrollPane() **public** ScrollPane(**int** *scrollbarPolicy*)	Creates a ScrollPane with the default SCROLLBARS_AS_NEEDED or with an explicit SCROLLBARS_ALWAYS or SCROLLBARS_NEVER policy.

instance methods	
public int getScrollbarDisplayPolicy()	Obtains the scrollbar display policy.

Public void setScrollPosition(**int** *x*,
                      int *y*)
 public void setScrollPosition(
                  Point *here*)
 public Point getScrollPosition()
	Sets, or obtains, the ScrollPosition of the child Component. This is the position on the child Component which is shown at the top left of the ScrollPane window.

TABLE 2.21   Major resources of the ScrollPane class.

To illustrate the use of this class it will be implemented with a much larger Canvas-based *CrossDoodle* instance contained within it. The *CrossDoodle* class is so called because it overrides the *paint()* method to draw a four-lined cross within itself. The appearance of the *ScrollPaneExample* class with the Scrollbars adjusted to show the upper left, middle, and lower right of the contained *CrossDoodle* (as indicated by the location of the Scrollbar's sliders) is shown in Figure 2.20.

The implementation of the *CrossDoodle* class, contained within the *ScrollPane-Example*'s class file, is as follows.

```
0041   class CrossDoodle extends Canvas {
0042
0043       protected CrossDoodle( int width, int height) {
0044           super();
0045           this.setSize( width, height);
0046       } // End CrossDoodle constructor.
0047
0048
0049       public void paint( Graphics context) {
0050
0051       int width  = this.getBounds().width;
0052       int height = this.getBounds().height;
0053
0054           context.drawLine( 0, 0, width, height);
0055           context.drawLine( 0, height, width, 0);
0056           context.drawLine( width/2, 0, width/2, height);
0057           context.drawLine( 0, height/2, width, height/2);
0058       } // End paint
0059   } // End class CrossDoodle.
```

The constructor is comparable to the previous *Doodle* and *PoppingDoodle* constructors. The *paint()* method draws four lines: from top left to bottom right on line 0054, from bottom left to top right on line 0055, vertically down the middle on line 0056, and horizontally across the middle on line 0057. An instance of this class is added to a ScrollPane instance in the *ScrollPaneExample* classes' *init()* method, as follows.

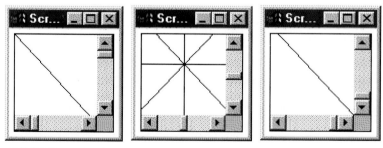

FIGURE 2.20 The *ScrollPaneExample* showing the top left, middle, and bottom right of the contained *CrossDoodle*.

```
0001   // Filename ScrollPaneExample.java.
0002   // Provides an initial example of the AWT ScrollPane class.
0003   // Written for the Java interface book Chapter 2 - see text.
0004   //
0005   // Fintan Culwin, v 0.2, August 1997.
0006
0007   import java.awt.*;
0008   import java.awt.event.*;
0009   import java.applet.*;
0010
0011
0012   public class ScrollPaneExample extends Applet {
0013
0014   private CrossDoodle aCrossDoodle;
0015   private ScrollPane   aScrollPane;
0016
0017      public void init() {
0018          aCrossDoodle = new CrossDoodle( 500, 550);
0019          aScrollPane  = new ScrollPane( ScrollPane.SCROLLBARS_ALWAYS);
0020          aScrollPane.add( aCrossDoodle);
0021          this.add( aScrollPane);
0022      } // End init.
```

On line 0018 a 500 by 500 (pixel) *CrossDoodle* instance called *aCrossDoodle* is constructed and, on line 0019, an instance of the *ScrollPane* class called *aScrollPane* is constructed with its scroll bar policy set to SCROLLBARS_ALWAYS. On line 0020 the *CrossDoodle* instance is added to the *ScrollPane* instance, and the *ScrollPane* instance is added to the applet Panel on line 0021. This is all that is required for the scrolling behavior illustrated in Figure 2.20 to be implemented, the *ScrollPane* automatically supplying the connection between the user's interactions with the Scrollbars and panning the *CrossDoodle* underneath its window.

Chapter Summary

- The Java AWT supplies a number of interface component classes. These include the Label, Button, Checkbox, Choice, Listbox, Canvas, TextField, TextArea, and ScrollPanel classes.

- FlowLayout, GridLayout, and BorderLayout managers can be used for different layout policies.

- The Component class is at the root of the AWT hierarchy and all of its attributes and methods are inherited by all other classes.

- The Component foreground, background, and font attribute values are inherited via the instance hierarchy.

- The MenuComponent hierarchy supplies the objects which can be used to construct menus.

- A popup menu has the advantage of saving screen space but has the disadvantage of not having any obvious indication of its presence.

- Applications should, in general, register event listeners with its components and should not explicitly enable and process events.

- An application can be its own listener object by registering itself with its included components.

- Extended components should, in general, explicitly enable and process their own events.

Exercises

2.1   The tables in this chapter provide only a brief overview of the AWT APIs. The most definitive version is in the documentation and source code for the AWT, which is provided as part of all Java environments. Consolidate your understanding of the classes in this chapter, and familiarize yourself with the format of this documentation, by reading the entries for the classes discussed.

2.2   While using your IDE to develop Java applets or any other commercial GUI product (for example your word processor), examine how the various components described in this chapter have been used in panels and dialogs.

2.3   Construct an applet from three Checkbox components configured as radio buttons and a single Label. Each radio button should identify one possible alignment, and the Label should change its label and alignment attributes to illustrate the selected button.

2.4   The output from the Scrollbar example is not very well formatted. Re-implement the example so that the decimal value is always three digits long and the hexadecimal value is always two digits long. Hint: Revisit the *ClickCounter* applet from Chapter 1.

2.5   Extend the Scrollbar example to add octal and binary values.

2.6   Adapt the Scrollbar example to implement a Centigrade to Fahrenheit converter with a range of 0°C to 100°C. Unlike the example in this chapter, this applet should make use of a separate (application) class to perform the conversion and a separate (translation) listener class to provide its behavior.

2.7   Extend the *Doodle* applet to give continuous feedback of the location of the pointer. This will require additional Label components and an extended *processMouseMoveEvent()* method.

2.8   Implement a TextField which will only allow the input of integer values, so that any non-digit characters should be removed from the display as soon as the user types them in. Adapt this applet for the input of floating point values which allow a single decimal point.

2.9   Extend the *Password* applet so that it locks with a suitable message after three unsuccessful attempts.

CHAPTER 3

Extending Pre-Supplied AWT Components

This chapter will illustrate the production of user interfaces which require specialized components to be developed by extending the pre-supplied Java components. Such specialized components are developed by extending a standard Component from the AWT, most commonly the Canvas class.

The first artifact which will be developed is a *StikNote* application, which provides the functionality of the pads of small pieces of paper (each of which has a strip of adhesive on its reverse). They are used by writing a short note on the top of the pad, then tearing it off and sticking it on a convenient surface. When the note has served its purpose, it can be taken down and thrown away.

The second artifact is a *DateEntry* component, which is intended to be used as a constituent part of a more complex interface. It allows the user to enter a calendar date in an unambiguous and error-free manner.

3.1 The *StikNote* Application, Visual Appearance, and STD Design

The visual appearance of the *StikNote* application is shown in Figure 3.1

The StikNote application main window is shown in the middle of the figure and can be identified by the button labeled "*Stik Note*" at the bottom. All of the other windows are *NoteWindow* windows containing various notes produced from the main window. When the "*Stik Note*" button on the main window is pressed the contents of the text area above the button, if any, are transferred to a new *NoteWindow* window. A *NoteWindow* will remain visible until its "*OK*" button is pressed, when it will be destroyed.

One other consideration of the visual appearance of the application is not shown on this illustration. The real-world sticky notes are most commonly yellow, in order to take advantage of this association in the user's mind, the background of all windows in the application is yellow and the text is displayed in blue using a large font to make sure that it is readable.

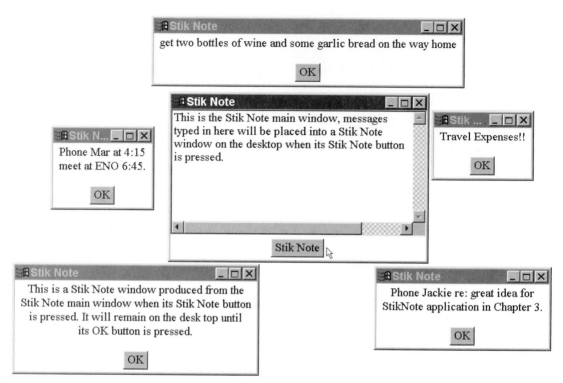

FIGURE 3.1   The *StikNote* application.

> **Design Advice**
>
> Take advantage of the user's prior experience by making the appearance and behavior of an application as similar as possible to their expectations.

A STD design for this application is given in Figure 3.2.

The initial transition, at the top of the diagram, indicates that the *StikNote Main Window* will be shown when the application is started. The single control, the *Stik Note* button, will only cause a transition to be followed if the user has entered some text into the text area part of the main window. The artifact has no terminal state and so no terminal transition.

The doubled lines on the main window's only transition indicate that every time the *StikNote* button is pressed, if there is any text in the *Main Window*, a new *Note Window* will be created containing the text from the main window. The action part of the transition label indicates that the text will also be cleared from the text area part of the main application window as the transition is followed. The unlabeled transition back from the *Note Window* state to the *StikNote Main Window* state indicates that after creating an instance of the *Note Window* the artifact will automatically return to the *StikNote Main Window* state. Each *Note Window* also has a single transition, which

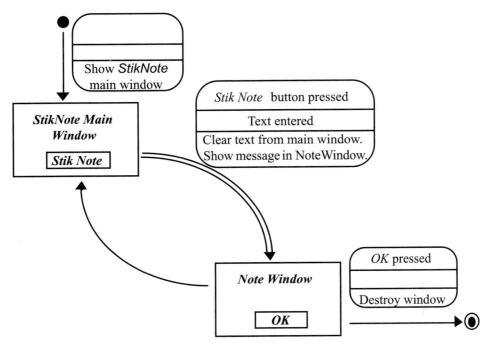

FIGURE 3.2   A *StikNote* state transition diagram.

is taken every time its *OK* button is pressed and will cause the *Note Window* to be destroyed leading to its, but not the artifact's, terminal state.

3.2 *StikNote* Design Overview

An instance diagram illustrating the overall design of this application is presented in Figure 3.3.

The diagram shows that the *client program*, in the middle, is supplied by an instance of the *StikNote* class which extends the Applet class. It also implements the ActionListener interface in order for it to be able to listen to events generated by the *mainWindow*, shown on the left, which is an instance of the *StikNoteWindow* class. In response to these events the client program will create anonymous instances of the *NoteWindow* class, shown on the right, which extends the Frame class. By extending the Frame class, *NoteWindow* instances are able to exist on the desktop with an independent top-level window, as illustrated in Figure 3.1.

In order to be able to display the multi-line messages, each *NoteWindow* has an encapsulated instance of the *MessageCanvas* class, which is an extension of the Canvas class. This class will be reused by other applications throughout the book and so, unlike the *StikNote*, *StikNoteWindow*, and *NoteWindow* classes, it is not contained within the *StikNote* **package** of classes.

The *StikNoteWindow* and *NoteWindow* classes can be considered as the *presentation* parts of this application, providing the user with interactive components and

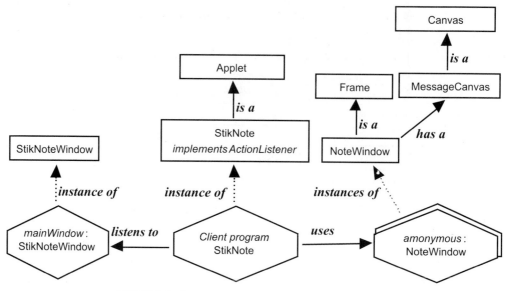

FIGURE 3.3   Instance diagram for the *StikNote* application.

presenting information and feedback to them. The StikNote class can be thought of as the *translation* part, mediating messages between the two presentation parts. In this artifact there is no application part. However if the messages were destined to be sent somewhere else, for example logged to a file, then this would provide an *application* component for the artifact.

3.3 The *StikNoteWindow* Class

The *StikNoteWindow* class provides the main window, shown in Figure 3.1 as the window containing the "*Stik Note*" button. The instance hierarchy for the *StikNoteWindow* is shown in Figure 3.4.

Figure 3.2 shows that the main window interface is constructed within the Applet's window and consists of a TextArea instance (called *theMessage*) with a Button instance (called *stikNoteButton*) mounted on its own Panel (called *buttonPanel*) beneath it. The *buttonPanel* is required in order that the *stikNoteButton* can present itself centered within the width of the Applet's window. If the panel were not used, then the Button would be stretched to fill the entire width of the window. This hierarchy is created in the *StikNoteWindow* constructor whose implementation is as follows.

```
0001   // Filename StikNoteWindow.java.
0002   // Provides StikNote application main window whose events
0003   // are listened to by the StikNote translation application.
0004   //
0005   // Written for the JI book, Chapter 3.
0006   // Fintan Culwin, v 0.2, August 1997.
0007
```

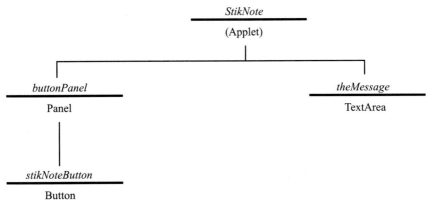

FIGURE 3.4   The *StikNoteWindow* instance hierarchy.

```
0008   package StikNote;
0009
0010   import java.awt.*;
0011   import java.awt.event.*;
0012   import java.applet.*;
0013
0014
0015   class StikNoteWindow extends Object {
0016
0017   private TextArea theMessage;
0018
0019
0020     protected StikNoteWindow( StikNote itsApplet) {
0021
0022     Panel   buttonPanel    = new Panel();
0023     Button stikNoteButton = new Button( "Post It");
0024
0025       theMessage = new TextArea( 10, 20);
0026
0027       stikNoteButton .addActionListener( itsApplet);
0028       buttonPanel.add( stikNoteButton );
0029
0030       itsApplet.setLayout( new BorderLayout());
0031       itsApplet.add( theMessage,  "Center");
0032       itsApplet.add( buttonPanel, "South");
0033     } // End StikNoteWindow constructor.
```

The constructor, commencing on line 0020, is declared with the visibility modifier **protected** which ensures that it can only be called from classes contained within the same package. Line 0008 has already declared this class to be part of the *StikNote* **package** and line 0015 does not declare it as a **public** class, restricting its visibility to other classes within the same package.

The constructor takes a *StikNote* argument which, as shown on the instance diagram, extends the Applet class and implements the ActionListener interface. The constructor will install the *StickNote* main window interface into the Applet window of this argument and will dispatch events from the *Stick Note* button to it. On lines 0022 and 0023 the *buttonPanel* and *stickNotetButton* from Figure 3.4 are created, following which the *theMessage* TextArea, declared as an instance attribute on line 0017, is constructed with a 10 row by 20 column input area. Before the interface is assembled on line 0027, the ActionListener attribute of the *stickNoteButton* is registered as the *itsApplet* argument, ensuring that events generated when it is pressed are dispatched to it.

The constructor concludes, on lines 0028 to 0032, by assembling the components to produce the interface as illustrated in Figure 3.1, using the instance hierarchy shown in Figure 3.4. The *stickNoteButton* is added to the *buttonPanel*, which in turn is added to the "*South*" location of the Applet's window which has already had a BorderLayout policy established. (The BorderLayout policy was described in Chapter 2, Section 2.10) The *theMessage* TextArea is added above the *buttonPanel* into the Applet window's "*Center*" location. When the interface is assembled within an Applet Panel, it will automatically become visible to the user as the application commences.

This interface will allow the user to enter, and edit, text within its TextArea component and, when its "*Stik Note*" button is pressed, will send an ActionEvent to its registered listener. It supplies two other **protected** methods, as follows, which its listener can make use of; one to obtain the contents of its TextArea and one to clear its contents.

```
036      protected String getMessage() {
0037         return theMessage.getText().trim();
0038      } // End getMessage.
0039
0040      protected void clearMessage() {
0041         theMessage.setText( "" );
0042      } // End clearMessage.
0043   } // End class StikNoteWindow.
```

Both of these methods manipulate the text attribute of the *theMessage* TextArea. The *getMessage()* method retrieves the text as a String, and then uses the String trim() method to remove any white space at the start and end of the text. So if the user has only pressed the space bar, and not typed in any characters, this will cause the *getMessage()* method to return an empty String. The *clearMessage()* method removes any existing text from *theMessage* by using its *setText()* action, passing as an argument an empty String.

3.4 The *StikNote* Class

Before considering the *NoteWindow* class, the *StikNote* class which implements the *client program* will be presented. Its major purpose is to configure, construct, and show the *mainWindow* and then to respond to presses of its "*Stik Note*" button by creating and showing new instances of the *NoteWindow* class containing the messages from the *mainWindow*. Its implementation, as far as the end of its constructor, is as follows.

```
0001   // Filename StikNote.java.
0002   // Contains the StikNote applet, responsible for creating
0003   // and showing the main window and then creating and
0004   // showing NoteWindow windows when its button is pressed.
0005   //
0006   // Written for the JI book, Chapter 3.
0007   // Fintan Culwin, v 0.2, August 1997.
0008
0009
0010   package StikNote;
0011
0012   import java.awt.*;
0013   import java.awt.event.*;
0014   import java.applet.*;
0015
0016   import StikNote.NoteWindow;
0017   import StikNote.StikNoteWindow;
0018
0019
0020   public class StikNote extends      Applet
0021                            implements ActionListener {
0022
0023   private StikNoteWindow mainWindow;
0024
0025      public void init() {
0026         this.setFont( new Font( "Serif", Font.PLAIN, 20));
0027         this.setBackground( Color.yellow);
0028         this.setForeground( Color.blue);
0029         mainWindow = new StikNoteWindow( this);
0030      } // End init.
```

On line 0010 this class also declares itself to be contained within the *StikNote* **package** and, on lines 0016 and 0017, **import**s the two other classes contained in the package. Its class declaration, commencing on line 0020, states that it implements the ActionListener interface in order for it to be able to respond to ActionEvents generated from the *mainWindow*, which is declared as an instance attribute of the class on line 0023.

The *init()* method commences, on lines 0026 to 0028, by configuring the Applet's physical appearance. On line 0026 the Font to be used by the Applet is set to 20-point plain Serif. On line 0027 its background Color is set to yellow and on line 0028 its foreground to blue. The configuration of these aspects of an interface's physical appearance is accomplished by using the setForeground(), setBackground(), and setFont() methods, which are inherited from the Component class and so are available to all components.

The argument to the setForeground() and setBackground() methods is an instance of the Color class and the most convenient way of obtaining a suitable value is to use one of the manifest class-wide constants supplied by the class. These constant Color values are listed in Table 3.1.

gray	lightGray	darkGray	white	black	red	pink
orange	yellow	green	magenta	cyan	blue	

TABLE 3.1   Class-Wide Manifest Constants Supplied by the Color Class

The argument to the **setFont()** method is an instance of the **Font** class which can be constructed by specifying the font to be used, its style, and its size. Thus, in the previous example a 20-point plain *Serif* font has been specified as the font to be used in the *StikNote* main window. Serif is a virtual font name which is mapped onto a physical font in the Java run-time environment's configuration, thus a user can change the mapping in order to accommodate their own preferences and requirements. Other virtual fonts which can be specified include *Sans-serif, Monospaced, Dialog*, and *DialogInput*. Alternatively physical fonts, including *Times, Helvetica, Courier, Symbol* and *ZapfDingabats*, can be specified. However as using physical font specifications will prevent the user from reconfiguring the font to be used to their own requirements, only virtual font specifications should be used.

Design Advice

Specify fonts in source code using virtual, not physical, names in order to allow the user to reconfigure them to their own requirements.

The font style can be specified using one of the class-wide **Font** manifest constants **PLAIN, BOLD,** or **ITALIC.** A bold italic font can be specified by a bitwise anding of the two constants (`Font.BOLD | Font.ITALIC`).

These **font, foreground,** and **background** physical appearance resources are inherited via the instance hierarchy. Consequently all components which are added to this **Applet** window will use a 20-point plain serif font with yellow backgrounds and blue foregrounds. Not all components take advantage of this inheritance; for example, as can be seen on Figure 3.1, **Button** instances do not use the inherited **background** color although they do use the inherited **foreground** and **font** resources. The inheritance does not extend to any **Frames** which are added to the **Applet** window; techniques for accommodating to this consideration will be explained later.

Having established the physical appearance of the application on line 0029, the *mainWindow* is created by calling its *StikNoteWindow* constructor passing as its argument the identity of the **Applet** which is currently being constructed. This, as previously explained, will create and install the main window interface into the **Applet** window and will cause it to be registered as the *stikNoteButton*'s listener. When the **init()** method concludes, the main window interface will be automatically presented to the user on the desktop display.

In order to satisfy the requirement of the **ActionListener** interface, the *StikNote* class must supply an *actionPerformed()* method, as follows.

```
0033        public void actionPerformed( ActionEvent event) {
0034
0035        NoteWindow theNote;
0036        String     itsContents = mainWindow.getMessage();
0037
0038          if ( itsContents.length() > 0) {
0039              theNote = new NoteWindow( itsContents, this);
0040              mainWindow.clearMessage();
0041          } // End if.
0042        } // End actionPerformed.
```

The method commences, on line 0036, by retrieving the String from the *main-Window*'s message area using its **protected** *getMessage()* method. If the message is empty as indicated by the condition, on line 0038 using the String length() method, then the *actionPerformed()* method concludes with no further steps. Otherwise, on line 0039, a new instance of the *NoteWindow* class is created passing as arguments the message which it is to display and the identity of the Applet. Before the method concludes, the message area in the *mainWindow* is cleared, on line 0040, by calling the *mainWindow*'s *clearMessage()* method.

The effect of this method, when the *stikNote* button on the main window is pressed, is to retrieve the contents of the TextArea if any, pass them to a new instance of the *NoteWindow* class, and then to clear the message from the main window. The user will see the message transferred from the main window to a new window that pops up onto the desktop.

3.5 The *NoteWindow* Class

The instance hierarchy for an instance of the *NoteWindow* class is shown in Figure 3.5. This hierarchy is very similar to that of the *StikNoteWindow* hierarchy shown in Figure 3.4. The root of the hierarchy, shown as *noteWindow*, is not an application in its own right but only a separate top-level window of the *StikNote* application. Consequently it is extended from the Frame class but not the Applet class. The other difference is that

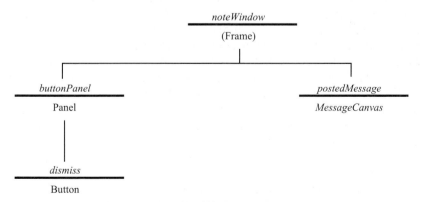

FIGURE 3.5   The *NoteWindow* instance hierarchy.

above the *buttonPanel* an instance of the *MessageCanvas* class, called *postedMessage*, is required. The *MessageCanvas* class is a specialized extension of the **Canvas** class, whose implementation will be described. Briefly it constructs a **Canvas** which is just large enough to display the text passed to it and arranges for it to be shown. The implementation of the *NoteWindow* class, as far as the start of its constructor, is as follows.

```
0001   // Filename NoteWindow.java.
0002   // Provides the NoteWindows for the StikNote applet.
0003   //
0004   // Written for the JI book, Chapter 3.
0005   // Fintan Culwin, v 0.2, August 1997.
0006
0007   package StikNote;
0008
0009   import java.awt.*;
0010   import java.awt.event.*;
0011
0012   import MessageCanvas;
0013
0014
0015   class NoteWindow extends     Frame
0016                    implements ActionListener {
```

This class also declares itself to be a non-**public** member of the *StikNote* package, but the *MessageCanvas* class **import**ed on line 0012 is not. This is because it is recognized that the *MessageCanvas* class is capable of being reused in a number of different interface components, as will be demonstrated, and so should not be thought of as associated with any particular **package.**

The declaration of the *NoteWindow* class, on lines 0015 and 0016, indicates that it implements the **ActionListener** interface as it will respond itself to presses of its own "*OK*" button, as will be described. The implementation of its constructor is as follows.

```
0019      protected NoteWindow( String     message,
0020                            Component itsParent) {
0021
0022      Button        dismissButton;
0023      Panel         buttonPanel   = new Panel();
0024      MessageCanvas postedMessage;
0025
0026      Point         itsParentsLocation;
0027      Dimension     itsParentsSize;
0028      Point         itsLocation;
0029      Dimension     itsSize;
0030
0031         this.setTitle( "Stik Note");
0032         this.setFont( itsParent.getFont());
0033         this.setBackground( itsParent.getBackground());
0034         this.setForeground( itsParent.getForeground());
```

```
0035
0036              postedMessage = new MessageCanvas( message);
0037              this.add( postedMessage, "Center");
0038
0039              dismissButton = new Button( "OK");
0040              dismissButton.addActionListener( this);
0041              buttonPanel.add( dismissButton);
0042              this.add( buttonPanel, "South");
0043              this.pack();
0044
0045              itsParentsLocation = itsParent.getLocationOnScreen();
0046              itsParentsSize     = itsParent.getSize();
0047              itsSize            = this.getSize();
0048              itsLocation        = new Point();
0049
0050              itsLocation.x = itsParentsLocation.x +
0051                              (itsParentsSize.width/2) -
0052                              (itsSize.width/2);
0053              itsLocation.y = itsParentsLocation.y +
0054                              (itsParentsSize.height/2) -
0055                              (itsSize.height/2);
0056
0057              this.setLocation( itsLocation);
0058              this.setVisible( true);
0059          } // End NoteWindow constructor.
```

This method can be divided into two parts. The first part, from lines 0019 to 0042, constructs the interface within the Frame window. The second part of the method, from lines 0043 to 0058, is concerned with positioning the window on the desktop centered within the main application window.

The constructor commences, on lines 0031 to 0034, by configuring its physical appearance. As this class extends the Frame class it has a separate top-level window and, as previously mentioned, does not inherit its physical attributes from its instance parent, as the *StikNoteWindow* class did. The Applet passed in its second argument, when its constructor was called in the *StikNote* class, is received by this class as a Component instance. On lines 0032 to 0034 the font, background, and foreground attributes are obtained from itsParent, using only Component methods, and installed into this Component using the equivalent attribute-setting methods. Before this, on line 0031 the title for the Frame is specified as "*Stik Note*" using the Frame setTitle() method, as can be confirmed in Figure 3.1.

The constructor continues, on line 0036 and 0037, by creating a new instance of the *MessageCanvas* class and adding it to the *NoteWindow*'s central location. There is no need to explicitly specify a BorderLayout management policy as this is the default policy for all Frames. Lines 0039 to 0042 continue assembling the interface as required from the instance diagram in Figure 3.5 and registering the *NoteWindow* instance itself as the listener for the *ActionEvent*s generated by the *dismissButton*.

Once this has been accomplished, on line 0043, the Frame's pack() method is called to perform the layout negotiations for the Frame and so establish its size, although this does not result in the interface becoming visible. Lines 0045 to 0055 are concerned with ensuring that when the *NoteWindow* is shown to the user it is centered within the main *StikNote* window.

To accomplish this first, on line 0045, the location and size of *itsParent* is obtained using the Component getLocationOnScreen() method. This method returns an instance of the Point class. This is a simple class which contains two **public** primitive **int** instance attributes called x and y. As **public** attributes their values can be set, or obtained, directly by referencing their name rather than by using methods of the class. This technique is used by a small number of Java pre-supplied classes but, in general, this technique should not be used. Instance attributes should always be declared **private** and methods to set and obtain their value supplied.

On line 0046 the size of the main window is obtained by use of its getSize() method. This method returns an instance of the Dimension class. Like the Point class, the Dimension class contains two **public** instance attributes, this time called width and height. The constructor continues by determining the size of the new *NoteWindow* using its own getSize() method.

Knowing the size and location of the main window, and the size of the new *NoteWindow*, it requires some simple arithmetic to calculate the location on the screen where the new window has to be positioned in order for it to be centered within the main window. This is accomplished on lines 0050 to 0055 with the x and y co-ordinates calculated stored as the x and y **public** attributes of a new instance of the Point class, called *itsLocation,* constructed on line 0048.

This Point instance is then passed as an argument to the *NoteWindow*'s setLocation() method, on line 0057, causing the new window to be positioned. The *NoteWindow* is then made visible by calling its setVisible() method, with the argument **true**, as the constructor's final step on line 0058. If this positioning of the *NoteWindow* were not done, the location of the *NoteWindow* on the desktop could not be guaranteed and the window manager might place it anywhere, at its discretion.

It might seem that devoting the majority of the effort in this constructor to the physical appearance of the interface and the location on the screen where it will appear is overkill. For example, the note could appear anywhere on the screen and the user can then drag it to where they want it, as they probably will do anyway. However, paying attention to details such as this differentiates excellent interfaces from good interfaces: an interface design principle known as *details matter*.

> **Design Advice**
>
> Details matter! Once the essential functionality of the application is assured, users will judge an interface on the care which has been taken to enhance its usability and aesthetic appeal.

The final method of the *NoteWindow* class is the *actionPerformed()* method which will be called when its "*OK*" button is pressed. It should result in the *NoteWindow* being removed from the desktop and being destroyed, and is implemented as follows.

```
0062    public void actionPerformed( ActionEvent event) {
0063        this.dispose();
```

```
0064      } // End actionPerformed.
0065   } // End NoteWindow.
```

The **dispose()** method of the **Frame** class called on line 0063 results in the **Frame** and all its contents being removed from the desktop and destroyed. This method is encapsulated within the *NoteWindow* class rather than being included within the *StikNote*'s *actionPerformed()* method because it is seen as being totally the concern of the *NoteWindow*, having no effect upon any other application component.

3.6 The *MessageCanvas* Class

The *MessageCanvas* class is the most complex of the classes required for the *StikNote* application. It is not possible to use a **Label** instance to show the note's contents because a **Label** can only show a single line of text. It would be possible to use a non-editable **TextArea** but it would be difficult to ensure that it was sufficiently large to just contain the text. The solution to these shortcomings is to extend the **Canvas** class to produce a specialized **Canvas** class capable of displaying a multi-line **String** in just sufficient space. This is the only class in the **StikNote** application which is sufficiently complex to merit a class diagram, as shown in Figure 3.6.

The diagram indicates that it supplies a single constructor and four **public** methods: *addNotify()*, *paint()*, *getPreferredSize()*, and *getMinimumSize()*. These are a minimum set of **Component** methods, which should be overridden for any specialized component to be able to inter-operate effectively with other components. The constructor requires a **String** as an argument and will display this **String** in a window just

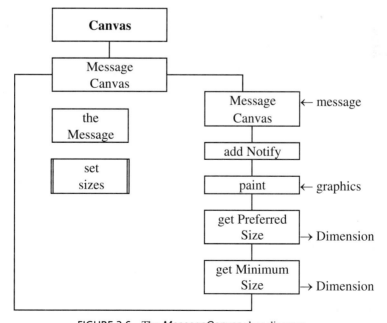

FIGURE 3.6   The *MessageCanvas* class diagram.

large enough to accommodate it. Once the *MessageCanvas* has been constructed there is no facility in this implementation for the contents of its window to be queried or changed.

The *addNotify()* method is called by the Java run-time environment when the component's peer object has been created. It can be used to ensure that certain methods, such as the **private** *setSizes()* method in this class, are not called until it is certain that the peer has been created. The *paint()* method is called by the Java run-time environment every time it is necessary to restore the contents of the component. This will happen when the component is shown for the first time and thereafter whenever it becomes visible after being hidden by another window.

The *getPreferredSize()* and *getMinimumSize()* methods may be called during *layout negotiations*. These happen when the contents of a Container are packed before being shown. Briefly a Container determines its own preferred size by asking all of its children for their preferred size and performing the appropriate calculations. For example a FlowLayout manager with three children would set its preferred width, based upon the combined preferred width of all of its children, and would set its preferred height to the tallest. Sometimes the preferred size of a component cannot be easily accommodated and then the getMinimumSize() method is asked for the component's minimum requirements. There is never a guarantee that the component will be given even its minimum requirements, and any methods which need to know the size of the component should ask for it, as will be demonstrated.

The implementation of the *MessageCanvas* class, which is not included in the *StikNote* **package**, as far as the end of its constructor, is as follows.

```
0001   // Filename MessageCanvas.java.
0002   // Provides a reusable centred multi-line label component.
0003   //
0004   // Written for the JI book, first used in Chapter 3.
0005   // Fintan Culwin, v 0.2, August 1997.
0006
0007
0008   import java.awt.*;
0009   import java.awt.event.*;
0010   import java.util.StringTokenizer;
0011
0012
0013   public class MessageCanvas extends Canvas {
0014
0015   private int     maximumWidth   = 0;
0016   private int     characterHeight;
0017   private String theMessage[];
0018
0019
0020       public MessageCanvas( String message) {
0021
0022       StringTokenizer tokenizer     = new StringTokenizer( message, "\n");
0023       int             numberOfLines = tokenizer.countTokens();
0024       int             index;
```

```
0025
0026            theMessage = new String[ numberOfLines];
0027            for ( index =0; index < numberOfLines; index++){
0028               theMessage[ index] = ((String) tokenizer.nextToken()).trim();
0029            } // End for.
0030         } // End MessageCanvas constructor.
```

A multiline *message* String will have to be rendered onto the *MessageCanvas* one line at a time and so the major responsibility of the constructor is to store each line of the message in a separate element of the String array instance attribute *theMessage*. To accomplish this, a StringTokenizer instance is constructed on line 0022 that will split the String argument *message* on its newline ("\n") boundaries.

Having prepared the *tokenizer*, its countTokens() method can be used to find out the *numberOfLines* in the message and this value is subsequently used to specify the size of *theMessage* array. Each line from the *message* String can then be extracted in turn, using the *tokenizer nextToken()* method, and stored in the array. There is no need for this class to configure its physical appearance as it will inherit the required attributes from its instance parent.

The purpose of the *addNotify()* method is to ensure that certain steps are not taken until the peer interface component is created. In this class the *setSizes()* method has the responsibility of ensuring that the *getPreferredSize()* and *getMinimumSize()* methods can reply in order that the *MessageCanvas* will be just large enough to accommodate *theMessage*. It does this by setting the value of the *maximumWidth* attribute to the screen width of the longest line of the message and the *characterHeight* attribute to the height of one character of the font being used. This cannot happen until its peer has been constructed because, until then, specific details of the precise font which will be used cannot be known. Accordingly, the implementation of the *addNotify()* and *setSizes()* methods is as follows.

```
0033      public void addNotify() {
0034         super.addNotify();
0035         this.setSizes();
0036      } // End addNotify.
0037
0038
0039      private void setSizes(){
0040
0041      FontMetrics   theMetrics = this.getFontMetrics( this.getFont());
0042      int           thisWidth;
0043      int           index;
0044
0045         characterHeight = theMetrics.getHeight();
0046         for ( index =0; index < theMessage.length; index++){
0047            thisWidth = theMetrics.stringWidth( theMessage[ index]);
0048            if ( thisWidth > maximumWidth) {
0049               maximumWidth = thisWidth;
0050            } // End if.
0051         } // End for.
0052      } // End setSizes.
```

The *addNotify()* method calls its parent's (Canvas) addNotify() method and then calls the *setSizes()* method. This method obtains a FontMetrics instance by using its own getFont() and getFontMetrics() methods. A FontMetrics instance encapsulates information concerning the size each character in the font will take up when rendered. Every character has the same height and this value is obtained, and stored in the instance attribute *characterHeight*, on line 0045. The loop between lines 0046 and 0051 uses *theMetrics stringWidth()* method to determine the width of the maximum line when rendered, and stores this value in the *maximumWidth* attribute. The *getPreferredSize()* and *getMinimumSize()* methods make use of these attributes, as follows.

```
0055     public Dimension getPreferredSize() {
0056        return new Dimension( maximumWidth +20,
0057                          (characterHeight * theMessage.length) +20);
0058     } // End getPreferredSize.
0059
0060     public Dimension getMinimumSize() {
0061        return new Dimension( maximumWidth,
0062                          (characterHeight * theMessage.length));
0063     } // End getMinimumSize.
```

The *getMinimumSize()* method returns the *maximumWidth* and *characterHeight* times the number of lines as the Dimension's horizontal and vertical components, respectively. The *getPreferredSize()* method returns the same values plus 20 (pixels) in order to allow for a border around the message. The *paint()* method is responsible for rendering the message onto the window and will be called by Java whenever it is required. Its implementation is as follows.

```
0066     public void paint( Graphics context) {
0067
0068     int      index;
0069     int      leftOffset;
0070     int      totalHeight = theMessage.length * characterHeight;
0071     int      itsWidth    = this.size().width;
0072     int      fromTop     = ((this.size().height - totalHeight) /2) +
0073                            characterHeight/2;
0074     FontMetrics theMetrics = this.getFontMetrics( this.getFont());
0075
0076        for ( index =0; index < theMessage.length; index++){
0077          leftOffset = ( itsWidth - theMetrics.stringWidth(
0078                                        theMessage[ index]))/2;
0079          context.drawString( theMessage[ index],
0080                            leftOffset, fromTop);
0081          fromTop+= characterHeight;
0082        } // End for.
0083     } // End paint.
```

The implementation of this method makes use of a Graphics instance called *context*; the use of *graphics contexts* will be described in detail in the next chapter. Briefly they encapsulate the precise knowledge required to produce output on the Component's window. Java will ensure that an appropriate Graphics instance is passed as an argument whenever the *paint()* method is called.

The first part of the method ensures that the message will be (approximately) horizontally and vertically centered within the window. To accomplish this, the Component size() method is used to determine the actual size of the window as no assumptions should be made regarding its size. The size() method returns a Dimension instance whose **public** width and height attributes can be accessed directly, as on lines 0071 and 0071. At the end of the local declarations, on line 0072, the variable *fromTop* contains the offset from the top of the window for the first line of the message, and the *itsWidth* to the width of the window,

The loop between lines 0076 and 0082 renders each line in turn from *theMessage* array using the Graphics *context* drawString() method. The three arguments to this method are the String to be rendered and the **int**eger horizontal and vertical locations at which to start. Lines 0077 and 0078 ensure that each line is horizontally centered within the window and 0081 that each line is vertically spaced from the previous line by the height of one character. The effect is that this method will *paint()* the message into a *MessageCanvas* window, which hopefully has at least its *getMinimumSize()* dimensions to be rendered within.

This completes the implementation of the *StikNote* application. It illustrates the techniques that can be used to extend a pre-supplied Component class to supply an extended class whose behavior is more suited to the requirements of a particular application. The *MessageCanvas* class, developed for this application, will be reused in other applications throughout the rest of this book. Some of its design decisions were made with this consideration in mind. In general, an extended Component class should be designed and implemented in a manner which allows for it to be easily reused. The techniques for extending the pre-supplied Component classes will be further considered in the remainder of this chapter.

3.7 The *DatePanel*, Visual Design and Behavior

The second artifact to be developed in this chapter is intended to be used for the input of a calendar date in an unambiguous and error-free manner. When a user is asked to input a calendar date into a text field, there is the possibility that they might type in an invalid date (for example, the 30th February in any year).

There is also a potential ambiguity if the date is required as a sequence of two digits, two digits and two or four digits; for example, 12/06/1996. In the conventional European format this is interpreted as the twelfth day of the sixth month in 1996: however, in the American convention this would be interpreted as the sixth day of the twelfth month in 1996. This problem could be minimized by using a prompt such as '*Please enter the date (dd/mm/yyyy)*'. However, this requires the user to be trained to realize that *dd* means the day of the month, *mm* the month number, and *yyyy* the year. It is also possible, if not probable, that an American user would not attend to this and still enter the date using the *mm/dd/yyyy* format.

Requiring the date to be input in a format such as *12 Dec 1996* also has problems with internationalization. The literal "Dec" assumes that the user understands English, and the format is also prone to input errors (for example, the mis-typing of "Dec" as "Drc"). The *DatePanel* which will be developed in this part of the chapter is intended to remove these possible ambiguities and problems. The appearance of a *DatePanel* is shown in Figure 3.7.

The upper left part of a *DatePanel* allows the user to indicate (from left to right) the century, the decade, and the year using option menus. The upper right-hand part of the panel allows the user to indicate the month, using another option menu. Every time a different year or a different month is selected the lower part of the panel will reconfigure itself to show the days of the month selected. For example, Figure 3.7 shows that there are 31 days in January in the year 2000 and that the first day of the month falls on a Saturday. Figure 3.8 shows that there are 29 days in February in the year 2000 (2000 is a leap year) and that the first day of the month falls on a Tuesday.

The labels used on the *DatePanel* in this illustration are in English, and the implementation as presented in this chapter will assume that English will always be used. The techniques which can be used to allow a *DatePanel* instance to be automatically configured to the different linguistic environments where it is used will be introduced in Chapter 9. Ideally an artifact such as this should be prepared for international use right from the very beginning of its design. However, this would additionally complicate what is already a rather complex example: accordingly, internationalization considerations will be left to another chapter.

Figure 3.8 indicates that the current date represented by the panel is the 29th Feb, shown by the *highlight* surrounding 29. The mouse pointer is currently over 17 and this is indicated to the user by the light *border* surrounding it. As the user moves the mouse pointer around the days of the month, the border is drawn and un-drawn around the

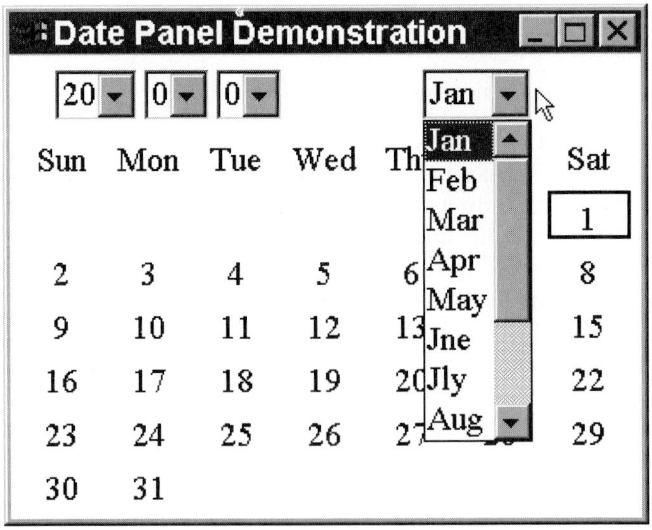

FIGURE 3.7   A *DatePanel* component showing 1st January 2000.

Date Panel Demonstration ▭ ▢ ✕

| 20 ▾ | 0 ▾ | 0 ▾ | | Feb ▾ |

Sun	Mon	Tue	Wed	Thu	Fri	Sat
		1	2	3	4	5
6	7	8	9	10	11	12
13	14	15	16	17	18	19
20	21	22	23	24	25	26
27	28	29				

FIGURE 3.8   A *DatePanel* component showing February 2000.

date which it is currently over. If the user presses and releases the mouse button while it is over a date then it will become the current date, confirmed to the user by the moving of the highlight from the old date to the new current date. The state transition diagram for this behavior is given in Figure 3.9.

This state transition diagram uses numbers to label the transitions which are keyed to Table 3.2. This has been done in order to keep the STD uncomplicated; although in this example the effect might be minimal, more complicated STDs benefit from this convention. The dashed arrows leaving the diagram indicate the generation

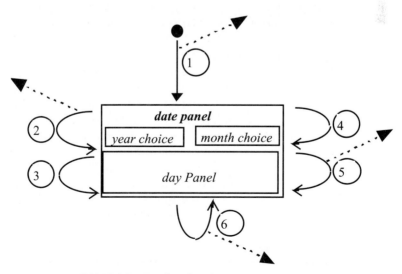

FIGURE 3.9   The *DatePanel* state transition diagram.

transition	action	pre-condition	consequence
1	none	none	post interface with default date highlighted, generate action event.
2	year choice	none	reconfigure day panel, generate action event.
3	month choice	none	reconfigure day panel, generate action event.
4	mouse exit	within day panel leaving bordered box	un-draw border around box.
5	mouse enter	within day panel entering active box	draw border around box.
6	mouse up	within day panel on active date box	move highlight to current day, generate action event.

TABLE 3.2   State Table for the *DatePanel* STD in Figure 3.9

of events by this component which can be listened to by registered listeners who wish to be informed that the date has changed. The diagram also provides names for the constituent components of a *DatePanel*, with all three of the *year choice* option menus collected together for convenience.

The single state on the STD and the minimal pre-conditions in the state table suggest again that the interface should be simple and intuitive to use. Transition 1 occurs when a *date panel* is first shown and generates an **ActionEvent** as it is configured for some specified initial date.

Transition 2 is taken when the user selects a different year either by selecting a different century, different decade, or different year. The consequence of this transition is for the *day panel* to reconfigure itself to indicate the pattern of days in the year and month now selected. Transition 3 is essentially identical but is triggered by the user choosing a different month from the *month choice* option menu.

The reconfiguration of the day panel results in the *day box*es within it being changed to indicate the pattern of days in the current month and year indicated by the year choice and month choice components. For example, in Figure 3.6 thirty-one days are laid out starting at the rightmost box on the top row, whereas in Figure 3.7 only twenty-nine days are laid out starting at the third box from the left on the top row. Whatever the configuration, a box containing a day number is regarded as an *active* box and a blank box is regarded as an *inactive* box.

Transition 4 occurs when the user moves the mouse pointer outside the scope of the day box currently bordered and results in that box becoming unbordered. Transition 5 occurs when the mouse pointer moves into the scope of an active box and results in it becoming bordered. The border is the thin rectangle surrounding the day number and is provided to confirm to the user the day currently primed for selection, which might not always be obvious from the location of the pointer. The use of two distinct transitions for this behavior implies that if the mouse pointer is ever outside the scope of any of the active boxes then none of the day boxes will be bordered.

Transition 6 can only occur when the mouse pointer is within an active box and is triggered by a mouse button up event. It results in the highlight being moved from the currently highlighted day to the day which triggered the mouse up event. Unlike the bordering of a day box, one, (and only one) day box must always be highlighted and is shown as a thick rectangle surrounding the day number.

The four transitions result in the currently indicated date being changed, 1, 2, 3 and 6, also have the consequence of generating an **ActionEvent**. A client of this component can intercept this event and handle it in order to inform the other parts of the interface that the date indicated by the user has changed. This will be illustrated in the demonstration client.

Design Advice

It is better to prevent the user from making 'errors' than to allow them to make 'errors' and have to 'correct' them.

3.8 The *DatePanel* Design Overview

The instance diagram for the *DatePanel* class is given in Figure 3.10.

The *DatePanel* contains an instance of the *MonthPanel* class, which it listens to in order to be informed when the user selects a date in the month. The *MonthPanel* instance contains an iteration of *DayBox* instances, which it listens to in order to be informed that a date has been selected. Both the *DatePanel* and *MonthPanel* class make use of the *DateUtility* class, which provides various class-wide methods for the

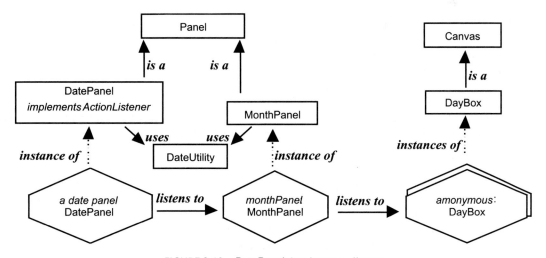

FIGURE 3.10   *DatePanel* class instance diagram.

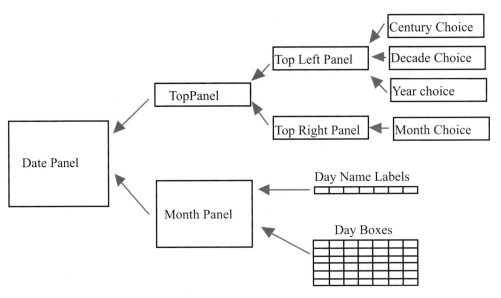

FIGURE 3.11   *DatePanel*, physical layout.

manipulation of dates. The layout relationships between these instances, and other components which do not have to be developed, are illustrated in Figure 3.11.

The *TopPanel*, *TopLeftPanel*, and *TopRightPanel* are needed to provide the required layout of the option Choice menus shown at the top of Figure 3.7. The *Month-Panel* has a row of *DayName* Labels above the grid of *DayBox*es, which provide the lower part of the interface shown in Figure 3.7.

3.9 The *DateUtility* Class

The *DateUtility* class provides a collection of class-wide methods which can be used to obtain the current data and determine various things about dates in general. Its class diagram is given in Figure 3.12

All of the methods in this class are class wide, as indicated by heavy boxes. The first method *daysThisMonthIs()* will return the number of days in the year and month supplied, allowing for the possibility of a leap year. The *isLeapYear()* method will return **true** if the year supplied is a leap year and **false** otherwise. The *dayOfWeekIs()* method will return a **int**eger in the range 0 to 6, indicating which day of the week the *dayNumber*, *month*, and *year* supplied falls on. A returned value of 0 indicates a Sunday and subsequent values the corresponding day of the week. The *firstDayOfMonthIs()* method returns an **int**eger value, using the same convention, for the day of the week on which the first day of the month and year supplied falls on. The final three methods: *yearIs()*, *monthIs()*, and *dayOfMonthIs()* return the year, month, and day of month as indicated by the computer's internal clock. The implementation of this class is not vital to an understanding of the implementation of the *DatePanel* artifact and can be found in Appendix B.

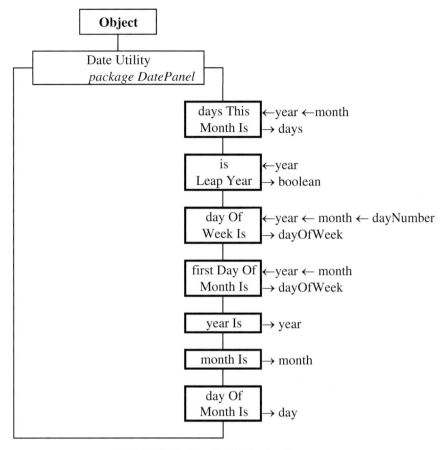

FIGURE 3.12   The *DateUtility* class diagram.

3.10 The *DayBox* Class

Instances of the *DayBox* class are used in the *DatePanel* artifact to supply each of the positions in the *MonthPanel,* which can be used to display a day of the month. Each instance can be *active*, displaying a number indicating a date in the month, or *inactive* in the current configuration and shown without a number. Only active boxes respond to the entry and exit of the mouse pointer, showing a border as it traverses through it, and only active boxes will respond to a mouse click generating an event which its listener can respond to. A *DayBox* instance is located at an ordinal location with respect to other boxes in a *MonthPanel.* The class diagram for the *DayBox* class is given in Figure 3.13.

The *ordinal* data attribute records the position of the *DayBox* in relation to all other *DayBox*es in the *MonthPanel*, its *ordinal* location is supplied to the constructor and can be obtained by the *ordinalIs()* method but cannot be changed after construction. The *dayNumber* attribute is the day of the month which the box will display and can be changed by the *setDayNumber()* method or queried by the *getDayNumber()*

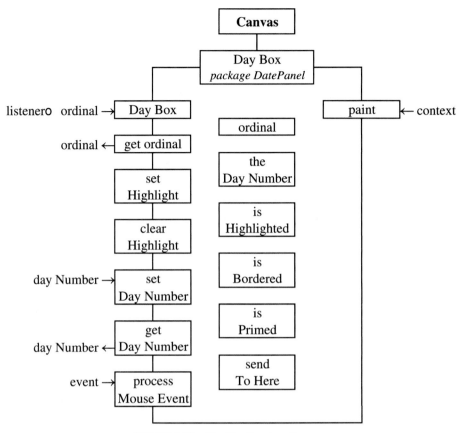

FIGURE 3.13   The *DayBox* class diagram.

method. The *isHighlighted* attribute indicates if the box should be highlighted and the *setHighlight()* and *clearHighlight()* methods support it.

The *isPrimed* attribute is used internally to indicate that a mouse down event has occurred so a mouse up event should be responded to. The *isBordered* attribute indicates if the box should be displayed with a border, between the time the mouse pointer enters and leaves it.

The *processMouseEvent()* method is needed for the class to process mouse events happening within itself, and the *sendToHere* attribute is the listener to which this method will dispatch events generated when the mouse button is released within it. The identity of the listener object is supplied to the instance in the *listener* attribute of its constructor.

The public *paint()* method will render the box onto the screen showing its *the-DayNumber*, if valid, and with highlighting and bordering as appropriate. The implementation of this class, as far as the end of its constructor, is as follows.

```
0001  // Filename DayBox.java.
0002  // Provides the individual boxes which contain the
```

```
0003    // day numbers in a MonthPanel.
0004    //
0005    // Written for JI book, Chapter 3 see text.
0006    // Fintan Culwin, v0.2, August 1997.
0007
0008    package DatePanel;
0009
0010    import java.awt.*;
0011    import java.awt.event.*;
0012
0013
0014    class DayBox extends Canvas {
0015
0016    private int            ordinal       = -1;
0017    private int            theDayNumber  = 0;
0018    private boolean        isHighlighted = false;
0019    private boolean        isBordered    = false;
0020    private boolean        isPrimed      = false;
0021    private ActionListener sendToHere;
0022
0023
0024       protected DayBox( int              itsLocation,
0025                         ActionListener listener) {
0026          super();
0027          ordinal = itsLocation;
0028          this.enableEvents( AWTEvent.MOUSE_EVENT_MASK);
0029          sendToHere = listener;
0030       } // End DayBox constructor.
```

The header and attribute declarations contain no surprises, with line 0014 indicating that this class is a non-**public** member of the *DatePanel* **package**. The constructor commences by calling its parent (Canvas) constructor, stores the two arguments in their corresponding instance attributes, and then, on line 0028 enables *MouseEvents* on this component. The methods which manipulate its attributes are as follows.

```
0033       protected int getOrdinal() {
0034          return ordinal;
0035       // End getOrdinal.
0036
0037
0038       protected void setHighlight() {
0039          isHighlighted = true;
0040          this.repaint();
0041       } // End setHighlight.
0042
0043       protected void clearHighlight() {
0044          isHighlighted = false;
0045          this.repaint();
0046       } // End clearHighlight.
```

```
0047
0048
0049    protected void setDayNumber( int dayNumber) {
0050        theDayNumber = dayNumber;
0051    } // End setDayNumber
0052
0053    protected int getDayNumber() {
0054        return theDayNumber;
0055    } // End getDayNumber
```

The *setHighlight()* and *clearHighlight()* methods not only manipulate the value of the appropriate attribute but also call the instance's *repaint()* method, which will indirectly call the *paint()* method whose implementation is as follows. The calling of *repaint()* will ensure that the effects of this change of state become visible to the user in a timely manner.

```
0058    public void paint( Graphics context) {
0059
0060    Dimension    location;
0061    String       numString;
0062    FontMetrics  metrics;
0063    int          stringHeight;
0064    int          stringWidth;
0065
0066        location = this.getSize();
0067        context.setColor( this.getBackground());
0068        context.fillRect( 0, 0,
0069                          location.width-1,
0070                          location.height-1);
0071        context.setColor( this.getForeground());
0072
0073        if ( theDayNumber != 0 ) {
0074            numString    = Integer.toString( theDayNumber);
0075            metrics      = this.getFontMetrics( this.getFont());
0076            stringHeight = metrics.getHeight();
0077            stringWidth  = metrics.stringWidth( numString);
0078            context.drawString( numString,
0079                                (location.width  - stringWidth)/2,
0080                                (stringHeight + 2));
0081
0082            if ( isHighlighted) {
0083                context.drawRect( 2, 2,
0084                                  location.width   - 4,
0085                                  location.height - 4);
0086                context.drawRect( 3, 3,
0087                                  location.width   - 6,
0088                                  location.height - 6);
0089            } // End if.
0090
0091            if ( isBordered ) {
```

```
0092                    context.drawRect( 1,1,
0093                                      location.width  - 2,
0094                                      location.height - 2);
0095                } // End if.
0096            } // End if
0097        } // End paint.
```

The first part of this method, on lines 0066 to 0071, clears the entire *DayBox*'s window to its background color by setting the drawing color of the Graphics *context* to the background color of the *dayBox* component and then drawing a filled rectangle over its entire extent. Before continuing, the drawing color of the *context* is reset to the *dayBox*'s foreground color. If the *theDayNumber* attribute is zero, indicating that the *dayBox* is inactive, the method concludes.

If the *dayBox* is active, lines 0074 to 0080 render *theDayNumber* in the center of its window, using techniques which are comparable to those used to render a line of text into the *MessageCanvas* in the previous part of this chapter. The *DayBox* class does not attempt to establish its own size, however it can be guaranteed that its size will be large enough to contain the day number, for reasons which will be explained in the next section.

If the *isHighlighted* attribute is set, lines 0082 to 0089 then draw the highlight around the box by drawing two concentric outline rectangles within the limits of its extremity. Lines 0091 to 0095 then draw the single lined border, if the *isBordered* attribute is set as a single outline rectangle at its extremity. Both parts of this method make use of the *drawRectangle()* method of the Graphics class, which will be described in more detail in the next chapter.

The final *DayBox* method, *processMouseEvent()*, will be called every time a mouse event occurs on the component and is required to cause the component to react only if it is currently active. It should border the component when the mouse enters it, unborder the component as it leaves, and dispatch an ActionEvent to its listener object if the mouse button is pressed and released within the component. Its implementation is as follows.

```
0100    protected void processMouseEvent( MouseEvent event) {
0101        if ( this.getDayNumber() != 0) {
0102            switch ( event.getID()) {
0103
0104                case MouseEvent.MOUSE_ENTERED:
0105                    isBordered = true;
0106                    repaint();
0107                    break;
0108
0109                case MouseEvent.MOUSE_EXITED:
0110                    isBordered = false;
0111                    isPrimed   = false;
0112                    repaint();
0113                    break;
0114
0115                case MouseEvent.MOUSE_PRESSED:
```

```
0116                       isPrimed = true;
0117                       break;
0118
0119                    case MouseEvent.MOUSE_RELEASED:
0120                       if ( this.isPrimed){
0121                          sendToHere.actionPerformed(
0122                                      new ActionEvent( this,
0123                                      ActionEvent.ACTION_PERFORMED,
0124                                      "DateSelected"));
0125                       } // End if.
0126                       break;
0127                 } // End switch.
0128           } // End if.
0129     } // End processMouseEvent.
```

Line 0101 prevents the method from being triggered if *theDayNumber* attribute of the *DayBox* is zero, which indicates that it is inactive. Otherwise, the ID attribute of the event is used to select between different courses of actions in the **switch** structure between lines 0102 and 0127. If the ID indicates that the mouse pointer has entered the component, lines 0104 to 0107 set the *isBordered* attribute to **true** and then *repaint()* is called to provide feedback to the user. If the ID indicates that the mouse pointer has left the component, lines 0109 to 0113 set the *isBordered* attribute to **false** and *repaint()* is called. The *isPrimed* attribute, which may have been set **true** by a mouse down event, is also set **false** in this situation to prevent an ActionEvent from being generated when it is not supposed to be.

On lines 0115 to 0117 the *isPrimed* attribute is set **true** when the mouse button is pressed down, but as this has no visible feedback repaint() is not called. Lines 0122 to 0125 are executed when the mouse button is released within a primed component, and cause the *actionPerformed()* method of the listener object referenced by *sendToHere* to be called with a **new** ActionEvent passed as its event argument. The three arguments to the *ActionEvent* constructor, on lines 0122 to 0124, are the identity of the component which generated the event (**this**), the ID of the event (ActionEvent.ACTION_PERFORMED), and the actionCommand attribute of the event ("*DateSelected*")

The mouse events do not directly cause the highlighting of a *DayBox* component. This is the responsibility of the listener object, which is always the instance of the *MonthPanel* class within which all *DayBox* instances are contained. The implementation of this class will be described next.

3.11 The *MonthPanel* Class

The *MonthPanel* class is responsible for laying out and configuring an iteration of *DayBox*es so as to reflect the year and month required of it. It also has the responsibility to maintain knowledge of the currently highlighted day number in order that it can unhighlight it when required and to report the currently highlighted day number when asked. The class diagram for the *MonthPanel* class is given in Figure 3.14.

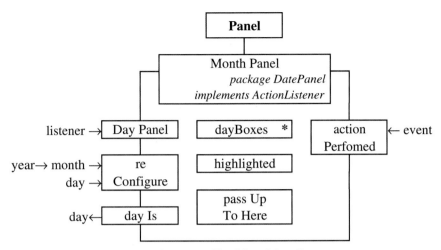

FIGURE 3.14   The *MonthPanel* class diagram.

The class indicates that an iteration of *DayBox* instances, called *dayBoxes*, is contained within each instance of this class as well as a primitive **int**eger indicating which one is *highlighted*. The constructor requires only the identity of a listener object, which is stored in the *passUpToHere* attribute. The constructor creates the *MonthPanel* without configuring it for a particular month, which is the responsibility of the *reConfigure()* method. This method will lay out the day numbers as appropriate to its year and month arguments, and highlight the day given. The *actionPerformed()* method is required to respond to the *ActionEvents* which will propagate from the contained *dayBox* instances, as described earlier. The *dayIs()* method is supplied to allow its instance parent, a *DatePanel*, to find out which date is currently highlighted. The implementation of this class, as far as the end of its constructor, is as follows.

```
0001   // Filename MonthPanel.java.
0002   // Provides an Panel which can be configured to show
0003   // the pattern of days in any particular month.
0004   //
0005   // Written for JI book, Chapter 3 see text.
0006   // Fintan Culwin, v0.2, August 1997.
0007
0008   package DatePanel;
0009
0010   import java.awt.*;
0011   import java.awt.event.*;
0012
0013   import DatePanel.DateUtility;
0014   import DatePanel.DayBox;
0015
0016
```

```
0017   class MonthPanel extends    Panel
0018                   implements ActionListener {
0019
0020   private static final int MAX_BOXES = 37;
0021
0022   private DayBox            dayBoxes[]  = new DayBox[ MAX_BOXES];
0023   private int              highlighted;
0024   private int              theFirstBox;
0025   private ActionListener   passUpToHere;
0026
0027   private static String dayNames[] = { "Sun", "Mon", "Tue", "Wed",
0028                                        "Thu", "Fri", "Sat"  };
0029
0030
0031      protected MonthPanel( ActionListener listener) {
0032
0033      int    thisOne;
0034      Label dayLabels[]  = new Label[ 7];
0035
0036         this.setLayout( new GridLayout( 7, 7, 0, 0));
0037         for ( thisOne = 0; thisOne < 7; thisOne++) {
0038            dayLabels[ thisOne] = new Label( dayNames[ thisOne],
0039                                             Label.CENTER);
0040            this.add( dayLabels[ thisOne]);
0041         } // End for.
0042
0043         for ( thisOne = 0; thisOne < MAX_BOXES; thisOne++) {
0044            dayBoxes[ thisOne] = new DayBox( thisOne, this);
0045            this.add( dayBoxes[ thisOne]);
0046         } // End for.
0047
0048         passUpToHere = listener;
0049      } // End MonthPanel constructor.
```

The constructor can be divided into a sequence of actions. It starts by establishing its' layout policy and then installs the day name Labels at the top of its area before creating all of the *DayBox* instances below the Labels.

The *dayBox*es are laid out in rows of 7 and the longest month contains 31 days. The worst-case scenario is illustrated in Figure 3.7 and occurs where the first day of the month falls on a Saturday. In this situation the first six boxes on the first row are inactive, requiring a further 31 active boxes and a total of 37 *DayBox* instances. The *Day-Box*es are contained within the array *dayBox*es, which is declared and has its size established on line 0022. The private *highlighted* attribute is then declared on line 0023. The *theFirstBox* attribute, declared on line 0024, is used to record which is the first active box in the panel; because it is not a logical component of the class, it is not shown on the class diagram. The value of this attribute will be set as the boxes are laid out in the *reConfigure()* method. The remaining attribute, *passUpToHere*, declared on line 0025, stores the identity of the listener object to which ActionEvents are to be dispatched when a date is selected.

In the constructor, the layout policy of the *DayPanel* is specified as a 7 by 7 grid layout. The first row of this grid is used for the names of the days and, on lines 0037 to 0041, these are created as instances of the Label class. The text which each Label will display is supplied from a class-wide array of Strings called *dayNames*, which is declared and initialized on lines 0027 and 0028.

On lines 0043 to 0046 the 37 *dayBoxes* are created and added to the grid, with each being informed of its ordinal position and its listener as it is constructed. As a GridLayout policy is used, all of the components on the Panel have to be the same size. As any day number, when rendered, will take up less width than the widest of the day names, it can be guaranteed that the *DayBox*es will be large enough to accommodate the day number string. Likewise, as the day names and the day numbers are using the same Font they will also be high enough. This implies that there is a close coupling between the *MonthPanel* and the *DayBox* classes, which is acceptable as they are not intended to be (re)used separately.

Before concluding, the *MonthPanel* constructor stores the identity of the listener object, passed in its listener argument, in the *passUpToHere* attribute. The *DayPanel* is constructed in an unconfigured state and has to be configured by a call of the *reConfigure()* method, whose implementation is as follows.

```
0052    protected void reConfigure( int year, int month, int day) {
0053
0054    int maxDay   = DateUtility.daysThisMonthIs(   year, month);
0055    int startDay = DateUtility.firstDayOfMonthIs( year, month);
0056
0057    int thisOne;
0058
0059       theFirstBox = startDay;
0060       if ( day > maxDay) {
0061          day = maxDay;
0062       } //End if.
0063
0064       dayBoxes[ highlighted].clearHighlight();
0065
0066       for ( thisOne = 0; thisOne < MAX_BOXES; thisOne++) {
0067          if ( (thisOne <   startDay) ||
0068               (thisOne >= (startDay + maxDay)) ){
0069             dayBoxes[ thisOne].setDayNumber( 0);
0070          } else {
0071             dayBoxes[ thisOne].setDayNumber( thisOne - startDay +1);
0072          } // End if.
0073          dayBoxes[ thisOne].repaint();
0074       } // End for.
0075
0076       dayBoxes[ theFirstBox + day -1].setHighlight();
0077       highlighted = theFirstBox + day -1;
0078    } // End reConfigure.
```

The *reConfigure()* method is responsible for setting the *dayBoxes* to indicate the year and month specified in its arguments. Its first step is to obtain the number of days in the month requested and the day of the week which *theFirstDay* falls on, using the appropriate *DateUtility* methods. The *day* argument indicates which day is to be highlighted, and it is possible that this might specify a day number which is larger than the maximum day of the month; for example, requesting the 31st day of February. To prevent this, lines 0060 to 0062 limit the value of *day* to the maximum day of the required month.

On line 0064 any existing highlight is cleared by calling the *clearHighlight()* method of the *dayBox[]* array element indicated by the *highlighted* attribute. When the *MonthPanel* is configured for the first time, none of the *DayBox*es will be highlighted and so this step will clear the highlight of a box which is not currently highlighted, however, as this has no adverse effects it need not be circumvented.

The loop between 0066 and 0074 sets all the *dayBoxes* to their appropriate state. The **if** condition on lines 0067 and 0068 will be **true** for all inactive boxes at the start and end of the array, and these will have their *dayNumber* attribute set to zero to indicate this. All other boxes will have the appropriate *dayNumber* as specified on line 0071. The final steps, on lines 0076 and 0077, are concerned with highlighting the *day* specified and recording it in highlighted.

The *dayIs()* method uses the *highlighted* attribute and the offset to the first active box, *theFirstBox*, to determine the day number which the *MonthPanel* currently indicates, as follows.

```
0081        protected int dayIs(){
0082            return highlighted - theFirstBox +1;
0083        } // End dayIs;
```

The remaining method, *actionPerformed()*, is needed in order for the *MonthPanel* class to satisfy the requirement of the ActionListener interface. As explained earlier, it is called whenever a mouse release event occurs in a primed *dayBox*. It has to move the highlight to the *dayBox* indicated by the user, and propagate the event up to its listener. Its implementation is as follows.

```
0086        public void actionPerformed( ActionEvent event)  {
0087            dayBoxes[ highlighted].clearHighlight();
0088            ((DayBox) event.getSource()).setHighlight();
0089            highlighted = ((DayBox) event.getSource()).getOrdinal();
0090            passUpToHere.actionPerformed( event);
0091        } // End actionPerformed.
```

On line 0087 the existing highlight is cleared, and on lines 0088 and 0089 the highlight of the *dayBox* which generated the *event* is set and its *ordinal* location stored in *highlighted*. Finally, on line 0090, the *event* passed to this method in its argument is passed onward to its stored *passUpToHere* ActionListener attribute. The ActionListener of a *MonthPanel* is always the *DatePanel* upon which it is mounted and whose implementation is as follows.

3.12 The *DatePanel* Class

The *DatePanel* class has to implement the entire interface shown in Figure 3.7 and designed in Figure 3.11, including an instance of the *MonthPanel* class. It is responsible for configuring the *MonthPanel* when it is first constructed and for reconfiguring it whenever the year or month is changed by the user. It is also responsible for generating an action event every time the user changes the date, and for providing inquiry methods to allow a client to determine what the date has been changed to. It also offers the set of methods, i.e., *setCommandString()*, *getCommandString()*, *addActionListener()* and *removeActionListener()*, that allow it to be used by a client in a manner essentially identical to pre-supplied AWT components such as Button, which also generate ActionEvents for arbitrary components to listen to. The *DatePanel* class diagram is given in Figure 3.15.

The first, default, constructor will create a *DatePanel* showing the current date. The second constructor allows a particular date to be specified, and the *setDate()* method allows a particular date to be set once an instance has been created. The *yearIs()*, *monthIs()*, and *dayIs()* methods will return the current settings of the interface.

The *actionPerformed()* method and *itemStateChanged()* methods are needed to satisfy the requirements of the *ActionListener* and the *ItemListener* interfaces, respectively. It has to implement these interfaces as it listens to the ItemEvents events generated by its own Choice components and also listens to the ActionEvents generated by its own *MonthPanel* component. The final four public methods are needed for this component to interoperate with other AWT Components, as will be explained. The implementation of this class, as far as the end of its first constructor, is as follows.

```
0001    // Filemake DatePanel.java.
0002    // Provides an interactive calendar panel allowing
0003    // safe an unambiguous input of a calendar date.
0004    //
0005    // Written for JI book, Chapter 3 see text.
0006    // Fintan Culwin, v 0.2, August 1997.
0007
0008    package DatePanel;
0009
0010    import java.awt.*;
0011    import java.awt.event.*;
0012
0013    import DatePanel.DateUtility;
0014    import DatePanel.MonthPanel;
0015
0016    public class DatePanel extends      Panel
0017                           implements ActionListener, ItemListener {
0018
0019    private MonthPanel monthPanel;
0020    private Choice      centuryChoice;
0021    private Choice      decadeChoice;
0022    private Choice      yearChoice;
0023    private Choice      monthChoice;
0024
0025    private String         actionCommand = null;
0026    private ActionListener itsListener;
```

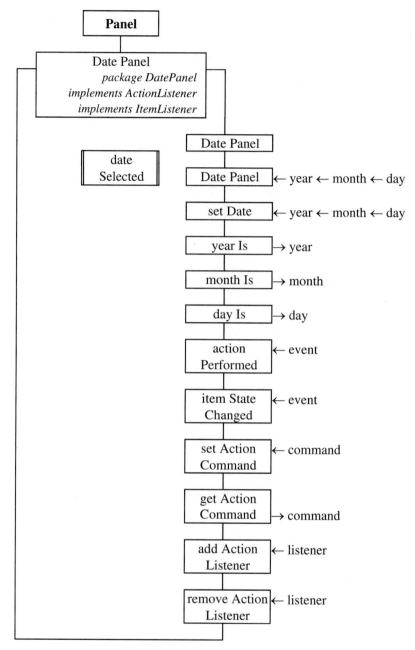

FIGURE 3.15   The *DatePanel* class diagram.

```
0027
0028   private static String monthNames[] = { "Jan", "Feb", "Mar", "Apr",
0029                                          "May", "Jne", "Jly", "Aug",
0030                                          "Sep", "Oct", "Nov", "Dec" };
```

```
0031
0032      public DatePanel() {
0033
0034         this( DateUtility.yearIs(),
0035              DateUtility.monthIs(),
0036              DateUtility.dayOfMonthIs());
0037      } // End DatePanel default constructor.
0038
```

The default constructor, on lines 0032 to 0037, indirects to the alternative constructor passing the current year, month, and day number obtained from the *DateUtility* class. In the alternative constructor, the components indicated in Figure 3.11 are constructed and assembled as follows.

```
0040      public DatePanel( int year, int month, int day) {
0041
0042      int     thisOne;
0043      Panel   topPanel       = new Panel();
0044      Panel   topLeftPanel   = new Panel();
0045      Panel   topRightPanel  = new Panel();
0046
0047         this.setLayout(          new BorderLayout( 4, 4));
0048         topPanel.setLayout(      new GridLayout( 1, 2, 4, 4));
0049         topLeftPanel.setLayout( new FlowLayout( FlowLayout.CENTER, 4, 4));
0050         topRightPanel.setLayout(new FlowLayout( FlowLayout.CENTER, 4, 4));
0051
0052         monthPanel = new MonthPanel( this);
0053
0054         centuryChoice  = new Choice();
0055         centuryChoice.addItemListener( this);
0056         centuryChoice.addItem( "19");
0057         centuryChoice.addItem( "20");
0058         centuryChoice.addItem( "21");
0059
0060         decadeChoice = new Choice();
0061         decadeChoice.addItemListener( this);
0062
0063         yearChoice   = new Choice();
0064         yearChoice.addItemListener( this);
0065
0066         for ( thisOne = 0; thisOne < 10; thisOne++){
0067             decadeChoice.addItem( Integer.toString( thisOne));
0068             yearChoice.addItem( Integer.toString(   thisOne));
0069         } // End for.
0070
0071         monthChoice   = new Choice();
0072         monthChoice.addItemListener( this);
0073         for ( thisOne = 0; thisOne < 12; thisOne++){
0074             monthChoice.addItem( monthNames[ thisOne]);
0075         } // End for.
```

```
0076
0077            topLeftPanel.add( centuryChoice);
0078            topLeftPanel.add( decadeChoice);
0079            topLeftPanel.add( yearChoice);
0080
0081            topRightPanel.add( monthChoice);
0082
0083            topPanel.add( topLeftPanel);
0084            topPanel.add( topRightPanel);
0085            this.add( topPanel,     "North");
0086            this.add( monthPanel, "Center");
0087
0088             this.setDate( year, month, day);
0089        } // End DatePanel constructor.
```

The constructor commences by constructing the three **Panels** indicated in Figure 3.11, on lines 0043 to 0045 and, together with the **Applet Panel**, have appropriate layouts specified on lines 0047 to 0050. The *monthPanel* is constructed on line 0052, with its **ActionListener** specified as itself. The *centuryChoice* **Choice** component is constructed on lines 0054 to 0058, with its **ItemListener** specified as itself and three **Items** indicating the centuries added to it. The loop on lines 0066 to 0069 populates the *decadeChoice* and *yearChoice* **Choice** components, which are constructed on lines 0060 and 0063, with their **ItemListeners** also specified as the *DatePanel* currently being constructed. The *monthChoice* is then constructed, has itself registered as its listener, and is populated on lines 0071 to 0075 using **Strings** obtained from the class-wide *monthNames[]* array declared on lines 0028 to 0030.

Having constructed all the constituent **Components**, they are added to their appropriate **Panels** and the **Panels** then added together to produce the required visual layout on lines 0077 to 0086. Finally the *setDate()* method is called on line 0088, passing on the arguments received by the constructor. The implementation of the *setDate()* method is as follows.

```
0092        public void setDate( int year,
0093                                 int month,
0094                                 int dayOfMonth) {
0095
0096            centuryChoice.select( (year / 100)  - 19);
0097            decadeChoice.select(   (year % 100) / 10);
0098            yearChoice.select( year % 10);
0099            monthChoice.select( month -1);
0100            monthPanel.reConfigure( year, month, dayOfMonth);
0101            dateSelected();
0102        } // End setDate.
```

In this method the *centuryChoice*, *decadeChoice*, and *yearChoice* select() methods are called on lines 0096 to 0098, passing as arguments a suitably arithmetically manipulated value derived from the *year* argument. On line 0099 the *monthChoice* select() method is called, passing on the *month* argument. This argument is received in the conventional 1 to 12 range of values but the indexes of the items on the Choice menu are in the range 0 to 11, so its decremented value is passed. The effect of these methods is to set the Choice menus at the top of the panel to indicate the year and month required. On line 0100 the three arguments are passed to a call of the *month-Panel reConfigure()* method which, as explained, will cause it to lay itself out as appropriate to the *year* and *month* specified with the *day* highlighted. The final step is to call *dateSelected()* which, as will be explained, will cause an ActionEvent to be generated by the *DatePanel*.

The three inquiry methods retrieve the appropriate value from the appropriate components of the interface, as follows.

```
0104        public int yearIs() {
0105            return Integer.valueOf( centuryChoice.getSelectedItem() +
0106                                    decadeChoice.getSelectedItem() +
0107                                    yearChoice.getSelectedItem()
0108                                  ).intValue();
0109        } // End yearIs.
0110
0111
0112        public int monthIs(){
0113            return monthChoice.getSelectedIndex() +1;
0114        } // End monthIs.
0115
0116
0117        public int dayIs(){
0118            return monthPanel.dayIs();
0119        } // End dayIs.
```

The *yearIs()* method returns the year indicated on the interface by catenating together the Strings obtained from the three Choice component *getSelectedItem()* methods and then converting the String to a primitive **int**. As with the setting of an item on the *monthChoice* menu, the range of values returned by *monthIs()* is converted from the 0 to 11 range into the 1 to 12 range when the index of the selected item is obtained using the *Choice getSelectedIndex()* method on line 0113. The *dayIs()* method determines which day of the month is currently indicated by using the *dayIs()* action of the encapsulated *monthPanel*.

As explained the *actionPerformed()* method is called whenever a new date is selected on the *monthPanel* and, as it does not need to reconfigure the *monthPanel*, indirects immediately to the **private** *dateSelected()* method in order to generate an ActionEvent to notify listeners that the date has changed. The *itemStateChanged()* method will be called whenever one of the Choice menus has a different item selected and, as this will cause the pattern of days in the month now indicated to change, the *monthPanel reConfigure()* method is called before it too indirects to the *dateSelected()* method. The implementation of these two methods is as follows.

```
0122        public void actionPerformed( ActionEvent event) {
0123            dateSelected();
```

```
0124        } // End actionPerformed.
0125
0126
0127    public void itemStateChanged( ItemEvent event) {
0128        monthPanel.reConfigure( this.yearIs(), this.monthIs(),
0129                                    this.dayIs());
0130        dateSelected();
0131    } // End itemStateChanged.
```

The implementation of the *dateSelected()* method makes use of the *actionCommand* and *itsListener* attributes which have yet to be considered. Unlike the dispatching of ActionEvents from a *dayBox* to a *monthPanel*, or from a *monthPanel* to a *datePanel*, it is possible for an ActionEvent generated by the *DatePanel* to be sent to a number of registered listeners. This requires the *addActionListener()* and *removeActionListener()* methods to be supplied. As there can be a number of *DatePanels* in an interface, the *setCommandString()* and *getCommandString()* methods are supplied in order to allow the origin of the events to be determined. The implementation of these methods, and of the **private** *dateSelected()* method which makes use of them, is as follows.

```
0134    public void setActionCommand( String command) {
0135        actionCommand = command;
0136    } // End setActionCommand.
0137
0138    public String getActionCommand() {
0139        if ( actionCommand == null) {
0140            return "Date Panel";
0141        } else {
0142            return actionCommand;
0143        } // End if.
0144    } // End getActionCommand.
0145
0146
0147    public void addActionListener( ActionListener listener) {
0148        itsListener = AWTEventMulticaster.add( itsListener, listener);
0149    } // End addActionListener.
0150
0151
0152    public void removeActionListener( ActionListener listener) {
0153        itsListener = AWTEventMulticaster.remove(itsListener, listener);
0154    } // End removeActionListener.
0155
0156
0157    private void dateSelected() {
0158        if ( itsListener != null) {
0159            itsListener.actionPerformed( new ActionEvent( this,
0160                                        ActionEvent.ACTION_PERFORMED,
0161                                        this.getActionCommand())));
0162        } // End if.
```

```
0163      } // End dateSelected.
0164   } // End class DatePanel.
```

The *setActionCommand()* stores the *command* String passed as an argument in the *actionCommand* attribute, and *getActionCommand()* returns the attribute or the literal "*Date Panel*" if it has not been set. Adding and removing ActionListeners (or any other Listener classes) is facilitated by the provision of the AWTEventMulticaster class, which will automatically maintain the list of listener objects to which events are to be dispatched to. Within *addActionListener()*, on line 0148, the AWTEventMulticaster *add()* method is used to add the new *listener* passed as an argument to the list held in *itsListener*. Likewise, the AWTEventMulticaster *remove()* method is used on line 0153 within *removeActionListener()* to remove a *listener*.

Having done all this, the actionPerformed() methods of all the listener objects which have been added to the *itsListener* attribute can be called with a single call, as on lines 0159 to 0161, passing as an argument to the called method a **new** ActionEvent containing the identity of the *DatePanel*, that generated it and its *commandString*. The *dateSelected()* method which effects this will be called every time the date is changed, either by clicking on a *dayBox* in the *MonthPanel* or by using one of the Choice menus. Any ActionListener objects which have been registered with the *DatePanel* by its *addActionListener()* method will be informed of this by having their *actionPerformed()* methods invoked. Each will be sent an individual copy of the ActionEvent created on lines 0159 to 0161, and the sequence in which they will be called is indeterminate.

This technique, making use of the class-wide AWTEventMulticaster methods, can be used whenever a specialized component has to allow a number of listeners to be registered and dispatch events, of any type, to each of them.

3.13 The *DatePanelDemonstration* Class

The *DatePanelDemonstration* client is presented next. Briefly it constructs a *DatePanel* instance using the default constructor, which should cause it to initially show the current date. It registers itself as its own listener object, and its *actionPerformed()* method will output the date from the *DatePanel* onto the terminal. The appearance of this demonstration harness was illustrated in Figures 3.7 and 3.8.

```
0001   // Filename DatePanelDemonstration.java.
0002   // Demonstration harness for the DatePanel.
0003   //
0004   // Written for the Java Interface book Chapter 3.
0005   // Fintan Culwin, v 0.2, August 1997.
0006
0007
0008   import java.awt.*;
0009   import java.applet.*;
0010   import java.awt.event.*;
0011
0012   import DatePanel.DatePanel;
```

```
0013
0014
0015   public class DatePanelDemonstration extends      Applet
0016                                     implements ActionListener {
0017
0018   DatePanel   aDatePanel;
0019
0020      public void init() {
0021         aDatePanel = new DatePanel();
0022         aDatePanel.setActionCommand( "date panel demo");
0023         aDatePanel.addActionListener( this);
0024         this.add( aDatePanel);
0025      } // End init.
0026
0027      public void actionPerformed( ActionEvent event)   {
0028         System.out.println( "Action Event received by " +
0029                              "demonstration harness.");
0029         System.out.print( "Originating from " +
                                 event.getCommandString());
0029         System.out.println( ", " aDatePanel.yearIs()  + "/" +
0030                                   aDatePanel.monthIs() + "/" +
0031                                   aDatePanel.dayIs() + " .");
0032   } // End actionPerformed.
```

The demonstration harness's *init()* method commences by creating an instance of the *DatePanel* class using the default constructor, which should result in it displaying the current date when it first becomes visible. It registers itself as its own *ActionListener* on line 0023, having installed a *commandString* on line 0022. Whenever the date on the panel is changed by the user a message should be output on the console, as follows, which gives an initial indication that the *DatePanel* seems to be working.

```
Action Event received by demonstration harness.
Originating from date panel demo, 1999/12/31.
```

Chapter Summary

- Specialized user interface components can be constructed by extending one of the pre-supplied **AWT Components**, most commonly the **Canvas** class.

- A separate top-level window, associated with an application window, is derived from a **Frame** instance.

- The user's prior experience should be taken advantage of in the design of an interface.

- A double-lined arrow on a STD indicates a transition which will result in a new part of the interface being created every time it is followed.

- Complex STDs should have state tables associated with them, keyed to the transitions on the diagram.

- It is better to prevent the user from making 'errors' than to have to correct them.

- National conventions should be considered when designing user interfaces.

- Specialized interface components should allow multiple listener objects to be registered with them.

- Attention to fine detail is an important part of effective user interface design.

Exercises

3.1   Color can be used in the *StikNote* application to indicate the relative importance of the notes—for example a red note to indicate an important message, yellow for routine, and green for non-important. Re-design and re-implement the *StikNote* application to provide three buttons marked *Urgent*, *Routine,* and *Trivial* at the bottom to produce a note of the required color.

3.2   Following on from Exercise 3.1, different fonts can also be used. Use the AWT documentation to find out what fonts are available and use different fonts for different priorities of message.

3.3   Extract the first word, or two, from the contents of a *StikNote* and use it as the window's title rather than have them all titled "*Stik Note.*"

3.4   Test the *DatePanel*. Produce a formal black box test plan and apply it to the component in order to increase your confidence that it is working correctly.

3.5   Place the *DatePanel* within a realistic application, for example one which asks you to indicate your date of birth and then informs you how many days you have lived.

3.6   Re-design and re-implement the *DatePanel* so that it has a minimum date below which a date cannot be selected. For example, an airline booking system should only allow a return flight to be booked on a date later than, or equal to, the date of the outward flight. Demonstrate the *MinimumDatePanel* in a suitable harness.

3.7   The *DatePanel* in this chapter takes up a large amount of screen space. This design attempts to

provide the same functionality in a much smaller space. Pressing the appropriate » button will increase its field and pressing « will decrease it. Design, implement, and demonstrate this design. How would you find out which was favored by users?

3.8   Implement a *MinimalClockPanel* based on the design idea from Exercise 3.7, allowing a time to be specified some time ahead of the current time. Include an instance of it on the *StikNote* interface, allowing an alarm time to be set on the *NoteWindow.* When the time has arrived, the note should indicate this to the user by reversing its colors every half second.

3.9   Re-implement the *MessageCanvas* class so that it has an attribute and methods to control the layout LEFT, RIGHT, or JUSTIFIED of the message.

3.10   Adapt the *DatePanelDemonstration* class so that it registers two object listeners with the *DatePanel* contained within it, then show that both are called when the date is changed.

3.11   There is a bug in the positioning of the *NoteWindow* instances. If the main *StikNote* window is in the top left of the desktop, the instance's top left corner may be positioned somewhere beyond the top left corner. Demonstrate and correct this bug.

3.12   The *MessageCanvas* class is not fully secure or compliant with the pre-declared AWT components. For example it inherits the **setFont()** method from the **Component** class, which should result in its minimum and preferred sizes changing. Make a list of all the methods which it inherits and decide which need to be overridden in order to make it fully compliant.

Drawing and Image Processing with Java—the *Tuttle* Class

This chapter will introduce a class which implements a style of graphical output known as *turtle graphics*. In this style of graphics it is imagined that a turtle, or other small creature, is crawling across the surface of the screen and sometimes leaves a trail as it goes. Instructions such as crawl forward, or backwards, so many steps; turn right, or left, so many degrees or pull your pen up, or down, can be given to the turtle and result in the expected output being produced on the screen. Due to a typing error during a project involving turtle graphics several years ago, these became known as *tuttle* graphics to the author and the name has stayed.

In the previous chapter, the Canvas class was extended to produce specialized interface components and the *Tuttle* class will be similarly produced in this chapter. To enable sophisticated components to be produced, Java's drawing facilities will have to be understood in greater detail and the implementation of *Tuttle* graphics will more than satisfy this requirement. This will also afford an opportunity for an introduction to the algorithmic manipulation of images to be provided. Because this book is only a primer these introductions will necessarily only provide an initial understanding and competence. The intention is that they will be sufficient for more advanced discussions of the topics to be approached, suggestions concerning suitable references are made in Appendix A.

The *Tuttle* class is also being developed at this stage so that various different styles of user interfaces, which will be used to control the *Tuttle*, can be introduced in the chapters which follow. It may be that the details of Java's graphical capabilities are found very complex when they are considered for the first time. If this is the case, then the details can be glossed over and all that needs to be understood for the chapters which follow are the **public** features of the *Tuttle* class and how to use them.

4.1 The Public Resources of the *Tuttle* Class

Figure 4.1 shows an instance of the *Tuttle* class contained within a very simple demonstration harness, which will be introduced at the end of this chapter. The harness supplies the text buttons at the bottom of the application and reports the status of the *Tuttle* at the top.

The feedback area at the top of the screen indicates that the tuttle is at x location -105, y location 60, heading in direction 300 and that its pen is up. The origin (0,0) of the tuttle's *frame of reference* is the center of the screen, and direction 0 indicates that it is heading directly toward the top of the screen. The screen is always 1000 tuttle steps wide and 1000 tuttle steps high, no matter what the physical size of the screen might be.

Directions are measured in degrees and increase as the tuttle rotates clockwise, so that a direction of 90° would indicate that the tuttle is heading directly towards the right of the screen. The representation of the tuttle changes to indicate the direction in which it is heading, and its color also changes to indicate what color trail will be left when its pen is down. The hexagon beside the tuttle was constructed by telling the tuttle to move forward and turn right by 60° six times; its pen was then raised and the tuttle moved clear of the hexagon before the image was produced.

The *Tuttle* class diagram is given in Figure 4.2.

A *Tuttle* instance has six obvious data attributes: the tuttle's *xLocation, yLocation,* its *direction* on the screen; the *currentForeground* and *currentBackground* color; and its *penDown*, either **true** or **false**. There are a number of other attributes within the class which will be described in detail later. There are also a number of other methods, as suggested by the dotted lines at the bottom of the diagram, which will be introduced in Chapter 8.

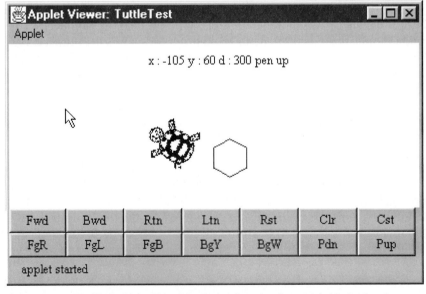

FIGURE 4.1   The *Tuttle* class within a simple user interface harness (with the drawing area reduced in height).

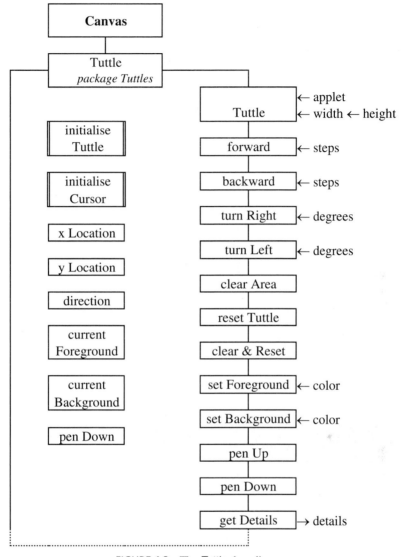

FIGURE 4.2   The *Tuttle* class diagram.

The constructor creates a new *Tuttle* centered within an area whose physical *width* and *height* are as specified in its arguments. It also requires the identity of the applet it is executing within, for reasons which will be explained. The creation of a *Tuttle* also includes calls of the two **private** methods, *initialiseTuttle()* and *intitialiseCursor()*, described later.

The remaining methods are all concerned with the *Tuttle*'s essential actions. The *forward()* and *backward()* methods move the tuttle the number of tuttle steps specified in its current direction, unless this would take it outside its area—in which case it is not moved. The steps are expressed in terms of the *Tuttle*'s *virtual* size, which is always 1000 by 1000 steps, and not in terms of its *physical* size determined by its constructor.

The *turnRight()* and *turnLeft()* methods rotate the tuttle clockwise and anti-clockwise, respectively—the argument indicating the number of *degrees* to turn. The tuttle cursor will always be rotated to indicate the direction in which the tuttle will move forward. The *clearArea()* method will clear all drawings from the tuttle's drawing area by filling it with the current background color, leaving the tuttle with its current location and direction. The *reset()* method will move the tuttle back to the center of the screen (0, 0) and set its direction to 0, without disturbing the contents of the screen. The *clearAndReset()* method will combine the *clearArea()* and *reset()* methods to fully restore the initial state.

The *setForeground()* and *setBackground()* methods change the color of the tuttle and its drawing area, respectively. When the *setForeground()* method is called the color of the tuttle cursor will change to indicate the color it will draw with. When the *setBackground()* method is called, any parts of the drawing shown in the old background color will be changed to the new background color. The *penUp()* and *penDown()* methods cause the tuttle to leave, or not to leave, a trail as it moves. The final method, *getDetails()*, returns a string of the form "*x: nnn y: nnn d: nnn pen {up/ down}*"; that is, the virtual x and y location and the direction and state of the pen, either up or down, as shown at the top of Figure 4.1.

The prototypes of the methods which are of interest to a client, which needs only to control a *Tuttle*, are given in Table 4.1.

4.2 The **Graphics and Color Classes**

The implementation of the *Tuttle* class will require a detailed consideration of the Graphics class and the ways in which it can be used for drawing on component windows. The Graphics class was briefly introduced in Chapter 2, where it was used to produce the drawings on the *Doodle*'s window. It was also used in Chapter 3 when text had to be rendered onto the windows of the *StikNote* application and the *DateBox*es drawn in the *DatePanel* class.

Whenever graphical, as opposed to textual, output has to be produced, an instance of the Graphics class is required. It encapsulates a large amount of information, including which object to draw on, what its dimensions are, what drawing color is to be used, which font is to be used for rendering, and so on. If a Graphics *context* were not used, then much of this information would have to be passed as arguments to every drawing method. For example, the call of the method to draw a line on the *Doodle*'s window in Chapter 2 was as follows.

```
context.drawLine( lastX, lastY, currentX, currentY);
```

The four arguments supplied to the call are the minimum information required to draw a line, where to start, and where to end. If a context were not used, then the call might have to be specified as follows.

```
drawLine( whichWindowToDrawOn,
```

```
public Tuttle( Applet applet int width, int height)

public void forward(    int steps)

public void backward(    int steps)

public void turnRight( int degrees)

public void turnLeft(   int degrees)

public void clearTuttleArea()

public void resetTuttle()

public void clearAndReset()

public void setForeground( Color newColor)

public void setBackground( Color newColor)

public void setPenUp()

public void setPenDown()

public String getDetails()
```

TABLE 4.1   Public Methods of the *Tuttle* Class which are of Interest to a Client

```
whichColorToDrawIn,
whichBackgroundColorToUse,
whatLimitsToDrawWithin,
whatDrawingModeToUse,
whatOriginToUse,
lastX, lastY, currentX, currentY);
```

Thus, the use of a Graphics instance simplifies calls of drawing methods although the necessity of using it may initially suggest that it might make their use more complex. The major resources of the Graphics class are given in Table 4.2.

The *drawRect(), drawPolygon(), drawOval()*, and *drawArc()* methods are accompanied by equivalent *fillRect(), fillPolygon(), fillOval()*, and *fillArc()* methods that differ only by filling the area with the current drawing color.

The Graphics class is an **abstract** class, many of its methods are **abstract**, as it is extended and implemented by the peer windowing system. This is necessary in order that the same Java methods can be used to produce output upon a number of different operating and windowing systems. Many of the methods in the table will be used when the detailed construction of the *Tuttle* class is considered.

A Graphics frame of reference has its default origin (0,0) at the top left of the drawing area, with x values increasing to the right and y values increasing downward. Direction 0 points to the 3 o'clock position, directly to the right of the screen, and

---

<div align="center">**constructor**</div>	
`protected Graphics()`	A null method; Graphics instances are not constructed but obtained with the Component getGraphics() method or the Graphics create() method.

<div align="center">**instance methods**</div>	

`public abstract Graphics create()`
`public Graphics create( int x, int y,`
`            int width, int height)`
	Obtains a copy of the whole Graphics instance or one whose output is constrained (clipped) to the area specified.

`public abstract void dispose()`	Releases the peer resources.
`public void finalize()`	Releases the peer resources and destroys the instance.
`public abstract void translate(` `                int x, int y)`	Translates the origin (0,0) point from the top left-hand corner to the point specified.

`public abstract void clipRect(`
`            int x, int y,`
`        int width, int height)`
`public abstract Rectangle`
`            getClipBounds()`
	Constrains (clips) graphics output to the area specified, or obtains the extent of the current clipping area. This will be the whole window if clipRect() has not been called.

`public abstract void setColor(`
`            Color newColor)`
`public abstract Color getColor()`
	Sets, or obtains, the drawing Color.

`public abstract void setFont(`
`            Font newFont)`
`public abstract Font getFont()`
	Sets, or obtains, the Font to be used when text is rendered.

`public FontMetrics getFontmetrics()`	Obtains the FontMetrics for the current Font.
`public abstract void setPaintMode()`	Sets the drawing mode so that the current Color overwrites the existing color.
`public abstract void setXORMode(` `            Color xorColor)`	Sets the drawing mode so that the current Color is exclusively *or*ed, with the existing color allowing drawings to be undone.

`public abstract boolean drawImage(`
`            Image toDraw,`
`        int atX, int atY,`
`    ImageObserver observer)`
	Draws the Image at the location specified, informing the ImageObserver if the Image is incomplete. Returns **false** if the Image could not be drawn and **true** otherwise.

`public abstract boolean drawImage(`
`            Image toDraw,`
`        int atX, int atY,`
`    int width, int height,`
`    ImageObserver observer)`
	Draws the Image at the location specified, scaling to width and height, and informing the ImageObserver if the Image is incomplete. Returns **false** if the Image could not be drawn and **true** otherwise.

TABLE 4.2 Major Resources of the Graphics Class

`public abstract void` copyArea (
     `int` *fromX,* `int` *from Y*
     `int` *width,* `int` *height,*
     `int` *toX,*   `int` *toY)*
	Copies the area of the image specified as fromX, fromY, width, and height to the location toX,　Y.

`public abstract void` drawLine (
     `int` *fromX,* `int` *fromY,*
     `int` *toX,*   `int` *toY)*
	Draws a line between the points specified.

`public abstract void` drawRect(
     `int` *atX,*   `int` *atY,*
     `int` *width,* `int` *height)*
	Draws a rectangle whose top left corner is at atX and atY, with the width and height specified.

`public void` fill3DRect(`int` *x,* `int` *y,*
     `int` *width,* `int` *height,*
     `boolean` *raised)*
	Draws a pseudo three-dimensional rectangle, as for **drawRect()**, with the **raised** argument indicating if it should appear raised (**true**) or sunken (**false**).

`public abstract void` drawPolygon(
     `int` *xPoints[],* `int` *yPoints[],*
     `int` *numberOfPoints)*
	Draws a polygon whose corners are stored in the two arrays connecting the last point to the first.

`public abstract void` drawOval(
     `int` *atX,*   `int` *atY,*
     `int` *width,* `int` *height)*
	Draws an oval inscribed within the area supplied. If width is equal to height, a circle is drawn.

`public abstract void` drawArc(
     `int` *atX,*   `int` *atY,*
     `int` *width,* `int` *height,*
     `int` *startAngle,* `int` *arcAngle)*
	Draws an arc within the area supplied, starting at startAngle and extending for arcAngle. Angles are measured in degrees, with the 3 o'clock direction being 0 and increasing clockwise.

`public abstract void` drawString(
     String *toRender,*
     `int` *atX,*   `int` *atY)*
	Renders the String supplied, using the current Font at the location specified.

TABLE 4.2 (continued)

directions increase in a clockwise manner. The origin can be moved to any location in the drawing area by using the translate() method but the zero direction cannot be changed. This frame of reference differs from that used by the *Tuttle* class, which will cause some complications in the *Tuttle*'s implementation as will be described. The two frames of reference are illustrated in Figure 4.3.

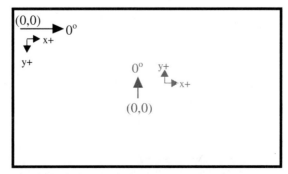

FIGURE 4.3   The Graphics' frame of reference (black) and the *Tuttle*'s frame of reference (gray).

The use of the Graphics class requires some knowledge of the Color class, whose major resources are given in Table 4.3.

A color within a computer system can be represented by its red, green, and blue (RGB) components. If the red, green, or blue values are set to zero, then black is indicated, if all components are set to their maximum value, then white is specified. Different values for the different components specify different colors; some examples are given in Table 4.4.

The first Color constructor will create a color from the three values supplied, the second constructor contains the three components in the lower 24 bits of its 32-bit integer argument, as shown in Figure 4.4. This also explains why the RGB values are limited to eight bit values between 0 and 255. This color model will allow a total of 2^{24}, or over 65 million, different colors to be specified which, as this is more colors than a human eye can resolve, should be sufficient. The Color class also supplies a number of pre-declared color constants, as shown in the table. The final two methods, *lighter()* and *darker()*, are supplied to facilitate the pseudo-three-dimensional bordering of an area.

---

constructor

public Color(**int** *red*, **int** *green*, **int** *blue*) **public** Color(**int** *redGreenBlue*)	Creates a new Color with the *red, green* and *blue* components in the range 0 to 255, as specified, or from appropriate fields of *redGreenBlue*.

constants

black	blue	cyan	darkGray	gray	lightGray
magenta	green	orange	pink	red	yellow	white

instance methods

public int getRed()	Obtains the red component of the Color.
public int getGreen()	Obtains the green component of the Color.
public int getBlue()	Obtains the blue component of the Color.
public Color brighter()	Obtains a brighter shade of the Color.
public Color darker()	Obtains a darker shade of the Color.

TABLE 4.3   Major Resources of the Color Class

	Red	Green	Blue
white	FF	FF	FF
red	FF	00	00
green	00	FF	00
blue	00	00	FF
gray	80	80	80
light gray	40	40	40
dark gray	B0	B0	B0
black	00	00	00

TABLE 4.4   Common RGB Color Values in Hexadecimal

4.3 The Construction of the *Tuttle* Class

The instance diagram for the *Tuttle* class is presented in Figure 4.5. It shows that every *tuttle* is an instance of the *Tuttle* class, which extends the **Canvas** class. Each *tuttle* also has a *rotatingCursor*, which is an instance of the *TuttleCursor* class.

The *Doodle* applet from Chapter 2 suffered from one major failure. When the applet's window was covered by another window and subsequently uncovered, any drawings on the window were lost and a blank window was redisplayed. This behavior would be unacceptable for the *Tuttle* class, and a technique known as *double buffering* is used to provide the required *save under* capability. It is accomplished by not drawing directly onto the component's window but upon a hidden **Image** and copying it to the window whenever required. This technique is illustrated in Figure 4.6.

Image is a Java AWT class which effectively provides a 'window' in the computer's memory, where an image can be stored or manipulated. The contents of an **Image** can be obtained by loading a graphics image file, for example a **.gif* (*G*raphics *I*mage *F*ormat) file from disk or from the Internet. Alternatively, the contents of an **Image** can be obtained by drawing onto it using a **Graphics** context constructed for the purpose. Both of these techniques will be described.

The context clause of the *Tuttle.java* source code file and the declaration of its data attributes are as follows.

bit positions

31 - 24	23-26	15-8	7-0
AA	RR	GG	BB

FIGURE 4.4   The RGB components of a 32-bit color value.

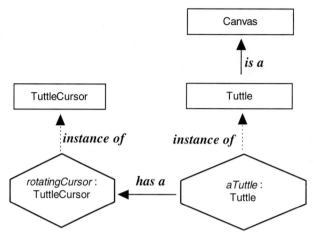

FIGURE 4.5 *Tuttle* instance diagram.

```
0001  // Filename Tuttle.java.
0002  // Providing tuttle (turtle) graphics capabilities by
0003  // extending the Canvas class.
0004  //
0005  // Written for the Java Interface Book Chapter 4.
0006  // Fintan Culwin, v 0.2, August 1997.
0007
0008
0009  package Tuttles;
0010
0011  import java.awt.*;
0012  import java.applet.*;
0013  import java.awt.image.*;
0014  import java.lang.Math;
```

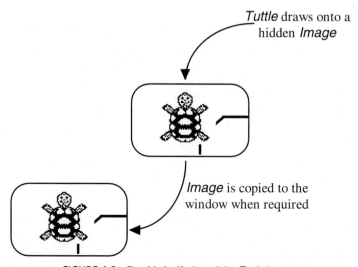

Tuttle draws onto a hidden *Image*

Image is copied to the window when required

FIGURE 4.6 Double buffering of the *Tuttle* image.

```
0015
0016    import Tuttles.TuttleCursor;
0017
0018
0019    public class Tuttle extends Canvas {
0020
0021    private static final int SCREEN_STEPS = 500;
0022
0023    private Image        tuttleImage;
0024    private Image        theCursor;
0025    private Graphics     tuttleGraphics;
0026    private TuttleCursor rotatingCursor;
0027    private Applet       itsApplet;
0028
0029    private int     xLocation = 0;
0030    private int     yLocation = 0;
0031    private int     direction = 0;     // The tuttle's virtual location.
0032
0033    private int     screenX   = 0;
0034    private int     screenY   = 0;     // The tuttle's screen location.
0035
0036    private int     screenWidth;
0037    private int     screenHeight;      // The physical dimensions of the
screen area.
0038
0039    private double  horizontalScale;
0040    private double  verticalScale;     // Virtual to physical conversion
factors.
0041
0042    private boolean penDown              = true;
0043    private Color   currentForeground = Color.blue;
0044    private Color   currentBackground = Color.yellow;
```

The context establishes that this class is contained within the *Tuttles* **package** and makes use of the *TuttleCursor* class from the same package. The constant *SCREEN_STEPS* is used to define the virtual distance between the center of the screen and the edge. The *tuttleImage* attribute is the image upon which all drawing will take place in order to implement double buffering and the *tuttleGraphics* attribute will be used to draw upon it. The *theCursor* and *rotatingCursor* attributes are used to support the cursor and will be described next, as will the use made of the *itsApplet* Applet attribute.

Design Advice

Drawing methods should always use a virtual frame of reference and translate to a physical frame of reference only when absolutely required.

The *xLocation*, *yLocation* and *direction* attributes define the location of the tuttle within the virtual space. The *screenX* and *screenY* attributes record the position of the tuttle on the physical screen, whose dimensions are stored in *screenWidth* and *screen-Height*. The *horizontalScale* and *verticalScale* store the conversion factors between the virtual and physical screen. The *currentForeground* and *currentBackground* attributes store the colors to be used and *penDown* the state of the tuttle's pen. It is the responsibility of the constructor and *addNotify()* methods to ensure that all of these attributes are initialized into a well-defined state, as follows.

```
0046        public Tuttle( Applet applet, int width, int height) {
0047           this.setSize( width, height);
0048           itsApplet = applet;
0049        } // End Tuttle constructor.
0050
0051
0052        public void addNotify() {
0053           super.addNotify();
0054           this.initialiseTuttle();
0055           this.initialiseCursor();
0056        } // End addNotify.
0057
0058
0059        private void initialiseTuttle() {
0060           screenWidth     = this.getSize().width;
0061           screenHeight    = this.getSize().height;
0062           tuttleImage     = this.createImage( screenWidth, screenHeight);
0063           tuttleGraphics = tuttleImage.getGraphics();
0064           tuttleGraphics.setColor( currentBackground);
0065           tuttleGraphics.fillRect( 0, 0, screenWidth, screenHeight);
0066           tuttleGraphics.setColor( currentForeground);
0067           tuttleGraphics.translate( screenWidth /2, screenHeight /2);
0068           horizontalScale = ((double) screenWidth /
0069                                        (double) (SCREEN_STEPS * 2));
0070           verticalScale   = ((double) screenHeight /
0071                                        (double) (SCREEN_STEPS * 2));
0072        } // End initialiseTuttle.
```

The constructor merely sets the size of the component to the dimensions supplied and stores the identity of its applet. The remaining initialization of the *Tuttle* is deferred until the *addNotify()* method is called, after its component peer has been created. The *addNotify()* method first calls its parent addNotify() method and then calls the **private** *initialiseTuttle()* and *initialiseCursor()* methods.

Because the component's window has been created the *initialiseTuttle()* method can commence, on lines 0060 and 0061, by determining the size of the physical drawing area. It would not be safe for the *Tuttle* simply to assume that the setSize() method, called in its constructor, had obtained the dimensions requested because layout negotiations may have given it a different size. Once the size of the screen window is known, on line 0062, the *tuttleImage* is created with exactly the same sizes using the Component createImage() method.

Having created an Image its getGraphics() method is used, on line 0063, to obtain a context for drawing onto it. Lines 0064 to 0066 then ensure that the image is cleared to the background color, by drawing a filled rectangle of the background color onto it, and the context is prepared for drawing in the foreground color. Line 0067 translates the origin $(0, 0)$ from the top left-hand corner of the Image to the center of the Image, for the convenience of the drawing methods. Finally the scaling factors, *horizontalScale* and *verticalScale*, are initialized to allow conversion between the virtual and physical locations on the screen. The implementation of the *initialiseCursor()* method will be considered later.

The contents of the *tuttleImage* need to be copied to the *Tuttle*'s window whenever its *paint()* method is called in order to provide double buffering. A component's paint() method is always called by Java from the update() method, whose default implementation, in the Component class, will first clear the visible window before indirecting to the paint() method. If the update() method were not overridden in the *Tuttle* class, this would cause the window to flicker as it is first cleared and immediately afterwards has the *TuttleImage* copied on to it. To avoid this behavior, an overriding *update()* method is declared in the *Tuttle* class as a method which only calls the *Tuttle*'s *paint()* method, without first clearing the visible window.

```
0110      public void update( Graphics systemContext) {
0111          this.paint( systemContext);
0112      } // End update.
0113
0114      public void paint( Graphics systemContext) {
0115
0116      int cursorCenterX;
0117      int cursorCenterY;
0118
0119          systemContext.drawImage( tuttleImage, 0, 0, this);
0120          cursorCenterX = ((screenWidth /2) + screenX) -
0121                          (theCursor.getWidth( this) /2);
0122          cursorCenterY = ((screenHeight /2) + screenY) -
0123                          (theCursor.getHeight( this) /2);
0124          systemContext.drawImage( theCursor,
0125                                   cursorCenterX,
0126                                   cursorCenterY,
0127                                   this);
0128      } // End paint.
```

The *paint()* method commences, on line 0119, by copying the *tuttleImage* from memory into the *Tuttle*'s visible window using the *systemContext drawImage()* method. The four arguments to his call indicate the Image to be copied, the location on the destination to place its top left corner; the last formal argument requires an ImageObserver to be supplied.

Java was intended from the outset for use on the Internet, and the latency inherent in this environment was taken into account during its implementation. In particular it was designed so that the presentation of information would not be unnecessarily impeded by delays waiting for images, or other multimedia resources, to be downloaded or otherwise manipulated. Accordingly many operations on Images, and other comparable multimedia resources, take place on a different thread from the main thread of control in Java programs. In order to allow synchronization of the separate threads to be achieved, the ImageObserver Interface is supplied. This Interface mandates methods which allow the main thread to determine from the subordinate thread the status of various operations, for example the loading or other time-consuming manipulation, of an Image.

As the Component class implements the ImageObserver interface, any AWT component can be supplied where the API requires an ImageObserver as a formal argument. In the call of the drawImage() method, on line 0119, currently being considered, the actual argument supplied for the fourth argument is the identity of the current *Tuttle* instance (**this**). The use of ImageObservers, including techniques for synchronization, will be continued throughout this chapter.

The *Tuttle paint()* method continues, on lines 0120 to 0127, by the drawing of *theCursor* onto the window, centered at the *Tuttle*'s current (*screenX, screenY*) location. The overall effect of the *paint()* method is to show the contents of the *tuttleImage* on the *Tuttle*'s window and then superimpose the cursor, which is maintained in the *theCursor* Image. The only method which actually draws onto the *tuttleImage* is the *forward()* method, whose implementation is as follows.

```
0132      public void forward( int steps) {
0133
0134      int     possibleNewX;
0135      int     possibleNewY;
0136      int     localDegrees = (direction + 270 ) % 360;
0137      double radians      = (((double) localDegrees) / 180.0) * Math.PI;
0138
0139         possibleNewX = xLocation +
0140                 (int) (Math.cos( radians) * (double) steps);
0141         possibleNewY = yLocation +
0142                 (int) (Math.sin( radians) * (double) steps);
0143
0144      if ( (possibleNewX >= -SCREEN_STEPS) &&
                                    (possibleNewX <= SCREEN_STEPS) &&
0145          (possibleNewY >= -SCREEN_STEPS) &&
                                    (possibleNewY <= SCREEN_STEPS) ){
0146
0147          int NewX = (int)(((double) possibleNewX) * horizontalScale);
0148          int NewY = (int)(((double) possibleNewY) * verticalScale);
0149
0150          if ( penDown) {
0151              tuttleGraphics.drawLine( screenX, screenY, NewX, NewY);
0152          } // End if.
0153
0154          xLocation = possibleNewX;
0155          yLocation = possibleNewY;
0156          screenX   = NewX;
0157          screenY   = NewY;
0158          repaint();
0159      } // End if.
0160      } // End forward.
0161
0162      public void backward( int steps) {
```

```
0163            this.forward( -steps);
0164        } // End backward.
```

The purpose of this method is to move the *Tuttle* from its current location by the number of steps specified in its current direction, providing this will not take it outside the bounds of the screen, and leave trail if the *penDown* flag is set. The *Tuttle* is constructed so that its zero degree direction is in the 12 o'clock position, pointing to the top of the window. However, the Graphics zero degree direction is in the 3 o'clock position, pointing to the right of the window. The declaration of the local variable *localDegrees*, on line 0136, converts the *Tuttle's* direction into an equivalent Graphics direction and then line 0137 expresses this value in radians rather than degrees.

The method itself commences, on lines 0139 to 0142, with the calculation of the possible new virtual location by using the appropriate trigonometric functions from the Math class. The **if** structure which follows then ensures that the new location is within the allowed area. If so the *newX* and *newY* variables, declared local to the **if** structure, are initialized to the new screen location and, if the pen is down, a line is drawn from the currently recorded screen location to the new location. As the *Tuttle* is now known to have moved, on lines 0154 to 0157 the attributes which record its virtual and physical location are updated. The final step is to call the repaint() method which will, in due course, cause the Tuttle's *update()* and hence its *paint()* methods to be called, thus making any new line drawn visible to the user and moving *theCursor*[1].

The *backward()* method, on lines 0162 to 0164, is implemented as a call of the *forward()* method with its argument negated. For example, moving backward 100 steps is the same as moving forward -100 steps. The implementation of the *penUp()* and *penDown()* methods is straightforward, manipulating the encapsulated *penDown* attribute as follows.

```
0167        public void setPenUp() {
0168            penDown = false;
0169        } // End setPenUp.
0170
0171        public void setPenDown() {
0172            penDown = true;
0173        } // End setPenDown.
```

The implementation of the *turnRight()* and *turnLeft()* methods are as follows.

```
0177        public void turnRight( int degrees) {
0178            direction += degrees;
0179            while ( direction < 0) {
0180                direction += 360;
0181            } // End while.
0182            direction %= 360;
0183            theCursor = rotatingCursor.rotate( direction);
0184            repaint();
```

---

[1] There is what some people might regard as an error in this implementation, details of how it manifests itself and how it can be circumvented are contained in Appendix B.

```
0185        } // End turnRight.
0186
0187        public void turnLeft( int degrees) {
0188            turnRight( -degrees);
0189        } // End turnLeft.
```

The *turnLeft()* method is implemented as a call of the *turnRight()* method passing the negated value of its argument. For example, turning left 30° is the same as turning right -30°. The first part of the *turnRight()* method is to add the number of *degrees* needed to turn to the current *direction*. Because a left turn is implemented as a negative right turn, the value of *direction* may become negative, the loop on lines 0179 to 0181 ensures that an equivalent positive value in the range 0 to 359 is obtained. Likewise, a right turn may take the value of direction above 359 so the modular division on line 0182 constrains it to the equivalent 0 to 359 value. On line 0183 *theCursor* is recreated to reflect the new *direction,* and finally the repaint() method is called to ensure that the new cursor is visible to the user.

The implementation of the *clearTuttleArea(), resetTuttle(),* and *clearAndReset()* methods are as follows.

```
0193        public void clearTuttleArea() {
0194            tuttleGraphics.setColor( currentBackground);
0195            tuttleGraphics.fillRect( -( screenWidth/2),
0196                                     -( screenHeight/2),
0197                                     screenWidth, screenHeight);
0198            tuttleGraphics.setColor( currentForeground);
0199            this.repaint();
0200        } // End clearTuttleArea.
0201
0202        public void resetTuttle() {
0203            xLocation = 0;
0204            yLocation = 0;
0205            screenX  = 0;
0206            screenY  = 0;
0207            direction = 0;
0208            theCursor = rotatingCursor.rotate( direction);
0209            this.repaint();
0210        } // End resetTuttle.
0211
0212        public void clearAndReset() {
0213            this.resetTuttle();
0214            this.clearTuttleArea();
0215        } // End clearAndReset;
```

On lines 0194 to 0198, the *Tuttle* area is cleared by filling it with a solid rectangle of the *currentBackground* color. As the *tuttleGraphics* context is used for this and as its origin has been transposed to the center of the Image, the upper left-hand corner of the rectangle has been re-transposed to the upper left corner of the image. When the context has had its drawing color restored to the *currentForeground* color, the *Tuttle*'s repaint() method is called to make the cleared image visible.

The *resetTuttle()* method resets the appropriate *Tuttle* attributes and then creates a new cursor, as the direction to be indicated by it may have changed, and *repaint*s the image onto the screen. The *clearAndReset()* method is implemented as calls of the *resetTuttle()* and *clearTuttleArea()* methods.

The *setForeground()* method stores the current color, changes the current color of the *tuttleGraphics* context, changes the color of the *rotatingCursor* instance, and obtains a new cursor before finally calling the repaint() method to show the new cursor.

```
0219    public void setForeground( Color newColor) {
0220        currentForeground = newColor;
0221        tuttleGraphics.setColor( currentForeground);
0222        rotatingCursor.setCursorColor( newColor);
0223        theCursor = rotatingCursor.rotate( direction);
0224        this.repaint();
0225    } // End setForeground.
```

The implementation of the **setBackground()** method is more complex and will be considered when the *TuttleCursor* class is considered. The final method of the *Tuttle* class is the *getDetails()* method, whose implementation is as follows.

```
0288    public String getDetails() {
0289
0290    StringBuffer buffer = new StringBuffer();
0291
0292        buffer.append( "x : "  + xLocation +
0293                        " y : " + (yLocation * -1) +
0294                   .     " d : " + direction);
0295        if ( penDown) {
0296            buffer.append( " pen down");
0297        } else {
0298            buffer.append( " pen up");
0299        } // End if.
0300        return buffer.toString();
0301    } // End getDetails.
```

On line 0293 the *yLocation* value has to be multiplied by -1 as, in the Graphics frame of reference, y values increase down the area while they increase up the area in the *Tuttle*'s frame of reference, as shown in Figure 4.3. Thus, when the *Tuttle* is above the midpoint of the screen it will have a negative Graphics value, which has to be reported as the equivalent positive value by the *Tuttle*.

4.4 The *TuttleCursor* Class

The *TuttleCursor* class supplies a cursor to the *Tuttle* class. The cursor has to be capable of being rotated to indicate the direction of the *tuttle* and has to be capable of being re-colored to indicate the foreground color of the *tuttle*. Its class diagram is given in Figure 4.7. This class is being introduced not only to supply the *Tuttle* class with a suitable

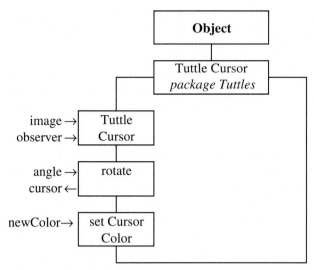

FIGURE 4.7   The *TuttleCursor* class diagram.

cursor but also to introduce the techniques by which an Image can be algorithmically processed by a Java artifact. As with the *Tuttle* class itself a detailed knowledge of the implementation of this class is not required for the use of the *Tuttle* object, although the techniques are essential for the development of any Java image processing applications.

The image which is to be used as the cursor is supplied to the *TuttleCursor* constructor from the private *initialiseCursor()* method of the *Tuttle* class whose implementation, which was omitted earlier, is as follows.

```
0078        private void initialiseCursor(){
0079
0080        MediaTracker tuttleTracker;
0081
0087            theCursor = ( itsApplet.getImage(
0088                            itsApplet.getCodeBase(), "Tuttles/tuttle.gif"));
0089            tuttleTracker = new MediaTracker( this);
0090            tuttleTracker.addImage( theCursor, 0);
0091            try {
0092                tuttleTracker.waitForID( 0);
0093            } catch ( InterruptedException exception) {
0094                // Do nothing!
0095            } // End try/ catch.
0096
0097            if ( (theCursor == null)                ||
0098                (theCursor.getWidth( this) < 1)  ||
0099                (theCursor.getHeight( this) < 1)  ){
0100                System.out.println( "Empty cursor image ... abending");
0101                System.exit( -1);
0102            } // End if.
0103            rotatingCursor = new TuttleCursor( theCursor, this);
```

```
0104            rotatingCursor.setCursorColor( currentForeground);
0105            theCursor = rotatingCursor.rotate( direction);
0106        } // End initialiseCursor.
```

The tuttle cursor is stored as a GIF format image in a file called "*tuttle.gif,*" which is assumed to be located in a sub-directory, (called *Tuttles*) of the directory containing the *Tuttles* package. This image has to be retrieved from the file and imported into the applet as a Java Image instance.

In order to accomplish this, the Applet getImage() method is called on lines 0087 and 0088. The arguments to this method are the *codeBase* of the Applet, which is the Internet location where the applet was downloaded from, and the name of the file at this location. The second argument indicates that the file which contains the image ("*tuttle.gif*") is contained in the *Tuttles* sub-directory of the *Tuttles* package directory. This method executes asynchronously in a separate thread of control, and lines 0089 to 0095 involve the use of a MediaTracker instance to suspend the current thread until the image has completely loaded.

MediaTrackers allow monitoring and synchronization of the separate threads which are loading multimedia files, as mentioned earlier. In this example, on line 0090, the *tuttleTracker* is asked to monitor the loading of the *theCursor* Image. The second argument to the addImage() method indicates the degree of priority to be used and allows one of a number of activities which a MediaTrackers instance might be monitoring to be identified. Lines 0091 to 0095 then effectively suspend the main thread until the image in the "*tuttle.gif*" file has been fully loaded.

It is possible that the image will not load, possibly because the file containing it could not be found or does not contain a valid image. Accordingly, lines 0097 to 0102 contain a guard which abends the program if the cursor image cannot be obtained. Once it is certain that the cursor image has loaded, and thus that *theCursor* Image is complete on line 0103, the *TuttleCursor* constructor is called passing *theCursor* image and identity of the Tuttle component being constructed as arguments. Finally on lines 0104 and 0105 the *setCursorColor()* and *rotate()* methods of the **new**ly constructed *TuttleCursor* instance, *rotatingCursor*, are called to ensure that *theCursor* is ready for use.

The declaration of the *TuttleCursor* class, as far as the start of its constructor, is as follows.

```
0001   // Filename TuttleCursor.java.
0002   // Provides a rotating cursor capability for the
0003   // Tuttle class.
0004   //
0005   // Written for the Java Interface Book Chapter 4.
0006   // Fintan Culwin, v 0.2, August 1997.
0007
0009   package Tuttles;
0011
0012   import java.awt.*;
0013   import java.awt.image.*;
0014   import java.lang.Math;
0016
0017   class TuttleCursor extends Object {
```

```
0018
0019   private int        imageWidth;
0020   private int        imageHeight;
0021   private int        pixels[];
0022   private int        rotatedPixels[];
0023   private Component  component;
0024   private Image      rotatedImage;
```

The *TuttleCursor* class encapsulates two arrays of **int**egers. One, called *pixels*, contains a copy of the cursor Image. The second, called *rotatedPixels*, is used to contain a rotated copy of the first, which will be transferred as an Image into the *rotated-Image* attribute when rotation is required. The *imageWidth* and *imageHeight* attributes store the size of the cursor image.

This provides a common pattern for image processing operations that can be adapted for use when other operations are required. The pattern of operations is illustrated in Figure 4.8. It shows that the Image has to be first converted into a one-dimensional array of **int**, which can then be processed (in this example, rotated) before it is converted back into an Image.

The implementation of the *TuttleCursor* constructor is as follows.

```
0028       protected TuttleCursor( Image           toRotate,
0029                               ImageObserver observer) {
0030
0031       PixelGrabber grabber;
0032       boolean      status;
0033
0034          component     = observer;
0035          imageWidth    = toRotate.getWidth( observer);
0036          imageHeight   = toRotate.getHeight( observer);
0037          pixels        = new int[ imageWidth * imageHeight];
0038          rotatedPixels = new int[ imageWidth * imageHeight];
0039
0040          grabber       = new PixelGrabber( toRotate, 0, 0,
0041                                          imageWidth, imageHeight,
0042                                          pixels, 0, imageWidth);
0043       try {
0044          status = grabber.grabPixels();
0045          if ( !status) {
```

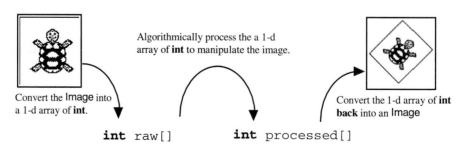

Algorithmically process the a 1-d array of **int** to manipulate the image.

Convert the Image into a 1-d array of **int**.

Convert the 1-d array of **int** **back** into an Image

int raw[]   **int** processed[]

FIGURE 4.8   Algorithmic processing of an Image.

```
0046                    throw new InterruptedException();
0047                 } // End if.
0048            } catch ( InterruptedException exception) {
0049                System.err.println("Exception grabbing pixels ... abending");
0050                System.exit( -1);
0051            } // End try/catch.
0052        } // End TuttleCursor constructor.
```

The *TuttleCursor* constructor requires the Image to be used for the cursor and also an *ImageObserver*, for reasons discussed earlier and as elaborated on later. The first part of the constructor, on line 0034, stores the identity of the *ImageObserver* in the component instance attribute. The width and height of the cursor image are then obtained, using the *toRotate* getWidth() and getHeight() methods that require an ImageObserver argument. Having established the size of the cursor image on lines 0037 and 0038, the sizes of the **int** *pixels* array, which will contain the raw image and the **int** *rotatedPixels* array, which will contain the processed image, can be established.

On lines 0040 to 0042, an instance of the PixelGrabber class is constructed whose arguments ensure that it will be capable of extracting all the pixels from the *toRotate* Image into the pixels array. This will comprise the first part of the image processing pattern shown in Figure 4.8. The grabbing is accomplished within the **try/ catch** structure guarding the call of the grabPixels() method on line 0044, whose **catch** part abends the program should it fail.

The outcome of the constructor is that the *pixels* array contains a representation of the *toRotate* Image containing the cursor. This representation will be processed into the *rotatedPixels* array, implementing the second stage from Figure 4.8. The implementation of the *rotate()* method is as follows.

```
0058    protected Image rotate( int angle) {
0059
0060    int    x, y;
0061    int    fromX, fromY;
0062    int    toX,   toY;
0063    int    transparent = 0x00000000;
0064    double radians  = (((double) (-(angle -180) ) %360) /
0065                                            180.0)  * Math.PI;
0066    double cosAngle = Math.cos( radians);
0067    double sinAngle = Math.sin( radians);
0068
0069
0070      for ( y = 0; y < imageHeight; y++) {
0071        for ( x = 0; x < imageWidth; x++) {
0072            // Rotate around the center of the image.
0073            toX   = ( imageWidth  /2) - x;
0074            toY   = ( imageHeight /2) - y;
0075            fromX = (int)( ( toX * cosAngle) - ( toY * sinAngle));
0076            fromY = (int)( ( toX * sinAngle) + ( toY * cosAngle));
0077            fromX += imageWidth  /2;
0078            fromY += imageHeight /2;
0079
```

```
0080            if ( (fromX < 0) || (fromX >= imageWidth)  ||
0081                 (fromY < 0) || (fromY >= imageHeight) ){
0082               // Rotated point is outside the image
0083               rotatedPixels[ (y * imageWidth) + x] = transparent;
0084            } else {
0085               rotatedPixels[ (y * imageWidth) + x] =
0086                      pixels[ (fromY * imageWidth) + fromX];
0087            } // End if.
0088          } // End x loop.
0089        } // End y loop.
0090
0093        rotatedImage =  component.createImage(
0094                    new MemoryImageSource( imageWidth, imageHeight,
0095                                 rotatedPixels, 0, imageWidth));
0096        return rotatedImage;
0097      } // End rotate.
```

Before considering the details of this method, the 32-bit RGB pixel value as shown in Figure 4.4 needs to be reconsidered. The upper eight bits in locations 24 to 31, shown as *AA*, control the *transparency* of the pixel. A pixel value has all of these bits set (the hexadecimal value 0xFF) is completely opaque, and the RGB color in the remaining 24 bits will be rendered exactly as specified onto the image. A pixel value which has all of these bits clear (the hexadecimal value 0x00) is completely transparent, and the RGB color in the remaining 24 bits is irrelevant because it will not be rendered. Intermediate values produce a varying degree of transparency. This information is known as the *alpha channel,* and a full 32-bit pixel value in this format is known as an *ARGB* value.

The image is used as the cursor has been prepared so that it contains only two colors, and all the pixels in the image which do not form a part of the cursor have their alpha values set so as to be transparent. When the cursor is rendered, the transparent parts will have no effect upon the existing background of the *Tuttle* area. This consideration is also required when the image is rotated; any parts of the rotated image which would have come from outside the cursor are set to the value of the transparent mask, as declared on line 0063 of the listing. This consideration is illustrated in Figure 4.9.

FIGURE 4.9   Rotating an image, the gray areas indicate the parts of the rotated image which originated outside the original image.

Design Advice

When rotating an image, calculate the location where each pixel of the rotated area comes from and not the location where each pixel on the original image will be rotated to. This will avoid gaps appearing in the image.

The rotating of the cursor takes place within the double loop between lines 0070 and 0089. Each pixel on the rotated image is considered in turn, and the location on the original image where it might have originated from is determined using the appropriate trigonometric transformation. If the **if** decision on lines 0080 and 0081 indicates that the original location is outside the bounds of the original image, the rotated pixel is set to the transparent mask. Otherwise, the location is known to be within the bounds and the pixel value is copied from the original image to the rotated image on lines 0085 and 0086.

This implementation is further complicated by two other factors. First the image is rotated around its center point, so the locations where the pixel is to be moved to (*toX* and *toY*) and where it is moved from (*fromX* and *fromY*) have to be expressed as displacements from the center as the rotation is performed in lines 0083 to 0086. However, the *y* and *x* indices of the loops are expressed in the normal top left/bottom right scan line sequence and the *fromX* and *fromY* are converted to this convention in lines 0077 and 0078.

The second complication is that the *pixel* and *rotatedPixel* arrays are single dimensional, as required by the PixelGrabber class, and the two coordinate values have to be combined when the array is accessed between lines 0083 to 0086.

Once the original image in the *pixels* array has been rotated into the *rotatedPixels* array, the *rotatedPixels* array is used to construct an Image instance on lines 0093 to 0095, implementing the third part of Figure 4.8. This step employs an instance of the MemoryImageSource class to accomplish the conversion, and the Image produced from it is **return**ed from the method and used by the *Tuttle* class to indicate the direction of the *tuttle*.

The implementation of the *setCursorColor()* method is simpler. Its requirement is to consider each pixel in the pixel array and, if it is not a transparent pixel, replace its value with a non-transparent *newColorMask* obtained from the *newColor* argument. Its implementation is as follows.

```
0100        protected void setCursorColor( Color newColor) {
0101
0102        int x, y;
0103        int newColorMask    = 0;
0104        int transparentMask = 0xFF000000;
0105
0106            newColorMask = transparentMask           |
0107                        (newColor.getRed()   << 16) |
0108                        (newColor.getGreen() << 8)  |
0109                         newColor.getBlue();
0110
0111            for ( y = 0; y < imageHeight; y++) {
0112                for ( x = 0; x < imageWidth; x++) {
0113                    if ( (pixels[ (y * imageWidth) + x] & transparentMask)
```

```
0114                                             == transparentMask ) {
0115                 pixels[ (y * imageWidth) + x] = newColorMask;
0116              } // End if.
0117           } // End x loop.
0118         } // End y loop.
0119      } // End setCursorColor.
```

The *newColorMask* is constructed from the *transparentMask* and the RGB components of the *newColor*, obtained using the getRed(), getGreen(), and getBlue() methods on lines 0106 to 0109. This is accomplished by using the bitwise left shift operator (<<) and bitwise *or*ing (|) of the resulting values so as to produce a 32-bit ARGB value, as illustrated in Figure 4.4. The *pixels* array is then processed by having every value considered, and if it is not transparent is replaced with the *newColorMask* on line 0015. This will ensure that the next time a cursor is requested by using the *rotate()* method, the color of the cursor will have changed.

The techniques used in the *TuttleCursor* class are also used in the *Tuttle setBackground()* method, which was omitted earlier. Its implementation is as follows.

```
0228     public void setBackground( Color newColor) {
0229
0230     int     x, y;
0231     int     pixels[];
0232     Image   newImage;
0233     int     newColorMask;
0234     int     oldColorMask;
0235     Color   oldColor;
0236
0237     PixelGrabber grabber;
0238     boolean      status;
0239
0240         pixels         = new int[ screenWidth * screenHeight];
0241         newColorMask   = 0xFF000000                      |
0242                          (newColor.getRed()    << 16) |
0243                          (newColor.getGreen() << 8)  |
0244                          newColor.getBlue();
0245         oldColorMask   = 0xFF000000                              |
0246                          (currentBackground.getRed()    << 16) |
0247                          (currentBackground.getGreen() << 8)  |
0248                          currentBackground.getBlue();
0249
0250         newImage = createImage( tuttleImage.getSource());
0251         grabber = new PixelGrabber( newImage,
0252                               0, 0,
0253                               screenWidth, screenHeight,
0254                               pixels, 0, screenWidth);
0255
0256         try {
0257            status = grabber.grabPixels();
0258            if ( !status) {
0259               throw new InterruptedException();
```

```
0260              } // End if.
0261          } catch ( InterruptedException exception) {
0262              System.err.println("Exception grabbing pixels ... abending");
0263              System.exit( -1);
0264          } // End try/catch.
0265
0266          for ( y = 0; y < screenHeight; y++) {
0267              for ( x = 0; x < screenWidth; x++) {
0268                  if ( pixels[ (y * screenWidth) + x] == oldColorMask) {
0269                      pixels[ (y * screenWidth) + x]   =  newColorMask;
0270                  } // End if.
0271              } // End x loop.
0272          } // End y loop.
0273
0274          newImage = this.createImage( new MemoryImageSource(
0275                                          screenWidth, screenHeight,
0276                                          pixels, 0, screenWidth));
0277          tuttleGraphics.drawImage( newImage, -(screenWidth /2),
0278                                  -(screenHeight /2), this);
0279
0280          currentBackground = newColor;
0281          repaint();
0282      } // End setBackground.
```

This method operates by obtaining a copy of the Image as an array of pixels between lines 0250 and 0264, which is the first part of Figure 4.8. The method then iterates through the array, and replaces any pixel which has the *oldColorMask* value, with the *newColorMask* value, which is the second part of Figure 4.8. It then recreates an Image in *newImage* from the *pixel* array on lines 0274 to 0276, which is the third part of Figure 4.8. It concludes by copying the processed *newImage* into the *tuttleImage* attribute on lines 0277 and 0278, causing it to be displayed when the *repaint()* method is called on line 0281, after it has noted the *newColor* in its *currentBackground* attribute. The effect is for any pixels of the old background color to be replaced with pixels of the new background color and leave the rest of the image unchanged.

The pattern for the processing of an Image, shown in Figure 4.8, has been demonstrated twice in this section. It was used in the *rotate()* method of the *TuttleCursor* class and also in the *setBackground()* method of the *Tuttle* class. This pattern of actions, and the Java techniques to implement them, can be adapted for other image processing operations; some possible operations are suggested in the end of chapter exercises.

4.5 The *TuttleTest* Demonstration Class

To conclude this chapter, the *TuttleTest* class used to provide the illustration in Figure 4.1 will be briefly introduced. The following chapters will present some more sophisticated interfaces for the *Tuttle* class. The implementation of this class, as far as its *init()* method, is as follows.

```
0001   // Filename TuttleTest.java.
0002   // First attempt at a Tuttle Interface,
```

```
0003   // interim version only.
0004   //
0005   // Written for the Java Interface Book Chapter 4.
0006   // Fintan Culwin, v 0.2, August 1997.
0007
0008
0009   import java.awt.*;
0010   import java.awt.event.*;
0011   import java.applet.*;
0012
0013   import Tuttles.Tuttle;
0014
0015
0016   public class TuttleTest extends      Applet
0017                          implements ActionListener {
0018
0019   private Tuttle theTuttle;
0020   private Label   feedbackLabel;
0021   private Panel   feedbackPanel;
```

The context imports the *Tuttle* class from the *Tuttles* package and the *TuttleTest* class is declared as implementing the **ActionListener** interface, as it will be its own listener when ActionEvents are generated by its buttons. Three instance attributes are declared on lines 0019 to 0021: an instance of the *Tuttle* class called *theTuttle*, a Label called *feedbackLabel* and a Panel called *feedbackPanel* upon which it will be mounted.

```
0023       public void init() {
0024
0025       Panel   tuttlePanel, tuttleButtonsPanel;
0026       Button fwdButton, bwdButton, rtnButton, ltnButton, rstButton,
0027              clrButton, cstButton, fgrButton, fglButton, fgbButton,
0028              bgyButton, bgwButton, pdnButton, pupButton;
0029
0030         this.setLayout( new BorderLayout());
0031
0032         tuttlePanel = new Panel();
0033         tuttlePanel.setBackground( Color.white);
0034         theTuttle = new Tuttle( this, 400, 400);
0035         tuttlePanel.add( theTuttle);
0036
0037         tuttleButtonsPanel = new Panel();
0038         tuttleButtonsPanel.setLayout( new GridLayout( 2, 7));
0039
0040         fwdButton = new Button( "Fwd");
0041         fwdButton.setActionCommand( "Fwd");
0042         fwdButton.addActionListener( this);
0043         tuttleButtonsPanel.add( fwdButton);
0044
0045         bwdButton = new Button( "Bwd");
0046         bwdButton.setActionCommand( "Bwd");
```

```
0047            bwdButton.addActionListener( this);
0048            tuttleButtonsPanel.add( bwdButton);
—       //Other Button construction and configuration omitted!
0114            feedbackPanel = new Panel();
0115            feedbackPanel.setBackground( Color.white);
0116            feedbackLabel = new Label();
0117            feedbackPanel.add( feedbackLabel);
0118
0119        this.add( tuttleButtonsPanel,  "South");
0120        this.add( tuttlePanel,          "Center");
0121        this.add( feedbackPanel,        "North");
0122        this.feedback();
0125     } // End init.
```

This method declares two *Panel*s, which will be required for layout control on line 0025 and, on lines 0026 to 0028, the fourteen buttons which are shown at the bottom of the interface. The first part of the method, on line 0030, establishes a **Border-Layout** policy for the **Applet**. The *Tuttle* instance, *theTuttle*, is then created and mounted in its own *Panel* in lines 0032 to 0035.

Following this, the *Panel* to mount the buttons on is created and its layout policy set to a 2 row by 7 column *GridLayout*. Each **Button** in turn is then created, has its *ActionCommand* attribute set, has the **Applet** registered as its *ActionListener,* and is added to the *tuttleButtonsPanel*. Once all **Buttons** have been processed, lines 0114 to 0117 create the *feedbackLabel* and install it onto its own **Panel**. The *init()* method concludes by assembling the interface and calls the *feedback()* method, as follows, to produce the initial information display at the top of the interface.

```
0187        private void feedback() {
0188            feedbackLabel.setText( theTuttle.getDetails());
0189            feedbackPanel.doLayout();
0190        } // End feedback.
```

The *feedback()* method obtains the information it needs by calling *theTuttle*'s *getDetails()* method and installs this **String** into the *feedbackLabel*, calling the *feedbackPanel*'s doLayout() method to ensure that the size of the **Label** is changed, if necessary.

All **ActionEvents** generated by the **Buttons** are sent to the *actionPerformed()* method, which extracts the *commandString* from it and calls the appropriate *Tuttle* method with the required argument, if any, as follows. As indicated in the implementation, a movement forwards or backwards is limited to 25 *tuttle* steps and a turn of right or left to 30°. This limitation will be addressed in the chapters which follow.

```
0129        public void actionPerformed( ActionEvent event) {
0130
0131        String itsCommand = event.getActionCommand();
0132
0133            if ( itsCommand.equals("Fwd")) {
0134                theTuttle.forward( 25);
0135            } else if ( itsCommand.equals("Bwd")) {
```

```
0136            theTuttle.backward( 25);
0137        } else if ( itsCommand.equals("Rtn")) {
0138            theTuttle.turnRight( 30);
—           // Other branches omitted!
0176        } else if ( itsCommand.equals("Pup")) {
0177            theTuttle.setPenUp();
0178        } // End if.
0179
0180        this.feedback();
0181    } // End actionPerformed.
```

Pressing all of the buttons at the bottom of the interface will ensure that each of the methods which the *Tuttle* class offers is called at least once, thus producing an initial confidence that the *Tuttle* class seems to be working correctly.

Chapter Summary

- *Tuttle* graphics involve considering a small creature crawling around the surface of the drawing area.

- The Graphics class provides the facilities for drawing upon a Component window or an Image, collectively known as *drawables*.

- Colors can be defined as 32-bit ARGB values.

- Drawings should always be made in terms of a virtual space and mapped to the physical space when they are rendered onto the drawable.

- The Component update() method first clears the drawable and then calls the paint() method. This will cause a visible image to flicker, and the update() method should be overridden to avoid this.

- Image processing can be accomplished by copying an Image to an **int**eger array, processing the contents of the array, and then creating a new Image from the array.

Exercises

4.1 Revisit the *Doodle* application from Chapter 2 and re-implement it to provide *save under* capability.

4.2 Extend the *Tuttle* class to provide a facility to render a String onto the drawing area at the current *Tuttle* location. This will also require methods to support a Font attribute to be provided.

4.3 Re-implement the *Tuttle* class, removing the *update()* method, so that the flickering effect becomes visible.

4.4   Extend the *Tuttle* class to produce a *GeometricTuttle* class which has the capability to draw rectangles, polygons, ovals, arcs, etc.

4.5   The execution of the *Tuttle setBackground()* method can take some time even on a fast machine. One way to avoid the usability problems caused by nothing apparently happening is to process the image one row at a time. This will take longer but the user will see the background changing slowly from the top to the bottom of the drawing. Re-implement the *setBackground()* method making use of this technique.

4.6   Design and implement a *ColorValue* applet which contains three Scrollbars, a Canvas, and a Label. The user should be able to interactively use the sliders to indicate the red, blue, and green components of a color. The applet should respond by filling the Canvas with the specified color and the Label should display the hexadecimal RGB values.

4.7   Implement an image processing class. This class should be capable of loading an image from a GIF file and then applying various filters to it. For example, a color can be converted to its gray scale equivalent using the formula GG = (RR + GG + BB) / 3 and then setting the RR, GG, and BB bytes to GG. A cut-off filter can then be produced which converts all pixels above a certain GG value to black and all below it to white.

4.8   Extend the application from 4.5 to provide an image-intensity histogram. The GG value is a measure of the intensity of the pixel and has a range of 0 to 255. By counting the number of pixels from the image which have each possible intensity value and then displaying these numbers as lines of different heights, an intensity histogram can be produced.

4.9   The decision not to move the tuttle beyond the bounds of the virtual space was somewhat arbitrary. Other possible decisions might have been to move the tuttle up to the limits of the space rather than to refuse to move it at all, to allow the tuttle to get lost in tuttle space to reappear when it moves back into view, or when the tuttle moves beyond the right (top) of the space to reappear on the left (bottom) of the space. Implement one, or all, of these alternative behaviors.

CHAPTER 5

Semi-Direct User Interfaces

In this, and the following two chapters, four possible styles of user interface will be developed for the *Tuttle* class as developed in the previous chapter. The interface presented in this chapter is a *semi-direct* style of interface, where the *Tuttle* will be controlled from a collection of buttons below its drawing area which display iconic representations of the action they control. This interface style is described as semi-direct because *direct* manipulation would allow the user to control the tuttle by selecting and manipulating it with the pointer and mouse. For example, to move the tuttle it might be selected and dragged. Selecting the *Tuttle* while a specific key on the keyboard is held down might cause the tuttle to rotate as the mouse pointer is moved around it.

The semi-direct interface will require buttons capable of displaying icons, but the 1.1 release of the AWT does not supply a *Button* class which is capable of displaying an image, only one which is capable of displaying a text label. Consequently the first part of this chapter will implement a *TuttleButton* class which provides this facility. This will still be a valuable exercise even if a subsequent release of the AWT does supply an *ImageButton* class because it will consolidate the understanding of supplying specialized components, and the requirements of a *TuttleButton* may differ significantly from any *ImageButton* class which might be supplied.

This interface, and those in the following chapters, may not be the best style of interface for the control of a tuttle. They are being introduced so that the considerations and techniques for the construction of these interface styles can be used where they are more appropriate. When all four styles of interface have been introduced, the techniques which can be used to evaluate an interface will be discussed.

5.1 The *TuttleButton* Class

The *TuttleButton* class will supply a button which implements push-button behavior and is capable of displaying an image, instead of the text label of the pre-supplied Java

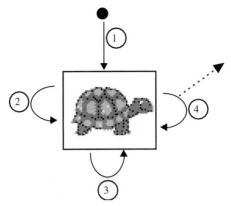

FIGURE 5.1   The *TuttleButton* state transition diagram.

AWT Button class. The state transition diagram of the behavior of a push-button is presented in Figure 5.1 and Table 5.1.

The behavior indicates that a button becomes *primed* when the mouse button is pressed while the mouse pointer is inside the button; this is confirmed to the user by a visual feedback which shows the button as if it were depressed. If the button is released while the mouse pointer is still inside the button, the button is raised and an action event is generated, as indicated by the dashed arrow leaving transition 4. However, if the mouse pointer is moved outside the button after being primed, the button will be un-primed and raised, and when the mouse pointer is subsequently released no action event will be generated.

The mechanism for showing a raised and depressed button is illustrated in Figure 5.2. The button is surrounded by a pseudo three-dimensional border, which has been emphasized in this illustration. It is imagined that the button is illuminated by a light shining from the top left. In the left-hand illustration the button is raised so the right and bottom of the button are in shade and are shown in a darker hue. In the right-hand

Transition	Event	Pre-Condition	Consequence
1	none	none	post button, raised.
2	mouse button down	none	prime button for action, depress button.
3	mouse exit	none	un-prime button for action, raise button.
4	mouse button up	button primed	generate action event, raise button.

TABLE 5.1   State Table for the *TuttleButton* STD in Figure 5.1

FIGURE 5.2   Highlighting of
buttons (the reversal of the
icon is not significant).

illustration the button is depressed so the left and top of the button are in the shade
and are shown in a darker hue.

The class diagram for the *TuttleButton* class is given in Figure 5.3. The first constructor requires the identity of the **Applet** and the source of the image to be used by
the button to be specified and will use a default, gray, border color. The second constructor allows the color to be used for the bordering to be explicitly specified, as well
as the **Applet** and the source for the image. The *addNotify()* method is used to initialize
the button after its peer has been constructed. The *getMinimumSize()*, *getPreferred-
Size()*, *update()*, and *paint()* methods are used by the button to interact with layout
negotiations and to display itself using the techniques previously described. The
processMouseEvent() method will implement the behavior shown in the STD in Figure 5.1, and is supported by the *setActionCommand()*, *getActionCommand()*, *addAc-
tionListener()*, and *removeActionListener()* methods. These are provided to allow
instances of this class to interact with other **Compoenents** in a manner directly comparable to the AWT **Button** class, as described in the previous chapter. The implementation of this class, as far as the end of the constructors, is as follows.

```
0001   // Filename TuttleButton.java.
0002   // Contains an extended Canvas component to supply
0003   // button behaviour with an image as its label.
0004   //
0005   // Written for the Java Interface book, Chapter 5.
0006   // Fintan Culwin, v 0.2, August 1997.
0007
0008   package Tuttles;
0009
0010   import java.awt.*;
0011   import java.awt.event.*;
0012   import java.applet.*;
0013   import java.awt.image.*;
0014
0015
0016   public class TuttleButton extends Canvas {
0017
0018   private static final int     BORDER_WIDTH        = 2;
0019   private static final Color   DEFAULT_BORDER_COLOR =
0020                                        new Color( 0x80, 0x80, 0x80);
0021
0022   private Image          buttonImage   = null;
0023   private String         imageSource   = null;
0024   private int            buttonWidth   = -1;
```

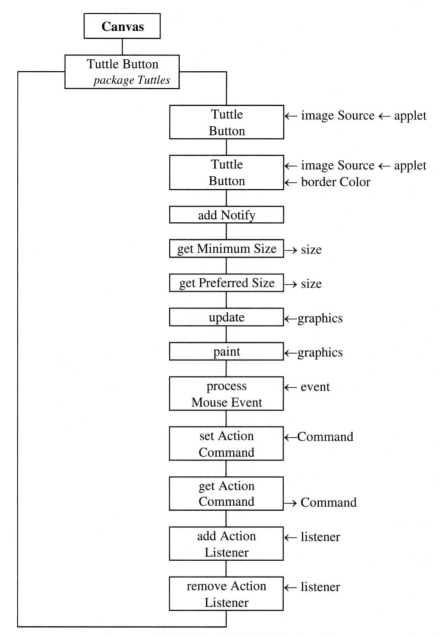

FIGURE 5.3   The *TuttleButton* class diagram.

```
0025  private int             buttonHeight  = -1;
0026  private boolean         pressed       = false;
0027  private Color           borderColour;
0028  private String          actionCommand = null;
0029  private ActionListener  itsListener   = null;
0030  private Applet          itsApplet;
0031
```

```
0032
0033    public TuttleButton( String theSource,
0034                           Applet applet) {
0035        this( theSource, applet,  DEFAULT_BORDER_COLOR);
0036    } // End TuttleButton constructor.
0037
0038    public TuttleButton( String theSource,
0039                           Applet applet,
0040                           Color  colorForBorder) {
0041        super();
0042        imageSource = new String( "Tuttles/Images/" + theSource);
0043        itsApplet = applet;
0044        this.setForeground( colorForBorder);
0045        this.enableEvents( AWTEvent.MOUSE_EVENT_MASK);
0046    } // End TuttleButton constructor.
```

The class-wide constant attributes, *BORDER_WIDTH* and *DEFAULT_BOR-DER_COLOR*, determine the size of the pseudo three-dimensional border and the default border color, if no color is explicitly specified as the button is constructed. The instance attributes indicate the Image which is to be used and *theSource* filename where it can be obtained from, the overall *buttonWidth* and *buttonHeight*, the *pressed* state of the button, its *borderColor* of the button, the *commandString* and *itsListener* object, and finally the identity of *itsApplet*.

The first constructor indirects to the second, passing the *DEFAULT_BOR-DER_COLOR* as the Color argument. The second constructor calls the **super** constructor and then, on line 0042, catenates the *theSource* argument, identifying the file containing the image for this button with a path string which indicates that it is expected to be found in the *Images* sub-directory of the *Tuttles* package directory. The full pathname and filename string is stored in the *imageSource* instance attribute. The *applet* argument is stored in the *itsApplet* attribute, on line 0043, and *colorForBorder* is passed as an argument to the inherited *setForeground()* method. The final step of the constructor is to enable mouse events on the *TuttleButton* in order that its *process-MouseEvent()* method will be called every time the mouse is used within its extent. The *addNotify()* method will complete the initialization of the *TuttleButton*, and is implemented as follows.

```
0050    public void addNotify() {
0051
0052    MediaTracker aTracker;
0053
0054        super.addNotify();
0055
0056        buttonImage = ( itsApplet.getImage(
0057                           itsApplet.getCodeBase(), imageSource));
0058        aTracker = new MediaTracker( this);
0059        aTracker.addImage( buttonImage, 0);
0060        try {
0061            aTracker.waitForID( 0);
0062        } catch ( InterruptedException exception) {
```

```
0063                // Do nothing!
0064            } // End try/ catch.
0065
0066        if ( buttonImage == null              ||
0067            buttonImage.getWidth( this)  < 1 ||
0068            buttonImage.getHeight( this) < 1 ){
0069          System.err.println( "The image " + imageSource +
0070                            "\nCould not be loaded, abending ...");
0071          System.exit( -1);
0072        } // End if.
0073        buttonWidth  = buttonImage.getWidth( this) + BORDER_WIDTH *2;
0074        buttonHeight = buttonImage.getHeight(this) + BORDER_WIDTH *2;
0075        this.setSize( buttonWidth, buttonHeight);
0076     } // End addNotify;
```

The first part of this method, which loads the image from a file on the server that provided the applet, is essentially identical to the loading of an image in the previous chapter. It uses the *itsApplet* attribute as an argument in the getImage() call on line 0056, to load the file into the *buttonImage* Image attribute. Should the image not load successfully, for example if the file cannot be found, then the condition on lines 0066 to 0068 will evaluate **true** and the program will abend. If the image is loaded successfully then the *buttonWidth* and *buttonHeight* attributes are initialized to the width and height of the image, plus an allowance for the border at each edge, and on line 0075 the size of the Component is established based upon these dimensions. These attributes are used by the *getMinimumSize()* and *getPreferredSize()* methods, as follows.

```
0081      public Dimension getMinimumSize() {
0082         return( new Dimension( buttonWidth, buttonHeight));
0083      } // End getMinimumSize.
0084
0085      public Dimension getPreferredSize() {
0086         return this.getMinimumSize();
0087      } // End getPreferredSize.
```

The implementation of the *update()* and *paint()* methods are as follows.

```
0089      public void update( Graphics systemContext) {
0090         this.paint( systemContext);
0091      } // End update.
0092
0093      public void paint( Graphics systemContext) {
0094
0095      int index;
0096
0097         systemContext.drawImage( buttonImage, BORDER_WIDTH,
0098                             BORDER_WIDTH, this);
0099         for ( index=0; index < BORDER_WIDTH; index++) {
0100            systemContext.draw3DRect( index, index,
0101                                 buttonWidth  - index -1,
0102                                 buttonHeight - index -1, !pressed);
```

```
0103            } // End for.
0104        } // End paint.
```

The *update()* method indirects to the *paint()* method for the reasons explained in the last chapter. The *paint()* method commences, on line 0098, by drawing the *button-Image* into the button's window offset from the top left of the window by the width of the border. Once this has happened, the border is drawn around the image as a sequence of concentric *draw3Drect()* calls. The last argument of a *draw3Drect()* call is a **boolean,** which if **true** causes the rectangle to be drawn as if raised and if **false** depressed. Those parts of the border shown as dark gray in Figure 5.2 are drawn using a darker hue of the component's foreground drawing color, those parts of the border shown as light gray are drawn using a lighter hue. The negated value of the *pressed* attribute is used to supply this last argument and its value is controlled by the *process-MouseEvent()*, as follows.

```
0107    protected void processMouseEvent( MouseEvent event) {
0108        switch ( event.getID()) {
0109
0110        case MouseEvent.MOUSE_EXITED:
0111            pressed = false;
0112            repaint();
0113            break;
0114
0115        case MouseEvent.MOUSE_PRESSED:
0116            pressed = true;
0117            repaint();
0118            break;
0119
0120        case MouseEvent.MOUSE_RELEASED:
0121            if ( (pressed)              &&
0122                (itsListener != null) ){
0123              itsListener.actionPerformed( new ActionEvent( this,
0124
                                                ActionEvent.ACTION_PERFORMED,
0125                                          this.getActionCommand())));
0126            } // End if.
0127            pressed = false;
0128            repaint();
0129            break;
0130        } // End switch.
0131    } // End processMouseEvent.
```

The MOUSE_EXITED branch of the **switch** structure ensures that the *pressed* attribute is **false** and calls the *repaint()* method to, indirectly, cause the *paint()* method to be called. As *pressed* is **false,** the last argument of the *draw3Drect()* method will be **true** and so the button will be drawn in a raised fashion. The MOUSE_PRESSED branch primes the button by setting the *pressed* attribute **true** and calls *repaint()*, which will draw the button in a depressed state. Finally the MOUSE_RELEASED method, if the *pressed* attribute is **true** and an *ActionListener* has been registered, calls the *actionPerformed()* method of *itsListener* passing as an argument a new Action-Event containing the *TuttleButton*'s *actionCommand*. This branch concludes by setting the *pressed* attribute **false** and *repaint*ing the button. The list of ActionListeners in *itsListeners* and the *commandString* attribute are maintained by the remaining four methods, whose implementations are directly comparable with those in the *DatePanel* class from the previous chapters, as follows.

```
0134      public void setActionCommand( String command) {
0135          actionCommand = command;
0136      } // End setActionCommand.
0137
0138      public String getActionCommand() {
0139          if ( actionCommand == null) {
0140              return "Tuttle Button";
0141          } else {
0142              return actionCommand;
0143          } // End if.
0144      } // End getActionCommand.
0145
0146
0147      public void addActionListener( ActionListener listener) {
0148          itsListener = AWTEventMulticaster.add( itsListener, listener);
0149      } // End addActionListener.
0150
0151      public void removeActionListener( ActionListener listener) {
0152          itsListener = AWTEventMulticaster.remove( itsListener, listener);
0153      } // End removeActionListener.
```

Before using instances of the *TuttleButton* in the semi-direct interface it should be demonstrated to be working correctly; a demonstration harness might be as follows.

```
0001  // Filename TuttleButtonDemonstration.java.
0002  // A demonstration test harness for the TuttleButton class.
0003  //
0004  // Written for the Java Interface book, Chapter 5.
0005  // Fintan Culwin, v 0.2, August 1997.
0006
0007
0008  import java.awt.*;
0009  import java.applet.*;
0010  import java.awt.event.*;
0011
0012  import Tuttles.TuttleButton;
0013
0014  public class TuttleButtonDemonstration extends    Applet
0015                                         implements ActionListener {
0016
0017    public void init() {
0018
0019    TuttleButton leftTuttleButton;
```

```
0020      TuttleButton rightTuttleButton;
0021
0022        this.setBackground( Color.white);
0023
0024        leftTuttleButton  = new TuttleButton( "greyltutt.gif", this);
0025        leftTuttleButton.setActionCommand( "Left  button");
0026        leftTuttleButton.addActionListener( this);
0027        this.add( leftTuttleButton);
0028
0029        rightTuttleButton = new TuttleButton( "greyrtutt.gif", this,
                                                       Color.red);
0030        rightTuttleButton.setActionCommand( "Right button");
0031        rightTuttleButton.addActionListener( this);
0032        this.add( rightTuttleButton);
0033      } // End init.
0034
0035
0036      public  void actionPerformed( ActionEvent event) {
0037        System.out.println( event.getActionCommand() + " pressed.");
0038      } // End actionPerformed.
0039    } // End class TuttleButtonDemonstration.
```

The *init()* action constructs two *TuttleButtons*, one initialized to display a grey left-facing tuttle image (*greyltutt.gif*) with the default grey border and the other a grey right-facing tuttle image (*greyrtutt.gif*) with a red border. These two GIF files are stored in the *Images* sub-directory of the directory on the server which contains the *Tuttles* package. Figure 5.2 illustrates the appearance of this demonstration harness.

The *TuttleButtonDemonstration* class implements the ActionListener interface and registers itself as the listener object for both buttons. Its *actionPerformed()* method will display a message on the console, containing the button's *actionCommand*, when each of the buttons is pressed. This indicates that the *TuttleButtons* are calling their registered listener object's *actionPerformed()* method when they are pressed by the user and that the method can determine which button was pressed. This client class does not have a *main()* action because the loading of the images from the server relies upon the top-level window being an Applet. Consequently the demonstration can only be run from a Web browser or an appletviewer utility.

5.2 The *SemiDirectTuttle* Interface

The semi-direct interface uses a collection of *TuttleButtons* to allow the user to control a *tuttle* instance. The appearance of the interface is illustrated in Figure 5.4.

There is a total of 21 *TuttleButtons* in the *tuttleControl* Panel at the bottom of the interface, and grouping has been used to help indicate to the user the different functions the buttons control. The collection of six buttons at the top left of the Panel is used to control the tuttle's drawing color; the color of the tuttle in each button indicating the color it will draw with. The collection of six buttons below it control the background color of the drawing area, with the button's background illustrating the color it

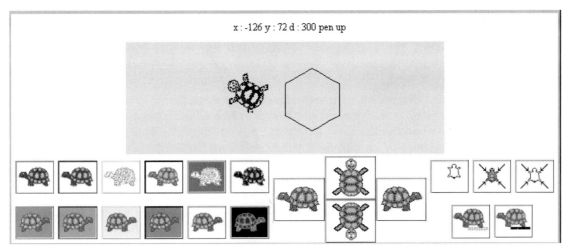

FIGURE 5.4   The *SemiDirectTuttle* interface (with the drawing area reduced in height).

will be cleared to. Apart from the black and white buttons at the right of each collection, each button uses a border color appropriate to its effect.

The collection of buttons at the top right of the panel control the screen functions and indicate, from left to right, clearing the drawing without resetting the tuttle, resetting the tuttle without clearing the drawing, and both clearing and resetting the tuttle. The two buttons below this collection indicate pen up and pen down. The collection of four larger buttons in the center of the panel control the movement of the tuttle. The two buttons in the center indicate moving forward (up) and backward (down), and the remaining two turning to the left and turning to the right.

As well as using the spatial position of the buttons to indicate their effect, both by grouping related effects together and, in the case of the movement buttons, their relative locations, the appearance of the buttons is used to communicate their effect. For the color buttons this is done by using the appropriate color for their foreground and background, all the other buttons are presented with gray-scale images. The use of left-facing tuttles for the foreground and right-facing tuttles for the background buttons is intended to reinforce this distinction.

The image used on each button, hopefully, gives an iconic representation of the button's effect. For example the dotted line below the pen up button indicates that as the tuttle moves it will leave no trace, particularly in comparison with the other button in the group which has a solid line below the tuttle. The icons used on the buttons should ideally be designed, and produced, by a graphic artist who is trained to communicate ideas by images in an aesthetically pleasing manner (unlike these buttons, which were designed by a complete amateur–the author!).

However there are very few images which clearly and unambiguously communicate the essence of an object or an action in a culturally independent manner, and it is likely that all of these have already been discovered. Accordingly, even though techniques can be used to improve the communicative impact of icons, it should not be assumed that the users will always be able to derive the meaning of an icon from its appearance and a help system, or training, should be available for the users of an iconic interface.

5.3 *SemiDirectTuttle,* Construction Overview

The instance diagram for the *SemiDirectTuttle* applet is presented in Figure 5.5. It shows that *theApplet* is an instance of the *SemiDirectTuttle* class that extends the Applet class and implements the ActionListener interface. This allows it to listen to events generated by an instance of the *SemiDirectTuttleInterface*, which extends the Panel class and contains the *TuttleButton*s the user will press to command the *Tuttle*. The events listened to by the *SemiDirectTuttle* application result in calls of the *theTuttle* actions, causing the *Tuttle* to react. In terms of the application, translation, and presentation design philosophy: the *Tuttle* instance contains the application and also provides its own presentation aspects, the *SemiDirectTuttleInterface* instance presents the controls to the user, and the *SemiDirectTuttle* instance supplies the translation aspects. All of these classes will be implemented within a package called *SemiDirect-Tuttle.*

5.4 The *SemiDirectTuttleInterface* Class

The *SemiDirectTuttleInterface* class is responsible for supplying the collection of *TuttleButtons*, shown at the bottom of Figure 5.4, and also for dispatching events generated by the user's interactions with the buttons to its listener object. It contains only a constructor so a class diagram will not be presented.

The layout managers introduced in previous chapters are not sufficiently sophisticated for the layouts required in the *SemiDirectTuttleInterface*. In order to produce

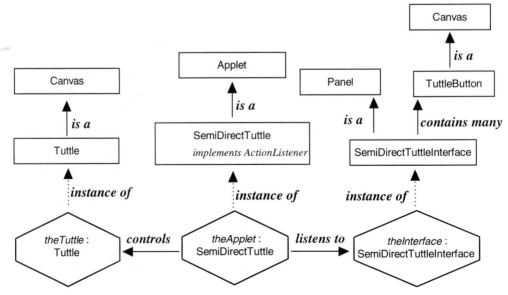

FIGURE 5.5 *SemiDirectTuttle* instance diagram.

the required groupings, the *GridBagLayout* layout manager has to be used. This is the most complex of the Java AWT layout managers and only a brief introduction to its full capabilities will be given here; further details can be obtained from the AWT documentation.

The basis of using a *GridBagLayout* layout manager is to imagine the area which will be occupied by a collection of components divided in a grid containing an arbitrary number of columns and rows. Figure 5.6 shows the panel upon which the four movement buttons were laid out, with a suitable grid superimposed.

The top-left cell of all grids must have the co-ordinates $(0,0)$ but the grid can contain any number of rows and columns. A component can then be placed onto the grid by specifying the cell where its top-left corner should appear and the width and height it should occupy, in cells. So the backward movement button is located in cell $(1,2)$ and has a width of 1 cell and a height of 2 cells. This information, known as *constraints*, is summarized for all four *TuttleButtons* in Table 5.2.

To apply these constraints an instance of the *GridBagConstraints* class has to be constructed, configured, and communicated to the *GridBagLayout* instance specified as the Panel's layout manager. This will be described in detail when the four *TuttleButtons* are constructed and added to their Panel in the *SemiDirectTuttleInterface* constructor, which commences as follows.

```
0018        public SemiDirectTuttleInterface( Applet itsApplet) {
0019
0020        ActionListener sendToHere = (ActionListener) itsApplet;
0021
0022          Panel foreGroundPanel  = new Panel();
0023          Panel backGroundPanel  = new Panel();
0024          Panel screenPanel      = new Panel();
0025          Panel penPanel         = new Panel();
0026          Panel movementPanel    = new Panel();
```

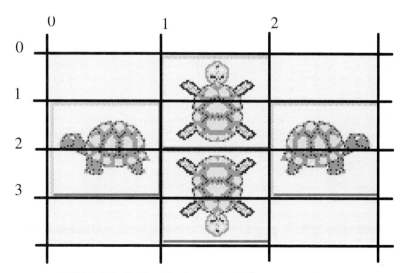

FIGURE 5.6   Grid used to layout the *Tuttle* movement buttons.

	gridx	gridy	gridwidth	gridheight
turnLeft	0	1	1	2
goForward	1	0	1	2
gobackward	1	2	1	2
turnRight	2	1	1	2

TABLE 5.2   Layout Constraints for the *Tuttle movementPanel*

```
0027
0028        GridBagLayout        tuttleLayout    = new GridBagLayout();
0029        GridBagLayout        movementLayout  = new GridBagLayout();
0030        GridBagConstraints constraints       = new GridBagConstraints();
0031
0032
0033        TuttleButton goForward;
0034        TuttleButton goBackward;
0035        TuttleButton turnLeft;
0036        TuttleButton turnRight;
—           Other TuttleButton declarations omitted.
```

The constructor requires as an argument the identity of the Applet that implements the ActionListener interface to which it is to send the *ActionEvents* generated by its *TuttleButtons*. This identity is established, for convenience, on line 0020 because both the identity of the Applet and of its ActionListener are required for the construction of the *TuttleButtons* and a single cast here prevents multiple casts later.

The five *Panels*, declared and constructed on lines 0022 to 0026, are used to mount the five groups of *TuttleButtons* in order to implement the groupings as described. The *SemiDirectTuttleInterface* itself and the *movementPanel* require a *GridbagLayout* policy, and two suitably named instances of the *GridBagLayout* class are declared and constructed on lines 0028 and 0029 to provide these. An instance of the *GridBagConstraints* class, called *constraints*, is declared and constructed on line 0030. The 21 *TuttleButtons* are then declared on lines 0033 to 0054.

Following these declarations, the *movementPanel* is prepared as follows. The first step, on line 0059, is to set the layout policy of the *movementPanel* to *GridBagLayout* by passing the *GridBagLayout* instance *movementLayout* as an argument to its *setLayout()* method.

```
0059        movementPanel.setLayout( movementLayout);
```

When the Components contained within the *movementPanel* are laid out, during layout negotiations, the Constraints associated with each Component are consulted to determine where it should be positioned. For this to be accomplished each *TuttleButton* in turn is constructed, has its *actionCommand* and *actionListener* attributes set, and then is added to the *movementPanel* after its *Constraints* are associated with it by a call of the *movementLayout setConstraints()* method. The first *TuttleButton* to be prepared is the *turnLeft* button, as follows.

```
0061          turnLeft = new TuttleButton( "greyltutt.gif", itsApplet);
0062          turnLeft.setActionCommand( "Turn left");
0063          turnLeft.addActionListener( sendToHere);
0064          constraints.gridx = 0;
0065          constraints.gridy = 1;
0066          constraints.gridwidth  = 1;
0067          constraints.gridheight = 2;
0068          movementLayout.setConstraints( turnLeft, constraints);
0069          movementPanel.add( turnLeft);
```

On line 0061 the *TuttleButton* is constructed, specifying as arguments the image it is to display and the identity of *itsApplet* required to obtain the Image for its button, as described earlier. On lines 0062 and 0063 its *actionCommand* and *actionListener* attributes are specified, the latter of which specifies as its argument the ActionListener cast value, *sendToHere*, of *itsApplet*. Lines 0064 to 0067 set the public attributes of the *constraints* object to those shown in Table 5.2, as required by the *turnLeft TuttleButton*. Line 0068 associates these *constraints* with the *turnLeft* button within the *movementLayout* GridBagLayout instance, by calling its *setConstraints()* method. Finally, on line 0069, the *turnLeft TuttleButton* is added to the *movementPanel*. Each of the other three *TuttleButton*s on the *movementPanel* are prepared and added in a similar way, specifying the appropriate constraints from Table 5.2.

The other four Panels (*foreGroundPanel, backGroundPanel, screenPanel,* and *penPanel*) use their default FlowLayout policy as their TuttleButtons are constructed, configured, and added. For example, the *penPanel* is prepared as follows.

```
0118          penUpButton = new TuttleButton( "penup.gif", itsApplet);
0119          penUpButton.setActionCommand(    "Penup");
0120          penUpButton.addActionListener(  sendToHere);
0121          penPanel.add( penUpButton);
0122
0123          penDownButton = new TuttleButton( "pendown.gif", itsApplet);
0124          penDownButton.setActionCommand(    "Pendown");
0125          penDownButton.addActionListener(  sendToHere);
0126          penPanel.add( penDownButton);
```

All five Panels, the four described in the preceding paragraph and the *movementPanel*, are also subject to a GridBagLayout policy in order to produce the required positionings. The grid required to lay out the Panels is illustrated in Figure 5.7, and the layout attributes derived are listed in Table 5.3.

The widths of the Panels were derived from the consideration that each of the small buttons is two-thirds of the width of each of the large buttons. Thus the panels have a width ratio of 6, 4½ and 3, which has been doubled to produce the integer ratio 12, 9 and 6. The anchor attribute is used by the layout manager to decide what to do when the space allocated to the component is larger than it requires. For example, if the area allocated to the *foregroundPanel* is larger than it requires it will be positioned in the lower right (SOUTHEAST) of the area. The anchor values were chosen so as to

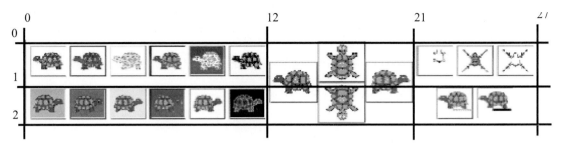

FIGURE 5.7 Grid used to layout the *TuttleControl* Panels.

preserve the functional and aesthetic properties of the interface under these circumstances. The part of the *init()* action responsible for positioning the *penPanel* is as follows.

```
0233            constraints.gridx      = 21;
0234            constraints.gridy      = 1;
0235            constraints.gridwidth  = 6;
0236            constraints.gridheight = 1;
0237            constraints.anchor     = GridBagConstraints.NORTHWEST;
0238            tuttleLayout.setConstraints( penPanel, constraints);
0239            this.add( penPanel);
0240        } // End SemiDirectTuttleInterface constructor.
```

The *tuttleLayout GridbagLayout* instance has been specified as the layout manager of the *SemiDirectTuttleInterface;* when it is informed, on line 0238, of the *constraints* to be applied to the *penPanel,* it is ready to use this information in layout negotiations after the *penPanel* has been added to it on line 0239.

All the data attributes of the *GridBagConstraints* class, and the effect which they have on the layout of the components, are summarized in Table 5.4. Additional details can be found in the API documentation.

	gridx	gridy	gridwidth	gridheight	anchor
foregroundPanel	0	0	12	1	SE
backgroundPanel	0	1	12	1	NE
movementPanel	12	0	9	2	CENTER
screenPanel	21	0	6	1	SW
penPanel	21	1	6	1	NW

TABLE 5.3 Layout Constraints for the *tuttleControlPanel*

Attributes of the GridBagConstraints class

`gridx` `gridy`	The location of the top-left cell of the **Component** .
`gridwidth` `gridheight`	The width and height, in cells, of the **Component**. **REMAINDER** can be specified for the last in a sequence and **RELATIVE** for the penultimate.
`weightx` `weighty`	The relative amount of additional space which the **Component** will take when the **Container** is larger than the minimum required.
`ipadx` `ipady`	The internal padding of the **Component**; in pixels, added to each of its edges in addition to its minimum size.
`fill`	The behavior when the area allocated to the component is larger than the minimum required. **HORIZONTAL** causes it to expand its width but not its height. Can also specify **VERTICAL** or **BOTH**.
`insets`	(Of class **Insets**) The external padding of the **Component**, in pixels; an **Insets** instance allows all four possibilities to be individually specified.
`anchor`	Used to determine where to place the **Component** when it is smaller than its allocated area. Values are the eight compass directions of **NORTH**, **NORTHEAST**, etc.

TABLE 5.4   Attributes of the GridBagConstraints Class

5.5 The *SemiDirectTuttle* Class

The *SemiDirectTuttle* class is responsible for constructing the interface by creating the *Tuttle* and *SemiDirectTuttleInterface* instances, together with a feedback **Panel** as used in the *TuttleTest* applet in the previous chapter, and subsequently responding to the ActionEvents dispatched to it from the *TuttleButtons*. The implementation of this class, as far as the end of its *init()* method, is as follows.

```
0001   // Filename SemiDirectTuttle.java.
0002   // Supplies a semi-direct interface the Tuttle class
0003   // using TuttleButtons.
0004   //
0005   // Written for Java Interface book chapter 5.
0006   // Fintan Culwin, v 0.2, August 1997.
0007
0008   package SemiDirectTuttle;
0009
0010   import java.awt.*;
0011   import java.applet.*;
0012   import java.awt.event.*;
0013
0014   import Tuttles.Tuttle;
0015   import SemiDirectTuttleInterface;
0016
0017   public class SemiDirectTuttle extends     Applet
0018                                 implements ActionListener {
0019
```

```
0020   private Label    feedbackLabel;
0021   private Tuttle theTuttle;
0022   private Panel    feedbackPanel;
0023
0024      public void init() {
0025
0026      Panel      tuttlePanel = new Panel();
0027      SemiDirectTuttleInterface theInterface;
0028
0029         this.setFont( new Font( "TimesRoman", Font.PLAIN, 14));
0030         feedbackLabel = new Label();
0031         feedbackPanel = new Panel();
0032         feedbackPanel.add( feedbackLabel);
0033
0034         theTuttle = new Tuttle( this, 500, 500);
0035         tuttlePanel.add( theTuttle);
0036
0037         theInterface  = new SemiDirectTuttleInterface( this);
0038
0039         this.setLayout( new BorderLayout());
0040         this.add( feedbackPanel, "North");
0041         this.add( tuttlePanel,   "Center");
0042         this.add( theInterface,  "South");
0043
0044         this.feedback();
0045      } // End init.
```

The *init()* method commences, on line 0029, by specifying the Font to be inherited by the *feedbackLabel* and used to display the *Tuttle*'s status information. It continues, on lines 0030 to 0032, by constructing the *feedbackLabel* and adding it to the *feedbackPanel*.

On lines 0034 and 0035 the *Tuttle* instance, *theTuttle*, is then constructed specifying a 500 by 500 pixel drawing area and is added to its Panel. Line 0037 constructs the *SemiDirectTuttleInterface*, *theInterface*, passing as its argument the identity of the *SemiDirectTuttle* applet (**this**) currently being constructed.

Having prepared the three parts of the interface, these are added in the appropriate BorderLayout locations of the Applet Panel to provide the complete interface shown in Figure 5.4. The last action of the *init()* method is to call the *SemiDirectTuttle*'s private *feedback()* method, to cause the *Tuttle*'s initial status to be shown when the interface is first presented to the user.

As the *SemiDirectTuttle* class states that it implements the ActionListener interface, it has to implement an *actionPerformed()* method as follows.

```
0048      public void actionPerformed( ActionEvent event) {
0049
0050      String theCommand = event.getActionCommand();
0051
0052         if ( theCommand.equals( "Forwards")) {
0053            theTuttle.forward( 25);
```

```
0054              } else if ( theCommand.equals( "Backwards")) {
0055                   theTuttle.backward( 25);
0056              } else if ( theCommand.equals( "Turn left")) {
0057                   theTuttle.turnLeft( 15);
—             Other if branches omitted.
0094              } // End if.
0095
0096              this.feedback();
0097         } // End actionPerformed.
```

The first stage of this method, on line 0050, is to retrieve the *theCommand* String from the *event* dispatched to it from the *SemiDirectTuttleInterface*. A 21-way **if/ else if** structure then provides a branch for each possible *commandString* associated with the 21 *TuttleButton*s, calling the appropriate *theTuttle* method and passing the appropriate argument if required.

For example, if the user were to press the *turnLeft* button the ActionEvent generated would contain the *commandString* "*Turn left.*" This would cause the condition on line 0056 to evaluate **true** and the *turnLeft()* method of *theTuttle* would be called on line 0057, causing the *tuttle* to turn 15° to the left. Likewise, pressing the *forwardButton* would result in the *tuttle* moving 25 steps forward when *theTuttle*'s *forward()* method is called on line 0053. Unfortunately, this interface does not allow the user any choice in the amounts of turn or movement which are associated with the buttons.

The final stage of the *actionPerformed()* method, on line 0096, is to call the *feedback()* method so that any changes in the *Tuttle*'s status are reported back to the user. The implementation of this method is identical to that of the comparable method presented in the *TuttleTest* applet at the end of the last chapter and is presented here for the sake of completeness.

```
0100         private void feedback() {
0101             feedbackLabel.setText( theTuttle.getDetails());
0102             feedbackPanel.doLayout();
0103         } // End feedback.
0104   } // End SemiDirectTuttle.
```

This completes the *SemiDirectTuttle* implementation, details of how to obtain the parts of the source code omitted for the sake of brevity can be found at the start of Appendix B.

Chapter Summary

- The AWT does not supply an *ImageButton* class, but a possible class has been supplied in this chapter.

- The GridBagConstraint class makes use of the GridBagLayout class to provide sophisticated layout management.

- Grouping of components on a Panel, and their appearance, should be used to assist in the communication of their function.

- Iconic representation of actions or objects should not be assumed to be unambiguous.

Exercises

5.1   The *ImageButton* class does not fully conform to the essential requirements of the Component class; for example, it does not supply a suitable setEnabled() method. Review the required actions of a Component, decide upon an appropriate behavior for an *ImageButton,* and extend the class to implement the behavior. For example, an *ImageButton*'s Image might be converted to gray scale as in Exercise 4.6 and then have its contrast reduced when it is set insensitive.

5.2   The Applet showStatus() method takes a single String argument and displays it somewhere in the Applet's window, for example the place where "applet started" is shown in Figure 4.1. Re-implement the *ImageButton* class so that it encapsulates the identity of the Applet it is running within as it is constructed and then displays a short message in this area when the mouse pointer enters it and clears the area when it leaves.

5.3   The *Pen Up* and *Pen Down* buttons on the *SemiDirectInterface* are essentially a toggle. Extend the *TuttleButton* class to provide a *ToggleTuttleButton* class that will toggle between two images when pressed. Replace the two *TuttleButton*s on the *SemiDirectInterface* with a single *ToggleTuttleButton.*

5.4   The two color panels on the *SemiDirectInterface* are essentially radio buttons. Extend the *TuttleButton* class to provide a *CheckboxTuttleButton* which has a *Status* attribute and visual indicator. Replace the *TuttleButtons* on the interface with *CheckboxTuttleButton*s.

5.5   The interface, as presented in this chapter, will only allow the tuttle to be moved 25 steps at a time or turned 15° at a time. Devise and design a semi-direct interface that would allow the user to move or turn the tuttle an arbitrary number of steps or degrees. For example, one possibility is to have a set of large buttons that move or turn 10 units and a set of small buttons that move or turn 1 unit. So if the user wanted to turn the tuttle 47° to the right, they could press the large turn right button four times and the small turn right button seven degrees.

5.6   Extend the *SemiDirectTuttle* interface to add controls for the *GeometricTuttle* class from Exercise 4.4.

5.7   Experiment with different groupings of the controls. For example, the foreground and background controls can be added as vertical rows of *TuttleButton*s to the left and right of the tuttle, where they would occupy the *East* and *West* locations of the BorderLayout management policy.

C H A P T E R   6

Application-Level Pull-Down Menus

The second interface which will be presented is a standard *application-level menu* style. This style consists of a sequence of *menu buttons* mounted on a *menu bar* at the top of the application. Each menu button, when activated, causes a *pull-down* menu of items to be presented. An item may be an *action button* which causes an action to occur, a *menu button* which causes a *cascading menu* to appear, or a *dialog button* which causes a *dialog panel* to appear.

    This style of interface has become ubiquitous for a very large number of applications and hence has a major advantage that, because of this widespread use, users will feel very familiar with it. However, it is probably the least suitable style of interface for the control of a *tuttle*, it is being introduced so that the techniques for the construction of this style of interface can be used where an application-level menu style of interface is more suitable.

    This chapter will also introduce the techniques and mechanisms which can be used to deploy a *dialog panel* within an application. This is a temporary window which appears on top of the main application window and informs the user of some occurrence or error or obtains some information from the user. Although dialog panels are being introduced in the context of application-level menus, they can also be used with other styles of user interface.

6.1 The *MenuBarTuttle* Interface

The appearance of the *MenuBarTuttle* interface, under Windows '95, is illustrated in Figure 6.1. It shows the main menu bar at the top of the interface, the feedback panel at the bottom, and the tuttle in the middle.

    The various *pull-down menus* attached to the *menu buttons* on the *menu bar* at the top of the application are shown in Figure 6.2.

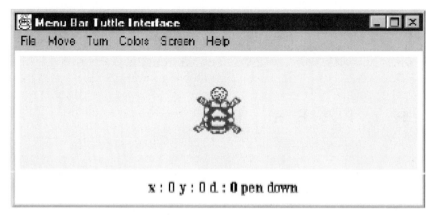

FIGURE 6.1 The MenuBarTuttle interface (with the drawing area reduced in height).

The first pull-down menu, the *File* menu, has a single **MenuItem** labeled *Exit....* The three dots following the label on the button indicate that, when it is activated, a *dialog* will be posted which the user will interact with to complete the operation. In this example, it is a *yes/no* confirmation of the request to exit the application, as will be described.

The second pull-down menu, the *Move* menu, has two items labeled *Forward* and *Backward*. Each item is followed by a right-facing triangle which indicates that, when activated, the item will post a second, cascading, menu. Both of these *cascading menus* are shown in Figure 6.2 and each consists of three items allowing the *tuttle* to be moved by 5, 10, or 25 steps. The third pull-down menu, the *Turn* menu, is essentially identical in its structure having two items labeled *Turn Right* and *Turn Left*, each of which leads to a cascading menu with options to turn by 5, 15, or 45 degrees.

The fourth pull-down menu, the *Colors* menu, also has two cascading menus controlled by items labeled *Foreground* and *Background*. Each cascading menu contains six **CheckboxMenuItems** behaving as if they were radio buttons allowing only one item to be selected at a time, the currently selected item indicated by a preceding tick. The menus in Figure 6.2 indicate that the current foreground color is *Blue* and the background is *Yellow*.

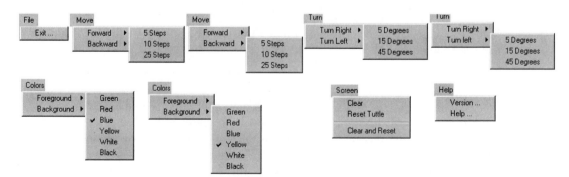

FIGURE 6.2 The MenuBarTuttle interface menu structure.

The *Screen* menu commences with three simple items which cause the screen to be cleared without moving the *tuttle*, moving the *tuttle* to the center of its area, and for both a re-centering of the *tuttle* and clearing of the screen to be performed. The last option of this part of the menu is separated from the previous two by use of a *separator*. The *Screen* menu is completed, following another separator, by two check box items allowing the state of the *tuttle*'s pen to be controlled. The final menu, the *Help* menu, offers access to two dialogs labeled *Version…* and *Help….*

Thus, the complete menu system contains five main menu buttons and associated pull-down menus, six cascading menus, three dialog panels, eighteen menu items which will have an effect upon the tuttle or its interface, and fourteen check box items. In addition, there are three dialog panels: the *exit, help,* and *version* dialogs which are shown when the appropriate menu item is activated by the user.

In this part of the chapter, only a selection of these elements will be described in detail, the remaining items are essentially identical, and details of how to obtain the complete source code is located at the start of Appendix B.

6.2 The MenuComponent Hierarchy

The facilities for the construction of menus are supplied by the Java AWT in a class hierarchy based upon the MenuComponent class, which is a sibling class of the Component class whose hierarchy has been used so far. The MenuComponent class hierarchy diagram was given in Figure 2.16 and is repeated in Figure 6.3 for convenience, again, the Object class is not part of the AWT but has been included to show the relationship between the AWT classes and it.

The base of the hierarchy is the abstract MenuComponent class which, like the Component class, provides a collection of resources which are common to all other MenuComponents. Its most important resources are given in Table 6.1.

The MenuBar, class supplies a menu bar upon which the main menu buttons, and their pull-down menus, can be attached. Its major resources are given in Table 6.2.

A MenuBar, once constructed, can only be added to a Frame instance using the Frame's setMenuBar() method. As mentioned in Chapter 3 a Frame is not an exten-

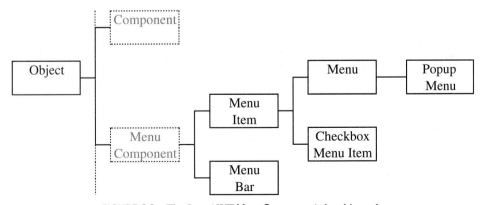

FIGURE 6.3   The Java AWT MenuComponent class hierarchy.

constructor	
public MenuComponent()	Constructor.

instance methods	
public MenuContainer getParent()	Obtains the instance parent.
public **void** setFont(Font *setTo*) **public** Font getFont()	Sets or obtains the Font to be used.
public String toString()	Obtains a String representation of the component.

TABLE 6.1   Major Resources of the MenuComponent Class

sion of, or a parent class of, the Applet class and provides an independent top-level window on the desktop. This means that application-level main menus cannot be presented within a Applet window inside a browser, but only in a separate top-level window on the desktop.

The reason for this restriction is that the provision of a top-level menu within an applet might result in two top-level menus being presented to the user. For example: when the applet is executed within a browser, the browser would supply a top-level menu and if the applet were to provide a second then this would undoubtedly be confusing to a user. Within the Apple, NextStep, and OpenStep environments this would be particularly confusing as these environments support only a single top-level menu, visible at the top of the screen, and change the options on the menu as the user moves focus from application to application. By insisting that a top-level menu in a Java artifact must be associated with a Frame instance, this problem is avoided.

constructors	
public MenuBar()	Constructor.

instance methods	

public **synchronized** Menu add(
                    Menu *addThis*)
public **synchronized** Menu remove(
            MenuComponent *fromHere*)
	Adds, or removes, the Menu to the menu bar. Menus are added to the next available location.

public Menu getMenu(**int** *here*) **public** **synchronized** **void** remove(**int** *here*)	Obtains the identity of the menu located at position *here*, or removes that menu from the menu bar.
public **void** setHelpMenu(Menu *toThis*) **public** Menu getHelpMenu()	Sets, or obtains the identity of, the help menu item.

TABLE 6.2   Major Resources of the MenuBar Class

constructors

`public` `MenuItem()`
 `public` `MenuItem( String label)`
 `public` `MenuItem( String label,`
 `            MenuShortCut shortcut)`
	Constructs an item, possibly with a *label* and *shortcut* specified.

instance methods

`public` `setLabel( String newLabel)` `public` `String getLabel()`	Sets, or obtains, the item's label.

`public` `void` `setEnabled(`
 `            boolean onOroff)`
 `public` `boolen` `isEnabled()`
	Enables (**true**) or disables (**false**) the item, or obtains the enabled state.

`public` `void` `setShortcut(`
 `            MenuShortcut shortCut)`
 `public` `MenuShortcut getShortcut()`
 `public` `void` `deleteShortcut()`
	Sets, obtains, or removes the shortCut associated with this item

`public` `void` `addActionListener(`
 `            ActionListener listener)`
 `public` `void` `removeActionListener(`
 `            ActionListener listener)`
 `public` `void` `setActionCommand(`
 `            String command)`
 `public` `String getActionCommand()`
	Adds, or removes, the ActionListener for this item and sets, or obtains, its ActionCommand. More than one ActionListener can be registered, but there is no guarantee on the order in which they will be called.

TABLE 6.3   Major Resources of the MenuItem Class

If a MenuBar contains a *help* menu button, as nomiated by the use of the setHelpMenu() method, it is always presented as the right-most button on the menu bar. All other buttons are presented in a left/right location determined by the sequence they were added to the menu bar.

The MenuItem class provides the entries which can appear on the pull-down and cascading menu panes; its major resources are presented in Table 6.3.

The Menu class provides the *menu panes* which provide the pull-down and cascading menus and the buttons which they are connected to. Its major resources are given in Table 6.4.

A TearOff menu can be detached from the top-level menu and remains available to the user in a separate window, allowing them to make extensive use of it without having to continually re-post it from the top-level menu. Finally, the CheckboxMenuItem class is used to supply check box items on a menu, its major resources are given in Table 6.5.

There is no support in the AWT for a set of CheckboxMenuItems to behave as a set of radio buttons, allowing only one of them to be checked at a time. If this behavior is required then it has to be supplied by the developer, as will be illustrated below. The use of *menu accelerators*, supplied by the MenuShortcut class, will also be described.

constructors

public Menu() **public** Menu(String *label*) **public** Menu(String *label*, **boolean** *tearOff*)	Constructs a new menu pane, with the label specified and with tear-off capability if *tearOff* is **true**.

instance methods

public synchronised MenuItem add(
            MenuItem *toAdd*)
public synchronized void insert(
            MenuItem *toInsert*,
            int   *insertHere*)
public synchronized void remove(
            MenuComponent *toRemove*)
public synchronized void removeAll()
public MenuItem getItem(**int** *thisOne*)
	Methods which allow **MenuItems** to be added, inserted, removed, or their identities obtained from the menu.

public void addSeparator() **public void** addSeparator(**int** here)	Adds a separator at the next, or specified, location in the menu.
public boolean isTearOff()	Returns **true** if the menu can be torn off.

TABLE 6.4   Major Resources of the Menu Class

constructors

public CheckboxMenuItem() **public** CheckboxMenuItem(String *label*) **public** CheckboxMenuItem(String *label*, **boolean** *checked*)	Constructs checkbox item with the *label* specified and indicator off, unless *checked* is **true**.

instance methods

public void setState(**boolean** *onOrOff*) **public boolean** getState()	Sets, or obtains, the checked state of the item.

public void addItemListener(
            ItemListener *listener*)
public void removeItemListener(
            ItemListener *listener*)
	Adds, or removes, the ItemListener for ItemEvents generated by this item. More than one ItemListener can be registered, but there is no guarantee on the order in which they will be called.

TABLE 6.5   Major Resources of the CheckboxMenuItem Class

6.3 *MenuBarTuttle* Construction Overview

The instance diagram for the *MenuBarTuttle* applet is presented in Figure 6.4. The upper part of this diagram is comparable to the instance diagram of the *SemiDirect-Tuttle* applet in Figure 5.5. It shows that *theApplet* is an instance of the *MenuBarTuttle* class, which extends the Applet class and implements the ActionListener interface. It listens to *theInterface*, which is an instance of the *MenuBarTuttleInterface* class and controls *theTuttle* which in an instance of the *Tuttle* class.

The lower part of the diagram shows the three *dialogs: helpDialog, exitDialog,* and *versionDialog,* all of which are instances of the appropriate class extended from

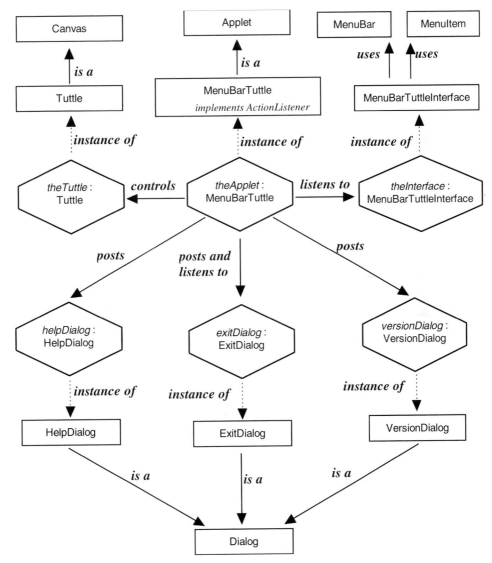

FIGURE 6.4   MenuBarTuttle instance diagram.

the AWT Dialog class. The *theApplet* instance needs only to listen to the *exitDialog* because, as will be explained later, it is the only dialog which will have any effect upon the behavior of the application. The classes making up this application will be implemented within a package called *MenuBarTuttle*.

6.4 The *MenuBarTuttleInterface* Class

The *MenuBarTuttleInterface* class supplies the entire menu system shown in Figure 6.2. To accomplish this it constructs an instance hierarchy, part of which is shown in Figure 6.5, and installs it into the **Frame** instance which is passed as an argument to its constructor.

The first part of the constructor, illustrating the construction of the *fileMenu* and *moveMenu*/ *moveForwardMenu*, is as follows.

```
0036      protected MenuBarTuttleInterface( Frame           itsFrame,
0035                                        ActionListener itsListener) {
0037
0039      MenuBar   mainMenuBar;
0040
0041      Menu      fileMenu;
0042      MenuItem  exitButton;
0043
0044      Menu      moveMenu;
0045
0046      Menu      moveForwardMenu;
0047      MenuItem  forward5;
0048      MenuItem  forward10;
0049      MenuItem  forward25;
----      Other Menu and MenuItem declarations omitted.
0080
0081          mainMenuBar = new MenuBar();
```

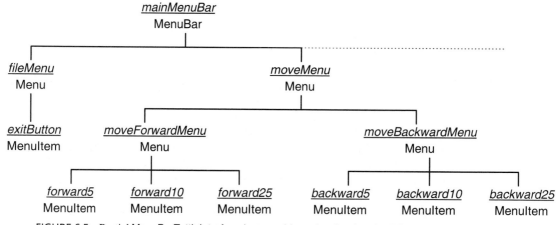

FIGURE 6.5   Partial **MenuBarTuttleInterface** instance hierarchy, showing the *File* and *Move* menu structure.

```
0082
0083              fileMenu = new Menu( "File");
0084                 exitButton  = new MenuItem( "Exit ...");
0085                 exitButton.setActionCommand( "exit show");
0086                 exitButton.addActionListener( itsListener);
0087                 fileMenu.add( exitButton);
0088
0089        mainMenuBar.add( fileMenu);
0090
0091             moveMenu = new Menu( "Move");
0092
0093              moveForwardMenu = new Menu( "Forward");
0094
0095                 forward5 = new MenuItem(  "5 Steps");
0096                 forward5.setActionCommand( "fd 5");
0097                 forward5.addActionListener( itsListener);
0098                 moveForwardMenu.add( forward5);
0099
0100                 forward10 = new MenuItem(  "10 Steps");
0101                 forward10.setActionCommand( "fd 10");
0102                 forward10.addActionListener( itsListener);
0103                 moveForwardMenu.add( forward10);
0104
0105                 forward25 = new MenuItem(  "25 Steps");
0106                 forward25.setActionCommand( "fd 25");
0107                 forward25.addActionListener( itsListener);
0108                 moveForwardMenu.add( forward25);
0109               moveMenu.add( moveForwardMenu);
----              // Construction of the moveBackwardMenu omitted.
0125
0127               moveMenu.add( moveBackwardMenu);
0128         mainMenuBar.add( moveMenu);
----        // Construction of the other menus omitted.
0285         mainMenuBar.add( helpMenu);
0286         mainMenuBar.setHelpMenu( helpMenu);
0287
0288         itsFrame.setMenuBar( mainMenuBar);
0289       } // End MenuBarTuttleInterface constructor.
```

This process is not particularly difficult, but it is complex and provides opportunity for confusing mistakes to creep in. To assist with understanding and maintaining the code it is suggested that indentation, which is conventionally used to indicate levels of program control structure, be used to indicate levels of the menu hierarchy. Thus, the *moveMenu* steps are indented one level from the *mainMenuBar* steps. Likewise, the cascading *moveForwardMenu* and *moveBackwardMenu* steps are indented to the right of the *moveMenu*, and the population of these two cascading menus is one further level of indentation to the right.

The two arguments to the constructor are the Frame instance, within which the menu is to be installed, and the identity of the ActionListener object to which all the active menu items are to dispatch ActionEvents when they are activated by the user. On lines 0039 to 0079 the MenuBar and all the Menus and MenuItems shown, or implied, in Figure 6.5 are declared. All the *CheckBoxMenuItems* which will populate the *Color* menus and the lower part of the *Screen* menu are declared, outside the scope of the constructor, as instance attributes of the class, for reasons which will be explained later.

The constructor's first step, on line 0081, is to construct the *mainMenuBar* as an instance of the MenuBar class. The *fileMenu* pane is then constructed on line 0083 and populated with a single item on lines 0084 to 0087. Line 0084 constructs the *exitButton* which, as it will control the posting of a dialog, has the conventional three dots (...) at the end of its label. Lines 0085 and 0086 then establish its actionCommand and action-Listener resources before the *exitButton* MenuItem is added to the *fileMenu* Menu on line 0087. As the *fileMenu* is now completely constructed, it is added to the *mainMenuBar* MenuBar instance on line 0089.

The construction of the *moveMenu*, on lines 0091 to 0127, continues this pattern. The *moveMenu* Menu instance is populated by two items, both of which are themselves Menu instances and so will behave as *cascading menus*. The first of these, *moveForwardMenu*, is constructed on line 0093 and, as it will subsequently be added to another Menu instance, Java is able to recognize it as a cascading menu. Because of this, the developer need not explicitly specify that its label should be followed by an arrow as Java will automatically supply one.

Before the *moveForwardMenu* is added to the *moveMenu*, on line 0109, it is populated with its three buttons. The construction, configuration, and installation of the three *MenuItems*: *forward5*, *forward10* and *forward25*, is accomplished on lines 0095 to 0108, using techniques which are essentially identical to those used for the *exitButton* described earlier.

The construction of the *moveBackwardMenu* is essentially identical to that of the *moveForwardMenu* and has been omitted from the listing. When, on line 0127, it has been added to the *moveMenu* the *moveMenu* is complete and is added to the *mainMenuBar* on line 0128.

The constructor continues with the construction of the remaining three menus, whose significant differences will be described, concluding with the addition of the *helpMenu* on line 0285. This menu is then nominated as the *helpMenu* on line 0286. This will ensure that this menu is always the right-most item on the menu bar and in some environments, for example X/ Motif, will be positioned at the extreme right of the menu bar. The final step of the *MenuBarTuttleInterface* constructor, on line 0288, is to install the MenuBar into the Frame passed as an argument to the constructor, using the Fame's setMenuBar() method.

This pattern of construction can be used whenever a top-level menu system needs to be constructed. The contents of each menu and, if required, of each cascading menu can be designed on paper using a technique similar to that in Figure 6.2. Having done this, the *init()* method from this example can be amended to implement the new requirements.

The construction of the *Color* menu differs a little from the construction of the *Move* menu as it is contains CheckBoxMenuItems, as shown in the instance hierarchy in Figure 6.6. This hierarchy is built in the constructor, as follows.

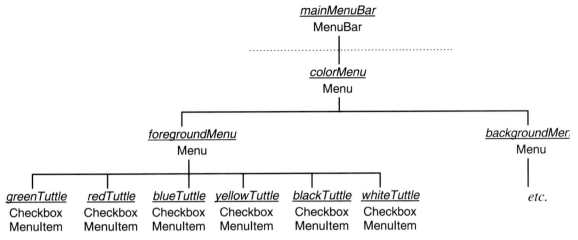

FIGURE 6.6   Partial mainMenuBar instance hierarchy and *Color* menu structure.

```
0168              colorMenu = new Menu( "Colors");
0169
0170                  foregroundMenu  = new Menu( "Foreground");
0171                      greenTuttle  = new CheckboxMenuItem ( "Green");
0172                      greenTuttle.setActionCommand( "fg green");
0173                      greenTuttle.addActionListener( itsListener);
0174                      foregroundMenu.add( greenTuttle);
----                     // Construction of other foreground CheckboxMenuItems
                         omitted.
0175
0236              colorMenu.add( foregroundMenu);
0203
0204                  backgroundMenu  = new Menu( "Background");
0205                      greenBack  = new CheckboxMenuItem ( "Green");
0206                      greenTuttle.setActionCommand( "bg green");
0207                      greenTuttle.addActionListener( itsListener);
0208                      backgroundMenu.add( greenBack);
0209
----                     // Construction of other background CheckboxMenuItems
                         omitted.
0235
0237              colorMenu.add( backgroundMenu);
0238          mainMenuBar.add( colorMenu);
```

The only significant difference in the construction of this menu structure is that the items added to the cascading menus are instances of the CheckboxMenuItem class, not the MenuItem class. This will allow each menu item to be accompanied on the menu by a state indicator, as shown in Figure 6.2. The CheckboxMenuItem constructor used in their construction does not explicitly specify the state of the indicator and so the default, unchecked, state is used for all of them. However these buttons have to the configured as *radio buttons*, ensuring that one, and only one, of the items is selected at any time. This is accomplished by another method of the *MenuBarTuttleInterface* class, *setForegroundCheckmark()*, implemented as follows.

```
0293        protected void setForegroundCheckmark( String toSet) {
0294           greenTuttle.setState(   false);
0295           redTuttle.setState(     false);
0296           blueTuttle.setState(    false);
0297           yellowTuttle.setState( false);
0298           whiteTuttle.setState(   false);
0299           blackTuttle.setState(   false);
0300
0301           if ( toSet.equals( "green")) {
0302              greenTuttle.setState( true);
0303           } else if ( toSet.equals( "red")) {
0304              redTuttle.setState( true);
0305           } else if ( toSet.equals( "blue")) {
0306              blueTuttle.setState( true);
0307           } else if ( toSet.equals( "yellow")) {
0308              yellowTuttle.setState( true);
0309           } else if ( toSet.equals( "white")) {
0310              whiteTuttle.setState( true);
0311           } else if ( toSet.equals( "black")) {
0312              blackTuttle.setState( true);
0313           } // End if.
0314        } // End setForegroundCheckmark.
```

The method commences, on lines 0294 to 0299, by ensuring that all check markers are set off. The six-way **if** structure on lines 0301 to 0313 then sets the state indicator of the item indicated by the *toSet* argument. It is the responsibility of the *MenuBarTuttle* class to ensure that this method is called to indicate the initial *Tuttle* foreground color before the menus are presented to the user for the first time. Similar *setForegroundCheckmark()* and *setPenUpCheckmark()* methods are supplied to ensure that the background color buttons and the pen buttons on the *Screen* menu also behave as radio buttons.

The only remaining significant difference is the inclusion of separators on the *Screen* menu, which are constructed and added by the following code fragment.

```
----
0250                 screenMenu.add( resetScreen);
0251
0252                 screenMenu.addSeparator();
0253
0254                 clsetScreen = new MenuItem( "Clear and Reset");
0255                 clsetScreen.setActionCommand( "cr");
0256                 clsetScreen.addActionListener( itsListener);
0257                 screenMenu.add( clsetScreen);
0258
0259                 screenMenu.addSeparator();
0260
```

```
0261                    penUpCheck   = new CheckboxMenuItem( "Pen up");
0262                    screenMenu.add( penUpCheck);
0263                    penDownCheck = new CheckboxMenuItem( "Pen down");
0264                    screenMenu.add( penDownCheck);
----
```

6.5 The *MenuBarTuttle* Class

The *MenuBarTuttle* class has the responsibility for constructing the *MenuBarTuttleInstance*, passing to it a **Frame** which it has created, and subsequently installing into it an instance of the *Tuttle* class and a feedback area before the **Fame**, and the interface it contains, is made visible to the user. It then listens to the **ActionEvents** sent to it by the *MenuBarTuttleInterface* and the *ExitDialog* instances, controlling *theTuttle* and the applet in response. The implementation of the *MenuBarTuttle* class, as far as the start of its *init()* method, is as follows.

```
0001   // Filename MenuBarTuttle.java.
0002   // Supplies a main menu interface for the Tuttle class.
0003   //
0004   // Written for Java Interface book chapter 6.
0005   // Fintan Culwin, v 0.2, August 1997.
0006
0007   package MenuBarTuttle;
0008
0009   import java.awt.*;
0010   import java.applet.*;
0011   import java.awt.event.*;
0012   import java.util.StringTokenizer;
0013
0014   import Tuttles.Tuttle;
0015   import MenuBarTuttle.MenuBarTuttleInterface;
0016
0017   import MenuBarTuttle.ExitDialog;
0018   import MenuBarTuttle.VersionDialog;
0019   import MenuBarTuttle.MenuBarTuttleHelpDialog;
0020
0021   public class MenuBarTuttle extends     Applet
0022                             implements ActionListener {
0023
0024   private Label   feedbackLabel;
0025   private Panel   feedbackPanel;
0026
0027   private Tuttle                   theTuttle;
0028   private MenuBarTuttleInterface   theInterface;
0029
0030   private ExitDialog               exitDialog;
0031   private VersionDialog            versionDialog;
0032   private MenuBarTuttleHelpDialog  helpDialog;
```

Lines 0014 to 0019 import the various classes indicated in the instance diagram in Figure 6.4 after the required Java packages, including the **StringTokenizer** class, have been imported. Following the class declaration on lines 0021 and 0022, the feedback **Label** and **Panel** are declared as instance attributes, as are *theTuttle Tuttle* instance and *theInterface MenuBarTuttleInterface* instances on lines 0024 to 0028. The instance attribute declarations conclude with the declaration of three specialized dialogs on lines 0030 to 0032. The *init()* method constructs the **applet**, as follows,

```
0036       public void init() {
0037
0038       Panel    tuttlePanel;
0039       Frame    tuttleFrame;
0040
0041           tuttleFrame = new Frame();
0042           tuttleFrame.setTitle( "Menu Bar Tuttle Interface");
0043           tuttleFrame.setBackground( Color.white);
0044           tuttleFrame.setFont( new Font( "TimesRoman", Font.PLAIN, 20));
0045
0046           feedbackPanel = new Panel();
0047           feedbackLabel = new Label();
0048           feedbackPanel.add( feedbackLabel);
0049
0050           tuttlePanel   = new Panel();
0051           theTuttle     = new Tuttle( this, 500, 500);
0052           tuttlePanel.add( theTuttle);
0053
0054           theInterface = new MenuBarTuttleInterface( tuttleFrame,
0055                                                 (ActionListener) this);
0056           theInterface.setForegroundCheckmark( "blue");
0057           theInterface.setBackgroundCheckmark( "yellow");
0058           theInterface.setPenUpCheckmark( false)
0059
0060           tuttleFrame.add( tuttlePanel,   "Center");
0061           tuttleFrame.add( feedbackPanel, "South");
0062
0063           tuttleFrame.setSize( tuttleFrame.getPreferredSize());
0064           this.feedback();
0065           tuttleFrame.setVisible( true);
0066
0067           helpDialog    = new MenuBarTuttleHelpDialog( tuttleFrame);
0068           exitDialog    = new ExitDialog( tuttleFrame, this);
0069           versionDialog = new VersionDialog( tuttleFrame,
0070                                           this.getAppletInfo());
0071       } // End init.
```

The *init()* method commences, on lines 0041 to 0044, by constructing and configuring an instance of the **Frame** class called *tuttleFrame*. Lines 0046 to 0048 then prepare the *feedbackPanel* and lines 0050 to 0052 the *tuttlePanel*, containing *theTuttle Tuttle* instance. Lines 0054 to 0055 then construct *theInterface*, passing as arguments the *tuttleFrame*, into which the menu bar will be installed; and the identity of the

MenuBarTuttle instance (**this**) being initialized as its listener object. Once constructed, the color and pen menus are configured as appropriate on lines 0056 to 0058. A Frame instance, by default, has a BorderLayout policy and the MenuBar is automatically added to its "*North*" location. Lines 0060 and 0061 place the *tuttlePanel* into its "*Center*" location and the *feedbackPanel* into its "*South*" location. Lines 0063 to 0065 set the size of the Frame, update the *feedbackPanel*, and then call the Frame setVisible() method to make the interface visible to the user. The final stage of the *init()* method, on lines 0067 to 0069, constructs the three specialized dialogs which will be considered in detail.

The *actionPerformed()* method of the *MenuBarTuttle* class will be called whenever the user activates any of the items on *theInterface*'s menus. The first part of this method is as follows.

```
0071    public void actionPerformed( ActionEvent event) {
0072
0073    StringTokenizer tokenizer = new StringTokenizer(
0074                                    event.getActionCommand());
0075    String theCommand  = tokenizer.nextToken();
0076    String theArgument = "";
0077
0078      if ( tokenizer.hasMoreTokens()) {
0079         theArgument = tokenizer.nextToken();
0080      } // End if.
0081
0082
0083      if ( theCommand.equals( "exit")) {
0084         if ( theArgument.equals( "show")) {
0085            exitDialog.setVisible( true);
0086         } else if ( theArgument.equals( "please")) {
0087            System.exit( 0);
0088         } // End if.
0089
0090      } else if ( theCommand.equals( "fd")) {
0091         theTuttle.forward( Integer.parseInt( theArgument));
0092      } else if ( theCommand.equals( "bd")) {
0093         theTuttle.backward( Integer.parseInt( theArgument));
0094
0095      } else if ( theCommand.equals( "tr")) {
0096         theTuttle.turnRight( Integer.parseInt( theArgument));
0097      } else if ( theCommand.equals( "tl")) {
0098         theTuttle.turnLeft( Integer.parseInt( theArgument));
```

The method commences by constructing a StringTokenizer instance, called *tokenizer*, initialized to process the commandString retrieved from the ActionEvent passed to *actionPerformed()* as an argument. The commandStrings installed into *theInterface*'s MenuItems included single-word commands such as "*cs*" for *clear screen* or "*pu*" for *pen up,* and two-word commands such as "*fd 10*" for *forward 10* or "*bg green*" for *background green.* The *tokenizer* will facilitate the scanning of the commandString to divide the multiple-word command into its constituent phrases. Line

0075 extracts the first word of the command into *theCommand* and lines 0076 to 0080 extract the second word, if any, into *theArgument*.

The remaining part of the *performAction()* method, starting on line 0083, consists of a multiple-way **if** structure containing a branch for each of the possible commands. To facilitate maintenance, the sequence of commands in the **if** structure corresponds to the sequence in which their MenuItems were added to the MenuBar in the constructor of the *MenuBarTuttleInterface* class. Consequently the first command to be considered, on lines 0083 to 0088, is the "*exit*" command; this part of the method will be described when the *ExitDialog* class is described.

Lines 0090 to 0098 process the commands originating from the *Move* and *Turn* menu. The commands passed will be "*fd,*" "*bd,*" "*tr,*" and "*tl*" for *forward, backward, turn right,* and *turn left,* respectively. Each of these commands is followed by an integer indicating the number of steps to move or the number of degrees to turn. The repeated phrase `Integer.parseInt(` `theArgument)` will convert the integer contained as a String in *theArgument* into a primitive **int** value. This value is passed as an argument to the appropriate *Tuttle* command.

For example, if the user activates the MenuItem labeled "*15 Degrees*" on the *Turn Right* menu, the *commandString* passed in the ActionEvent instance will be "*tr 15*". The *tokenizer* will place "*tr*" into the *theCommand* String and "*15*" into the *theArgument* String. The **if** condition on line 0095 will evaluate **true** and line 0096 will call *theTuttle*'s *turnRight()* method passing as an argument the **int** value 15. This will result in the *tuttle* shown to the user turning 15° to the right and, as will be demonstrated, the feedback shown to the user changing to show the *tuttle*'s new direction.

The next commands to be considered originate from the *Colors* menu and will contain the command "*fg*" (*foreground*) or "*bg*" (*background*) followed by the name of the color. The "*fg*" command is processed as follows.

```
0101            } else if ( theCommand.equals( "fg")) {
0102                if ( theArgument.equals( "green")) {
0103                    theTuttle.setForeground( Color.green);
0116                } else if ( theArgument.equals( "red")) {
----                // Other branches omitted
0114                } // End if.
0115                theInterface.setForegroundCheckmark( theArgument);
```

Line 0101 guards for the "*fg*" command and the **if** structure starting on line 0102 contains a branch for each allowed *tuttle* color, the branches containing a call of the *theTuttle*'s *setForeground()* method passing as an argument the appropriate manifest value from the Java Color class. Once the color has been changed, the *theInterface set-ForegroundCheckmark()* method is called to update the checkmarks on the interface's *foreground color* menu. The implementation of the processing of the "*bg*" command is essentially identical.

The processing of the commands from the *Screen* menu do not need to consider the value stored in *theArgument* as they are all single-word commands. The branches corresponding to the last three items on the menu are as follows.

```
0135            } else if ( theCommand.equals( "cr")) {
0136                theTuttle.clearAndReset();
```

```
0137              } else if ( theCommand.equals( "pu")) {
0138                  theTuttle.setPenUp();
0139                  theInterface.setPenUpCheckmark( true);
0140              } else if ( theCommand.equals( "pd")) {
0141                  theTuttle.setPenDown();
0142                  theInterface.setPenUpCheckmark( false);
```

The "*cr*" command calls *theTuttle*'s *clearAndReset()* method, which does not require an argument. The "*pu*" and "*pd*" commands not only call *theTuttle*'s *setPenUp()* and *setPenDown()* methods but also call *theInterface*'s *setPenStatus()* method to update the checkmarks on the *Screen* menu. The *actionPerformed()* method concludes by processing the commands originating from the *Help* menu.

```
0145              } else if ( theCommand.equals( "version")) {
0146                  versionDialog.setVisible( true);
0147              } else if ( theCommand.equals( "help")) {
0148                  helpDialog.setVisible( true);
0149              } // End if.
0150
0151              this.feedback();
0152      } // End actionPerformed.
```

The *versionDialog* and *helpDialog setVisible()* methods will be considered later. After the outer **if** structure concludes on line 0149, the *feedback()* method is called to update the feedback shown to the user at the bottom of the interface and the method concludes on line 0152.

6.6 The Dialog Class

The remainder of this chapter will introduce the three dialogs shown at the bottom of the context diagram in Figure 6.4. The presentation of a dialog to a user is an essential and valuable part of a wide variety of user interfaces. The pattern of construction and use which will be established in this part of the chapter can be used a template upon which more advanced dialogs can be constructed. All three of the classes providing the dialogs extend the Dialog class whose major resources, including those inherited from the Window class, are given in Table 6.6.

A Dialog *is a*n extension of the Window class, which in turn *is a*n extension of the Container class and hence can control the layout of its instance children. A Dialog is constructed in an invisible state and should be **packed** after its instance children are added, before it is shown using *setVisible()* with the argument **true**. Once visible, its *stacking* relationship with other windows can be controlled with toFront() and toBack(). When it is no longer required, it can be hidden by using the Component setVisible() method with the argument **false**.

A *modal* dialog will prevent the user from having any other interactions with the application until it has been attended to and dismissed, and will always remain in front of any other windows. In contrast, a *non-modal* dialog does not prevent the user from interacting with the application while it is posted and can be hidden behind other windows.

constructors

public Dialog(Frame   *itsFrame*)
public Dialog(Frame   *itsFrame*,
                boolean *modal*)
public Dialog(Frame   *itsFrame*,
                String *itsTitle*)
public Dialog(Frame   *itsFrame*,
                String *itsTitle*,
                boolean *modal*)
	Constructors allowing the modality, default non-modality, possibly with a *itsTitle* specified. All Dialogs are initially invisible and have to be explicitly made visible to the user.

instance methods

public void setModal(**boolean** *modality*) **public boolean** isModal()	Sets, or retrieves, the *modality* of the Dialog.
public void setTitle(String *setTo*) **public** String getTitle()	Sets, or retrieves, the title of the Dialog.
public void setResizable(**boolean** *canBe*) **public boolean** isResizable()	Determines, or decides if, the Dialog *canBe* resized by the user, by using the window controls.
public void setVisible(**boolean** *showing*) **public boolean** isVisible()	Ensures that the Dialog is (**true**) visible on the desktop by raising it above all other windows, or removes it from the desktop (**false**). Finds out if it is visible.
public void pack()	Lays out the components in the Window.
public void toBack() **public void** toFront()	Moves the Window above (toFront) or behind (toBack) any other windows.

public void addWindowListener(
            ItemListener *listener*)
public void removeWindowListener(
            ItemListener *listener*)
	Registers or removes a listener for the WindowEvents generated by the button. More than one listener can be registered, but there is no guarantee on the sequence in which they will be called.

TABLE 6.6   Major Resources of the Dialog Class, Including Those Inherited from Window

---

Design Advice

Modal dialogs should only be used when the functionality of the application depends on the modality. In general, non-modal dialogs should be favored.

The user can iconify, maximize, minimize, and close the window using the window controls supplied by the peer environment and these will cause appropriate Window-Events to be generated. The user can only resize a window, using the window controls, if its resizable attribute has been set. All WindowEvents can be intercepted by the registered windowListener and the requested methods confirmed or denied. Examples of handling WindowEvents will be given.

There are two design approaches to using Dialogs, and other sub-windows, within an application. The first approach is to create all the windows in an invisible state as the application initializes itself. These windows are then shown in response to the user's actions and are subsequently hidden when they are no longer required. The alternative approach is not to create any windows upon initialization but to create them each time they are required and destroy them when they are no longer required.

The first approach causes the time an application takes to initialize itself to increase but allows a window to be posted very quickly. The second approach allows an application to appear faster but there may be a delay when a sub-window is requested by the user. In practice, a combination of these approaches can be used with windows which are frequently required or whose contents do not change, being created as the application is initialized. Those windows which are infrequently required, or those whose contents change each time they are shown, can be created upon demand. Both of these techniques will be used in the remainder of this book.

A more advanced approach to this problem may involve the construction and presentation of the main window to the user as quickly as possible on the artifact's main thread. At the same time, the dialogs can be constructed on separate threads which have a lower level of priority. The user can then commence work with the application as quickly as possible, with Java preparing the dialogs when it is not busy attending to the user. Details of this technique are outside the scope of this book.

6.7 The *ExitDialog* Class

The *exitDialog* used by the *MenuBarTuttle* class, attached to the *File* menu *Exit …* item, is an instance of the *ExitDialog* class whose appearance and behavior is shown in Figure 6.7.

The dialog is posted in a modal manner, in response to the user pressing the *Exit …* item on the *File* menu. It is appropriate for this dialog to be presented to the user in a modal manner as the possibility of an application terminating is sufficiently important for the user to be forced to attend to it. Once posted pressing either of the buttons will un-post the dialog, causing a transition to the STD's terminal state. If the *yes* button is pressed this transition will generate an action event, allowing the *MenuBarTuttle* class to be informed that the user indicated that the application should be shut down.

The dialog is constructed with a *MessageCanvas* instance, as described in Chapter 3, containing a two-line message mounted in its "*Center*" location and a Panel containing the two Buttons in its "*South*" location. The *ExitDialog* instance attribute declarations and constructor are as follows.

```
0018  class ExitDialog extends     Dialog
0019                     implements ActionListener {
0020
0021  private Window         itsParentWindow;
0022  private ActionListener itsListener;
```

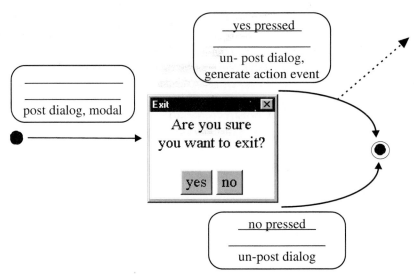

FIGURE 6.7 The ExitDialog appearance and behavior.

```
0023
0024    private Panel            buttonPanel;
0025    private MessageCanvas    message;
0026    private Button           yesButton;
0027    private Button           noButton;
0028
0029       protected ExitDialog( Frame         itsParentFrame,
0030                             ActionListener listener) {
0031
0032          super( itsParentFrame, "Exit", true);
0033          this.setFont( itsParentFrame.getFont());
0034          this.setBackground( itsParentFrame.getBackground());
0035          itsParentWindow = (Window) itsParentFrame;
0036          itsListener = listener;
0037
0038          message = new MessageCanvas( "Are you sure\nyou want to exit?");
0039          message.setBackground( Color.white);
0040
0041          buttonPanel = new Panel();
0042          buttonPanel.setBackground( Color.white);
0043
0044          yesButton = new Button( "yes");
0045          yesButton.setActionCommand("yes");
0046          yesButton.addActionListener( this);
0047          buttonPanel.add( yesButton);
0048
0049          noButton = new Button( "no");
0050          noButton.setActionCommand("no");
0051          noButton.addActionListener( this);
0052          buttonPanel.add( noButton);
```

```
0053
0054            this.add( message,      "Center");
0055            this.add( buttonPanel, "South");
0056            this.pack();
0057        } // End ExitDialog constructor.
```

The constructor commences, on line 0032, by calling its parent (**super**) constructor, specifying as the first argument the Frame instance which this dialog window is to be associated with. This argument is received as the first argument of the *ExitDialog* constructor. The remaining two arguments of the Frame constructor call are the title to be used for the dialog window and the modal state (**true**) of the dialog. The constructor continues, on lines 0033 and 0034, by configuring the appearance of the dialog and, on lines 0035 and 0036, storing the identities of the arguments to the constructor in instance attributes.

Lines 0038 to 0056 then construct, configure, and assemble the components of the dialog: a *MessageCanvas* instance in its "*Center*" location and a Panel containing two buttons in the "*South*" location, producing the appearance shown in Figure 6.7. The ActionListener of both buttons is specified as the *ExitDialog* instance itself, which accordingly declares itself to implement the ActionListener interface. The constructor creates the dialog ready for use but it does not become visible to the user until its *setVisible()* method, implemented as follows, is called with a **true** argument.

```
0063        protected void setVisible( boolean showIt) {
0064
0065        Point       itsParentsLocation;
0066        Dimension   itsParentsSize;
0067        Point       itsLocation;
0068        Dimension   itsSize;
0069
0070          if ( showit) {
0071              itsParentsLocation = itsParentWindow.getLocationOnScreen();
0072              itsParentsSize     = itsParentWindow.getSize();
0073              itsSize            = this.getSize();
0074              itsLocation        = new Point();
0075
0076              itsLocation.x = itsParentsLocation.x +
0077                              itsParentsSize.width/2 -
0078                              itsSize.width/2;
0079              itsLocation.y = itsParentsLocation.y +
0080                              itsParentsSize.height/2 -
0081                              itsSize.height/2;
0082            this.setLocation( itsLocation);
0083          } // End if.
0084          super.setVisible( showIt);
0085        } // End show.
```

The **boolean** *showIt* argument indicates if the dialog should be made visible to the user or hidden from them. This method only need be concerned with intervening when the dialog is to be shown and the **if** structure between lines 0070 to 0083 effects this. The contents of this decision are identical to a part of the implementation of the *PostItNote setVisible()* method in Chapter 3, and ensure that the dialog is always presented to the user centered within its parent, *MenuBarTuttle*, window. Following the **if** structure on line 0084, the parent, Dialog, setVisible() method is indirected to passing onward the *showIt* argument to actually make the dialog visible, or hide it if *showIt* is **false**.

The only other method of the *ExitDialog* class is the *actionPerformed()* method, as follows.

```
0085        public void actionPerformed( ActionEvent event) {
0086            this.setVisible( false);
0087            if ( event.getActionCommand().equals( "yes")) {
0088                itsListener.actionPerformed( new ActionEvent( this,
0089                                        ActionEvent.ACTION_PERFORMED,
0090                                        "exit please")));
0091            } // End if.
0092        } // End actionPerformed.
0093    } // End ExitDialog.
```

This method can only be called in response to a press of either of the buttons on the ExitDialog and commences by calling the *ExitDialog*'s setVisible() method, with the argument **false**, to un-post it from the desktop. If this method was called as a consequence of the "*yes*" button being pressed, the user has confirmed that the applet should terminate. This results, on lines 0088 to 0090, in the *actionPerformed()* method of the ActionListener passed to the constructor being called with an ActionEvent argument containing the commandString "*exit please.*"

The *MenuBarTuttle* constructs its *exitDialog* instance at the end of its *init()* method as follows.

```
0065        exitDialog = new ExitDialog( tuttleFrame, this);
```

Hence the identity of the *ActionListener* to which the *ActionEvent* is dispatched when the "*yes*" button is pressed is the *MenuBarTuttle* instance, whose processing of "*exit*" commands within its *performAction()* method, given in detail earlier, is as follows.

```
0083        if ( theCommand.equals( "exit")) {
0084            if ( theArgument.equals( "show")) {
0085                exitDialog.setVisible( true);
0086            } else if ( theArgument.equals( "please")) {
0087                System.exit( 0);
0088            } // End if.
```

The *Exit ...* button on the *File* menu of the interface will send the *commandString* "*exit show*" to this method and this will result, in line 0085, in the *exitDialog setVisible()* method being called, with the argument **true**, making the dialog visible to the user in the middle of the applet's window. If the user confirms that the applet should terminate, this method will be called again with the *commandString* "*exit please*" resulting in the System.exit() call, on line 0087, terminating the applet. The argument 0 to the exit() method call indicates that the application concluded normally.

A common novice's design error would be to call the System.exit() method within the *ExitDialog*'s implementation. With this approach, the applet is not made aware that the user has confirmed that the applet should conclude before it terminates and so has no opportunity to tidy up, for example closing any open streams, before the applet finishes.

Design Advice

Only the applet, or application, class should be responsible for finishing and should conclude gracefully, closing any streams and releasing any other resources as required.

As the applet stands at the moment, the application can also be immediately terminated by using the appletviewer's window frame exit control. In the Windows '95 illustrations used in this book, this is the X button at the top right. To prevent this from happening, or cause it to happen in some environments, the WindowEvents dispatched to the Frame will have to be intercepted and handled. To accomplish this, the declaration of the *MenuBarTuttle* class will have to be amended to indicate that it implements the WindowListener interface, as follows.

```
0022   public class MenuBarTuttle extends    Applet
0023                              implements ActionListener,
0024                                         WindowListener {
```

The *tuttleFrame* will have to be informed of the identity of its WindowListener object by calling its addWindowListener() method, as follows.

```
0047       tuttleFrame.addWindowListener( this);
```

Having done this, the *MenuBarTuttle* class will have to supply the seven methods required by the WindowListener interface of which only one, the *windowClosing()*, method need actually do anything. The implementation of these methods is as follows.

```
0168   public void windowClosing( WindowEvent event) {
0169       exitDialog.setVisible( true);
0170   } // End windowClosing .
0171
0172   public void windowOpened( WindowEvent event)    {} // End
0173   public void windowClosed( WindowEvent event)    {} // End
0174   public void windowIconified( WindowEvent event {} // End
0175   public void windowDeiconified(WindowEvent event){} // End
0176   public void windowActivated( WindowEvent event){} // End
0177   public void windowDeactivated( WindowEvent event){} // End
```

The *windowClosing()* method calls the *exitDialog setVisible()* method to post the dialog onto the desktop and, as it does not dispatch to its **super** *windowClosing()* method, prevents the window from actually closing. The remaining six methods are dummy methods which do nothing, but have to be supplied in order to satisfy the WindowListener interface, and have been laid out in a manner which emphasizes this to anyone reading the code. The consequence of these changes is that when the exit control on the **Frame** is pressed the *exitDialog* will be posted and, only if the user confirms the exit by pressing the "*yes*" button, will the **applet** actually terminate.

In this implementation the only instance attributes which strictly require visibility outside the scope of the constructor are *itsParentWindow*, required by the *setVisible()* method, and *itsListener*, required by the *actionPerformed()* method. However Java has a rule that when a constructor calls its parent (**super**) constructor, this call has to be the very first statement in the constructor. This rule prevents the remaining instance declarations, on lines 0024 to 0027, from being declared as local variables of the constructor. A more elegant solution would be to include an additional private *constructDialog()* method within the class, declaring the components as local variables, and calling the method from the constructor; but in a class as simple as this declaring them as private instance attributes seems acceptable.

6.8 The *VersionDialog* Class

The appearance of the *versionDialog* for this applet is shown in Figure 6.8. It is posted onto the desktop, in a non-modal manner, when the *Version…* item on the *Help* menu is activated and is un-posted from the desktop when its **OK** button is pressed.

The *VersionDialog* class is essentially identical to the *ExitDialog* containing a constructor which assembles the dialog but does not display it, a *setVisible()* method which posts it onto the desktop centered within the applet's **Frame** window, and an *actionPerformed()* method which is called as a consequence of the "*OK*" button being pressed and un-posts the dialog. The implementation of the class is given in Appendix B. The *VersionDialog*'s constructor is called from the *MenuBarTuttle*'s *init()* method as follows.

```
0066        versionDialog = new VersionDialog( tuttleFrame,
0067                                          this.getAppletInfo());
```

FIGURE 6.8 The MenuBarTuttle
version dialog.

The first argument to the constructor is the **Frame** which the dialog is to be associated with. The second is the **String** which the *versionDialog* is to display in its *MessageCanvas* component; this argument is specified as the **String** returned from the *MenuBarTuttle*'s *getAppletInfo()* method, implemented as follows.

```
0162    public String getAppletInfo() {
0163      return "Menu Bar Tuttle\nVersion 2.0\n " +
0164             "Fintan Culwin, August 1997\n"    +
0165             "fintan@sbu.ac.uk";
0166    } // End getAppletInfo.
```

The *getAppletInfo()* method is intended to be used by the developer to allow a client of the applet, for example an appletviewer utility, to obtain a **String** which provides some information about the version, and any other details that seem appropriate. It is being used here only to supply the contents of the *versionDialog*. VersionDialogs are customarily more complex than this and many use animated images to draw attention to the prowess of the development team.

6.9 The *HelpDialog* Class

The *HelpDialog* class has a somewhat similar overall pattern to the other two dialogs but uses the remaining layout manager, the *CardLayout* class, to allow the various help panels to be displayed. The appearance of the *helpDialog* for this applet is shown in Figure 6.9.

The dialog consists of a set of radio buttons at the top, a *dismiss* button at the bottom, and an area for the help messages to be displayed in the middle. When a radio button is pressed the help message in the middle will change, as indicated in the illustration. The middle part of the dialog, providing the help messages, is implemented using a CardLayout manager. A CardLayout manager supports a sequence of components, any of which can be selected for display by using the methods supplied by the manager.

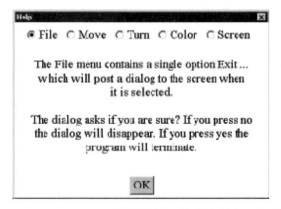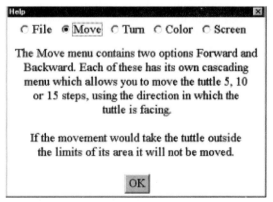

FIGURE 6.9   The helpDialog, showing help for the *File* and *Move* menus.

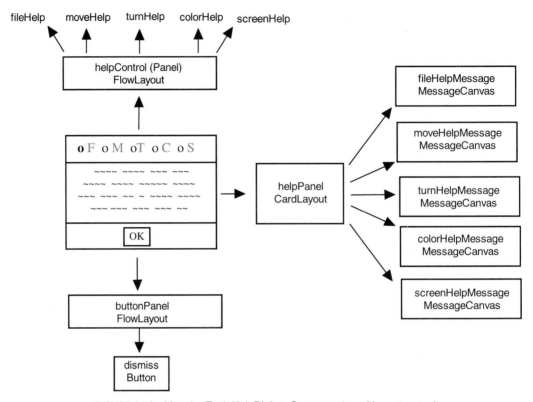

FIGURE 6.10 MenubarTuttleHelpDialog, Components, and layout control.

The **Components** required, and the layout management, of the *MenuBarTuttle-HelpDialog* are illustrated in Figure 6.10. The Dialog itself has a default BorderLayout, with a *helpControl* Panel in its "*North*" location, a *helpPanel* in its "*Center*" location, and a *buttonPanel* in its "*South*" location. The *helpControl* Panel has a FlowLayout and contains five *Checkbox* instances, while the *buttonPanel* also has a FlowLayout and contains a single Button instance called *dismiss*. The *helpPanel* has a CardLayout and contains five *MessageCanvas* instances, only one of which will ever be visible at any instant. These **Components** are declared as instance attributes of the class, in the header of its declaration, as follows.

```
0018   class MenuBarTuttleHelpDialog extends    Dialog
0019                                 implements ActionListener,
0020                                            ItemListener   {
0021
0022   private static final String FILE   = "File";
0023   private static final String MOVE   = "Move";
0024   private static final String TURN   = "Turn";
0025   private static final String COLOR  = "Color";
0026   private static final String SCREEN = "Screen";
0027
0028   private Panel           helpControl;
```

```
0029   private CheckboxGroup  theGroup;
0030   private Checkbox      fileHelp;
0031   private Checkbox      moveHelp;
0032   private Checkbox      turnHelp;
0033   private Checkbox      colorHelp;
0034   private Checkbox      screenHelp;
0035
0036   private Panel         helpPanel;
0037   private CardLayout    manager;
0038   private MessageCanvas fileHelpMessage;
0039   private MessageCanvas moveHelpMessage;
0040   private MessageCanvas turnHelpMessage;
0041   private MessageCanvas colorHelpMessage;
0042   private MessageCanvas screenHelpMessage;
0043
0044   private Panel         buttonPanel;
0045   private Button        dismiss;
0046
0047   private Window        itsParentWindow;
```

The class implements the **ActionListener** interface in order to respond to the user pressing its dismiss button, by un-posting the dialog, and implements the **ItemListener** interface in order to be able to respond to the user pressing one of the **Checkbox** buttons, as will be described. The use of the manifest values declared on lines 0022 to 0026, and the instance attributes declared on lines 0028 to 0047, will be described as the constructor, which commences as follows, is explained.

```
0051      protected MenuBarTuttleHelpDialog( Frame itsParentFrame) {
0052
0053        super( itsParentFrame, "Help", false);
0054        itsParentWindow = (Window) itsParentFrame;
0055        this.setFont( itsParentFrame.getFont());
0056
0057        helpControl = new Panel();
0058        helpControl.setBackground( Color.white);
0059
0060        theGroup = new CheckboxGroup();
0061        fileHelp = new Checkbox( FILE, theGroup, true);
0062        fileHelp.addItemListener( this);
0063        helpControl.add( fileHelp);
0064
0065        moveHelp = new Checkbox( MOVE, theGroup, false);
0066        moveHelp.addItemListener( this);
0067        helpControl.add( moveHelp);
0068
0069        turnHelp = new Checkbox( TURN, theGroup, false);
0070        turnHelp.addItemListener( this);
0071        helpControl.add( turnHelp);
0072
0073        colorHelp = new Checkbox( COLOR, theGroup, false);
0074        colorHelp.addItemListener( this);
```

```
0075            helpControl.add( colorHelp);
0076
0077            screenHelp = new Checkbox( SCREEN, theGroup, false);
0078            screenHelp.addItemListener( this);
0079            helpControl.add( screenHelp);
```

The first stage of the constructor, on lines 0052 to 0054, constructs and configures the Dialog as before. Lines 0057 to 0079 then construct the five Checkbox items as members of the same CheckboxGroup, *theGroup*, in a manner comparable to the Checkbox example in Chapter 2. The label to be used for each Checkbox is specified using one of the manifest Strings, for reasons which will be explained, and each has its itemListener object specified as **this**. The five Checkboxes are added to the *helpControl* panel, using its default FlowLayout policy, to produce the appearance at the top of the images in Figure 6.9. The next part of the constructor is responsible for the middle part of the interface, as follows.

```
0081            manager   = new CardLayout();
0082            helpPanel = new Panel();
0083            helpPanel.setBackground( Color.white);
0084            helpPanel.setLayout( manager);
0085
0086            fileHelpMessage =   new MessageCanvas( FILE_MESSAGE);
0087            helpPanel.add( fileHelpMessage, FILE);
0088
0089            moveHelpMessage =   new MessageCanvas( MOVE_MESSAGE);
0090            helpPanel.add( moveHelpMessage, MOVE);
0091
0092            turnHelpMessage =   new MessageCanvas( TURN_MESSAGE);
0093            helpPanel.add( turnHelpMessage, TURN);
0094
0095            colorHelpMessage =   new MessageCanvas( COLOR_MESSAGE);
0096            helpPanel.add( colorHelpMessage, COLOR);
0097
0098            screenHelpMessage = new MessageCanvas( SCREEN_MESSAGE);
0099            helpPanel.add( screenHelpMessage, SCREEN);
```

Lines 0081 to 0084 construct an instance of the CardLayout class and install it as the layout manager of the *helpPanel*, upon which the help messages will be displayed. Each help message in turn is then constructed as an instance of the *MessageDialog* class. The text for the help messages is obtained from class-wide constant attributes which, in order not to clutter the header part of the class source code file, are declared at the end of the file. For example, the *FILE_MESSAGE* String value is declared as follows.

```
0155    private static final String FILE_MESSAGE =
0156                    "The File menu contains a single option Exit ...\n" +
0157                    "which will post a dialog to the screen when \n" +
0158                    "it is selected.\n  \n" +
```

```
0159                        "The dialog asks if you are sure? If you press no\n" +
0160                        "the dialog will disappear. If you press yes the \n" +
0161                        "program will terminate.";
```

As each *MessageCanvas* instance is added to the *helpPanel* a name, specified by one of the manifest names which were used for the Checkbox buttons, is associated with it. For example, on line 0093 the *turnHelpMessage* is added to the *helpPanel* with the manifest value *TURN* ("*Turn*") specified in the second argument of the add() method. The *manager* CardLayout instance, which has been installed as the *help-Panel*'s layout manager, will keep track of these names as will be demonstrated. By default the first Component added to the Panel will be displayed when it becomes visible, and this has been anticipated by setting the *FileHelp* Checkbox button's marker on line 0061. The remaining parts of the constructor construct the *dismiss* Button and assemble the interface before packing it, as follows.

```
0102        dismiss = new Button( "OK");
0103        dismiss.setActionCommand( "OK");
0104        dismiss.addActionListener( this);
0105
0106        buttonPanel = new Panel();
0107        buttonPanel.setBackground( Color.white);
0108        buttonPanel.add( dismiss);
0109
0110        this.add( helpControl, "North");
0111        this.add( helpPanel,   "Center");
0112        this.add( buttonPanel, "South");
0113        this.pack();
0114    } // End MenuBarTuttleHelpDialog constructor.
```

The *setVisible()* method does not differ from the *setVisible()* method of the Exit-Dialog just given, ensuring that the dialog is centered within its parent window whenever it becomes visible. The *actionPerformed()* method is called as a consequence of the user pressing the *dismiss* button and un-posts the dialog from the desktop as follows.

```
0140    public void actionPerformed( ActionEvent event) {
0141        this.setVisible( false);
0142    } // End actionPerformed.
```

The *itemStateChanged()* method, as follows, will be called as a consequence of the user pressing any of the *Checkbox*es, because their ItemListener resource was specified as the dialog to which they belong (**this**). It calls the CardLayout *manager*'s show() method passing as arguments the *helpPanel* which it is associated with and the name of the *Component* to be shown. The name is retrieved from the *event* by using its getItem() method and contains the label which was specified by a manifest value when the Checkbox was constructed. The same manifest value was also associated with the corresponding MessageCanvas as it was added to the Panel and so this mechanism will ensure that the correct message is shown.

```
0145        public void itemStateChanged( ItemEvent event) {
0148            manager.show( helpPanel,(String) event.getItem());
0151        } // End itemStateChanged.
```

For example the manifest value TURN ("*Turn*") was specified as the label of the *turnHelp* Checkbox, and was also associated with the *turnHelpMessage Message-Canvas* as it was *add*ed to the *helpPanel*. When the user selects the *turnHelp* radio button, the ItemEvent generated will contain the value "*Turn*" as its item attribute, when this is retrieved and passed to the *manager*'s show() method, it will locate and display the *turnHelpMessage* in the Panel.

During layout negotiations a Container which has a CardBox layout manager will ask for sufficient screen space to show its largest Component and, assuming it is granted this dimension, will not need to resize itself as its various Components are shown. Components which are smaller than the size of the window will be presented centered within the available space. The major resources of the CardLayout manager are given in Table 6.7.

This component can be adapted for use with any application which provides help to the user on a dialog panel. It will be suitable for use in its current form so long as the number of help categories does not exceed about seven items. When the number of help items exceeds this, a different user interface will be required. One possibility is a dialog containing a List component showing the larger number of topics in its scrolling area. Selecting and activating a topic will un-post the list dialog and post a dialog containing a MessageCanvas, possibly within a ScrollPane, which contains the help information. When the help information dialog is dismissed, the list dialog will be represented and it too can be dismissed when help is no longer required.

constructors	

`public CardLayout()`
`public CardLayout( int horizontalSpace,`
`                   int verticalSpace)`
	Constructor possibly allowing the spacing between components to be specified.

instance methods	
`public void first( Container parent)` `public void last(  Container parent)`	Shows the first or last card.

`public void previous(`
`                   Container parent)`
`public void next(  Container parent)`
	Shows the previous or next card.

`public void show( Container parent,` `              String     name,)`	Shows the card identified by *name*.

TABLE 6.7   Major Resources of the CardLayout Class

6.10 Menu Accelerators

Before concluding this introduction to application-level main menu interfaces, the use and implementation of *menu accelerators* will be introduced. A menu accelerator, also known as a *keyboard shortcut*, allows the user to post a dialog which is associated with a menu item by pressing a combination of keys on the keyboard. For example, the key combination <CONTROL><E> may cause an application's exit dialog to be posted without having to navigate the *File* menu. Accelerators tend to be favored by expert users, who can also be expected to be the most critical of the overall interface design and notice their absence.

A menu accelerator can be associated with a MenuItem by using its setShortcut() method, which requires an argument of the MenuShortcut class. Such an argument can most conveniently be provided by creating an anonymous instance of the MenuShortcut class in the setShortcut() method call, specifying the key required by using its classwide manifest name from the KeyEvent class. For example, the following line added in the appropriate place in the *ManuBarTuttleInterface* class will associate the <CONTROL><E> shortcut with the *exitButton* MenuItem.

```
exitButton.setShortcut( new MenuShortcut( KeyEvent.VK_E));
```

It should be included, for purposes of maintainability, in the sequence of steps which creates and installs the *exitButton* into the *fileMenu*. The phrase **new** MenuShortcut(KeyEvent.VK_E) constructs the anonymous MenuShortcut instance, which is associated with the *exitButton* by means of its setShortcut() method. If this method is included, the Java run-time system is able to recognize the existence of the shortcut and advertise it upon the menu, as shown in the left hand image of Figure 6.11.

The accelerator shown on the right-hand image in Figure 6.11 was obtained by using the alternative MenuShortcut constructor, which has a second **boolean** argument indicating if the <SHIFT> key should also be associated with it, as follows.

```
exitButton.setShortcut( new MenuShortcut( KeyEvent.VK_E, true));
```

The nomination of the <CONTROL> key is a feature of the peer environment, not of Java. For example, if this were to be executed on a Macintosh computer the

FIGURE 6.11   The *File* menu with accelerators on the *Exit …* option.

nominated key would be the <APPLE> key. This completes the implementation of the *MenuBarTuttle* interface as described at the start of the chapter. Further development of this interface will be presented in Chapter 8.

Chapter Summary

- An application-level main menu, and its associated pull-down menus, have the major advantage of user familiarity.

- The MenuComponet hierarchy is a sibling of the Component hierarchy and supplies the facilities to implement menus.

- Only a Frame instance can contain a MenuBar, which means that only independent top-level Windows, (and not Applets) can use a standard pull-down menu interface.

- Dialogs cannot exist independently of a top-level Window and can be posted in a modal or non-modal manner.

- WindowEvents can be intercepted by a registered WindowListener object and responded to as appropriate.

- The CardLayout manager allows one of a number of Panels to be shown at any one time, and provides facilities to navigate between them.

- Menu accelerators allow the menus to be operated from the keyboard without having to navigate the menus with the mouse.

Exercises

6.1   Extend the *MenuBarTuttle* interface to add controls for the *GeometricTuttle* class from Exercise 4.4.

6.2   Redesign, and subsequently re-implement, the *MenuBarTuttle*'s *Move* and *Turn* menus so that the user can move or turn the tuttle an arbitrary number of units. This should be accomplished, for example when moving the tuttle forward, by interposing a cascading menu that offers two further cascading menus labeled *tens* and *units*. The *tens* menu should offer items which move the tuttle *10*, *20*, *30* steps, etc. and the *units* menu items to move it *1*, *2*, *3* steps, etc. Therefore, if the user wanted to move the tuttle 47 steps they could activate the *Move/ Forwards/ tens/ 40* item followed by the *Move/ Forwards/ units/ 7* item.

6.3   Redesign, and subsequently re-implement, the *MenuBarTuttle*'s *Move* and *Turn* menus so that the user can move or turn the tuttle an arbitrary number of units. This should be accomplished, for example when moving the tuttle, by a single item on the *Move* menu labeled *Steps* …. Activating this item should post a dialog which contains a feedback Label, a horizontal ScrollBar, and *Forward*, *Backward* and *Dismiss* buttons. Therefore, if the user wanted to move the tuttle 47 steps they could post the dialog, set the slider to 47 (confirming this in the feedback Label) and then pressing the *Forward* button.

6.4   How could you find out which of the interfaces from 6.2 and 6.3 was favored by the users?

6.5   Install suitable accelerators into the menu structure and attempt to determine by investigation if their presence assists users. Does the experience level of the user make them more likeley to use accelerators?

6.6   Provide an *Exit* button and a *Help ImageButton* for the *SemiDirectInterface* from Chapter 5 and cause them to post the appropriate dialog when they are pressed.

6.7   Design and implement the alternative help system as described in this chapter.

6.8   Re-implement the *ExitDialog* class so that an instance of the class is created each time the user activates the *File* menu *Exit …* item and is destroyed each time the user dismisses it. Attempt to determine if there are any significant differences in the time it takes for the application to initialize itself and the time it takes for the dialog to be posted between this implementation and the implementation as described in this chapter.

C H A P T E R   7

Text-Based User Interfaces

In this chapter, two further styles of user interface will be developed for the *Tuttle* class. The first interface to be presented is a *text menu* style of interface, where the *Tuttle* is controlled from a set of text menus displayed below the drawing area. The menu bar based pull-down menu, from the previous chapter, is not particularly suitable for controlling a *tuttle* due to the constant mouse movements required to use it. The text menu style of interface has many of the advantages of a pull-down menu system, but allows the menus to be used from the keyboard without having to continually locate the mouse and use it to navigate the menus.

The second interface style which will be presented in this chapter is a *command line* system. In this interface style, the user is presented with an empty text input area and is expected to learn and remember the commands, and their syntax, which the tuttle will respond to. This style of interface is the most difficult to learn but can be the most powerful for an experienced user to operate. It is also the traditional style of interface for a Logo style turtle.

In order to implement these interfaces, the *Tuttle* class from Chapter 4 will be extended to produce a *TextTuttle* class that will accept and process commands passed to it as *String*s. The advantages of this refinement for the text menu style of interface may not be immediately obvious; however, when the *Tuttle* hierarchy is further extended in the following chapter the advantages will become clearer.

7.1 The *TextTuttle* Class

The class diagram for the *TextTuttle* class is presented in Figure 7.1.

The constructor has the same effect as the *Tuttle* constructor, requesting a tuttle drawing area with the dimensions specified and passing the identity of the applet for use by the tuttle. The other public attributes shown on the diagram are the manifest values of all the commands the *TextTuttle* will respond to. The *identifyCommand()* method will attempt to return the manifest value of the command contained in the String argument *command*, or the value *UNKNOWN*, if it cannot be recognized. The remaining method, *doCommand()*, will take a complete *command* String and attempt

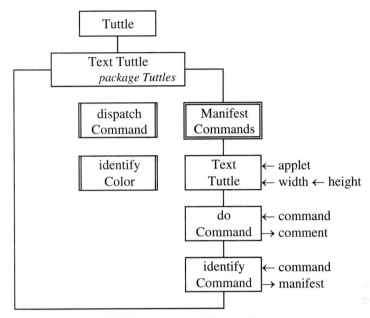

FIGURE 7.1   The *TextTuttle* class diagram.

to execute it. If it is possible for the *TextTuttle* to process the instruction, *doCommand()* will return an empty String in *comment*, otherwise it will contain an explanation of why the instruction could not be obeyed. The class diagram also shows two private methods called *dispatchCommand()* and *identifyColor()* whose use will be described. The implementation of this class, as far as the end of the constructor, is as follows.

```
0001   // Filename TextTuttle.java.
0002   // Extends the Tuttle class by providing a text
0003   // interface for its commands.
0004   //
0005   // Written for the Java Interface Book Chapter 7.
0006   // Fintan Culwin, v 0.2, August 1997.
0007
0008   package Tuttles;
0009
0010   import java.awt.*;
0011   import java.applet.*;
0012   import java.util.StringTokenizer;
0013
0014   import Tuttles.Tuttle;
0015
0016   public class TextTuttle extends Tuttle {
0017
0018   public static final int UNKNOWN       = -1;
0019   public static final int FORWARD       = 0;
0020   public static final int BACKWARD      = 1;
```

```
0021   public static final int TURN_RIGHT       = 2;
0022   public static final int TURN_LEFT        = 3;
0023   public static final int FOREGROUND       = 4;
0024   public static final int BACKGROUND       = 5;
0025   public static final int PEN_UP           = 6;
0026   public static final int PEN_DOWN         = 7;
0027   public static final int CLEAR            = 8;
0028   public static final int RESET            = 9;
0029   public static final int CLEAR_AND_RESET  = 10;
0030   public static final int EXIT             = 11;
0031   public static final int MAX_COMMANDS     = 11;
0032
0033   private static final String[] commands =
0034                        { "fd", "bd", "tr", "tl",
0035                          "fg", "bg", "pu", "pd",
0036                          "cl", "rs", "cr",
0037                          "exit" };
0038
0039
0040      public TextTuttle( Applet applet, int width, int height) {
0041         super( applet, width, height);
0042      } // End TextTuttle constructor.
```

The manifest values for the commands are enumerated on lines 0018 to 0031, with delimiting values for *UNKNOWN* commands and the maximum number of commands. The declaration of the **String** array *commands[]*, on lines 0033 to 0037, provides the corresponding two-letter abbreviation for each command, apart from the "*exit*" command. Finally, in this part, the constructor is implemented as a dispatching call of the parent, *Tuttle*, constructor. The *doCommand()* method relies upon the *identifyCommand()* method; the implementation of these two methods is as follows.

```
0045      public String doCommand( String theCommand) {
0046
0047      StringTokenizer tokenizer = new StringTokenizer( theCommand);
0048      String          firstTerm = null;
0049      String          theReply;
0050
0051      int thisCommand = UNKNOWN;
0052
0053         if ( tokenizer.hasMoreTokens()) {
0054            firstTerm   = tokenizer.nextToken().toLowerCase();
0055            thisCommand = identifyCommand( firstTerm);
0056
0057            if ( thisCommand == UNKNOWN ) {
0058               theReply = new String( "The command " + firstTerm +
0059                                      " is not known!");
0060            } else {
0061               theReply = dispatchCommand( thisCommand, tokenizer);
0062            } // End if.
0063         } else {
```

```
0064                  theReply = new String( "There does not seem to" +
0065                                          "be a command given!");
0066            } // End if.
0067          return theReply;
0068        } // End doCommand.
0069
0070        public int identifyCommand( String toIdentify) {
0071
0072        int thisCommand = MAX_COMMANDS;
0073        int identified  = UNKNOWN;
0074
0075          while ( ( identified  == UNKNOWN) &&
0076                  ( thisCommand != UNKNOWN) ){
0077            if ( toIdentify.equals( commands[ thisCommand])) {
0078               identified = thisCommand;
0079            } else {
0080               thisCommand--;
0081            } // End if.
0082          } // End while.
0083          return identified;
0084        } // End identifyCommand.
```

The *doCommand()* method commences, on line 0047, by constructing a StringTokenizer instance called *tokenizer* which will be used to split its single String argument, *theCommand*, into its constituent parts. The provision of a suitable command to this method is the responsibility of the tuttle text interfaces, as will be described.

Having initialized the *tokenizer* on line 0053, the *tokenizer* hasMoreTokens() method is used to make sure that *theCommand* is not empty and, if it is, *theReply* is prepared with a suitable message on line 0064. Otherwise the *firstTerm* is obtained from the *tokenizer* on line 0054 and identified, using *identifyCommand()*, on line 0055. If the *firstTerm* is not identified, a suitable reply is placed into *theReply* on lines 0058 and 0059. If this is not the case, then the *firstTerm* has been identified as a valid command and is processed by the **private** *dispatchCommand()* method on line 0061, passing as the second argument the *tokenizer* which still contains any remaining terms. In this case, the String returned by *dispatchCommand()* is stored in *theReply,* to be returned as the result of the *doCommand()* method on line 0066.

The *identifyCommand()* method, on lines 0070 to 0084, is a sequential search of the *commands[]* array. It returns the appropriate manifest value identifying the command contained in its *toIdentify* argument, or the value *UNKNOWN* if it does not contain a valid command. Should additional commands be added during maintenance, then additional manifest values can be added to the list and their string representation to the *commands[]* array, and this method will still operate correctly.

The *dispatchCommand()* method has the responsibility of checking any arguments of the *Tuttle* command and returning an appropriate message should too many, too few, or an inappropriate argument be supplied. If the arguments do prove to be acceptable the appropriate method of the parent, *Tuttle,* class should be called and an empty String returned.

The first part of its implementation, as follows, is concerned with processing those commands which require a single **int**eger argument: *forward*, *backward*, *turn left*, and *turn right*.

```
0087    private String dispatchCommand( int            theCommand,
0088                                    StringTokenizer arguments){
0089
0090    StringBuffer theResponse = new StringBuffer( "");
0091    boolean      processed    = false;
0092
0093      switch( theCommand) {
0094
0095      case FORWARD:
0096      case BACKWARD:
0097      case TURN_RIGHT:
0098      case TURN_LEFT:
0099          if (arguments.countTokens() == 1) {
0100          int toStepOrTurn;
0101            try {
0102                toStepOrTurn = Integer.parseInt( arguments.nextToken());
0103                switch ( theCommand) {
0104                case FORWARD:
0105                    this.forward( toStepOrTurn);
0106                    break;
0107                case BACKWARD:
0108                    this.backward( toStepOrTurn);
0109                    break;
0110                case TURN_RIGHT:
0111                    this.turnRight( toStepOrTurn);
0112                    break;
0113                case TURN_LEFT:
0114                    this.turnLeft( toStepOrTurn);
0115                    break;
0116                } // End switch.
0117                processed = true;
0118            } catch ( NumberFormatException exception) {
0119                processed = false;
0120            } // End try/ catch.
0121          } // End if.
0122          if ( !processed) {
0123              theResponse.append( commands[ theCommand] +
0124                        " should be followed by a single number.");
0125          } // End if.
0126          break;
```

The **switch** structure starting on line 0093 is controlled by the manifest value of *theCommand*, passed to *dispatchCommand()* from the *doCommand()* method. On lines 0095 to 0098 the first branch of the outer **switch** statement starting on line 0093 lists, as **case** selectors, the manifest values of the commands which require a single **int**eger argument.

The processing of these commands commences, on line 0099, with a check to make sure that only a single argument remains in the StringTokenizer instance called *arguments*, which was passed from the *doCommand()* method. If this is so then, on line 0102, an attempt is made, within a **try/ catch** structure, to interpret this argument as an **int**eger and store it in the local variable *toStepOrTurn*. Assuming that an exception is not throw, a second inner **switch** structure (between lines 0103 and 0116) dispatches to a call of the appropriate *Tuttle* method passing the value of *toStepOrTurn* as its argument. The final stage of the **try** part of the **try/ catch** structure sets the *processed* flag **true**.

If the command has not been processed, either because there are too many or too few argument, or because the single argument does not contain an **int**eger value, the value of *processed* will be **false**, unchanged from its declaration on line 0091. This will cause a suitable message to be placed into the StringBuffer *theResponse*, on lines 0123 to 0124. Finally, on line 0126, this part of the **switch** structure which started on line 0093 is completed with a **break** statement.

For example, if the *doCommand()* method were called with the String "*fd 30*".the *fd* part of the command would be extracted and identified by *identifyCommand()* as the manifest value *FORWARD*. This will cause *dispachCommand()* to be called with *FORWARD* as its first, *theCommand*, argument and the StringTokenizer, still containing "30," as its second argument. The value *FORWARD* will match the selector on line 0095 and cause the **switch** branch commencing on line 0099 to be executed. The **if** condition on line 0099 would evaluate **true** and so the **try/ catch** structure on line 0101 would be attempted. As "30" can be interpreted as the **int**eger value 30, no exception would be thrown on line 0102 and the inner **switch** structure on line 0103 would be considered. The value *FORWARD* in *theCommand* would cause line 0105 to be executed. This is a call of the *Tuttle forward()* method, inherited by the *TextTuttle* class, and will result in the tuttle moving forward 30 steps. The next line to be executed would be line 0117, setting the value of the *processed* flag **true** and avoiding any message being placed into *theResponse* on lines 0123 and 0124.

Alternatively, if the command received by the *doCommand()* method were "*fd*" or "*fd 30 please,*" the command would still be identified as *FORWARD* but the **if** condition on line 0099 would be **false** and result in lines 0123 and 0124 placing a suitable message in *theResponse*. This would also happen if the command were "*fd please*": the condition on line 0099 would now be **true** but the attempted conversion of "*please*" to an **int**eger on line 0102 would throw a *NumberFormatException* which, when caught on line 0118, would set the *processed* flag to cause the message to be placed in *theResponse*, as before.

The next part of the *dispatchCommand()* method processes those actions which require no arguments: *pen up*, *pen down*, *reset*, *clear,* and *clear and reset*. Its implementation, which follows, is similar to the previous fragment.

```
0128        case PEN_UP:
0129        case PEN_DOWN:
0130        case RESET:
0131        case CLEAR:
0132        case CLEAR_AND_RESET:
0133           if (arguments.countTokens() == 0) {
0134              switch ( theCommand) {
```

```
0135              case PEN_UP:
0136                  this.setPenUp();
0137                  break;
0138              case PEN_DOWN:
0139                  this.setPenDown();
0140                  break;
0141              case RESET:
0142                  this.resetTuttle();
0143                  break;
0144              case CLEAR:
0145                  this.clearTuttleArea();
0146                  break;
0147              case CLEAR_AND_RESET:
0148                  this.clearAndReset();
0149                  break;
0150              } // End switch.
0151              processed = true;
0152          } // End if.
0153          if ( !processed) {
0154              theResponse.append( commands[ theCommand] +
0155                          " should not  be followed by anything.");
0156          } // End if.
0157          break;
```

Line 0133 ensures that no arguments have been supplied; if this is so then an inner **switch** structure, between lines 0134 to 0150, dispatches to a call of the appropriate parent *Tuttle* method. Should any arguments be supplied, then lines 0154 to 0155 will place an appropriate message in *theResponse*. The next part of the method deals with the *foreground* and *background* commands, which require a single argument identifying one of the six acceptable *Tuttle* colors.

```
0158      case FOREGROUND:
0159      case BACKGROUND:
0160          if (arguments.countTokens() == 1) {
0161          Color theColor;
0162              theColor = identifyColor(
0163                                  arguments.nextToken().toLowerCase());
0164          if ( theColor != null) {
0165              if ( theCommand == FOREGROUND) {
0166                  this.setForeground( theColor);
0167              } else {
0168                  this.setBackground( theColor);
0169              } // End if.
0170              processed = true;
0171          } // End if.
0172          } // End if.
0173          if ( !processed) {
0174              theResponse.append( commands[ theCommand] +
0175                      " should only be followed by white, black, red, " +
0176                          "blue, green or yellow.");
```

```
0177            } // End if.
0178              break;
0179          } // End switch.
0180        return theResponse.toString();
0181     } // End dispatchCommand.
```

Line 0164 uses the **private** *identifyColor()* method to decide if a valid color name has been supplied in the single argument. The implementation of the *identifyColor()* method is given next. If the color name is recognized, the appropriate tuttle command is called; otherwise a message is placed into *theResponse*. The *dispatchCommand()* method concludes on line 0180 by returning the String contained in *theResponse*, which will be empty if the command has been passed to the tuttle or will contain a suitable message otherwise.

```
0185        private Color identifyColor( String possibleColor) {
0186
0187        Color theColor = null;
0188          if ( possibleColor.equals( "black")) {
0189            theColor = Color.black;
0190          } else if ( possibleColor.equals( "white")) {
0191            theColor = Color.white;
0192          } else if ( possibleColor.equals( "yellow")) {
0193            theColor = Color.yellow;
0194          } else if ( possibleColor.equals( "green")) {
0165            theColor = Color.green;
0196          } else if ( possibleColor.equals( "red")) {
0197            theColor = Color.red;
0198          } else if ( possibleColor.equals( "blue")) {
0199            theColor = Color.blue;
0200          } // End if.
0201        return theColor;
0202     } // End IdentifyColor.
```

The *dispatchCommand()* method does not attempt to process the *exit* command because, as explained in the previous chapter, exiting from an application must be the responsibility of a translation module and not of an application module. The processing of the exit command will be described in the two text interfaces later in this chapter.

This completes the implementation of the *TextTuttle* class but a complete demonstration of its effectiveness cannot be provided until the *CommandLineTuttle* interface is considered later in this chapter. However, a partial demonstration is contained with the *TextMenuTuttle* class which follows.

7.2 The *TextMenuTuttle* Interface

The instance diagram for the *TextMenuTuttle* applet does not differ significantly, apart from the names, from that of the *SemiDirectTuttle* given in Chapter 5. The appearance of the *TextMenuTuttle* interface when it is first launched is shown in Figure 7.2. An instance of the *TextMenuTuttleInterface* class is mounted at the bottom of the applet and contains a *TextArea* component that shows the *top-level menu*. The capitalization of

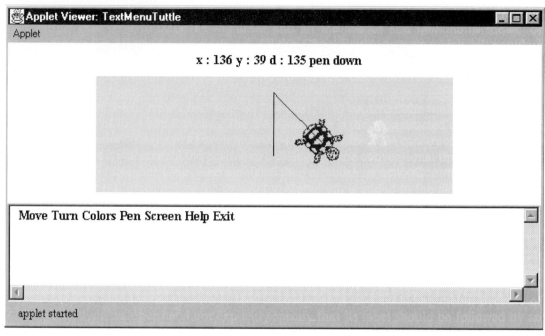

FIGURE 7.2   The *TextMenuTuttle* interface (with the drawing area reduced in height).

the terms used on the menu indicate to the user how to operate it. For example, pressing '*m*' or '*M*' on the keyboard will post the *Move* sub-menu, '*t*' or '*T*' the *Turn* sub-menu, and so on.

In the discussion which follows, only the *Move* menu system will be described in detail, the operation and implementation of the other menus are essentially identical. Details of how to obtain the complete implementation can be found in Appendix B.

Pressing '*m*' or '*M*' when the *top-level menu* is posted will post the *Move* menu whose appearance is shown in the top image of Figure 7.3. This menu has two visible options to move the tuttle forward or backward. It also has a third, invisible, option to cancel the *Move* menu and return to the *top-level menu* which is activated by pressing the <ESCAPE> key. Pressing the '*f*' or '*F*' key when the *Move* menu is posted will cause the *Move Forward* menu to be posted and likewise '*b*' or '*B*' will post the *Move Backward* menu. The appearance of the *Move Forward* menu is shown in the bottom image of Figure 7.3, the appearance of the *Move Backward* menu is essentially identical.

Pressing the '*5*', '*1*' or '*2*' key on the keyboard when the *Move Forwards* menu is posted will cause the tuttle to move forward 5, 10 or 25 steps respectively and leave the *Move Forward* menu posted. The behavior of the *Move* menu system can be shown in a state transition diagram, as in Figure 7.4.

Not all of the other menu systems are quite identical in their behavior with the *Move* menu system. For example, the *Colors* menu offers transitions to the *Foreground Color* or *Background Color* menus, each of which can be unposted by pressing the <ESCAPE> key. The *Foreground Color* menu offers the six color choices which

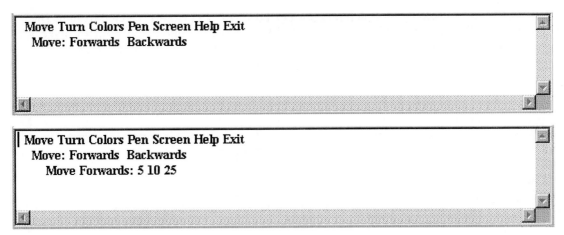

FIGURE 7.3   The *TextMenuTuttle* applet, showing the *Move* menu (top) and the *Move Forwards* menu (bottom).

have been offered by previous tuttle applets and can be cancelled by pressing the <ESCAPE> key, returning to the *Colors* menu without changing the current foreground tuttle color. However, if a color choice is made then the tuttle color is changed and the *Foreground* menu is unposted, leaving the *Colors* menu active. This differs from

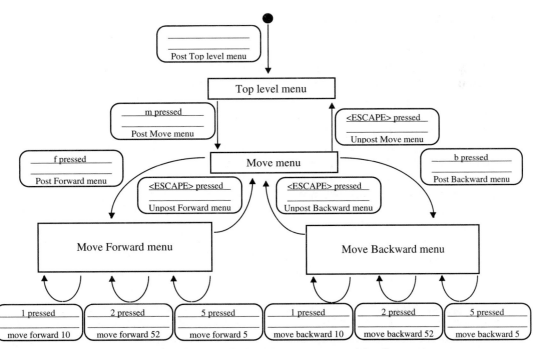

FIGURE 7.4   The *TextMenuTuttle Move* menu state transition diagram.

the *Move Forward* menu, which remains posted when an option is selected from it. This decision was taken as it was anticipated that the user would often want to make a sequence of movements, but would only want to select a single color at a time.

> **Design Advice**
>
> Although consistency is important in user interface design, functionality can sometimes be more important.

7.3 The *TextMenuTuttleInterface*

The *TextMenuTuttleInterface* class supplies the part of the interface shown at the bottom of Figure 7.2, consisting of a single non-editable TextArea instance. The implementation of this class, as far as the end of its constructor, is as follows.

```
0001   // Filename TextMenuTuttleInterface.java.
0002   // Supplies text menu interface for a Tuttle.
0003   //
0004   // Written for Java Interface book chapter 7.
0005   // Fintan Culwin, v 0.2, August 1997.
0006
0007   package TextMenuTuttle;
0008
0009   import java.awt.*;
0010   import java.applet.*;
0011   import java.awt.event.*;
0012
0013
0014   class TextMenuTuttleInterface extends Panel {
0015
0016   protected static final int TOP_LEVEL_MENU         = 0;
0017   protected static final int MOVE_MENU              = 1;
0018   protected static final int MOVE_FORWARD_MENU      = 2;
0019   protected static final int MOVE_BACKWARD_MENU     = 3;
0020   protected static final int TURN_MENU             = 4;
0021   protected static final int TURN_LEFT_MENU         = 5;
0022   protected static final int TURN_RIGHT_MENU        = 6;
0023   protected static final int COLOR_MENU            = 7;
0024   protected static final int FOREGROUND_COLOR_MENU = 8;
0025   protected static final int BACKGROUND_COLOR_MENU = 9;
0026   protected static final int PEN_MENU              = 10;
0027   protected static final int SCREEN_MENU           = 11;
0028   protected static final int HELP_MENU             = 12;
0029   protected static final int EXIT_MENU             = 13;
0030
0031   private int                 menuState            = TOP_LEVEL_MENU;
0032
0033   private TextArea menuArea;
```

```
0034
0035     protected TextMenuTuttleInterface( KeyListener itsListener) {
0036
0037         menuArea  = new TextArea( 5, 60);
0038         menuArea.setEditable( false);
0039         menuArea.addKeyListener( itsListener);
0040
0041         this.add( menuArea);
0042     } // End TextMenuTuttleInterface constructor.
```

The class declaration, on line 0014, indicates that it extends the Panel class. It commences, on lines 0016 to 0029, with the declaration of fourteen **protected** manifest values to represent the possible states of the interface and, on line 0031, an instance attribute called *menuState* to record the state of the menu. The intention is that the *menuState* attribute will always reflect the menu which the interface is currently showing. Two **protected** methods, *setMenuState()* and *menuStateIs(),* are provided to support the use of this attribute. As these resources are protected they can be seen by the only other class in the package, the *textMenuTuttle* class, but are not visible to classes outside the package. The use which the *textMenuTuttle* class makes of this knowledge will be described.

The constructor on lines 0035 to 0042 creates a non-editable TextArea instance, called *menuArea*, with 5 rows and 60 columns, and registers the KeyListener instance, *itsListener*, passed as an argument as its KeyListener attribute. This will cause the appropriate methods in *itsListener* to be called as the user operates the keyboard. The constructor concludes by adding the *menuArea* instance into itself as its only instance child. The implementation of the *setMenuState()* method is as follows.

```
0046     protected void setMenuState( int newState) {
0047
0048         menuState = newState;
0049
0050         switch( menuState) {
0051            case TOP_LEVEL_MENU:
0052                menuArea.setText( topLevelMenu);
0053                break;
0054
0055            case MOVE_MENU:
0056                menuArea.setText( topLevelMenu + moveMenu);
0057                break;
0058
0059            case MOVE_FORWARD_MENU:
0060                menuArea.setText( topLevelMenu + moveMenu + movefMenu);
0061                break;
—              // Other cases omitted.
0103            case EXIT_MENU:
0104                menuArea.setText( topLevelMenu + exitMenu);
0105                break;
0106         } // End switch.
0107     } // End setMenuState.
```

The method commences, on line 0048, by setting the value of *menuState* to the value of the argument passed to the method in *newState*. It continues with a multi-way switch structure containing a branch for each possible menu state and, within each branch, calls the *menuArea*'s *setText()* method to cause the appropriate menu to be shown to the user. To accomplish this, a number of Strings are declared at the end of the class; for example the Strings referred to in the fragment are declared as follows.

```
0115   private static final String topLevelMenu       =
0116                  "  Move Turn Colors Pen Screen Help Exit";
0117   private static final String moveMenu       =
0118                  "\n     Move: Forwards Backwards";
0119   private static final String movefMenu       =
0120                  "\n        Move Forwards: 5 10 25 ";
—              // Other cases omitted.
0141   private static final String exitMenu       =
0142                  "\n     Exit: Yes No";
0143   } // End class TextMenuTuttleInterface.
```

Thus on line 0060, as the interface moves into the *MOVE_FORWARD_MENU* state, the three strings on lines 0116, 0118, and 0120 are catenated together and displayed in the *menuArea* to produce the appearance shown in the lower illustration from Figure 7.3. The only other method of this class is the inquiry method *menuStateIs()*, whose implementation is as follows.

```
0110      protected int menuStateIs() {
0111         return menuState;
0112      } // End menuStateIs.
```

7.4 The *TextMenuTuttle* Class

As with the previous tuttle interfaces, this class (which extends the Applet class) has the responsibility, in its *init()* method, of configuring itself, creating an instance of the *TextTuttle* class, creating an instance of the *TextMenuTuttleInterface* class to control the tuttle, creating a feedback area, and then placing the interface into a well-defined initial state so that, on its conclusion, the interface becomes visible to the user. The implementation of the class, as far as the end of its constructor, is as follows.

```
0001   // Filename TextMenuTuttle.java.
0002   // Supplies a main application text menu
0003   // interface the TextTuttle class.
0004   //
0005   // Written for Java Interface book chapter 7.
0006   // Fintan Culwin, v 0.2, August 1997.
0007
0008   package TextMenuTuttle;
0009
0010   import java.awt.*;
0011   import java.applet.*;
```

```
0012    import java.awt.event.*;
0013
0014    import Tuttles.TextTuttle;
0015    import TextMenuTuttle.TextMenuTuttleInterface;
0016
0017    public class TextMenuTuttle extends    Applet
0018                               implements KeyListener {
0019
0020    private TextTuttle                theTuttle;
0021    private TextMenuTuttleInterface  theInterface;
0022
0023    private Panel                     feedbackPanel;
0024    private Label                     feedbackLabel;
0026
0027
0028        public void init() {
0029
0030        Panel tuttlePanel;
0031
0032            this.setLayout( new BorderLayout());
0033            this.setFont( new Font( "TimesRoman", Font.BOLD, 14));
0034            this.setBackground( Color.white);
0035
0036            tuttlePanel = new Panel();
0037            theTuttle   = new TextTuttle( this, 400, 400);
0038            tuttlePanel.add( theTuttle);
0039
0040            theInterface = new TextMenuTuttleInterface( this);
0041
0042            feedbackPanel = new Panel();
0043            feedbackLabel = new Label();
0044            feedbackPanel.add( feedbackLabel);
0045
0046            this.add( feedbackPanel, "North");
0047            this.add( tuttlePanel,   "Center");
0048            this.add( theInterface,  "South");
0049
0050            this.feedback();
0051            theInterface.setMenuState(
0052                               TextMenuTuttleInterface.TOP_LEVEL_MENU);
0053        } // End init.
```

The majority of this constructor is largely comparable to the corresponding constructors from the previous tuttle interfaces. The significant differences are that an instance of the *TextMenuTuttleInterface*, called *theInterface*, is constructed on line 0040 and subsequently added to the applet Panel in its "*South*" location on line 0048. It has its state set to *TOP_LEVEL_MENU*, on line 0051, before the method concludes. This will ensure that the interface, when first visible to the user, is something like that shown in Figure 7.2.

The identity of **this** instance of the *TextMenuTuttle* class is passed to *theInterface* as it is constructed and, in order for this to be allowed, the *TextMenuTuttle* class has to implement the KeyListener interface, as stated on line 0019. The KeyListener interface requires the class to supply *keyTyped()*, *keyPressed()*, and *keyReleased()* methods which will be called as appropriate when the user interacts with the keyboard. A KeyEvent instance will be passed as an argument to these methods which contains, among other things, an attribute called keyChar indicating which key on the keyboard was pressed. This class is only concerned with processing KeyTyped events, and the implementation of the three KeyListener methods is as follows.

```
0057      public void keyTyped( KeyEvent event) {
0058
0059      char pressed  = event.getKeyChar();
0060      int  newMenu  = TextMenuTuttleInterface.TOP_LEVEL_MENU;
0061
0062        switch ( theInterface.menuStateIs()) {
0063
0064        case TextMenuTuttleInterface.TOP_LEVEL_MENU:
0065          newMenu = topLevelMenu( pressed);
0066          break;
0067
0068        case TextMenuTuttleInterface.MOVE_MENU:
0069          newMenu = moveMenu( pressed);
0070          break;
0071
0072        case TextMenuTuttleInterface.MOVE_FORWARD_MENU:
0073          newMenu = moveForwardMenu( pressed);
0074          break;
0075
—         // Other cases omitted.
0116        case TextMenuTuttleInterface.EXIT_MENU:
0117          newMenu = exitMenu( pressed);
0118          break;
0119
0120        } // End switch menuState.
0121
0122      theInterface.setMenuState( newMenu);
0123      this.feedback();
0124      } // End keyTyped.
0125
0126      public void keyPressed(  KeyEvent event ) {}  // End keyPressed.
0127      public void keyReleased( KeyEvent event ) {}  // End keyReleased.
```

The *keyTyped()* method commences, on line 0059, by retrieving the identity of the key typed from the KeyEvent *event* and storing it in the local **char**acter variable *pressed*. A second local variable called *newMenu* of type **int** is declared on line 0060. This variable will be used to represent the menu which should be displayed after this KeyEvent has been processed and is initialized to a default value, indicating that the *TOP_LEVEL_MENU* should be shown.

The major part of the method, between lines 0062 and 0120, is a **switch** structure containing a branch for every possible menu state; its selector expression is a call of the *theInterface*'s *menuStateIs()* method. Each branch calls a **private** method, with a systematic name, to deal with the key *pressed*. For example, if the application has just been started then it will be in the *TOP_LEVEL_MENU* state as described earlier. If the user presses and releases the '*m*' key on the keyboard, a keyEvent containing '*m*' will be constructed and passed as the *event* argument to the *keyTyped()* method. The **switch** selector on line 0062 will identify the *TOP_LEVEL_MENU* state, causing the branch on line 0065 to be taken, calling the *topLevelMenu()* method, and passing as an argument the keyCharacter extracted from the *event* on line 0059. The *topLevelMenu()* method will process this character and return the identity of the menu state the interface is to transit to. All other possible states have associated methods, each of which takes as an argument the identity of the key *pressed* and returns the manifest value of the *newMenu* to be displayed; examples of these methods will be given.

Following the end of the **switch** structure in the *keyTyped()* method, the *setMenuState()* method of *theInterface* is called passing as an argument the *newMenu* to be displayed. The final action of the *keyTyped* method is to update the *feedback* Panel shown at the top of the interface. The other two required methods of the KeyListener interface, *keyPressed()* and *keyReleased(),* need not do anything and are declared as dummy methods on lines 0126 and 0127 in order to satisfy the requirements of the KeyListener interface which this class implements.

The *topLevelMenu()* method, called from *keyTyped()* whenever the interface is in its *TOP_MENU_STATE*, is implemented as follows. It consists of a **switch** statement, containing a branch for each possible combination of key presses which the menu is to respond to. Each branch sets the value of the local variable *newMenuState* to indicate the appropriate menu state which the interface is to transit to. On line 0171 this value is **return**ed from the method and, if none of the branches have been activated, will contain its default value *TOP_LEVEL_MENU*. The returned value will be used by the *keyTyped()* method to set the state of the menu. The effect is that if the user presses one of the expected keys, then the interface will transit to the appropriate state–otherwise it will remain in the *TOP_LEVEL_MENU* state.

```
0131      private int topLevelMenu( char pressed) {
0132
0133      int newMenuState = TextMenuTuttleInterface.TOP_LEVEL_MENU;
0134
0135        switch( pressed) {
0136        case 'M':
0137        case 'm':
0138           newMenuState = TextMenuTuttleInterface.MOVE_MENU;
0139           break;
0140
0141        case 'T':
0142        case 't':
0143           newMenuState = TextMenuTuttleInterface.TURN_MENU;
0144           break;
0145
--            // Other cases omitted.
```

```
0166              case 'E':
0167              case 'e':
0168                  newMenuState = TextMenuTuttleInterface.EXIT_MENU;
0169                  break;
0170              } // End switch.
0171              return newMenuState;
0172          } // End topLevelMenu
```

Following the example, which assumed that the user pressed '*m*', this will cause the branch on line 0143 to be followed–causing this method to return the value *TURN_MENU* on line 0171. As explained, this will result in the interface presenting the user with the text menu shown at the top of Figure 7.3. The next time the user uses the keyboard, the *keyPressed()* method will result in a call of the *moveMenu()* method whose implementation is as follows.

```
0175          private int moveMenu( char pressed) {
0176
0177              int newMenuState = TextMenuTuttleInterface.MOVE_MENU;
0178
0179              switch( pressed) {
0180              case KeyEvent.VK_ESCAPE:
0181                  newMenuState = TextMenuTuttleInterface.TOP_LEVEL_MENU;
0182                  break;
0183
0184              case 'F':
0185              case 'f':
0186                  newMenuState = TextMenuTuttleInterface.MOVE_FORWARD_MENU;
0187                  break;
0188
0189              case 'B':
0190              case 'b':
0191                  newMenuState = TextMenuTuttleInterface.MOVE_BACKWARD_MENU;
0192                  break;
0193              } // End switch.
0194              return newMenuState;
0195          } // End moveMenu.
```

The implementation of this method is directly comparable to the implementation of the *topLevelMenu()* method. It will respond to presses of the <ESCAPE> key by transiting back to the *TOP_LEVEL_MENU* state, the '*f*' or '*F*' key to the *MOVE_FORWARD_MENU* state, and the '*b*' or '*B*' key to the *MOVE_BACKWARD_MENU* state, any other key will leave the interface in the *MOVE_MENU* state. The identity of the <ESCAPE> key is established, on line 0180, by using the manifest value VK_ESCAPE (*Virtual Key Escape*) supplied by the KeyEvent class. Assuming that the user presses the '*f*' or '*F*' key, the interface will appear as shown at the bottom of Figure 7.3 and the next *KeyEvent* generated will cause the *KeyTyped()* method to call the *moveForwardMenu()* method, implemented as follows.

```
0198          private int moveForwardMenu( char pressed) {
0199
```

```
0200       int newMenuState = TextMenuTuttleInterface.MOVE_FORWARD_MENU;
0201
0202          switch( pressed) {
0203          case KeyEvent.VK_ESCAPE:
0204             newMenuState = TextMenuTuttleInterface.MOVE_MENU;
0205             break;
0206
0207          case '5':
0208             theTuttle.doCommand("fd 5");
0209             break;
0210
0211          case '1':
0212             theTuttle.doCommand("fd 10");
0213             break;
0214
0215          case '2':
0216             theTuttle.doCommand("fd 25");
0217             break;
0218          } // End switch.
0219          return newMenuState;
0220       } // End moveForwardMenu.
```

In this method, pressing the <ESCAPE> key effects a transit back to the *MOVE_MENU* state and other key presses will leave the interface in the *MOVE_FORWARD_MENU* state. However, pressing the '*5*', '*1*', or '*2*' key will cause the *theTuttle doCommand()* method to be called, passing as an argument a suitable command string. So if the user presses the '*1*' key the *tuttle* will move forward 10 steps. As the *keyPressed()* method concludes by calling the *feedback()* method, whose implementation does not differ from those presented in previous chapters, the new status of the *tuttle* will be reported at the top of the interface. The menu system will remain in the *MOVE_FORWARD_MENU* state until the <ESCAPE> key is pressed, allowing the user to rapidly move the *tuttle* in its current direction.

A consideration of the three methods described, and the corresponding *moveBackwardAction()*, will show that the behavior of the interface is as described in the STD from Figure 7.4. The remaining parts of the *TextMenuTuttle* class are essentially identical with a specific method for each of the possible menu states, whose implementations are comparable to those presented. The only significant difference is in the *exitMenu()* method, as follows, where pressing the '*y*' or '*Y*' key will cause the applet to terminate.

```
0512   private int exitMenu( char pressed) {
0513
0514   int newMenuState = theInterface.EXIT_MENU;
0515
0516       switch( pressed) {
0517       case KeyEvent.VK_ESCAPE:
0518          newMenuState = theInterface.TOP_LEVEL_MENU;
0519          break;
0520
0521       case 'Y':
```

```
0522        case 'y':
0523            System.exit( 0);
0524            break;
0525
0526        case 'N':
0527        case 'n':
0528            newMenuState = theInterface.TOP_LEVEL_MENU;
0529            break;
0530        } // End switch.
0531
0532        return newMenuState;
0533    } // End exitMenu.
```

The operation of this system provides a demonstration of the correct implementation of the *TextTuttle* class, which will be further demonstrated by the *Command-LineTuttle* class. Details of how to obtain the parts of the source code which have been omitted from this part of the chapter are contained in Appendix B.

7.5 The *CommandLineTuttle* Interface

The *CommandLineTuttle* interface provides the traditional method of instructing a tuttle and, for experienced users, provides the most efficient and powerful mechanism. The appearance of the *CommandLineTuttle* interface is shown in Figure 7.5.

The single-line *TextField* at the very bottom of the interface is used by the user to type in the commands. Above it, a *TextArea* records the commands which the user has issued and also outputs any messages from the tuttle to the user. Every command which the user inputs is echoed in the *TextArea*, preceded by a chevron (>), and any messages from the interface in response to the command are shown below it. The *TextArea* provides a *history list* of the commands which have been issued, which the user can use to refresh their memory of what has happened and copy commands from it to paste into the *TextField*.

The design of the language used to command the tuttle is implicit in the *TextTuttle* class. The commands should be constructed in a regular manner; in this example each command consists of a verb, for example *forward*, and is possibly followed by a single argument, for example *100*. This should never be reversed, for example stating the color followed by *background* or *foreground* (e.g., *green foreground*).

The abbreviations used for the verbs have likewise been chosen in a regular manner, using key letters from the full name of the command. Although it should not be assumed that these are always unambiguous, for example the command *turn right* (*tr*) could just as easily have been *right turn* (*rt*) or even *clockwise* (*cw*), an alternative technique for the selection of the abbreviations might be to use the first two unique letters of a command.

A more complete command line system might employ synonymous commands, for example the *turn right* command could be issued as *turn right*, *right turn*, *tr*, or *rt*. (One famous example of the misuse of this consideration is an interface which, when the command *exit* is given, responds "*If you want to exit the application you must type*

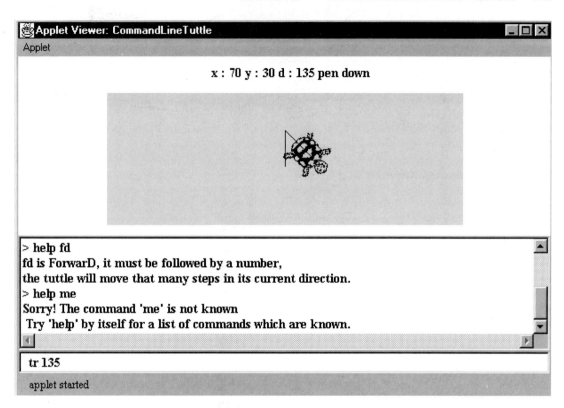

FIGURE 7.5   The *CommandLineTuttle* interface (with the drawing area reduced in height).

'quit'."). As with icons there are techniques which can be used to identify a set of verbs, and an associated syntax, which are most acceptable to the users.

Design Advice

The language of a command line interface should be constructed so as to be as regular and predictable as possible.

There is one exception to the regularity of the command language used in this interface. The *exit* command does not have an abbreviation and must be given as "*exit please.*" The reason for this is that the consequences of using the exit command by accident are so severe that the irregularity is intended to reduce the probability of this happening. However, it can also be predicted that for a very experienced user this effect will be lost. For example, the MS DOS delete command *del* will ask for a confirmation if it is used to delete all the files in a directory: (*C>del *.* \n Are you sure (Y/N) y*). An experienced user will conceptually compile this sequence of two operations into a single operation and, on occasion, will use the compiled sequence by accident.

As there is so much potential uncertainty, for the user, in the format of the commands an effective *help* facility is essential for all command line interfaces. This is vital for novice users of the interface who, when presented with a blank command line for the first time, may have no idea of what to do. It is also essential for very experienced users who may use many different command line systems and can become confused on a particular system. For example: the commands to exit from different command line systems include *exit*, *quit*, *logout*, *system*, and *bye*. The details of the help facility for the tuttle command line system are indicated in Figure 7.5 and will be presented in the description of its implementation.

7.6 The *CommandLineTuttleInterface* Class

Corresponding to the previous tuttle interfaces the *CommandLineTuttle* interface is provided by an instance of the *CommandLineTuttle* class, providing the translation layer, and an instance of the *CommandLineTuttleInterface* class, providing the interface presentation layer. The implementation of the *CommandLineTuttleInterface* class is as follows.

```
0001   // Filename CommandLineTuttleInterface.java.
0002   // Supplies the command line interface for
0003   // the Tuttle class.
0004   //
0005   // Written for Java Interface book chapter 7.
0006   // Fintan Culwin, v 0.2, August 1997.
0007
0008   package CommandLineTuttle;
0009
0010   import java.awt.*;
0011   import java.awt.event.*;
0012
0013   import Tuttles.TextTuttle;
0014
0015   class CommandLineTuttleInterface extends Panel {
0016
0017   private TextArea   commandFeedback;
0018   private TextField commandArea;
0019
0020      protected CommandLineTuttleInterface( ActionLineListener itsListener) {
0021
0022         this.setLayout( new BorderLayout());
0023
0024         commandFeedback = new TextArea( 6, 60);
0025         commandFeedback.setEditable( false);
0026
0027         commandArea = new TextField( 60);
0028         commandArea.addActionListener( itsListener);
0029
0030         this.add( commandFeedback, "Center");
0031         this.add( commandArea,      "South");
0032      } // End CommandLineTuttleInterface constructor.
0033
```

```
0034        protected void clearCommandArea() {
0035            commandArea.setText( "");
0036        } // End clearCommandArea.
0037
0038        protected void appendFeedback( String toAppend) {
0039            commandFeedback.append( toAppend);
0040        } // End clearCommandArea.
0041    } // End class CommandLineTuttleInterface class.
```

This interface, shown at the bottom of Figure 7.5, consists of a TextArea called *commandFeedback* mounted above a TextField called *commandArea*. The constructor, on lines 0020 to 0032, constructs these two instances and mounts them as appropriate using a BorderLayout policy. The *commandFeedback* area is configured to be non-editable, and the *commandArea* has the ActionListener argument of the constructor, *itsListener*, registered with it.

The only other methods of this class are *clearCommandArea()*, on lines 0034 to 0036, and *appendFeedback()* on lines 0038 to 0041. The *clearCommandArea()* method clears the contents of the lower area, and the *appendFeedback()* method appends the String in its argument to the text displayed in the upper text area.

7.7 The *CommandLineTuttle* Class

The *CommandLineTuttle* constructor is comparable to the other *tuttle* interface constructors: creating, configuring, and installing an instance of the *TextTuttle* class, the *CommandLineTuttleInterface* class, and a *feedbackPanel* into the interface. The ActionListener instance passed as an argument to the *CommandLineTuttleInterface* constructor is the instance of the *CommandLineTuttle* currently being initialized. Consequently this class has to implement the ActionListener interface and so an *actionPerformed()* method. The implementation of the class, presented without comment, as far as the end of its *init()* method, is as follows.

```
0001    // Filename CommandLineTuttle.java.
0002    // Supplies the command line translation for
0003    // the Tuttle class.
0004    //
0005    // Written for Java Interface book chapter 7.
0006    // Fintan Culwin, v 0.2, August 1997.
0007
0008    package CommandLineTuttle;
0009
0010    import java.awt.*;
0011    import java.awt.event.*;
0012    import java.applet.*;
0013
0014    import java.util.StringTokenizer;
0015
0016    import Tuttles.TextTuttle;
0017    import CommandLineTuttle.CommandLineTuttleInterface;
```

```
0018
0019
0020    public class CommandLineTuttle extends      Applet
0021                                  implements ActionListener {
0022
0023    private TextTuttle                    theTuttle;
0024    private CommandLineTuttleInterface theInterface;
0025
0026    private Panel                       feedbackPanel;
0027    private Label                       feedbackLabel;
0028
0029        public void init() {
0030
0031        Panel tuttlePanel = new Panel();
0032
0033            this.setLayout( new BorderLayout());
0034            this.setFont(   new Font( "TimesRoman", Font.BOLD, 14));
0035            this.setBackground( Color.white);
0036
0037            theTuttle = new TextTuttle( this, 400, 400);
0038            tuttlePanel.add( theTuttle);
0039
0040            theInterface = new CommandLineTuttleInterface( this);
0041
0042            feedbackPanel = new Panel();
0043            feedbackPanel.setBackground( Color.white);
0044            feedbackLabel = new Label();
0045            feedbackPanel.add( feedbackLabel);
0046
0047            this.add( feedbackPanel, "North");
0048            this.add( tuttlePanel,    "Center");
0049            this.add( theInterface,   "South");
0050
0051            this.feedback();
0052        } // End init.
```

As this class has been registered as the actionListener attribute of the single-line *commandArea* shown the user, its' *actionPerformed()* method will be called every time the user presses the <ENTER> key in the command area of the interface. The *action-Command* attribute of the *event* passed as an argument to the *actionPerformed()* method will contain the entire line of text from the *commandArea*.

The basis of the *actionPerformed()* method is to pass the command line, extracted from the ActionEvent argument of the method, to *theTuttle* instance. The method concludes by echoing the command, and any response received from *theTuttle*, in the feedback area before clearing the command area and updating the tuttle's feedback Panel. This outline is complicated by the need to process the *help* and *exit* commands separately. The implementation of the *actionPerformed()* method is as follows.

```
0055        public void actionPerformed( ActionEvent event) {
0056
```

```
0057        String          theCommand = event.getActionCommand();
0058        StringTokenizer tokenizer  = new StringTokenizer( theCommand);
0059        String          firstTerm  = tokenizer.nextToken().toLowerCase();
0060        String          theResponse;
0061
0062           if ( firstTerm.equals( "help")) {
0063              theResponse = obtainHelp( tokenizer);
0064           } else if ( firstTerm.equals( "exit")) {
0065              theResponse = checkExit( tokenizer);
0066           } else {
0067              theResponse = theTuttle.doCommand( theCommand);
0068           } // End if
0069
0070           theInterface.appendFeedback( "\n> " + theCommand);
0071           if ( theResponse.length() > 0 ) {
0072              theInterface.appendFeedback("\n" + theResponse);
0073           } // End if.
0074           theInterface.clearCommandArea();
0075           this.feedback();
0076        } // End actionPerformed.
```

Lines 0057 to 0059 prepare a **StringTokenizer** instance called *tokenizer*, initialized to parse the command extracted from the *event* argument by using its getAction-Command() method, and extract the first term of the command into the local **String** *firstTerm*. Line 0060 declares a **String** instance called *theResponse* ready to receive any reply from *theTuttle*.

Lines 0062 and 0063 deal with a *help* command by using the *obtainHelp()* method described later; likewise lines 0064 to 0065 deal with an *exit* command by using the *checkExit()* method. All other commands are passed to *theTuttle* on line 0067, by calling its' *doCommand()* method passing the entire command line retrieved from the *event* as its argument. As explained, the *doCommand()* method will attempt to interpret the command and, if it is valid, instruct the *tuttle* to obey it. If it cannot be interpreted as a valid tuttle command, the *doCommand()* method will return an explanation which will be stored in *theResponse*.

Line 0070 echoes *theCommand* to the feedback area on *theInterface*, preceded by a chevron ('>'), by using its *appendFeedback()* method. Lines 0071 to 0073 follow this by the contents of *theResponse*, if any. The method concludes, on lines 0074 and 0075, by clearing the command area on *theInterface*, which is then ready for the next command and by updating the *feedbackPanel* as usual.

As indicated on Figure 7.5 the command "*help*" by itself will provide a list of recognized commands, "*help*" followed by one of the possible tuttle commands will provide specific help for that command, and anything else will be reported as an unknown command with the further advice to try "*help*" by itself. The *obtainHelp()* method, implemented as follows, will be called from the *actionPerformed()* method when "*help*" is identified in the first term of the user's command, and will return a suitable response to be subsequently displayed in the text feedback area.

```
0090        private String obtainHelp( StringTokenizer tokenizer) {
0091
```

```
0092        StringBuffer theHelp = new StringBuffer( "");
0093        String        secondTerm;
0094        int           helpFor;
0095
0096          if ( ! tokenizer.hasMoreTokens()) {
0097              theHelp.append( "help is available for fd, bd, tr, tl " +
0098                             "fg bg pu pd cl rs cr and exit");
0099          } else {
0100              secondTerm = tokenizer.nextToken().toLowerCase();
0101              helpFor = theTuttle.identifyCommand( secondTerm);
0102
0103              switch ( helpFor) {
0104              case theTuttle.FORWARD:
0105                  theHelp.append("fd is ForwarD, it must be followed by a
                      number, " +
0106                                 "\nthe tuttle will move that many steps in
                                    its " +
0107                                 "current direction.");
0108                  break;
—              // Other branches omitted.
0187              case theTuttle.UNKNOWN:
0188                  theHelp.append("Sorry! The command '" + secondTerm +
0189                              "' is not known \n Try 'help' by itself for " +
0190                              "a list of commands which are known.");
0191                  break;
0192
0193              } // End switch.
0194          } // End if.
0195          return theHelp.toString();
0196      } // End obtainHelp.
```

The command "*help*" by itself will be detected on line 0096, by the absence of a second term in the StringTokenizer *tokenizer* argument, and causes a suitable message to be placed in *theHelp* StringBuffer on lines 0097 to 0098. Otherwise, on line 0100, the second term is extracted from the *tokenizer* and passed to the *TextTuttle identifyCommand()* method on line 0101. A fourteen-way **switch** structure, starting on line 0103, contains a branch for each recognized command each placing a suitable message for each into *theHelp*. The last branch of the **switch** structure, on lines 0187 to 0191, provides help if the second term of the command was not recognized by the *TextTuttle* as a valid command. The method concludes, on line 0195, by returning the String contained in *theHelp*.

Figure 7.5 illustrates the operation of this method. The "*help fd*" command was typed in by the user and the help obtained, from lines 0105 to 0107 of the *obtainHelp()* method, is shown following the command in the feedback area. This was followed by a "*help me*" request which causes the UNKNOWN branch to be taken, and the resulting message is shown.

The remaining *checkExit()* method is somewhat similar and is implemented as follows.

```
0078        private String checkExit( StringTokenizer tokenizer) {
0079            if ( (tokenizer.countTokens() == 1)  &&
0080                (tokenizer.nextToken().toLowerCase().equals( "please")) ){
0081                System.exit( 0);
0082                return "";
0083            } else {
0084                return new String( "To exit from this application you have " +
0085                                "to type 'exit', followed by 'please'!");
0086            } // End if.
0087        } // End checkExit.
```

Lines 0079 and 0080 check to see if there is a second term following the exit command and, if so, if it is *"please."* Only if both these conditions are satisfied will the applet terminate on line 0081; a more complete applet might have to perform some housekeeping at this stage before exiting. Otherwise if the command was not given as *exit please*, on lines 0084 and 0085 advice on how to exit from the applet is returned to be displayed in *theInterface*'s feedback area.

7.8 Evaluating the Interfaces

There are now four interfaces for the control of a *tuttle* and the question of which is the best interface might be raised, not only in the context of controlling a *tuttle* but also for any other application. However the question has no easy answer and will depend upon the nature of the application, the nature of the task which it is being used for, and the nature of the user who is performing the task. All that can be attempted is that, given a specific application and task with a particular type of user, a comparison of different interfaces can be made and some of these results might be generalized.

Any user interface should be *effective, efficient,* and *enjoyable.* Effective in the sense that it allows tasks to be performed, efficient in the sense that it allows the tasks to be performed without undue stress or effort, and enjoyable in the sense that the users will report that they take pleasure (or at least feel neutral) about using the interface. This description of user interfaces provides the basis of the techniques which can be used to evaluate them. A representative set of users can be selected, or obtained, and required to perform some task. Their actions while they are performing the task can be observed, recorded, or measured and their attitude towards the interface can be established after they have completed it.

To evaluate the four *tuttle* interfaces a specific task, or series of tasks, could be established and described to the user. In order to ensure that the task being presented to the user is one of controlling the *tuttle* and not a test of their trigonometric or artistic abilities, the instructions should include the lengths of the lines and the angles of the turns. A possible task is shown in Figure 7.6.

To conduct the investigation correctly the experiences of each group of users, known as *subjects*, should be as identical as possible. This relies upon an investigation protocol being produced which states exactly what the person conducting the investigation should say regarding the purpose of the investigation, what is expected of the subjects, and what the investigator can say if a subject asks for help. The protocol might

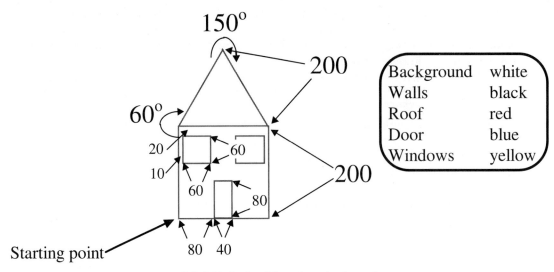

FIGURE 7.6   Possible *tuttle* evaluation task.

then allow a period of time, say about 15 minutes, during which the user is allowed to freely explore the interface before the specific task is introduced.

The measurements which can be made upon the subject's behavior while attempting the task include:

- the degree of completion of the task.

- the total time taken to complete the task.

- the number of commands used.

- the number of mistakes made.

- the number of times help is requested.

The attitude of the subject can be established by using a questionnaire after they have completed the task. A common form of questionnaire is made up from Leikert scales which have five possible responses, as shown in Figure 7.7. This can be converted

	Strongly agree	**Agree**	**Neither agree or disagree**	**Disagree**	**Strongly disagree**
I felt confident that I would be able to complete the task.	☐	☐	☐	☐	☐
Sometimes I was not certain what action to take next.	☐	☐	☐	☐	☐

FIGURE 7.7   Sample Leikert scale for evaluating the subject's attitude.

to a numeric response by scoring a middle response as 0, negative responses as -1 and -2, and positive responses as +1 and +2. As indicated in the sample given, to prevent the subject from just ticking all the boxes down a column a mixture of positive and negative statements should be used.

This approach can be used proactively as well as reactively. That is, a specification of the required usability of an interface can be produced while the functional specification of the software is being prepared. A very simple *usability specification* for a word processing system might be as follows.

> *The task is to open a new, empty document and type in a given paragraph which involves making some words bold and some italic. The paragraph should then be printed and the document stored in a file in the default directory.*
>
> *A subject who has very little experience of using computers should be able to complete this task within 30 minutes, making less than 10 errors, and report an overall neutral attitude. A subject who uses a computer on a semi-regular basis, at least once a week, should be able to complete the task in 15 minutes, making less than 5 errors, and report an overall positive attitude. A subject who uses a computer on a daily basis should be able to complete the task in less than 5 minutes, making no errors, and report an overall positive attitude.*

However, the major problem with this approach to usability engineering is the cost involved in performing the investigation. Improvements to the usability of an interface (or a proposed interface) can be more economically introduced by using a list of heuristics, particularly when the list is applied by an expert. One of the most widely used list of heuristics is that devised by Neilsen, and details of references which contain it are included in Appendix A.

Chapter Summary

- Text menus have many of the advantages of pull-down menu systems but they can be controlled from the keyboard and so avoid the necessity of having to transfer attention to the mouse.

- Command line systems can be the most powerful for experienced users but can be intimidating to novice users.

- The syntax of command line systems should be as regular as possible and designed with care.

- An effective help system is essential for command line interfaces.

- Feedback in a command line system should include a history list of commands issued.

- Any user interface should be effective, efficient, and enjoyable.

- Evaluation of an interface by the use of structured investigations can be very powerful, but it is also very expensive.

- Evaluation of an interface by the use of heuristics is the most cost-effective way of improving its usability, particularly when it is carried out by a usability expert.

Exercises

7.1   Extend the text menu and the command line interface to accommodate the additional facilities available in the *GeometricTuttle* class from Exercise 4.4.

7.2   Redesign, and subsequently re-implement, the *TextMenuTuttle*'s *Move* and *Turn* menus so that the user can move or turn the tuttle an arbitrary number of units. This could be accomplished, for example when moving the tuttle forward, by interposing a menu which offers two further menus labeled *tens* and *units*. The *tens* menu should offer items which move the tuttle *10, 20, 30* steps, etc. and the *units* menu items to move it *1, 2, 3* steps, etc. So if the user wanted to move the tuttle 47 steps they could activate the *Move/ Forwards/ tens/ 40* item followed by the *Move/ Forwards/ units/ 7* item.

7.3   Is the irregularity of the menu structures, some returning to the higher level after being activated and some remaining in the same state, in the *TextMenuTuttle* interface a problem for the users? To determine this, implement a version of the *TextMenuTuttle* interface which is regular in its behavior and then have two groups of users perform the same task. Observe and record their behavior.

7.4   Extend the *TextTuttle* class so that it will accept synonyms for the commands. As a minimum, each command should be allowed to be issued in its abbreviated and long form (e.g., fd and forward). Additionally, actual synonyms should be provided (e.g., tr and rt mean turn right and right turn).

7.5   Which of the four *tuttle* interfaces is the most effective? Which is the most efficient? And which is the most enjoyable? To decide upon these questions, design a standard task and have four groups of users perform the task and observe and record their behavior.

7.6   Are the results of Exercise 7.5 dependent upon the experience level of the users?

7.7   Decide upon the most acceptable name for *tuttle* commands by producing a series of diagrams which illustrate what action the *tuttle* will take and ask a sample of users what name they would give to the action. How much variability is there in the results you obtain? What is the most popular name for each action? How does the list of most popular names compare with the list of commands as presented in this chapter? What does this tell you about naming commands?

C H A P T E R   8

Undo, Load, and Save Capabilities

The *Tuttle* hierarchy lacks two aspects of functionality which are essential for a well-constructed interface and are fundamental to its usability. The first of these is an ability to *undo* a tuttle's actions, which is required to improve the *learnability* of an interface. When an undo facility is not available, a user will be reluctant to take any action as there is the possibility that the action will be incorrect and all preceding actions may have to be repeated. For example, in the sample evaluation task from the previous chapter the user may have almost completed the drawing of a house and might fear the possibility of incorrectly moving the tuttle and leaving a line in the wrong location.

When an undo facility is not available, the user is thus intimidated against actively exploring the interface. When a comprehensive undo facility is available the user is consequently encouraged to use the interface, secure in the knowledge that should a mistake be made it can easily be rectified. This is particularly so if the undo capability is complemented by a *redo* capability. However, not all actions are always undoable and this can cause its own problems if a naive user assumes that every action is undoable.

The second feature which is missing from the tuttle's functionality is one to save the drawing to a disk file and subsequently load it again. Again, for a general-purpose application, this is essential if the user is to have confidence in using the application. In the case of the *Tuttle* hierarchy, a variation of this capability can be used to log the users' actions in order to assist with the analysis of their behavior while performing the evaluation tasks.

8.1 The *Tuttle* Class Revisited

In order to extend the *TextTuttle* from the previous chapter to provide the *BufferedTuttle*, capable of implementing the undo and load/ save facilities, the *Tuttle* class from Chapter 5 will first require some small amendments. The most obvious of these are

protected inquiry methods for some **private** data attributes*: tuttleLocationIs(), tuttleDirectionIs(), penStatusIs(), tuttleForegroundIs(),* and *tuttleBackgroundIs().* Less obviously a new data attribute has to be introduced which determines if the drawing is to be updated each time a tuttle command is executed.

The reasons for these changes is that the undo capability is implemented by repeating all but the last command since the last time the screen was cleared, effectively redoing all but the last command. The commands are stored as text strings in a buffer within the *BufferedTuttle* class, which will be introduced shortly. As clearing the screen may leave the tuttle at any location, facing in any direction, with any foreground and background color, and with its pen up or down, these attributes have to be obtained and stored in order to reproduce this state at the start of an undo operation. In order to avoid the tuttle being seen to move around the screen while this happens, and to speed up the operation, the drawing on the screen is not updated while the undo is being effected. Instead the screen is only updated after all the replayed commands have been obeyed. The prototypes of the new *Tuttle* methods are listed in Table 8.1.

The Point class, an instance of which is returned by the *tuttleLocationIs()* method, contains two public integer data attributes called x and y; using it avoids having to provide two methods, which might be called *tuttleXLocationIs()* and *tuttleYLocationIs()*. The *showTuttle()* and *hideTuttle()* methods set the value of an additional *Tuttle* **private boolean** data attribute called *tuttleShowing*. This attribute is used only after each command has been processed to decide if the screen should be re*paint*ed when the *update()* method is called.

```
public void update( Graphics systemContext) {
    if ( tuttleShowing) {
        this.paint( systemContext);
    } // End if.
} // End update.
```

The *hideTuttle()* and *showTuttle()* methods are used when a sequence of methods are replayed and apparently allow the commands to be instantly repeated without the *Tuttle* being shown at the end of every action. This facility will be illustrated later in this chapter.

protected Point *tuttleLocationIs*()	Returns the current location of the tuttle.
protected int *tuttleDirectionIs*()	Returns the current direction of the tuttle.
protected boolean *penStatusIs*()	Returns **true** if the pen is down.
protected Color *tuttleForegroundIs*()	Returns the tuttle's drawing color.
protected Color *tuttleBackgroundIs*()	Returns the tuttle's background color.
protected void *clearAndReset*()	Combines a color change and a tuttle reset.
protected void *showTuttle*()	Causes the drawing not to be updated.
protected void *hideTuttle*()	Causes the drawing to be updated.

TABLE 8.1   Additional Protected *Tuttle* Methods

8.2 The *BufferedTuttle* Class, Undo Capability

The *BufferedTuttle* class introduces the capability to record the commands which have been issued to the tuttle in order that they can be replayed, or saved to a file, when required. The first part of the *BufferedTuttle* class diagram is given in Figure 8.1.

The instance attribute *commandBuffer* is where the list of commands is stored; it will be implemented as an instance of the Java **Vector** class. The single constructor is comparable with the previous *Tuttle* hierarchy constructors and the *doCommand()* method overloads the *TextTuttle doCommand()* method. The remaining **public** methods are concerned with the undo capability: the *undo()* method will undo the last undoable command, if any, and return a confirmation of the action. The *isUndoAvailable()* method will indicate if an undoable command is available and the *whatUndoIsAvailable()* method will supply a **String** describing the undoable command. The two **protected** methods store and restore the tuttle's current status. The implementation of this class, as far as the end of the constructor, is as follows.

```
0001  // Filename BufferedTuttle.java.
0002  // Extends the Tuttle class by providing a buffer to
0003  // store the commands and a text processing interface.
0004  // Provides undo, save and load capability.
0005  //
0006  // Written for the Java Interface Book Chapter 8.
```

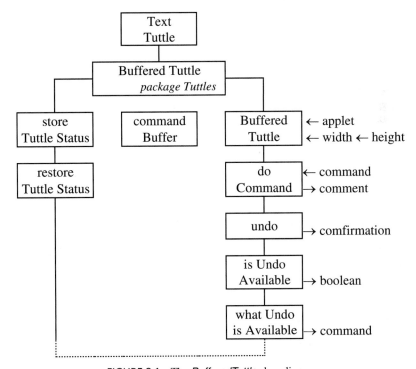

FIGURE 8.1   The *BufferedTuttle* class diagram.

```
0007   // Fintan Culwin, v 0.2, August 1997.
0008
0009   package Tuttles;
0010
0011   import java.awt.*;
0012   import java.applet.*;
0013
0014   import java.io.*;
0015   import java.util.StringTokenizer;
0016   import java.util.Vector;
0017
0018   import Tuttles.TextTuttle;
0019
0020   public class BufferedTuttle extends TextTuttle {
0021
0022   public static final int UNDO          = 12;
0023   public static final int LOAD          = 13;
0024   public static final int SAVE          = 14;
0025   public static int        MAX_COMMANDS = 15;
0026
0027   private int      startX;
0028   private int      startY;
0029   private int      startDirection;
0030   private Color    startForeground;
0031   private Color    startBackground;
0032   private boolean  startPenStatus;
0033
0034   protected Vector commandBuffer;
0035
0036      public BufferedTuttle( Applet applet, int width, int height) {
0037         super( applet, width, height);
0038         commandBuffer = new Vector();
0039         this.storeTuttleStatus();
0040      } // End BufferedTuttle constructor.
```

The manifest declarations, on lines 0022 to 0025, add manifest values for the new operations to those already provided by the *TextTuttle*. The six data attributes declared on lines 0027 to 0032 are used by the *storeTuttleStatus()* and *restoreTuttleStatus()* methods to record, or restore, the initial state of the tuttle prior to the storing, or replaying, of any undoable actions. The Vector instance, *commandBuffer*, declared on line 0034 is used to store the list of commands to be repeated when an undo action is requested. The Vector class is supplied by the JDK and instances of it are able to store an indeterminate number of Objects.

The constructor commences, on line 0037, by calling the **super** (*TextTuttle*) constructor. It then concludes by constructing an empty *commandBuffer* Vector and storing the initial tuttle status by calling the *storeTuttleStatus()* method, whose implementation is as follows.

```
0138      protected void storeTuttleStatus() {
0139
```

```
0140        Point localPoint = this.tuttleLocationIs();
0141
0142          startX           = localPoint.x;
0143          startY           = localPoint.y;
0144          startDirection   = this.tuttleDirectionIs();
0145          startForeground  = this.tuttleForegroundIs();
0146          startBackground  = this.tuttleBackgroundIs();
0147          startPenStatus   = this.penStatusIs();
0148          commandBuffer.removeAllElements();
0149      } // End storeTuttleStatus.
```

The inquiry methods of the *Tuttle* class, as previously described, are used to obtain details of the tuttle's current status which are stored in the appropriate data attributes. Before the method finishes, any commands stored in the *commandBuffer* are removed by using its *removeAllElements()* method. The implementation of the complementary *restoreTuttleStatus()* method is as follows.

```
0152        protected void restoreTuttleStatus(){
0153            this.setForeground( startForeground);
0154            this.clearAndReset( startBackground);
0155            this.setPenUp();
0156            this.turnRight( 90);
0157            this.forward( startX);
0158            this.turnLeft( 90);
0159            this.forward( startY);
0160            this.turnRight( startDirection);
0161            if ( startPenStatus) {
0162                this.setPenDown();
0163            } else {
0164                this.setPenUp();
0165            } // End if.
0166        } // End restoreTuttleStatus.
```

This method restores the tuttle's status to that when the *storeTuttleStatus()* method was last called, using methods of the *Tuttle* class and the stored data attributes. Briefly the colors are restored before the screen is cleared and the tuttle reset to its starting location. The pen is then raised and the tuttle is moved to the stored location and direction before the pen is lowered, if required.

A small optimization is included to avoid the delay in setting the foreground color which was commented upon in Exercise 4.5. Rather than setting the background color, which might result in a delay, and then immediately clearing and resetting the tuttle which would cause a further delay, a protected *clearAndReset()* method (taking a Color argument) is supplied by the *Tuttle* class this method not only clears the screen and resets the tuttle, but also sets the background color before it does so, thus avoiding any delay. This new method is called on line 0154, and is exactly equivalent to calling Tuttle.*currentBackground(anyColor)* immediately followed by Tuttle.*clearAndReset()*, but executes much faster. If this were not done, then each undo operation would take a significant time, causing users not to want to use it and resulting in reduced usability.

> **Design Advice**
>
> Optimization should only be performed when an artifact is known to be working. This usability problem was discovered, and the optimization implemented, only when the interface had been completed and was being tested.

The first part of the implementation of the *doCommand()* method is as follows. The basis of its design is to pass on the command to the *TextTuttle doCommand()* method unless the command is *undo*, *load,* or *save*, which require special consideration.

```
0045    public String doCommand( String theCommand) {
0046
0047    StringTokenizer tokenizer = new StringTokenizer( theCommand);
0048    String          firstTerm = null;
0049    String          theReply  = null;
0050    int             thisCommand;
0051
0052      if ( tokenizer.hasMoreTokens()) {
0053          firstTerm   = tokenizer.nextToken().toLowerCase();
0054          thisCommand = identifyCommand( firstTerm);
0055
0056          if ( thisCommand == UNDO) {
0057              theReply = this.undo();
0058          } else if ( thisCommand == LOAD) {
0059              theReply = this.loadDrawing( tokenizer);
0060          } else if ( thisCommand == SAVE) {
0061              theReply = this.saveDrawing( tokenizer);
0062          } else {
0063              theReply = super.doCommand( theCommand);
0064          } // End if.
```

The three new commands are detected on lines 0056 to 0061 and cause the appropriate method of the *BufferedTuttle* class to be called, otherwise the command is passed to the parent, *TextTuttle, doCommand()* method for the tuttle to attempt to execute it. In order for the new commands to be identified on line 0054, an overriding *identifyCommand()*, implemented as follows, is called.

```
0081    public int identifyCommand( String toIdentify) {
0082
0083    int identified  = UNKNOWN;
0084
0085      if ( toIdentify.equals( "undo")) {
0086        identified = UNDO;
0087      } else if ( toIdentify.equals( "load")) {
0088        identified = LOAD;
0089      } else if ( toIdentify.equals( "save")) {
0090        identified = SAVE;
0091      } else {
0092        identified = super.identifyCommand( toIdentify);
```

```
0093              } // End if.
0094              return identified;
0095          } // End identifyCommand.
```

On lines 0085 to 0090 the three new commands are checked and the manifest value from this class is stored in *identified* if any is recognized. Otherwise line 0092 calls the parent, *TextTuttle*, *identifyCommand()* method to attempt to identify it.

The implementation of the *undo()* command is as follows. Its basis is to restore the state of the tuttle at the start of the undoable sequence of operations stored in the *commandBuffer* and then repeat all but the last stored command.

```
0098          private String undo() {
0099
0100          int           thisCommand;
0101          StringBuffer  theReply = new StringBuffer("");
0102
0103              if ( commandBuffer.size() > 0) {
0104                  theReply.append( "undo " +
0105                  commandBuffer.elementAt( commandBuffer.size()-1));
0106                  commandBuffer.removeElementAt( commandBuffer.size()-1);
0107                  this.hideTuttle();
0108                  this.restoreTuttleStatus();
0109                  for ( thisCommand = 0;
0110                        thisCommand < commandBuffer.size();
0111                        thisCommand++) {
0112                      super.doCommand( (String) commandBuffer.elementAt(
0113                                                      thisCommand));
0114                  } // End for.
0115                  this.showTuttle();
0116              } else {
0117                  theReply.append( "Nothing to undo!");
0118              } // End if.
0119              return theReply.toString();
0120          } // End undo.
```

Line 0103 tests to make sure that there are commands stored in the *command-Buffer* and, if there are none, a suitable comment is placed into *theReply* StringBuffer on line 116. Otherwise, on line 0106 the last command in the buffer is removed after being placed, preceded by "*undo*," into *theReply*. Following this, on lines 0107 to 0108 the tuttle is hidden (so that the commands about to be replayed will not have the drawing updated after each of them has executed) and the state of the tuttle is restored to that recorded in the *BufferedTuttle* instance attributes using *restoreTuttleStatus()*. The loop on lines 0109 to 0113 extracts each command stored in the *commandBuffer* and dispatches it to the *TextTuttle doCommand()* method for execution. Following this the tuttle is shown again, by calling the *showTuttle()* method which also updates the screen. The *undo()* method concludes on line 0119 by returning the contents of *theReply*. The effect for the user is that the drawing reverts to its appearance before the last tuttle command was executed.

The commands to be replayed are placed into the *commandBuffer* in the second part of the *BufferedTuttle doCommand()* method, after they have been executed, as follows.

```
0066            if ( theReply.length() == 0) {
0067                if ( thisCommand == CLEAR_AND_RESET ||
0068                    thisCommand == CLEAR          ){
0069                this.storeTuttleStatus();
0070            } else if ( thisCommand != CLEAR          &&
0071                        thisCommand != CLEAR_AND_RESET &&
0071                        thisCommand != SAVE            &&
0072                        thisCommand != LOAD            ){
0073                commandBuffer.addElement( theCommand);
0074            } // End if.
0075        } // End if.
0076    } // End if.
0077    return theReply;
0078 } // End doCommand.
```

Line 0066 ensures that only commands which do not return a comment are stored for a possible subsequent undo. This eliminates all commands which are not recognized, all requests for help, and also all undo commands, which will return either a comment that there is nothing that can be undone or a confirmation of which command has been undone. Otherwise the two commands which cause the screen to be cleared, *clear* and *clear and reset*, are considered undoable because the tuttle is unable to remember the state of the drawing prior to these operations. They both result, on line 0069, with the *storeTuttleStatus()* method being called–this will store the current state of the tuttle and clear the *commandBuffer*. All commands, other than these two commands and the *save* and *load* commands, are subsequently added to the *commandBuffer* so that they can be subsequently undone.

The final two methods associated with the undo capability are inquiry methods which inform a client if there are any commands to undo and details of the first command which can be undone. Their implementations, presented without comment, are as follows.

```
0122    public boolean isUndoAvailable() {
0123        return ! commandBuffer.isEmpty();
0124    } // End isUndoAvailable.
0125
0126
0127    public String whatUndoIsAvailable() {
0128
0129    StringBuffer isAvailable = new StringBuffer( "");
0130
0131        if ( this.isUndoAvailable()) {
0132            isAvailable.append( commandBuffer.elementAt(
0133                            commandBuffer.size()-1));
0134        } // End if.
0135        return isAvailable.toString();
0136    } // End whatUndoIsAvailable.
```

8.3 Incorporating the Undo Capability into the Interfaces

The easiest interface to adapt for the inclusion of the undo capability is the *Comand-LineTuttle* interface which, apart from the help system, will require no changes once all references to *TextTuttle* have been replaced with *BufferedTuttle*. The command *"undo"* will either cause the last command to be undone or produce a message that there is no command to undo. This is illustrated in Figure 8.2.

The help system requires minor changes to add *"undo"* to the list of available help topics and to allow it to respond to requests for help about undo. This interface will allow the undo capability to be easily demonstrated, and tested, before the more extensive changes to the other interfaces are implemented.

The next most straightforward change is to the *SemiDirectTuttle* interface, particularly if the *TuttleButton* class has been extended as suggested in Exercise 5.1 or the *ToggleTuttleButton Button* class from Exercise 5.3 is available. To demonstrate the changes an additional *TuttleButton* instance capable of being set insensitive, called *undoButton*, is added to the interface alongside the changed *penUpDown ToggleTuttleButton Button* instance. The appearance of this part of the revised interface is shown in Figure 8.3.

To implement undoability the *SemiDirectTuttleInterface* class will have to be extended to supply methods called *setUndoAvailable()* and *setUndoUnavailable()*, which will set the sensitivity of the *undoButton* as appropriate. The *actionPerformed()* method in the *SemiDirectTuttle* class will have to use *theTuttle*'s *isUndoAvailable()* method, every time it processes the command, and set the *undoButton*'s sensitivity as required. For example, if the forward command is executed the *isUndoAvailable()* method will return true and the interface's *setUndoAvailable()* method will be called to make sure that the undo button is sensitive, as shown as in the left-hand image in Figure 8.3. Alternatively, if the clear command is executed *isUndoAvailable()* will return false and *setUndoUnavailable()* will set the undo button insensitive, as shown in the right-hand image in Figure 8.3.

The *undoButton* itself will have its *actionCommand* attribute set to the string *"undo"* so that, whenever it is sensitive and pressed, the command *"undo"* will be sent to the *SemiDirectTuttle*'s *actionPerformed()* method and passed on the *BufferedTuttle theTuttle* instance to be executed, as previously described.

The changes to the *TextMenuTuttle* are a little more complex. The *TextMenuTuttleInterface* class will have to provide an additional manifest menu state value called *UNDO_MENU*, an additional **String** instance attribute called *undoCommand*, and a method to set the value of this attribute called *setUndoCommand()*. The value of the *undoCommand* attribute will be used to decide if the last command can be undone. If

FIGURE 8.2   The revised *CommandLineTuttle* interface showing undo capability.

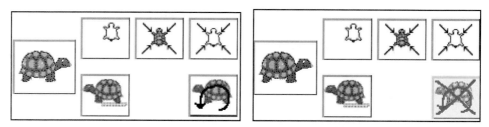

FIGURE 8.3   The revised *SemiDirectTuttle* interface showing undo available (left) and undo not available (right).

it contains an empty string, then undo is known to be unavailable. Otherwise, if *undo-Command* does not contain an empty string, not only is undo known to be available but the string also contains the text of the command to be undone.

Like the *SemiDirectTuttle* class, the *TextMenuTuttle* class will have to check if undo is available at the end of its *keyPressed()* listener method. If undo is not available, it will send an empty string as an argument to *theInterface*'s *setUndoCommand()*, otherwise undo is available and the command string obtained from *theTuttles*'s *whatUndoIsAvailable()* method will be sent as an argument, as follows.

```
// Changes required at the end of TextMenuTuttle doCommand()
if ( theTuttle.isUndoAvailable()) {
    theInterface.setUndoCommand( theTuttle.whatUndoIsAvailable());
} else {
    theInterface.setUndoCommand( "");
} // End if.
```

The new *UNDO_MENU* branch of the switch structure in the *TextMenuTuttleInterface*'s *setMenuState()* method will have to provide different menus depending upon the availability of an *undoCommand*, as follows.

```
// New branch in the TextMenuTuttle setMenuSate() method.
case UNDO_MENU:
if ( undoCommand.length() == 0) {
    menuArea.setText( topLevelMenu +
                "\n    Undo is not available.");
} else {
    menuArea.setText( topLevelMenu +
                "\n    Undo " + undoCommand +
                " : Yes No");
} // End if.
break;
```

This branch will be called when the user activates the new *Undo* option on the top-level menu by pressing '*U*' or '*u*'. The test on the **if** condition will be **true** if the *undoCommand* is empty and will result in the "*Undo is not available.*" message being shown to the user, as illustrated in the upper image in Figure 8.4. Otherwise, if *undo-*

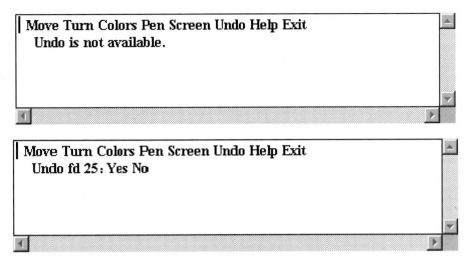

FIGURE 8.4   The revised *TextMenuTuttle* interface showing
undo not available (top) and undo available (bottom).

Command is not empty, its contents are catenated to ask the user if they want to undo the command which it contains. For example, if the last command executed by the tut-tle was "*fd 25*" the appearance of the menu would be as illustrated in the lower image in Figure 8.4.

The *TextMenuTuttle keyPressed()* method's **switch** structure will have to call a new method, called *undoMenu()*, whenever a key is pressed while the interface is in the *UNDO_MENU* state. This method is implemented as follows.

```
// New method in TextMenuTuttle to process key presses
// from the undo menu.
private int undoMenu( char pressed) {
int newMenuState = TextMenuTuttleInterface.UNDO_MENU;
    switch( pressed) {
    case KeyEvent.VK_ESCAPE:
    case 'N':
    case 'n':
        newMenuState = TextMenuTuttleInterface.TOP_LEVEL_MENU;
        break;
    case 'Y':
    case 'y':
        if ( theTuttle.isUndoAvailable()) {
           theTuttle.DoCommand( "undo");
        } // End if.
        newMenuState = TextMenuTuttleInterface.TOP_LEVEL_MENU;
        break;
    } // End switch.
    return newMenuState;
} // End undoMenu.
```

The method will cause the interface to remain in the *UNDO_MENU* state until either the <ESCAPE>, '*n*', '*N*', '*y*' or '*Y*' key is pressed, when it will transit back to the *TOP_LEVEL_MENU*. Before this, if the '*y*' or '*Y*' key is pressed and undo is available then the *doCommand()* method of *theTuttle* is called to effect the requested undo action. The only other changes required to the *TextMenuTuttle* interface are to the *help* system, which will have to be updated to offer help on the *undo* capability.

The changes required for the *MenuBarTuttle* interface require an additional top-level *Edit* menu containing a single *MenuItem* called *undoButton* to be added to the interface, this can be accomplished as follows.

```
// Change required in MenuBarInterface's constructor to add undo.
    editMenu = new Menu( "Edit");
        undoButton = new MenuItem( "can't undo!");
        undoButton.setEnabled( false);
        undoButton.setActionCommand( "undo");
        undoButton.addActionListener( itsListener);
        editMenu.add( undoButton);
    mainMenuBar.add( editMenu);
```

The initial state of the *undoButton MenuItem* is for it to be insensitive and show the label "*Can't undo!*"; as no commands have been issued so none can be undone. The state of the button can be changed by the new *MenuBarTuttleInterface setUndoCommand()* method, implemented as follows.

```
// New action in MenuBarInterface to control the File menu Undo item.
protected void setUndoCommand( String theCommand) {
    if ( theCommand.length() == 0) {
        undoButton.setLabel( "can't undo!");
        undoButton.setEnabled( false);
    } else {
        undoButton.setLabel( "Undo " + theCommand);.
        undoButton.setEnabled( true);
    } // End if.
} // End setUndoCommand.
```

This method is called from the end of the *MenuBarTuttle* classes' *actionPerformed()* method to indicate if undo is available and, if so, what command can be undone. The required fragment is as follows, and the appearance of the *Edit* menu in its different states is shown in Figure 8.5.

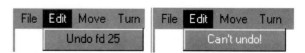

FIGURE 8.5   The revised *MainMenuTuttle* interface showing undo available (left) and undo not available (right).

```
// New step at the end of MenuBarTuttle's actionPerformed() method.
if ( theTuttle.isUndoAvailable()) {
    theInterface.setUndoCommand( theTuttle.whatUndoIsAvailable());
} else {
    theInterface.setUndoCommand( "");
} // End if.
```

When the *undoButton* MenuItem is sensitive and activated by the user, the actionCommand string "*undo*" will be passed in the ActionEvent to the *MenuBarTuttle*'s *actionPerformed()* method, where it will be passed onward to the *BufferedTuttle*'s *doCommand()* method to be effected. As with the other three interfaces, the *help* system will require minor changes to provide help for the undo capability.

8.4 The *BufferedTuttle* Class, Save and Load Capability

The second major addition to the functionality of the *TextTuttle* class is an ability to save and load drawings from and to the tuttle instance. This is accomplished by two additional methods called *saveDrawing()* and *loadDrawing()*, both of which require a *StringTokenizer* (assumed to contain a single String indicating a filename) to be passed to them. The save capability is implemented by writing the values of the eight attributes defining the initial state of the tuttle to the file and following them with the list of commands which are stored in the *commandBuffer*. The load capability is complementary to this–first restoring the state of the tuttle, using the first part of the file, and then executing all the commands remaining in the file. The implementation of the *saveDrawing()* method is as follows.

```
0171    private String saveDrawing( StringTokenizer tokenizer) {
0172
0173    int         thisCommand;
0174    String      theReply    = "";
0175    String      theFileName;
0176    PrintWriter saveHere;
0177
0178      if ( tokenizer.countTokens() != 1) {
0179         theReply = new String( "Save must be followed only by the " +
0180                        "name of the file to save the drawing to.");
0181      } else {
0182         theFileName = (String) tokenizer.nextToken();
0183         try {
0184            saveHere = new PrintWriter( new FileOutputStream(
0184                                                    theFileName));
0185            saveHere.println( this.identifyColorAsString(
0185                                                    startBackground));
0186            saveHere.println( "fg " +
0187               this.identifyColorAsString( startForeground));
0188            saveHere.println( "pu");
0189            saveHere.println( "tr 90");
```

```
0190                    saveHere.println( "fd " + startX);
0191                    saveHere.println( "tl 90");
0192                    saveHere.println( "fd " + startY);
0193                    saveHere.println(  "tr " + startDirection);
0194              if ( startPenStatus) {
0195                 saveHere.println( "pd");
0196              } else {
0197                 saveHere.println( "pu");
0198              } // End if.
0199
0200              for ( thisCommand = 0;
0201                      thisCommand < commandBuffer.size();
0202                      thisCommand++) {
0203                 saveHere.println( (String)
0204                                      commandBuffer.elementAt(
                                          thisCommand));
0205              } // End for.
0206              saveHere.close();
0207           } catch ( IOException exception) {
0208              theReply = new String( "The drawing could not be saved  +
0209                                    "to theFileName + ".");
0210           } // End try/ catch.
0211        } // End if.
0212        return theReply;
0213     } // End saveDrawing.
```

As with all other *Tuttle* methods, successful completion of the command will result in an empty String being returned from the method. If the save operation cannot be carried out successfully, the String returned will not be empty and will contain an explanation.

The *saveDrawing()* method commences by ensuring that there is a single token remaining in the *StringTokenizer* instance passed to the method from the *BufferedTuttle*'s *doCommand()* method. If it does not contain a single token, a suitable comment is placed into *theReply* on lines 0179 and 0180. Otherwise, on line 0182, the String is extracted from the *tokenizer* and stored in the local *theFileName* variable.

The actions which follow involve input–output operations which may cause an IOException to be thrown. Accordingly they are contained within a **try**/**catch** structure, between lines 0183 and 0210, which, if an exception is thrown, places a suitable message into *theReply*. The **try** part of the structure commences, on line 0184, by opening an anonymous *FileOutputStream*, using *theFileName* to identify a file on the local disk. This anonymous instance is used immediately as the argument to a PrintWriter constructor whose identity is recorded in *saveHere*. The Java PrintWriter class provides facilities for a Stream of unicode text characters to be output from an artifact, in this case to be output to a file on the local disk.

Having opened a Stream to the local disk, line 0184 writes the name of the tuttle's background color to the file, using the private class-wide *identifyColorAsString()* method whose implementation will be given later. This is followed by writing to the Stream the sequence of tuttle commands required to restore it to the state it was in before the first command was stored in its *commandBuffer*. These commands conclude, on lines 0194 to 0198, with a definite *pen down* or *pen up* command to ensure that there are always eight commands in this sequence, for reasons which will be explained when the *loadDrawing()* method is described. The reason why the background color is treated as a special case at the start of the sequence will also be explained.

After the initialization sequence has been written, lines 0200 to 0205 write all the commands from the *commandBuffer* to the **Stream** and the method will conclude by returning the contents of *theReply*, after the **Stream** has been closed on line 0206. The implementation of the *identifyColorAsString()* method is as follows, and is in some senses the inverse of the *identifyColor()* method from the *TextTuttle* class.

```
0259   private static String identifyColorAsString( Color toIdentify) {
0260
0261   String theString = null;
0262
0263     if ( toIdentify.equals( Color.black)) {
0264        theString = new String( "black") ;
0265     } else if ( toIdentify.equals( Color.white)) {
0266        theString = new String( "white");
0267     } else if ( toIdentify.equals( Color.yellow)) {
0268        theString = new String( "yellow");
0269     } else if ( toIdentify.equals( Color.green)) {
0270        theString = new String( "green");
0271     } else if ( toIdentify.equals( Color.red)) {
0272        theString = new String( "red");
0273     } else if ( toIdentify.equals( Color.blue)) {
0274        theString = new String( "blue");
0275     } // End if.
0276     return theString;
0277   } // End identifyColorAsString.
```

An initial demonstration of the *saveDrawing()* method can be accomplished by using a *CommandLineTuttle* implementation unchanged from when it was used to demonstrate *undo* commands. However, it cannot be guaranteed that an applet loaded across the Web will be allowed to open a file on the local disk; accordingly, this facility can only be guaranteed to work if the applet is executed locally, using an *appletviewer* utility with suitable security settings. The contents of the file produced if the *save* command, followed by a filename, is used as soon as the applet is launched should be as follows.

```
yellow
fg blue
pu
tr 90
fd 0
tl 90
fd 0
tr 0
pd
```

For example, typing in the command "*save test.tutt*" will save the commands to a file called "*test.tutt*," which can be opened in a text editor and its contents examined. If a second "*save test.tutt*" command is given, the contents of the file will be overwritten with the new drawing, as can be similarly confirmed. The **catch** part of the **try/catch** structure can be demonstrated by making the "*test.tutt*" file read only, which should cause the exception to be thrown when the Java run-time system attempts to overwrite it, and a message explaining that the drawing could not be saved should be shown on the interface.

The *loadDrawing()* method requires an argument of the StringTokenizer class containing a single String, which will identify the file from which it should read, (and execute) the commands which are stored in it. The basis of this method is to create an input stream using the filename supplied in its *tokenizer* instance and then to restore the drawing from the commands stored in the file opened. It has to be implemented defensively as it cannot be guaranteed that the user will always indicate a file of the correct type. The implementation of this method is as follows.

```
0216    public String loadDrawing( StringTokenizer tokenizer) {
0217
0218    int          loadCount    = 0;
0219    int          thisCommand;
0220    boolean      allDone      = false;
0221    String       theReply     = "";
0222    String       theFileName;
0223    String       theCommand;
0224    BufferedReader loadFromHere = null;
0225
0226        if ( tokenizer.countTokens() != 1) {
0227            theReply = new String( "Load must be followed only by the " +
0228                        "name of the file to load the drawing from.");
0229        } else {
0230            theFileName = (String) tokenizer.nextToken();
0231            try {
0232                loadFromHere = new BufferedReader(
0233                                    new FileReader( theFileName));
0234                this.hideTuttle();
0235                theCommand = loadFromHere.readLine();
0236                if ( this.identifyColor( theCommand ) != null) {
0237                    this.clearAndReset( theCommand);
0238                } else {
0239                    throw new IOException();
0240                } // End if.
0241                while ( !allDone) {
0242                    theCommand = loadFromHere.readLine();
0243                    if ( theCommand == null ) {
0244                        allDone = true;
0245                    } else {
0246                        this.doCommand( theCommand);
```

```
0247                    if ( loadCount++ == 8) {
0248                        this.storeTuttleStatus();
0249                      } // End if.
0250                  } // End if.
0251                } // End while.
0252                loadFromHere.close();
0253            } catch ( IOException exception) {
0254                theReply = new String( "The drawing could not be " +
0255                                "loaded from " + theFileName + ".");
0256            } // End try/ catch.
0257            this.showTuttle();
0258        } // End if.
0259        return theReply;
0260    } // End loadDrawing.
```

The first part of the implementation of this method, on lines 0226 to 0233, is somewhat similar to the *saveDrawing()* method. It will place a message in *theReply* if the *tokenizer* does not contain a single token or attempt to open a BufferedReader Stream, identified as *loadFromHere*, if it does.

After the tuttle has been hidden, the first line is read from the file on line 0235. If this file was written by the *saveDrawing()* class, then this line should contain one of the six recognized color names and this is tested on line 0236. If the name is recognized, the version of the *Tuttle clearAndReset()* method which requires the name of a color as an argument is called on line 0237, in order to clear the screen to the color indicated and prepare the tuttle in its initial state. If the first line of the file does not contain a recognized color name, an IOException is **throw**n on line 0244 to prevent any further attempt to read from the file and cause an error to be reported from the method. This special processing of the first line serves two purposes: first to attempt to guarantee that this is a file containing tuttle commands, and second to optimize the setting of a new background color, as discussed with the *restoreTuttleStatus()* method.

If the file is to be processed, the loop starting on line 0241 will read each command from the file and pass it the *doCommand()* method to be processed. After the first eight commands have been processed, which as emphasized earlier will restore the tuttle to its initial state, the *storeTuttleStatus()* method is called on line 0248 to initialize the instance attributes and clear the *commandBuffer*. The effect of this is to restore the *commandBuffer* to exactly the state it was in when the drawing was saved, allowing undo capability to be offered.

An attempt to read beyond the end of the file by using readLine() will not throw an exception but will return a **null** string. This consideration is used, on lines 0243 and 0244, to set the *allDone* flag which will terminate the loop; subsequently, the Stream will be closed and the empty contents of *theReply* returned from the method. However if an implicit or explicit IOException is thrown, lines 0254 to 0255 place an error message in *theReply* to be returned from the method.

As with the *saveDrawing()* method, this method can be conveniently demonstrated by using the *CommandLineTuttle* applet, running locally, to open a file ("*open test.tutt*") which was saved from the applet when the *saveDrawing()* method was demonstrated. The error message can be seen by requesting that a file which does not exist be opened or by opening a file which is known not to contain a suitable sequence of tuttle commands.

8.5 The *MenuBarTuttle* Interface, Open Operations

Only the *MenuBarTuttle* interface will be upgraded to allow drawings to be saved and loaded from the application; the *CommandLine* interface requires no further changes. The upgrading of the other two interfaces will be left for the end of chapter exercises.

A *load* operation has, by convention, become known as an *open* operation in an application main menu bar system, and the facility will be described as such in this discussion. The *open* facilities are being described before the *save* and *save as* facilities as they are very similar, but a little simpler. The design pattern which is presented in this, and the next section, can be used for any application main menu bar user interface which has to offer open and save capability.

The open capability is supplied by two classes. The first, called *TuttleOpenDialog*, extends the Java FileDialog class and allows the user to navigate the local disk structure and indicate the file which should be opened. The second class, called *TuttleOpenErrorDialog*, is used when the file indicated cannot be opened, for any reason, and informs the user of the failure of the open operation. The state transition diagram of the *openInterface* is presented in Figure 8.6.

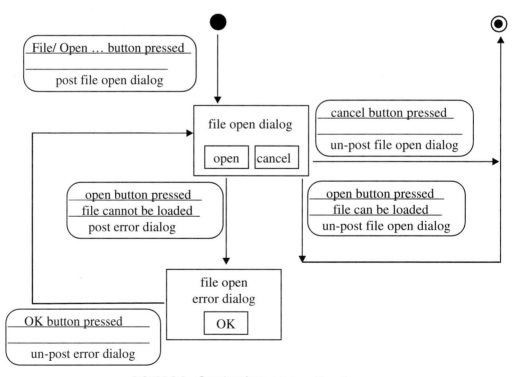

FIGURE 8.6 *OpenInterface*, state transition diagram.

The initial transition, shown on the top left of the diagram, is taken in response to the *Open …* button of the *File* menu being pressed and results in a *file open dialog* being posted. This dialog differs between environments, but allows the user to navigate the directory structure and select, or enter, a filename. All *file open dialog*s provide a *cancel* button which, if pressed, will cause the dialog to be un-posted and the interface will exit via its terminal transition, shown on the top right, without attempting to load the file.

Otherwise the user will at some stage press the *open* button and if they have selected, or entered, the name of a valid *tuttle* command file it will result in the drawing being successfully loaded, the *file open dialog* being un-posted, and the interface exiting via the transition shown at the lower right of the *file open dialog* state.

However, if the file indicated when the *open* button is pressed cannot be successfully loaded, for any reason, the *file open error dialog* will be posted, shown by the lower left transition of the *file open dialog* state This will inform the user that the file could not be opened; when the user presses the *OK* button the interface will return to the *file open dialog* state, from where a new file can be indicated, or the interface can be canceled.

In order to build this interface, an *Open …* MenuItem will have to be added to the *File* menu by using the same techniques introduced in Chapter 6. A *Save …* and a *Save As …* MenuItem will also have to be added, as well as separators, producing the completed *File* menu shown in Figure 8.7.

When the *Open …* menu item is activated the *MenuBarTuttle*'s *actionPerformed()* method, upgraded as follows, will identify the origin by the "*open*" *actionCommand* on line 0091. This will cause the *setVisible()* method of an instance of the *TuttleOpenDialog* named *openDialog*, which was constructed in the *MenuBarTuttle init()* method, to be called with the argument **true**. The class diagram of the *OpenDialog* class is presented in Figure 8.8.

```
——        // MenuBarTuttle actionPerformed() method, Open upgrade.
0091        if ( theCommand.equals( "open")) {
0092            openDialog.setVisible( true);
```

FIGURE 8.7   *MenuBarTuttle File* menu
including *Open*, *Save,* and *Save As* items.

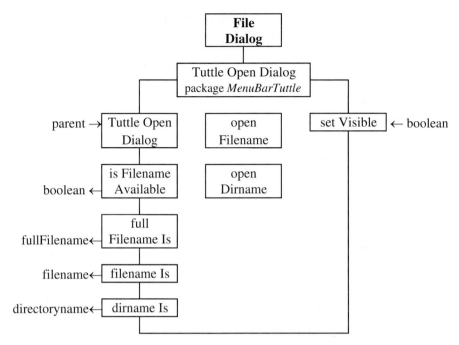

FIGURE 8.8 The *TuttleOpenDialog* class diagram.

```
0093            } else if ( theCommand.equals( "loadit")) {
0095              if ( openDialog.isFilenameAvailable()) {
0096                tuttlesReply = theTuttle.doCommand( "load " +
0097                                          openDialog.fullFilenameIs());
0098              if ( tuttlesReply.length() > 0 ) {
0099                openErrorDialog.setMessage( "The file " +
0100                                          openDialog.filenameIs() +
0101                                          "\nin the directory\n"   +
0102                                          openDialog.dirnameIs()   +
0103                                          "\ncould not be opened");
0104                openErrorDialog.setVisible( true);
0105              } // End if.
0106            } // End if.
0107
0108            } else if ( theCommand.equals( "exit")) {
—              // Rest of the method as before.
```

The *TuttleOpenDialog* class extends the AWT FileDialog class and encapsulates the filename and the directory name of any file indicated by the user when the dialog is posted, using its *setVisible()* method. The *isFilenameAvailable()* method returns **false** until the user has indicated the file to be opened and the *filenameIs()* and *dirnameIs()* methods return copies of the appropriate attribute. The *fullFilenameIs()* returns the two attributes catenated together. All of its methods are **protected** as they are only intended to be called from within the *MenuBarTuttle* package, however, the *setVisible()* method overrides an existing **public** method and so has to be declared **public**.

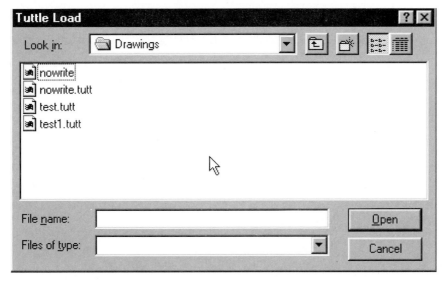

FIGURE 8.9   The *TuttleOpenDialog* in the Windows 95 environment.

The appearance of an *OpenDialog* instance, when running in the Windows 95 environment, is shown in Figure 8.9.

The major methods of the JAVA AWT FileDialog class, which itself extends the Dialog class, are given in Table 8.2.

The implementation of the *TuttleOpenDialog* class, as far as the end of its constructor, is as follows. The constructor is comparable to the Dialog constructors from Chapter 6. It commences, on line 0022, by calling its parent (FileDialog) constructor, explicitly indicating LOAD mode with the parent Frame indicated and a title passed in the first two arguments. The identity of the parent Window and its ActionListener are stored in its instance attributes before the constructor concludes.

```
0001  // Filename TuttleOpenDialog.java.
0002  // Supplies a Dialog containing an exit/ yes/ no
0003  // question and sends ActionEvent if yes replied.
0004  //
0005  // Written for Java Interface book chapter 8.
0006  // Fintan Culwin, v 0.2, August 1997.
0007
0008  package MenuBarTuttle;
0009
0010  import java.awt.*;
0011  import java.awt.event.*;
0012
0013  class TuttleOpenDialog extends FileDialog {
0014
0015  private String         openFilename = null;
0016  private String         openDirname  = null;
0017  private Window         itsParentWindow;
0018  private ActionListener itsListener;
```

constructors

FileDialog (Frame *itsParent*,
            String *itsTitle*)
 FileDialog (Frame   *itsParent*,
            String *itsTitle*,
            int   *itsMode*)
	Constructs a new FileDialog configured for loading a file, unless *itsMode* (*LOAD* or *SAVE*) indicates otherwise.

instance methods

public void setDirectory(String *setTo*) **public** String getDirectory()	Sets, or obtains, the current directory of the dialog, does not change if *setTo* is invalid.
public void setFile(String *setTo*) **public** String getFile()	Sets, or obtains, the current filename of the dialog, does not change if *setTo* is invalid.
public int *getMode*()	Returns the mode (LOAD or SAVE) of the dialog.

TABLE 8.2   Major resources of the FileDialog Class

```
0019
0020        protected TuttleOpenDialog( Frame          itsParentFrame,
0021                                    ActionListener listener) {
0022          super( itsParentFrame, "Tuttle Open", FileDialog.LOAD);
0023          itsParentWindow = (Window) itsParentFrame;
0024          itsListener = listener;
0025        } // End TuttleOpenDialog constructor.
```

The FileDialog setVisible() method differs from the Dialog setVisible() method in that, when called with the argument **true** to make it visible, it *blocks* until it is dismissed. So when a FileDialog is shown nothing else can happen in the application until it is dismissed, whereupon flow of control remains in the same method and continues with the next line in sequence. The overriding *TuttleOpenDialog setVisible()* method is implemented as follows.

```
0028        public void setVisible( boolean showIt) {
0029
0030          String     tempDirname;
0031          String     tempFilename;
0032          Point      itsParentsLocation;
0033          Dimension  itsParentsSize;
0034          Point      itsLocation;
0035          Dimension  itsSize;
0036
0037
```

```
0038               if ( showIt) {
0039                   itsParentsLocation = itsParentWindow.getLocationOnScreen();
0040                   itsParentsSize     = itsParentWindow.getSize();
0041                   itsSize            = this.getSize();
0042                   itsLocation        = new Point();
0043
0044                   itsLocation.x = itsParentsLocation.x +
0045                                       itsParentsSize.width/2 -
0046                                       itsSize.width/2;
0047                   itsLocation.y = itsParentsLocation.y +
0048                                       itsParentsSize.height/2 -
0049                                       itsSize.height/2;
0050               this.setLocation( itsLocation);
0051
0052                   openFilename = null;
0053                   openDirname  = null;
0054               this.setDirectory( "");
0055               this.setFile( "");
0056
0057               super.setVisible( true);
0058
0059                   tempDirname  = this.getDirectory();
0060               if ( ( tempDirname != null)) {
0061                   openDirname  = new String( tempDirname);
0062               } // End if.
0063                   tempFilename = this.getFile();
0064               if ( ( tempFilename != null)) {
0065                   openFilename = new String( tempFilename);
0066                   itsListener.actionPerformed( new ActionEvent( this,
0067                                               ActionEvent.ACTION_PERFORMED,
0068                                               "loadit"));
0069           } else {
0070               super.setVisible( false);
0071           } // End if.
0072       } // End setVisible.
```

The overriding aspect of this method is only concerned with situations where it is called with a **true** argument, because in situations where it is called with a **false** argument it indirects immediately to the **super** setVisible() method on line 0070. Otherwise, execution of the method commences between lines 0039 and 0050 by positioning the dialog with respect to *itsParent* window, as was first explained in Chapter 3. Before the dialog is actually made visible, on lines 0052 to 0055 the Directory and File attributes of the FileDialog are set to empty Strings and the two corresponding attributes of the *TuttleOpenDialog* class are set to **null** Strings.

The dialog is now shown to the user by calling its parent setVisible() method on line 0057. As explained this will block until it is dismissed, whereupon flow of control will continue with line 0059. Lines 0059 to 0066 retrieve the *directory* attribute from the FileDialog and, if it is not **null**, store a copy in the *TuttleOpenDialog openDirname* attribute. Lines 0063 to 0068 do the same for the **filename** attribute storing it in the *openFilename* attribute and also, if the value is not **null**, cause an ActionEvent argument containing the actionCommand "*loadit*" to be sent to *itsListener*'s *actionPerformed()* method. A **null** Filename would indicate that the *Cancel* button was pressed to dismiss the dialog; a non-**null** Filename indicates the *Open* button.

The implementation of the remaining *TuttleOpenDialog* methods can be presented, without comment, as follows.

```
0075        protected boolean isFilenameAvailable() {
0076            return ( openFilename != null);
0077        } // End isFilenameAvailable.
0078
0079        protected String filenameIs(){
0080            return new String( openFilename);
0081        } // End filenameIs.
0082
0083        protected String dirnameIs() {
0084            return new String( openDirname);
0085        } // End dirnameIs.
0086
0087        protected String fullFilenameIs() {
0088            return new String( openDirname + openFilename);
0089        } // End fullFilenameIs.
0090    } // End TuttleOpenDialog.
```

The ActionListener registered with the *TuttleOpenDialog* instance is the *MenuBarTuttle* applet and so is its *actionPerformed()* method, shown on page 242, which will be called when the user dismisses the *openDialog*. Line 0093 of the *actionPerformed()* method will detect the "*loadit*" actionCommand and if the *openDialog isFilenameAvailable()* returns **true**, indicating that the user dismissed the dialog with the *Open* and not the *Cancel* button, lines 0096 and 0097 will call *theTuttle doCommand()* method passing as an argument "*load*" followed by the full filename, obtained by using the *openDialog fullFilenameIs()* method.

If the file loads without any difficulties, then the *String* returned from *doCommand()* will be empty and no further steps need be taken. Otherwise there were difficulties in opening, or loading, the file and, on lines 0099 to 0104, an instance of the *TuttleOpenErrorDialog* class, called *openErrorDialog*, is shown after informing it of the reason why the file could not be opened. The class diagram for the *TuttleOpenError-Dialog* class is shown in Figure 8.10.

The design and implementation of this class is also very similar to the dialogs from Chapter 6. It differs by having to show the user a different message every time it is displayed and, to support this requirement, the *setReason()* method is supplied.

The constructor requires a *parent* Frame and an ActionListener as arguments, as with previous dialog classes. The dialog presented to a user contains a Button instance called *okButton* and a MessageCanvas instance called *message*. The *setReason()* will install its String argument explaining *theReason* why the dialog was posted in its MessageCanvas instance. The implementation of this class, as far as the end of its constructor, is as follows.

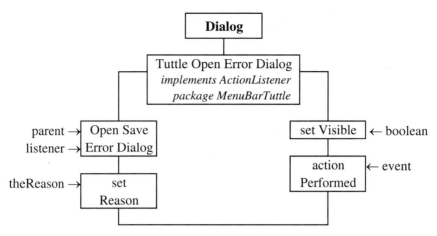

FIGURE 8.10   The *TuttleOpenErrorDialog* class diagram.

```
0001   // Filename TuttleOpenErrorDialog.java.
0002   // Supplies a Dialog containing to report any problems
0003   // encountered when opening a tuttle drawing file.
0004   //
0005   // Written for Java Interface book chapter 8.
0006   // Fintan Culwin, v 0.2, August 1997.
0007
0009   package MenuBarTuttle;
0010
0012   import java.awt.*;
0013   import java.awt.event.*;
0014
0015   import MessageCanvas;
0016
0017   class TuttleOpenErrorDialog extends    Dialog
0018                              implements ActionListener {
0019
0020   private Window         itsParentWindow;
0021   private ActionListener itsListener;
0022
0023   private Button         okButton;
0024   private Panel          buttonPanel;
0025   private MessageCanvas   message;
0026
0027      protected TuttleOpenErrorDialog( Frame           itsParentFrame,
0028                                   ActionListener listener) {
0029
0030         super( itsParentFrame, "Tuttle Open Error!", true);
0031         this.setFont( itsParentFrame.getFont());
0032         this.setBackground( itsParentFrame.getBackground());
0033         itsParentWindow = (Window) itsParentFrame;
0034         itsListener     = listener;
0035
```

```
0036          okButton = new Button( "OK");
0037          okButton.addActionListener( this);
0038          buttonPanel = new Panel();
0039          buttonPanel.setBackground( Color.white);
0040          buttonPanel.add( okButton);
0041
0042       this.add( buttonPanel, "South");
0043    } // End TuttleOpenErrorDialog constructor.
```

This constructor does not construct the MessageCanvas instance *message*, which is the responsibility of the *setReason()* method as follows.

```
0046    public void setReason( String theReason) {
0047       message = new MessageCanvas( theReason);
0048       message.setBackground( Color.white);
0049       this.add( message, "Center");
0050       this.pack();
0051    } // End setReason.
```

Each time the dialog is posted a new *MessageCanvas* instance is constructed and installed, requiring the dialog to be packed in order to allow the changed size of the *MessageCanvas* to be accommodated. Any existing *MessageCanvas* instance is effectively abandoned when the new instance is created and added, and will be garbage collected in due course. The *setVisible()* method does not differ significantly from previous *setVisible()* methods and is presented here for the sake of completeness.

```
0054    public void setVisible( boolean showIt) {
0055
0056    Point          itsParentsLocation;
0057    Dimension      itsParentsSize;
0058    Point          itsLocation;
0059    Dimension      itsSize;
0060
0061       if ( showIt) {
0062          itsParentsLocation = itsParentWindow.getLocationOnScreen();
0063          itsParentsSize     = itsParentWindow.getSize();
0064          itsSize            = this.getSize();
0065          itsLocation        = new Point();
0066
0067          itsLocation.x = itsParentsLocation.x +
0068                          itsParentsSize.width/2 -
0069                          itsSize.width/2;
0070          itsLocation.y = itsParentsLocation.y +
0071                          itsParentsSize.height/2 -
0072                          itsSize.height/2;
0073          this.setLocation( itsLocation);
0074       } // End if.
0075       super.setVisible( showIt);
0076    } // End setVisible.
```

The appearance of a *TuttleOpenErrorDialog* is shown in Figure 8.11.

FIGURE 8.11   The *TuttleOpenErrorDialog*
reporting an error opening a file.

The ActionListener registered with this dialog's "*OK*" button is itself, so when the button is pressed the *TuttleOpenErrorDialog ActionPerformed()* method will be called as follows.

```
0079    public void actionPerformed( ActionEvent event) {
0080        this.setVisible( false);
0081        itsListener.actionPerformed( new ActionEvent( this,
0082                                ActionEvent.ACTION_PERFORMED,
0083                                "open"));
0084    } // End actionPerformed.
```

The method first hides the dialog and then calls *itsListener*'s *actionPerformed()* method passing as an argument an ActionEvent containing "*open*" in its actionCommand attribute. The identity of *itsListener*, established as the dialog was constructed, is the *menuBarTuttle* applet and so it is the *actionPerformed()* method shown on page 241 which will be called. The "*open*" command received from this dialog is indistinguishable from an "*open*" command received from the '*Open …*' button of the *File* menu and so it will result in the *openFileDialog* being posted, as required by the STD shown in Figure 8.6.

8.6 The *MenuBarTuttle,* Save Operations

The *SaveInterface* is offered to the user as "*Save …*" and "*Save As …*" items on the *File* menu. A *save* request differs from a *save as* request in that *save* assumes that there is an *established filename* which can be used to save the file with, whereas *save as* will require the user to explicitly indicate the filename. A filename is *established* as a result of a successful open or save operation. The state transition diagram for the *Save interface* is presented in Figure 8.12.

In this design, if a *save* request is made when there is not an established filename then the same initial transition as the *save as* request, shown at the top of the diagram, is taken. This transition leads to a *file save dialog* and onwards from there, with further

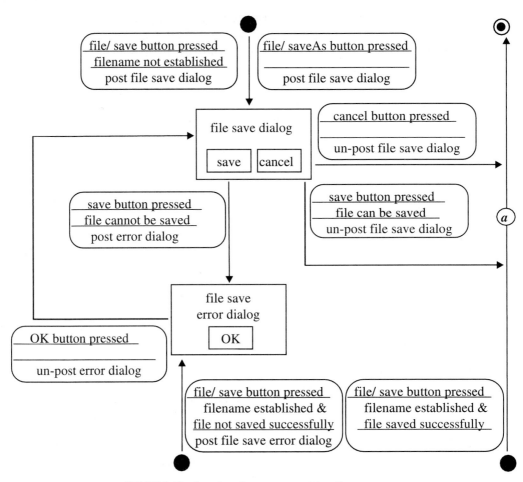

FIGURE 8.12   Save interface, state transition diagram.

transitions corresponding to those of the *Open interface*. However if there is an established filename which, for some reason, cannot be saved successfully then the lower left initial transition will be taken leading straight to the *file save error dialog*, and onwards from there to the *file save dialog*.

The last initial transition, on the lower right, is taken in response to a *save* request with an established filename and when the file is saved successfully. This transition has only one path and leads directly through the interface to the terminal state, without posting any dialogs. This behavior is very acceptable to an experienced user as it allows a *save* to be easily performed. However, it can be very unnerving to a very inexperienced user who might use the *save* option several times in succession, looking for a confirmation that the operation has completed successfully.

One possible solution to this problem might be to implement a *confirmation dialog* which can be posted from the right transition at the point labeled **a** in the diagram and, when its *OK* button is pressed, continues to the terminal state. To accommodate experienced users an *Options …* dialog can be attached to the *Help* menu, which allows the *confirmation dialog* to be bypassed. This refinement will be left to an end of chapter exercise. The open interface does not need such a confirmation because as the consequences of loading the file will be immediately visible to the user

---

Design Advice

Designing for inexperienced and experienced users increases the complexity of the interface and its implementation. However, the experienced users who it benefits are the most likely to notice the care you have taken.

The implementation of the *Save interface* is very similar to the *Open interface*, requiring *TuttleSaveDialog* and *TuttleSaveErrorDialog* classes. The *TuttleSaveDialog* supplies two additional **public** methods called *setFullFilename()* and *clearFullFilename()*, which allow the *saveFilename* and *saveDirname* instance attributes to be manipulated from outside the class. They are required in order to realize the established filename capability as described; they not only manipulate the attributes but also set the title shown on the applet's Frame, whose identity is recorded by the constructor, in order to indicate the full path of the established filename, if any. The implementation of the parts of the *MenuBarTuttle's actionPerformed()* method which deal with opening and saving are as follows.

```
0098        if ( theCommand.equals( "open")) {
0099            openDialog.setVisible( true);
0100        } else if ( theCommand.equals( "loadit")) {
0101            if ( openDialog.isFilenameAvailable()) {
0102                tuttlesReply = theTuttle.doCommand( "load " +
0103                                        openDialog.fullFilenameIs());
0104                if ( tuttlesReply.length() > 0 ) {
0105                    openErrorDialog.setReason( "The file " +
0106                                        openDialog.filenameIs() +
0107                                        "\nin the directory\n"    +
0108                                        openDialog.dirnameIs()   +
0109                                        "\ncould not be opened");
0010                    openErrorDialog.setVisible( true);
0111                    saveDialog.clearFullFilename();
0112                } else {
0113                    saveDialog.setFullFilename( openDialog.filenameIs(),
0114                                        openDialog.dirnameIs());
0115                } // End if.
0116            } // End if.
0117
0118        } else if ( theCommand.equals( "saveas")) {
0119            saveDialog.setVisible( true);
0120        } else if ( theCommand.equals( "save")) {
0121            if ( saveDialog.isFilenameAvailable()) {
0122                this.actionPerformed( new ActionEvent( this,
0123                                ActionEvent.ACTION_PERFORMED,
0124                                "saveit"));
0125            } else {
0126                saveDialog.setVisible( true);
```

```
0127                  } // End if.
0128               } else if ( theCommand.equals( "saveit")) {
0129                  tuttlesReply = theTuttle.doCommand( "save " +
0130                                          saveDialog.fullFilenameIs());
0131                  if ( tuttlesReply.length() > 0 ) {
0132                     saveErrorDialog.setReason(
0133                                 "The drawing could not be saved to " +
0134                                 "\nthe file " + saveDialog.filenameIs() +
0135                                 "\nin the directory\n"   +
0134                                 saveDialog.dirnameIs()   + ".");
0135                     saveErrorDialog.setVisible( true);
0136                     saveDialog.clearFullFilename();
0137                  } else {
0138                     saveDialog.setFullFilename( saveDialog.filenameIs(),
0139                                              saveDialog.dirnameIs());
0140                  } // End if.
```

The open part of this method has been upgraded to take account of the established filename requirement. A successful *open* operation will result, on lines 0113 and 0114, with a call of the *saveDialog setFullFilename()* method. This will result in the name of the file which has been opened being displayed in the title shown on the applet's Frame and allow a *Save* operation to save the drawing to the file whose identity is established by this call. An unsuccessful *open* operation will result, on line 0111, in the *saveDialog clearFullFilename()* method being called. This will ensure that there is no established filename which can be used by a save operation, and also changes the title on the Frame to indicate this.

A *Save As* ... request is detected on line 0118 and results in the *saveDialog* being made visible to the user. A *Save* request is detected on line 0120 and, if line 0121 indicates that a filename has been established, results, on lines 0122 to 0124, with the *actionPerformed()* method of **this** *MenuBarTuttle* instance being called with an Action-Event argument containing the actionCommand "*saveit*". The reasons why this is done will be explained later. If a *Save As* ... request is detected and a filename is not established, then line 0126 posts the *saveDialog()* onto the desktop in order to obtain a filename from the user.

The *TuttleSaveDialog* class is implemented in a very similar manner to the *TuttleOpenDialog* class just described. If the user selects, or enters, a filename it will cause the *actionPerformed()* method of the *MenuBarTuttle* instance being called with an ActionEvent argument containing the actionCommand "*saveit.*" The "*saveit*" actionCommand is detected on line 0128 and results, on lines 0129 and 0130, in *theTuttle*'s *doCommand()* method being called with an argument requesting a save to the established filename. This is why the *save* part of the method, on lines 0122 to 0124, indirected to this part of the method by recalling the *doCommand()* method with a "*saveit*" actionCommand.

Following the request to *theTuttle* to save the drawing, line 0131 establishes if the operation was successful by examining the reply from the tuttle. If this reply is not empty it indicates that an error occurred and, if so, lines 0132 to 0135 cause the *saveErrorDialog()* to be shown to the user with a suitable message contained within it;

following this, line 0135 clears any established filename. Otherwise, if the file was saved successfully, lines 0138 to 0139 establish the filename for any future save operations.

The *saveErrorDialog* is essentially identical to the *openErrorDialog* and, when its "*OK*" button is pressed, results in an *ActionEvent* whose *actionCommand* contains "*saveas*" being sent as an argument to a call of the *MenuBarTuttle*'s *actionPerformed()* method. The consequence, as described, will result in the *saveDialog* being shown on the screen. This, and the description just provided, indicates that this implementation conforms with the STD shown in Figure 8.12. The implementation of the *TuttleSaveDialog* class can be found in Appendix B; the *TuttleSaveErrorDialog* class does not differ significantly from the *TuttleLoadErrorDialog* class, and details of how to obtain it can be found at the start of Appendix B.

The *SaveInterface* can be demonstrated in a similar manner to the demonstration of the *OpenInterface*, ensuring that all possible paths through the state transition diagram are followed during the demonstration. This will include attempting to save using a filename which identifies a file set to read only, in order to demonstrate the ways in which the *file save error dialog* can be posted.

8.7 Logging the User's Actions

The final extension to the *Tuttles* hierarchy introduces the *LoggingTuttle* class, which supplies the facility to write a log of the user's actions to a text file. Each command logged on the file is preceded by the time, accurate to the nearest second, at which the *LoggingTuttle* instance received it.

The reason for including this class in the hierarchy is to allow the user's behavior to be recorded. This can be very useful when an elusive bug is being investigated, in order to determine exactly what actions the user took prior to the appearance of the bug. It can also assist in usability evaluations, as described in the previous chapter, by recording exactly what commands the user issued and when they were issued. As with the *BufferedTuttle* class, logging involves opening a file on the computer which is executing its client–this can only be guaranteed if it is running as a local applet within a suitably configured browser or appletviewer.

A specialized *Tuttle* interface to allow the logged commands to be replayed, either one at a time or in sequence with or without regard to the delays between the commands and, possibly, in a continual loop, would be useful for analyzing the log. The construction of such an interface will be a suggested end of chapter exercise.

In order for the user's actions to be stamped with the current time the *TimeStamp* class, whose class diagram is given in Figure 8.13, will be required. The implementation of this class is given in Appendix B. The default constructor will construct a *TimeStamp* instance with the manifest value *INVALID_TIME* as will the alternative constructor if the *stampNow* boolean argument is **false**; such a *TimeStamp* instance can subsequently be stamped with the *stamp()* method. Alternatively a *TimeStamp* instance can be stamped upon construction by using the alternative constructor with a **true** argument. The *elapsed()* method will return the time in seconds between this instance and the instance passed in the *anotherStamp* argument, or the *INVALID_TIME* value if either instance is unstamped. Finally the *toString()* method will return the string "**:**:**" for an unstamped instance and a string of the form

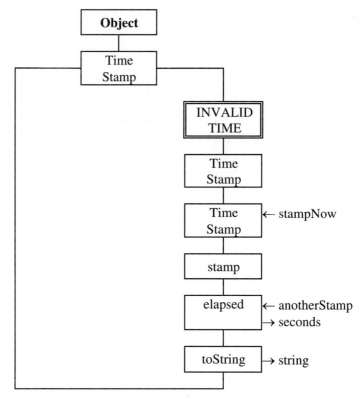

FIGURE 8.13 The *TimeStamp* class diagram.

"hh:mm:ss" for a stamped instance. The class diagram for the *LoggingTuttle* class is given in Figure 8.14.

The constructor is comparable to previous *Tuttle* classes, apart from requiring a MouseListener instance as an argument. The reason for this is that the user can start or stop logging by clicking the mouse on the tuttle's drawing area while holding down both the <SHIFT> and <CONTROL> keys, and this requires a suitable listener to respond to the event generated. The intention is that this facility will only be used by engineers investigating a bug or usability investigators, so general users need not know anything about it.

The *doCommand()* method, in addition to executing the command, will also log it to the *logFile* if the *loggingActive* attribute is **true**. This is accomplished by calling the **public** *logCommand()* method. The *startLogging()* and *stopLogging()* methods control the logging of commands by opening and closing the *logFile*. The *loggingActive* instance attribute is set as appropriate by these methods and its value can be obtained by the *isLoggingActive*() method. The implementation of this class, as far as the end of its constructor, is as follows.

```
0001  // Filename LoggingTuttle.java.
0002  // Extends the Tuttle class by providing the facility
0003  // for tuttle commands to be logged to a file.
```

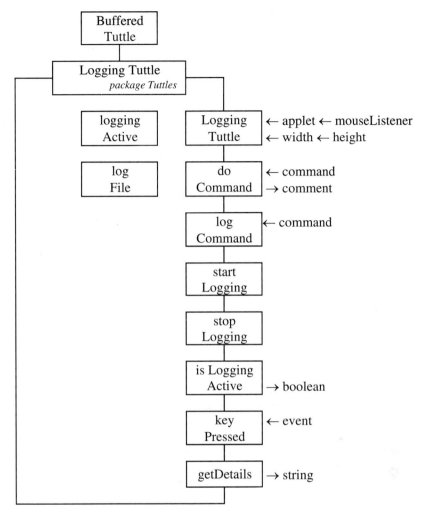

FIGURE 8.14   The *LoggingTuttle* class diagram.

```
0004   // Written for the Java Interface Book Chapter 8.
0005
0006   // Fintan Culwin, v 0.2, August 1997.
0007
0008   package Tuttles;
0009
0010   import java.awt.*;
0011   import java.applet.*;
0012   import java.awt.event.*;
0013   import java.io.*;
0014
0015   import TimeStamp;
0016   import Tuttles.BufferedTuttle;
0017
```

```
0018  public class LoggingTuttle extends BufferedTuttle {
0019
0020  private boolean      loggingActive   = false;
0021  private PrintWriter  logFile;
0022
0023      public LoggingTuttle( Applet applet, MouseListener itsListener,
0024                          int width, int height) {
0025          super( applet, width, height);
0026          this.addMouseListener( itsListener);
0027      } // End LoggingTuttle constructor.
```

The constructor indirects to the parent, *BufferedTuttle*, constructor before registering the *listener* attribute as its MouseListener attribute. The *doCommand()* and *logCommand()* methods are implemented as follows.

```
0029      public String doCommand( String theCommand) {
0030          logCommand( theCommand);
0031          return super.doCommand( theCommand);
0032      } // End doCommand.
0033
0034      public void logCommand( String theCommand) {
0035          if ( loggingActive) {
0036              logFile.println( new TimeStamp( true) + " " + theCommand);
0037          } // End if.
0038      } // End logCommand;
```

The *doCommand()* method indirects to the parent *doCommand()* method after the *logCommand()* method has been called. The *logCommand()* method contains a guard which, if logging is currently active, outputs onto the *logFile* the value of the anonymous *TimeStamp* constructed on line 0036 followed by the command to be logged. Logging is started and stopped by the *startLogging()* and *stopLogging()* methods which, together with the *isLoggingActive()* method, are implemented as follows.

```
0042      public void startLogging() {
0043
0044      String theTime  = new String( new TimeStamp().toString( true));
0045      String fileName = new String( "tlog" + theTime.substring( 0, 2)
0046                                          + theTime.substring( 3, 5)
0047                                          + theTime.substring( 6)
0048                                          + ".log");
0049          try {
0050              logFile = new PrintWriter( new FileOutputStream( fileName));
0051          } catch ( IOException exception) {
0052              System.err.println( "Log file could not be openend," +
0053                                  "logging to terminal.");
0054              logFile = new PrintWriter( System.out, true);
0055          } // End try/ catch.
0056          loggingActive = true;
```

```
0057            logCommand( "logging started");
0058        } // End startLogging.
0059
0060        public void stopLogging() {
0061            logCommand( "logging stopped");
0062            logFile.close();
0063            loggingActive = false;
0064        } // End stopLogging.
0065
0066        public boolean isLoggingActive() {
0067            return loggingActive;
0068        } // End isLoggingActive.
```

The *startLogging()* method commences by constructing a, (hopefully) unique filename by using the *TimeStamp* class. On line 0044 the String *theTime* is initialized to the String value of the current system time, for example "15:34:24". On lines 0045 to 0048 the numeric sub-strings from this String are extracted and catenated to the string "*tlog*" and are followed by the string ".*log*". This will cause the *fileName* String to have a value of the form "tlog*hhmmss*.log", for example "*tlog153424.log*", which is hopefully unique.

On lines 0049 to 0055 an attempt is made to open a file in the default directory with the established *fileName*. Should this attempt fail then a message is output onto the error stream, System.err, and the *logFile* is assigned to the standard output stream, System.out. Once this has occurred, the *loggingActive* attribute is set to indicate that logging is active and the "logging started" command is logged on the *logFile*.

The *stopLogging()* method first logs the command "logging stopped" and then closes the file. It is possible that this will be an attempt to close the System.out stream, an attempt which will not succeed but will not be regarded by Java as an error. The method concludes by setting the *loggingActive* attribute **false**. The *isLoggingActive()* method simply returns the value of the *loggingActive* attribute.

The final method *getDetails()* overrides the *getDetails()* method in the basic *Tuttle* class and provides a non-obvious (to the user) indication that logging is active. The String returned by the *Tuttle getDetails()* method is of the form "x: *nnn* y: *nnn* d: *nnn* pen {*up/down*}" and this is returned unchanged by this method if logging is inactive. However, if logging is active then the 'x', 'y' and 'd' are replaced by their uppercase equivalents. This is accomplished as follows.

```
0072        public String getDetails() {
0073
0074        StringBuffer buffer = new StringBuffer( super.getDetails());
0075
0076            if ( loggingActive) {
0077                buffer.setCharAt( buffer.toString().indexOf('x'), 'X');
0078                buffer.setCharAt( buffer.toString().indexOf('y'), 'Y');
0079                buffer.setCharAt( buffer.toString().indexOf('d'), 'D');
0080            } // End if.
0081            return buffer.toString();
0082        } // End getDetails.
0083    } // End LoggingTuttle.
```

On line 0074 the Tuttle *getDetails()* method is called and the String returned is stored in the StringBuffer *buffer.* On line 0077 the 'x' is transposed to 'X' by locating its position using the String *indexOf()* method and replaced using the *StringBuffer setCharAt()* method. Lines 0078 and 0079 do the equivalent for the 'y' and 'd' characters. The last step of the method is to return the unchanged or changed value of the *StringBuffer* as the result of the method.

This completes the implementation of the *LoggingTuttle* class, a log file produced when the user moves the *tuttle* forward 100 steps and then turns left 35 degrees might have the following contents.

```
10:34:23 logging started
10:34:25 fd 100
10:34:29 lt 35
10:34:29 logging stopped
```

Only the changes to the *BufferedCommandLineTuttle* interface which are required to produce the *LoggingCommandLineInterface* will be described, the changes to the other interfaces will be left as an end of chapter exercise. The *Logging-CommandLineTuttle* class has to declare that it implements the MouseListener as well as the ActionListener interface and, having done this, it can pass itself as the MouseListener argument of the *LoggingTuttle* constructor in its *init()* method as follows.

```
0019   public class LoggingCommandLineTuttle extends      Applet
0020                                         implements ActionListener,
0021                                                    MouseListener {
—          // Amended line in the init() method to construct a LoggingTuttle.
0037          theTuttle = new LoggingTuttle( this, this, 400, 400);
```

The MouseListener interface requires the class to provide four methods, which are implemented as follows.

```
0080      public void mouseClicked( MouseEvent event) {
0081
0082         if ( event.isControlDown() && event.isShiftDown()) {
0083           if ( theTuttle.isLoggingActive()) {
0084              theTuttle.stopLogging();
0085           } else {
0086              theTuttle.startLogging();
0087           } // End if.
0088           this.feedback();
0089         } // End if.
0090      } // End mouseClicked.
0091
0092      public void mousePressed(  MouseEvent event ) {}   // End
0093      public void mouseReleased( MouseEvent event ) {}   // End
0094      public void mouseEntered(  MouseEvent event ) {}   // End
```

```
0095        public void mouseExited(    MouseEvent event ) {}  // End
                mouseExited.
```

Only the *mouseClicked()* method needs to be supplied as a real method; the other three are provided as dummy methods on lines 0092 to 0095. The *mouseClicked()* method should only respond if both the <CONTROL> and <SHIFT> keys are held down and this is tested on line 0082 using the inquiry methods supplied by the MouseEvent class. If this test succeeds, on line 0084, logging is stopped if it is currently active and on line 0086 started if it is currently inactive. Whenever logging is stopped or started, line 0088 calls the *feedback()* method on order that the tuttle status, shown on the interface, changes as described to confirm the effect of the user's action.

The *actionPerformed()* method requires a small change in order that the *help* and *exit* commands, which are not passed to the LoggingTuttle *doCommand()* method, are logged to the file. The changes are implemented as follows.

```
--          // Changes required to actionPerformed() to log help and exit
                commands.
0062          if ( firstTerm.equals( "help")) {
0063             theTuttle.logCommand( theCommand);
0064             theResponse = obtainHelp( tokenizer);
0065          } else if ( firstTerm.equals( "exit")) {
0066             theTuttle.logCommand( theCommand);
0067             theResponse = checkExit( tokenizer);
0068          } else {
0069             theResponse = theTuttle.doCommand( theCommand);
0070          } // End if
—           // Rest if the method as before.
```

The final required change is in the *checkExit()* method to close the log file, by calling the *stopLogging()* method, before the applet exits. The changes are implemented as follows.

```
—           // Amended checkExit method to stop logging before exiting.
0141        private String checkExit( StringTokenizer tokenizer) {
0142          if ( (tokenizer.countTokens() == 1)  &&
0143             (tokenizer.nextToken().toLowerCase().equals( "please")) ){
0144             if ( theTuttle.isLoggingActive()) {
0145                theTuttle.stopLogging();
0146             } // End if.
0147             System.exit( 0);
0148             return "";
0149          } else {
—           // Rest if the method as before.
```

This completes the *Tuttles* hierarchy and its interfaces. The four chapters have introduced a number of different styles of interfaces whose design rationales can be adapted for other application areas.

Chapter Summary

- *Undo*, *save*, and *load* capabilities are essential to encourage a user to explore an interface.

- Multiple-level undo capability is more effective than single level undo.

- Not all commands are undoable.

- The *Tuttle* undo capability is implemented by storing and replaying commands, allowing multiple-level undo to be provided.

- Undo capability should be designed into an application, and its interface, from the outset.

- Standard *open*, *save*, and *save as* GUI STD designs can be readily adapted for a specific interface.

- The Java AWT **FileDialog** class is supplied to allow the host computer's file system to be navigated.

- Due to security restrictions on applets, interaction with the host computer's file system can only be guaranteed for applets running locally.

- Logging the users actions, and a capability to replay them, can be very useful when investigating obscure bugs and usability problems.

- An effective interface should be configurable by the user to satisfy their individual level of expertise.

Exercises

8.1   Extend the *CommandLineTuttle open* and *save* capability so that it requires a filename to be specified on the command line and provides either a confirmation that the action has completed successfully or error message otherwise.

8.2   An exception occurring while a file is being loaded may cause the *Tuttle* to be left with only a partially loaded drawing. Correct this potential fault by copying the *commandBuffer* before the *load* method starts and replaying the commands from the copied buffer if an exception occurs. Demonstrate the effectiveness of the change by deliberately throwing an exception after a number of commands have been executed during the *loadDrawing()* method.

8.3   Some applications of *Tuttle* graphics, for example drawing fractal patterns, require the *Tuttle*'s state to be stored and restored to and from a stack. This will allow the *Tuttle*'s state to be pushed onto the stack, a complex part of the pattern to be drawn, and the state restored by popping it from the stack. Use the **java.util.Stack** class to extend the *BufferedTuttle* class to offer this capability.

8.4   Upgrade the *SemiDirectTuttle* and *TextMenuTuttle* interfaces to allow loading and saving of the drawings.

8.5   Extend the *MenuBarTuttle* save interface capability to accommodate experienced users, as described in the chapter.

8.6   The *MenuBarTuttle* save interface, as described in this chapter, will overwrite any existing file with the same name without a confirmation from the user. Redesign and re-implement the interface to require an explicit confirmation to overwrite when an existing file is selected with the *file save dialog*.

8.7   Adapt the *LoggingTuttle* class so that it logs the elapsed time of the command instead of the current time. The "*logging started*" command should be logged at time 0 and subsequent commands logged from this time.

8.8   Design and implement an interface to allow *tuttle* logs to be replayed.

8.9   Upgrade the *MenuBarTuttle*, *SemiDirectTuttle,* and *TextMenuTuttle* interfaces to allow logging of the user's actions.

CHAPTER 9

Customization, Localization, and Internationalization

This final chapter will introduce some of the techniques by which an artifact can be configured by an individual user to their individual requirements, a process known as *customization*. This may be necessary, for example, in order that a partially sighted user can still use the application; possibly by indicating that they require a very large-sized font displayed in blue upon a yellow background. Many otherwise acceptable interfaces are unable to be customized in this or other ways, restricting their usability. For example assumptions about the font to be used, which determines the size of dialog panels and other components, might be hard coded in the artifact's source. Should the user require a different font, or should the interface be translated into a different language, this will require extensive re-engineering of the interface.

In general, and unlike the examples given so far in this book, such resources should not be hard coded into an artifact but should be obtained from resource specification and customization mechanisms as an application or applet is launched. The introduction of such mechanisms in the last chapter of this book should not be taken as any indication of their lack of importance. Indeed, to give them their due prominence they should have been introduced in the first chapter had it been possible.

Design Advice

An artifact should be designed and implemented for multi-lingual use from the outset, not adapted after it has been constructed.

The linguistic environment which an artifact is executed within is known as *localization*, not internationalization, as many national environments are multi-lingual. For example, any application developed for use within the European Union (EU) should be capable of presenting itself, and interacting with the user, in any one of the twelve official languages. (This is not yet a legal requirement for software developed with EU support but the three major languages of the EU–English, German, and French–are expected to be supported.) Localization may also be required to adapt an application to the particular hardware, or operating system, which it finds itself executing upon.

The phrase *internationalization*, often abbreviated to ***I18n*** as there are eighteen characters between the initial ***i*** and terminal ***n***, therefore does not define a particular linguistic group but purely national characteristics, such as the formats in which values representing such things as dates and currency are presented. Localization is correspondingly often referred to as ***L12n***.

Partly as a result of Java being developed for use on the Web, it has very advanced facilities for localization and internationalization. In particular, its character type **char** is defined from the outset as being capable of representing characters from a unicode character set. This avoids the problem in earlier languages of having to decide between using a non-unicode character type, capable only of representing most, (but not all) character glyphs from romanized alphabets, or of using the so-called wide character (unicode) types which are capable of representing virtually all glyphs from almost all alphabets from all linguistic communities.

The first part of this chapter will briefly introduce the techniques which can be used for customization, both of applets and of applications, before introducing the more powerful mechanisms which can be used for localization and internationalization. To accomplish this latter task, the *DatePanel* component from Chapter 3 will be revisited and re-implemented to allow it to automatically use different linguistic labels for the month and day names, correcting the weakness noted in that chapter.

9.1 System Properties

Customization can mean preparing an application for use with a particular hardware platform, for example a Windows or Macintosh PC or a Unix workstation, and consequently running under a particular operating system. It can also mean allowing an individual user, or a network administrator, to customize particular resources which the artifact will use. These customizations can refer to general resources used by all applications, for example the fonts and colors to be used, or can refer to customizations which are particular to a specific application. For example, a geographic information system may have a different set of icons depending upon the precise information it is representing or upon the choice of the user. This specific resource, determining which set of icons is used, is meaningless to other applications but may be controlled by an application-specific resource.

An application can find out about the environment which it is running upon by obtaining the system properties list using the static method System.getProperties(). Due to security restrictions designed to prevent applets from obtaining information about the system which they are executing on, it is possible for this method to throw a SecurityException. The System.getProperties() method returns an instance of the Properties class, which can be output to the terminal using its list() method. The following, very minimal, class illustrates the use of these facilities.

```
0001   // Filename PropertyDemo.java.
0002   // Program to retrieve and display the system properties list.
0003   //
```

```
0004  // Written for JI book, Chapter 9 see text.
0005  // Fintan Culwin, v 0.2, August 1997.
0006
0007
0008  import java.applet.*;
0009  import java.awt.*;
0010  import java.util.*;
0011
0012  public class PropertyDemo extends Applet {
0013
0014     public void init() {
0015
0016     Properties preset = System.getProperties();
0017
0018        preset.list( System.out);
0019     } // End init.
0020
0021
0022     public static void main( String args[]) {
0023
0024     Frame        frame    = new Frame("Property Demo");
0025     PropertyDemo theDemo  = new PropertyDemo();
0026
0027        theDemo.init();
0028        frame.add( theDemo, "Center");
0029        frame.setVisible( true);
0030        frame.setSize( frame.getPreferredSize());
0031     } // End main.
0032  } // End PropertyDemo
```

On line 0016 the System.getProperties() method is called and the Properties instance returned is referenced by *preset*, whose list() method is called on line 0018 specifying the System.out PrintStream as the destination of the output. When this was executed as a stand-alone application approximately twenty properties were listed, the most useful of which were reported as follows.

```
java.version=1.1_Final
java.class.version=45.3
os.arch=x86
os.name=Windows 95
os.version=4.0
file.separator=\
path.separator=;
line.separator=
user.language=en
user.region=GB
user.timezone=GMT
user.name=fintan
```

The first group gives information about the Java language and class versions which are being used. The next two groups give information concerning the operating system and other system-dependent properties. The final group gives information about the user and their locale. When *PropertyDemo* was executed as an applet, within a browser or an appletviewer utility, over sixty properties were listed including all of those just listed.

Once the system properties have been obtained, the value of any particular property can be determined by using the Properties getProperty() method. For example assuming the system properties are available in *preset*, the name of the user can be obtained with the following fragment.

```
String userName = new String( preset.getProperty( "user.name"));
```

This, assuming the same environment, would initialize the String *userName* to "*fintan.*" If it not possible for the getProperies() method to be used, then an alternative mechanism employing the System.getProperty() method may be successful. This method requires as an argument the name of the property to be retrieved and may not throw a SecurityException, for some properties, even if the getProperies() method does cause the exception to be thrown. For example the following fragment, if allowed, will also retrieve the user's name.

```
String userName = new String( System.getProperty( "user.name"));
```

One other important aspect about the environment of an artifact is to determine if it is executing as an applet or as an application. The easiest way to this is to attempt to obtain an AppletContext using the Applet getAppletContext() method. If the artifact is running as a stand-alone application, this method will throw a NullPointerException; otherwise, it will return an AppletContext instance as described in Chapter 4. The following fragment illustrates this capability.

```
AppletContext itsContext;
   try {
       itsContext = this.getAppletContext();
       // Actions appropriate to an applet here.
   } catch ( NullPointerException exception) {
       // Actions appropriate to a stand alone application here.
   } // End try/ catch.
```

9.2 User Customization

In this section the techniques by which an user can customize resources, both for applications and applets, will be introduced. In the interests of manageable simplicity, the example will be restricted to specifying only the foreground color the background color and the font to be used. These techniques can be readily adapted to allow any other resources to be stipulated by the user in a similar manner. The artifact which will

FIGURE 9.1 *CustomDemo* artifact in various configurations.

be developed in this section is called *CustomDemo* and contains only a label which greets the user by name, using the system properties described earlier to find out the user's name. The appearance of the artifact, with different resource specifications and running as an applet and as an application, is illustrated in Figure 9.1.

In Figure 9.1 the upper left image shows *CustomDemo* running as a stand-alone application using a blue 40-point TimesRoman italic font on a yellow background, the upper right image shows it running in an appletviewer utility using a blue 40-point Helvetica bold font on white background, the lower image shows it running in Netscape using a white 40-point Courier font on green background.

The *CustomDemo* class declares five **String** instance attributes to record the user's choices for these resources and initializes them to sensible default values, as follows.

```
0011   public class CustomDemo extends Applet {
0012
0013   private String fontName              = new String( "Times");
0014   private String fontStyle             = new String( "PLAIN");
0015   private String fontSize              = new String( "14");
0016   private String foregroundColorName   = new String( "black");
0017   private String backgroundColorName   = new String( "white");
```

Each of these attributes has a private state setting method to allow its value to be changed. For example, the *setFontName()* method is implemented as follows.

```
0043        private void setFontName( String setTo) {
0044            fontName = new String( setTo);
0045        } // End setFontName.
```

These attributes are used by a private *setResources()* method to set the Font, Foreground, and Background attributes of the Applet as follows.

```
0064        private void setResources() {
0065
0066        Font   theFont;
0067        int    theFontStyle = Font.PLAIN;
0068        int    theFontSize;
0069        Color theBackgroundColor;
0070        Color theForegroundColor;
0071
0072            if ( fontStyle.equalsIgnoreCase( "ITALIC")) {
0073                theFontStyle = Font.ITALIC;
0074            } else if ( fontStyle.equalsIgnoreCase( "BOLD")) {
0075                theFontStyle = Font.BOLD;
0076            } // End if.
0077
0078            try {
0079                theFontSize = Integer.parseInt( fontSize);
0080            } catch ( NumberFormatException exception) {
0081                theFontSize = 12;
0082            } // End try/ catch.
0083
0084            theFont = new Font( fontName, theFontStyle, theFontSize);
0085            if ( theFont != null) {
0086                this.setFont( theFont);
0087            } // End if.
0088
0089            theBackgroundColor = this.identifyColor( backgroundColorName);
0090            if ( theBackgroundColor != null) {
0091                this.setBackground( theBackgroundColor);
0092            } // End if.
0093
0094            theForegroundColor = this.identifyColor( foregroundColorName);
0095            if ( theForegroundColor != null) {
0096                this.setForeground( theForegroundColor);
0097            } // End if.
0098        } // End setResources.
```

On line 0067 a local primitive **int** called *theFontStyle* is declared and initialized to the manifest value Font.PLAIN. At the start of the method, lines 0072 to 0076 examine the value of the *fontStyle* instance attribute and change the value of *theFontStyle* from its default if required. In a somewhat similar manner, lines 0078 to 0082 attempt to interpret the value of the *fontSize* attribute as an integer setting the value of the local **int** *theFontSize* to the parsed value, or the default value 12 if it cannot be parsed. Line 0084 then attempts to create a Font instance, called *theFont*, using the two processed local values and the value of the *fontName* attribute. If a font specified by these arguments can be obtained, line 0086 sets the Font attribute of the Applet, otherwise, the value of *theFont* will be null and the Applet's default Font will not be changed.

Lines 0089 to 0092 set the Background attribute of the Applet, and lines 0094 to 0097 set the Foreground attribute. In order to accomplish this, a supporting method called *identifyColor()* is used. This method translates one of the twelve color names recognized by the Color class, as given in Table 3.1, into the corresponding manifest Color value. It is implemented as follows.

```
0101      private Color identifyColor( String toIdentify){
0102
0103      Color identifiedColor = null;
0104
0105         if ( toIdentify.equalsIgnoreCase( "red")) {
0106            identifiedColor = Color.red;
0107         } else if ( toIdentify.equalsIgnoreCase( "green")) {
0108            identifiedColor = Color.green;
—      // Other supported names omitted.
0131         } // End if.
0132
0133         return identifiedColor;
0134      } // End identifyColor.
```

The effect of the *setResources()* method is to change the Font and Color resources of the Applet to those indicated by the five instance attributes, assuming that they can be interpreted to identify a font and colors. These attributes are inherited, via the instance hierarchy, by most (but not all) of the Components which are contained within the Applet. The *setResources()* method is implemented in a very defensive manner. Any invalid arguments to one of the state setting methods, for example an unrecognized color name, will result in the Applet retaining its default values.

This part of the customization mechanism will allow the resources to be specified by calling any or all of the five state setting methods and is completed by mechanisms which allow the user to express and communicate their preferences. This is accomplished, in the case of applets, by indicating the preferences as <PARAM> tags within the <APPLET> tag in the HTML file which causes the *CustomDemo* applet to be loaded. For example, the HTML file used for the second image in Figure 9.1 is as follows.

```
<HTML>
<!- Filename CustomDemo.html.                              ->
<!- Loads the CustomDemo artefact as an applet and communicates ->
<!- the user's preferences via the <PARAM> tags.           ->
<!- Written for the JI book Chapter 9.                      ->
```

```
<!— Fintan Culwin, version 0.2, August 1997                    —>
<HEAD>
<TITLE>Custom Demo Applet</TITLE>
</HEAD>
<BODY>
<HR>
<CENTER>
<APPLET   CODE   = CustomDemo
          WIDTH  = 200
          HEIGHT = 100>
          <PARAM NAME=FONTNAME    VALUE=Helvetica>
          <PARAM NAME=FONTSTYLE   VALUE=bold>
          <PARAM NAME=FONTSIZE    VALUE=40>
          <PARAM NAME=FOREGROUND VALUE=blue>
          <PARAM NAME=BACKGROUND VALUE=white>
</APPLET>
</CENTER>
<HR>
</BODY>
</HTML>
```

Within the <APPLET> </APPLET> tag, the <PARAM> tag is used to indicate the NAMEs and VALUEs of the resources which are customizable by the user. The NAMEs are chosen by the applet's developer and have to be expressed exactly as required. In particular the case of the characters has to be respected and it is suggested, as a convention, that they should be expressed in upper case. These NAME/ VALUE pairs can be retrieved by the Applet getParameter() method, for example within CustomDemo's *init()* method, as follows.

```
0018        public void init() {
0019
0020        Properties      preset    = System.getProperties();
0021        String          userName  = new String(
0022                                        preset.getProperty( "user.name"));
0023        AppletContext itsContext;
0024        Label           demoLabel = new Label();
0025
0026           try {
0027              itsContext = this.getAppletContext();
0028              this.setFontName(  this.getParameter("FONTNAME"));
0029              this.setFontStyle( this.getParameter("FONTSTYLE"));
0030              this.setFontSize(  this.getParameter("FONTSIZE"));
0031              this.setBackgroundColorName( this.getParameter("BACKGROUND"));
0032              this.setForegroundColorName( this.getParameter("FOREGROUND"));
0033           } catch ( NullPointerException  exception) {
0034              // Do nothing.
0035           } // End try/ catch.
0036           this.setResources();
0037
0038           demoLabel.setText( "hello " + userName);
```

```
0039              this.add( demoLabel);
0040          } // End init.
```

Line 0027 is included in order that the artifact can decide if it is running as an applet or as an application. If it is running as an applet, then lines 0028 to 0032 attempt to obtain the values of the five allowed parameters. The *getParameter()* method takes a single argument identifying the <PARAM> NAME to be retrieved and will return the VALUE associated with it. If the named parameter has not been specified in the HTML file, then this method will return a **null** string and, in this example, can be safely passed onto the appropriate state setting method.

Having retrieved the values from the HTML file and having used them as arguments to their corresponding state setting methods, line 0036 calls the *setResources()* method to effect the installation of the resources into the Applet. The *init()* method ends by setting the text of the *demoLabel* component, which is then added to the applet. The effect is that the Label is displayed to the user using a font and colors which they can control by editing the <PARAM> tags within the HTML file which loads the *CustomDemo* applet.

This technique cannot be used when the artifact is used as an application. Instead the resource specifications have to be expressed on the command line which launches the application. For example, the command line used to launch the *CustomDemo* instance shown at the top left of Figure 9.1 was as follows.

```
java CustomDemo  FONTNAME=TimesRoman FONTSIZE=40 FONTSTYLE=italic
    FOREGROUND=blue BACKGROUND=yellow
```

This all has to typed onto the same line, but to facilitate specifying the options it could be contained in a MS/DOS batch file; a Unix script file, or a Macintosh launch utility could be used. The command line arguments are made available to the application's *main()* method in its *args*[] String array argument. The contents of this array can be examined to extract the name/ value pairs and passed to the *CustomDemo*'s state setting methods as follows.

```
0138      public static void main( String args[]) {
0139
0140      Frame       frame   = new Frame("Custom Demo");
0141      CustomDemo theDemo = new CustomDemo();
0142      String      parameter;
0143      int         argIndex;
0144
0145
0146         for (argIndex =0; argIndex < args.length; argIndex++) {
0147
0148             parameter = args[ argIndex].substring(
0149                                    args[ argIndex].indexOf( "=") +1,
0150                                    args[ argIndex].length());
0151
0152             if ( args[ argIndex].toLowerCase().startsWith( "fontname")) {
0153                 theDemo.setFontName( parameter);
```

```
0154                    } else if ( args[ argIndex].toLowerCase().startsWith(
                                                      "fontstyle")) {
0155                       theDemo.setFontStyle( parameter);
0156                    } else if ( args[ argIndex].toLowerCase().startsWith(
                                                      "fontsize")) {
0157                       theDemo.setFontSize( parameter);
0158                    } else if ( args[ argIndex].toLowerCase().startsWith(
                                                      "foreground")) {
0159                       theDemo.setForegroundColorName( parameter);
0160                    } else if ( args[ argIndex].toLowerCase().startsWith(
                                                      "background")) {
0161                       theDemo.setBackgroundColorName( parameter);
0162                    } // End if.
0163                } // End for.
0164
0165            theDemo.init();
0166            frame.add(theDemo, "Center");
0167            frame.setVisible( true);
0168            frame.setSize( frame.getPreferredSize());
0169        } // End main.
0170    } // End CustomDemo.
```

The loop between lines 0146 and 0163 will iterate over all arguments, or will not iterate at all if no arguments are supplied, in which case the default values of the customizable resources will be used. The first step of each iteration on lines 0148 to 0150 is to extract, and store in the local String *parameter*, that part of the argument string which follows the '=' symbol. Should the argument not contain an '=' symbol, this will result in the entire string being extracted and stored.

Lines 0152 to 0162 then attempt to determine if the argument string starts with one of the five recognized resource names and, if so, the appropriate state setting method is called passing as an argument the parameter which has already been extracted. Should no value be expressed for the parameter, or should it be an invalid value, the defensive implementation of the *setResources()* method will result in the default values being used. This mechanism is a little more friendly than the applet resource mechanism because it will allow the user to specify the name part of the name value pairs in upper or lower case.

Once the command line arguments have been processed, on line 0165, the *CustomDemo theDemo* instance's *init()* method is called. Within *init()* on line 0027, the attempt to get an application context will cause a NullPointerException to be thrown, thus preventing the method from attempting to retrieve the <PARAM> tag values. Following the **try/ catch** structure the *setResources()* method, called on line 0036, will incorporate any values which have been detected on the command line into the Applet, exactly as before.

9.3 Linguistic Localization of the *ExitDialog*

To start the introduction of the Java techniques for linguistic localization, the *ExitDialog* class from Chapter 5 will be redeveloped so that it automatically presents itself using phrasing appropriate to the user's language. Java is able to determine which language the user prefers by examining the system properties list user.language entry, as described earlier. Figure 9.2 illustrates *ExitDialog* instances in different linguistic locales.

The java.util.ResourceBundle class contains the facilities which allow the linguistic environment to be automatically determined and the appropriate, pre-prepared, resources to be loaded at run time as the interface is constructed. The java.util.ResourceBundle class is extended by the AWT to provide the java.util.ListResourceBundle class. The developer must further extend this class to provide resource bundles appropriate to each locale which they are supporting, and a default bundle which will be used if the user's specific locale is not being supported.

For the ExitDialog class, the ListResourceBundle class was extended to produce the *ExitDialogResources* class containing the English default resources for the *ExitDialog* class. The implementation of this class is as follows.

```
0001   // Filename ExitDialogResources.java.
0002   // Contains the default (English UK/USA) resources
0003   // for the ExitDialog class.
0004   //
0005   // Written for Java Interface book chapter 9.
0006   // Fintan Culwin, v 0.2, August 1997.
0007
0008   import java.util.ListResourceBundle;
0009
0010   public class ExitDialogResources extends ListResourceBundle {
0011
0012       static final Object[][] contents = {
```

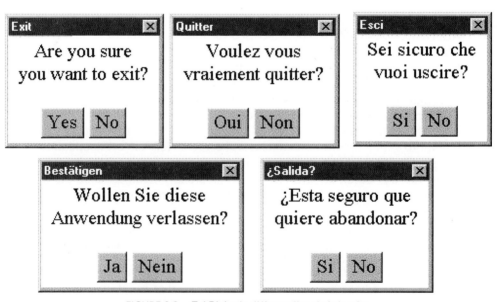

FIGURE 9.2 *ExitDialog* in different linguistic locales.

```
0013              { "exitDialogTitle",     "Exit"},
0014              { "exitDialogQuestion", "Are you sure \nyou want to exit?" },
0015              { "exitDialogYes",       "Yes"},
0016              { "exitDialogNo",        "No"}
0017          }; // End contents.
0018
0019     public Object[][] getContents() {
0020          return contents;
0021      } // End getContents.
0022  } // End class ExitDialogResources.
```

The four phrases on the dialog which will change from locale to locale have been identified and given the manifest names *exitDialogTitle*, *exitDialogQuestion*, *exitDialogYes*, *exitDialogNo*. On lines 0012 to 0017 a two-dimensional array of class-wide constant Objects, called *contents*, is declared and initialized. The first dimension of the array contains the manifest names, and the second dimension of the array contains the phrases which are to be associated with each name stored as a String. The only method which this class needs to provide is *getContents()*, which returns the entire *contents* array.

The *ExitDialog* class has to obtain the values of the Strings to be used in its interface by opening the ListResourceBundle contained in the *ExitDialogResources* class and retrieving the phrases by using the manifest names. The implementation of the revised *ExitDialog* constructor, and the additional instance attributes, is as follows.

```
0028     protected ExitDialog( Frame            parentFrame,
0029                           ActionListener listener) {
0030
0031     ResourceBundle  resources;
0032     String          dialogTitle;
0033     String          exitQuestion;
0034     String          yesLabel;
0035     String          noLabel;
0036
0037         super( parentFrame, true);
0038
0039         itsParentWindow = (Window) parentFrame;
0040         itsListener     = listener;
0041
0042         this.setFont(       itsParentWindow.getFont());
0043         this.setForeground( itsParentWindow.getForeground());
0044         this.setBackground( itsParentWindow.getBackground());
0045
0046         resources    = ResourceBundle.getBundle( "ExitDialogResources");
0047         dialogTitle  = (String) resources.getObject( "exitDialogTitle");
0048         exitQuestion = (String) resources.getObject(
                                                  "exitDialogQuestion");
0049         yesLabel     = (String) resources.getObject( "exitDialogYes");
0050         noLabel      = (String) resources.getObject( "exitDialogNo");
0051
0052         super.setTitle( dialogTitle);
```

```
0053
0054          message = new MessageCanvas( exitQuestion);
0055          message.setBackground( Color.white);
0056          this.add( message, "Center");
0057
0058          buttonPanel = new Panel();
0059          buttonPanel.setBackground( Color.white);
0060
0061          yesButton = new Button( yesLabel);
0062          yesButton.setActionCommand( "yes");
0063          yesButton.addActionListener( this);
0064          buttonPanel.add( yesButton);
0065
0066          noButton = new Button( noLabel);
0067          noButton.setActionCommand( "no");
0068          noButton.addActionListener( this);
0069          buttonPanel.add( noButton);
0070
0071          this.add( buttonPanel, "South");
0072          this.pack();
0073       } // End ExitDialog constructor.
```

The first change is in the call of the **super** (Frame) constructor, on line 0037, where the title for the dialog is no longer specified upon construction because at this stage it cannot be known. Line 0046 opens the ListResourceBundle *ExitDialogResources* using the ResourceBundle class wide-method getBundle(). It is this method which, as will be explained, automatically retrieves ResourceBundles appropriate for the linguistic locale if they are available. For the time being, it can be assumed that this will retrieve the *contents* of the *ExitDialogResource* bundle as shown earlier.

Lines 0047 to 0050 then use the getObject() method of the resources instance provided by the getBundle() method to retrieve the localized resources. A call of getObject() passes as an argument the identity of an Object in the first dimension of the array and returns the identity of the corresponding Object in the second dimension of the array. In this example both array dimensions contain Strings, so a String is passed as an argument and the Object returned is cast to a String, as it is stored in the instance attributes. If the argument passed to getObject() does not identify an entry in the first dimension of contents, it will return a **null** Object.

Having retrieved the Strings to be shown in the interface, lines 0052, 0054, 0061 and 0066 use them to specify the dialog Frame's title, the contents of the *Message-Canvas*, the label to be used on the *yesButton,* and the label to be used on the *noButton* respectively. This should be compared with the *ExitDialog* constructor in Chapter 5 which used String literals in these places.

The ResourceBundle getBundle() method, as used on line 0046, attempts to load a class file whose name is obtained by first catenating the user.language and user.region to the String passed as an argument. Assuming that the system properties list is as shown at the start of this chapter, this example would first attempt to load a ListResourceBundle class called "*ExitDialogResources_en_GB*". If this fails it then attempts to load a ListResourceBundle, omitting the user.region, in this example

"*ExitDialogResources_en*"; if this fails it uses the default name as specified in the call, in this example "*ExitDialogResources*". Thus for the default (English) linguistic locale, only the default *ExitDialogResources* class as shown earlier need be provided.

Each of the alternative linguistic locales requires an additional extended ListResourceBundle class to be provided, with a name ending with the appropriate language code. For example, the language code for French is "*fr*" and so the name of the class containing the *ExitDialog* ListResourceBundle would be "*ExitDialogResources_fr*". The implementation of this class is as follows.

```
0001   // Filename ExitDialogResources_fr.java.
0002   // Contains the French language resources
0003   // for the ExitDialog class.
0004   //
0005   // Written for Java Interface book chapter 9.
0006   // Fintan Culwin, v 0.2, August 1997.
0007
0008   import java.util.ListResourceBundle;
0009
0010   public class ExitDialogResources_fr extends ListResourceBundle {
0011
0012       static final Object[][] contents = {
0013           { "exitDialogTitle",     "Quitter" },
0014           { "exitDialogQuestion", "Voulez vous \nvraiement quitter?" },
0015           { "exitDialogYes",       "Oui"},
0016           { "exitDialogNo",        "Non"}
0017       }; // End contents.
0018
0019       public Object[][] getContents() {
0020          return contents;
0021       } // End getContents.
0022   } // End class ExitDialogResources_fr.
```

For a user in a French language locale, their user.language system property will be *fr* and so, using the mechanism explained earlier, the *ExitDialogResources_fr* class will be loaded by the ResourceBundle getBundle() method in preference to the *ExitDialogResources* class, as illustrated in the second image in Figure 9.2. In order to test the various resource classes, Java toolkits allow system properties to be expressed on the command line. For example, in order to obtain the French *ExitDialog* the command line used with the Sun appletviewer utility was:

```
%appletviewer -J-Duser.language=fr ExitDialogDemo.html
```

This causes the *ExitDialogDemo* applet, referenced from *ExitDialogDemo.html*, to be loaded and executed with the user.language system property temporarily set to *fr*. The user.region property can be used in conjunction with the user.language property to allow for situations where a common language has national variants. For example, resources in an *_en_UK* file might differ from the resources in an *_en_US* file in the spelling of such words as colour (color), centre (center), and through (thru (sic)).

Arabic	ar	Chinese	zh	Danish	da
Dutch	nl	English	en	Finnish	fi
French	fr	German	de	Greek	el
Hebrew	iw	Irish	ga	Italian	it
Japanese	ja	Korean	ko	Norwegian	no
Portugese	pt	Russian	ru	Spanish	es

TABLE 9.1 Common ISO 639:1998 Language Codes

Table 9.1 contains a list of the most common language codes, and Table 9.2 the most common national codes. Details of how to obtain the complete lists of language and region codes are contained in Appendix A.

9.4 Linguistic Localization of the *DatePanel*

The linguistic localization techniques described can be used with the *DatePanel* class to allow it to configure its interface using the user's language. For example, Figure 9.3 shows a *DatePanel* in a French environment.

The *ListResourceBundle* for the revised *DatePanel* is called *DatePanelResources* and so the French variant is called *DatePanelResources_fr*, implemented as follows.

```
0001  // Filename DatePanelResources_fr.java.
0002  // Contains the French language resources
0003  // for the DatePanel class.
0004  //
0005  // Written for Java Interface book chapter 9.
0006  // Fintan Culwin, v 0.2, August 1997.
0007
0008  import java.util.ListResourceBundle;
0009
0010  public class DatePanelResources_fr extends ListResourceBundle {
0011
0012  static final String dayNames[]   = { "Dim", "Lun", "Mar", "Mer",
0013                                       "Jeu", "Ven", "Sam"};
0014
0015  static final String monthNames[] = { "Jan", "Fév", "Mar", "Avr",
0016                                       "Mai", "Jun", "Jul", "Aoû",
0017                                       "Sep", "Oct", "Nov", "Déc"};
0018
```

Australia	AU	Brazil	BR	Canada	CA
China	CN	Denmark	DK	Finland	FI
France	FR	Germany	DE	Greece	GR
India	IN	Ireland	IE	Israel	IL
Italy	IT	Japan	JP	Korea (South)	KR
Mexico	MX	Netherlands	NL	New Zealand	NZ
Norway	NO	Portugal	PR	Russian Federation	RU
Singapore	SG	South Africa	ZA	Spain	ES
Sweden	SE	United King.	UK	United States	US

TABLE 9.2   Common ISO 3166 Region Codes

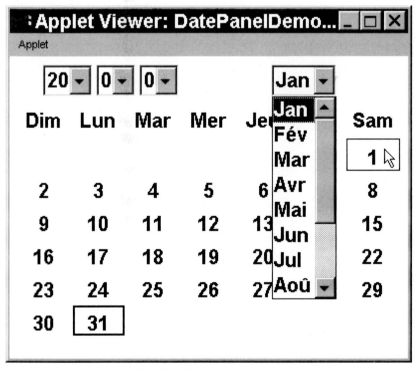

FIGURE 9.3   A *DatePanel* instance in a French linguistic locale.

```
0019      static final Object[][] contents = {
0020          { "dayNames",    dayNames },
0021          { "monthNames", monthNames },
0022      }; // End contents.
0023
0024      public Object[][] getContents() {
0025          return contents;
0026      } // End getContents.
0027
0028  } // End class DatePanelResources_fr.
```

The contents of each Object in the second dimension of the *contents* array is a one-dimensional array of Strings, containing either the twelve month names or the seven day names. These arrays are declared as **static final** attributes of the class on lines 0012 to 0017, and their identifiers are referenced in the declaration of the *contents* array on lines 0019 to 0022. This should be compared with the *ExitDemoResources* class above where a single String was stored, and emphasize the fact that Objects of any class can be stored in the *contents* array.

When these resources are retrieved from the ListResourceBundle in the *DatePanel* classes they have to be aware that they are retrieving arrays of Strings. For example, the fragment of the *MonthPanel* class which retrieves the *monthNames* from the resource bundle and installs them into the *menuChoice* component is as follows.

```
0046    String          monthNames[];
0047    ResourceBundle  resources;
0075        resources   = ResourceBundle.getBundle( "DatePanelResources");
0076        monthNames  = (String[]) resources.getObject( "monthNames");
0077        monthChoice = new Choice();
0078        monthChoice.addItemListener( this);
0079        for ( thisOne = 0; thisOne < 12; thisOne++){
0080            monthChoice.addItem( monthNames[ thisOne]);
0081        } // End for.
```

The *monthNames* String array is declared, but not initialized, on line 0046. Once the ResourceBundle *resources* has been opened, on line 0075, the array is retrieved from it on line 0076 and cast from Object to an array of Strings as it is assigned to the *monthNames*. Having done this, each String from the array is used to specify the label of a Choice item within the loop on line 0080. The effect is, as shown in Figure 9.3, to cause the drop-down *menuChoice* list to use the French language abbreviated month names. A similar set of changes was also required in the *MonthPanel* class for it to retrieve the day names from the same resource bundle class, as also shown in Figure 9.3.

9.5 Other Localization Facilities

Java provides some automatic localization facilities for such things as dates, times, currency values, and numbers in general. Table 9.3 shows how these values are conventionally represented in various locales.

The java.text.Format hierarchy provides a number of classes which can be used to automatically format a value according to the locale. For example, a child class of Format called NumberFormat provides two class-wide methods called getNumberInstance() and getCurrencyInstance() which return a class-wide NumberFormat instances suitable for the formatting of general numeric values and currency values, respectively. The following application illustrates their usage.

```
0001   // Filename NumberFormatDemo.java.
0002   // Program to illustrate formatting of numeric values.
0003   //
0004   // Written for JI book, Chapter 9 see text.
0005   // Fintan Culwin, v 0.2, August 1997.
0006
0007   import java.text.NumberFormat;
0008
0009   public class NumberFormatDemo {
0010
0011     public static void main( String args[]) {
0012
0013       Double aGeneralNumber  = new Double( 1234.56);
0014       Double aPositiveAmount = new Double( 12.34);
0015       Double aNegativeAmount = new Double( -12.34);
0016
0017         System.out.println( "\n\t Number Format Demo\n");
0018
0019         System.out.print( "Default formatting of a general number ... ");
0020         System.out.println( NumberFormat.getNumberInstance().
0021                                       format( aGeneralNumber) + ".");
0022
```

	Numeric	positive & negative currency	time: morning & afternoon	short date
U.S.	1,2345.67	$12.34 ($12.34)	7:07AM 10:20 PM	12/31/99
U.K.	1,2345.67	£12.34 -£12.34	07:07 22:20	31/12/99
Germany	1 2345.56	DM 12,34 -DM 12,34	07:07Uhr 22:20Uhr	31.12.1996
France	1 2345,56	12,34 F -12,34 F	07:07 22:20	31-12-1996

TABLE 9.3   Locale-Dependant Conventional Representations

```
0023            System.out.print("Default formatting of a positive amount ... ");
0024            System.out.println( NumberFormat.getCurrencyInstance().
0025                                        format( aPositiveAmount) + ".");
0026
0027            System.out.print("Default formatting of a negative amount ... ");
0028            System.out.println( NumberFormat.getCurrencyInstance().
0029                                        format( aNegativeAmount) + ".");
0030      } // End main.
0031   } // End NumberFormatDemo.
```

The format() methods declared in the Format hierarchy will only operate upon instance of the numeric classes, such as Double, and not upon instances of primitive variables such as **double**. Accordingly the three numeric values which will be used for illustration are declared as instances of the Double class on lines 0013 to 0015. On lines 0020 and 0021 the getNumberInstance() method of the NumberFormat class is called to obtain an anonymous NumberFormat instance, whose format() method is called to provide a String representation of the value appropriate for the current locale which is then output to the terminal. Lines 0023 to 0029 are similar outputting values formatted as currency. When this program was executed in the English UK locale, the output was as follows.

```
Number Format Demo
Default formatting of a general  number ... 1,234.56.
Default formatting of a positive amount ... £12.34.
Default formatting of a negative amount ... -£12.34.
```

Executing the program again, temporarily specifying a French locale as explained, produced the following output.

```
Number Format Demo
Default formatting of a general  number ... 1 234,56.
Default formatting of a positive amount ... 12,34 F.
Default formatting of a negative amount ... -12,34 F.
```

A similar program, as follows, can be used to illustrate the output of dates and times.

```
0001   // Filename TimeFormatDemo.java.
0002   // Program to illustrate formatting of times and dates.
0003   //
0004   // Written for JI book, Chapter 9 see text.
0005   // Fintan Culwin, v 0.2, August 1997.
0006
0007   import java.util.Date;
0008   import java.util.GregorianCalendar;
0009   import java.text.DateFormat;
```

```
0010
0011   public class TimeFormatDemo {
0012
0013     public static void main( String args[]) {
0014
0015     Date theNightBefore  = new GregorianCalendar(
0016                                   1999, 11, 31, 20, 20).getTime();
0017     Date theMorningAfter = new GregorianCalendar(
0018                                   2000, 0, 1, 07, 07).getTime();
0019
0020       System.out.println( "\n\t Date and Time Format Demo\n");
0021
0022       System.out.println("Default formatting of dates and times ... ");
0023       System.out.print(   "Before ");
0024       System.out.print(   DateFormat.getInstance().format(
0025                                              theNightBefore));
0025       System.out.print(   " after ");
0026       System.out.print(   DateFormat.getInstance().format(
0026                                              theMorningAfter));
0027       System.out.println( ".\n");
0028
0029       System.out.println( "Formatting of dates ... ");
0030       System.out.print(   "Before ");
0031       System.out.print(   DateFormat.getDateInstance( DateFormat.FULL).
0032                                            format( theNightBefore));
0033       System.out.print(   " after ");
0034       System.out.print(   DateFormat.getDateInstance(
0034       DateFormat.MEDIUM).
0035                                            format( theMorningAfter));
0036       System.out.println( ".\n");
0037
0038       System.out.println( "Formatting of times ... ");
0039       System.out.print(   "Before ");
0040       System.out.print(   DateFormat.getTimeInstance(
0041                            DateFormat.SHORT). format( theNightBefore));
0042       System.out.print(   " after ");
0043       System.out.print(   DateFormat.getTimeInstance( DateFormat.LONG).
0044                                                      format(
0044                                              theMorningAfter));
0045       System.out.println( ".");
0046     } // End main.
0047   } // End TimeFormatDemo.
```

Two **Date** instances are constructed on lines 0015 to 0018 and are subsequently output using various anonymous **DateFormat** instances on lines 0022 to 0045. The instances obtained can be configured by using one of the **DateFormat** manifest values SHORT, MEDIUM, FULL, and LONG, as illustrated. The output produced when this program was executed in the English UK locale was as follows.

```
Date and Time Format Demo
Default formatting of dates and times ...
Before 31/12/99 20:20 after 01/01/00 07:07.
Formatting of dates ...
Before Friday, 31 December 1999 after 01-Jan-00.
Formatting of times ...
Before 20:20 after 07:07:00 GMT.
```

Executing the program again, temporarily specifying a German locale, produced the following output with the appropriate time zone adjustment to the Date automatically applied.

```
Date and Time Format Demo
Default formatting of dates and times ...
Before 31.12.99 21:20 after 1.1.00 08:07.
Formatting of dates ...
Before Freitag, 31. Dezember 1999 after 1.1.2000.
Formatting of times ...
Before 21:20 after 08:07:00 GMT+01:00.
```

The ChoiceFormat class can be used when the output to be produced depends upon the value of some other Object. For example, a transaction reporting system would have to change its output depending upon the number of transactions, as follows, when reporting in both English and German

There were 0 transactions.	Gab es 0 Überweiungen.
There was 1 transaction.	Gab es 1 Überweiung.
There were *n* transactions.	Gab es *n* Überweiungen.

where *n* indicates any value greater than 1. In order to implement this requirement, a ListResourceBundle as described will have to be prepared for each locale. The German language version, called *ChoiceDemoFormat_de*, is as follows.

```
0001   // Filename ChoiceDemoResources_de.java.
0002   // German resources for the ChoiceFormatDemo program.
0003   //
0004   // Written for JI book, Chapter 9 see text.
0005   // Fintan Culwin, v 0.2, August 1997.
0006
0007
0008   import java.util.ListResourceBundle;
0009   import java.text.*;
0010
0011   public class ChoiceDemoResources_de extends ListResourceBundle {
0012
0013   static final double[]      limits = {0.0,1.0, 2.0};
0014
0015   static final String        initialPhrases[]  = {"Gab es ",
```

```
0016                                                    "Gab es ",
0017                                                    "Gab es "};
0018    static final ChoiceFormat initialFormatter =
0019                        new ChoiceFormat( limits,
                                              initialPhrases);
0020
0021    static final String       finalPhrases[]  = {" Überweiungen",
0022                                          " Überweiung",
0023                                          " Überweiungen"};
0024    static final ChoiceFormat finalFormatter =
0025                        new ChoiceFormat( limits,
                                              finalPhrases);
0026
0027       static final Object[][] contents = {
0028          { "initialFormatter", initialFormatter },
0029          { "finalFormatter",   finalFormatter   }
0030       }; // End contents.
0031
0032       public Object[][] getContents() {
0033          return contents;
0034       } // End getContents.
0035    } // End class ChoiceDemoResources_de.
```

A ChoiceFormat instance is constructed from an array of **double** values and a corresponding array of Objects. When its format() method is called, it must be supplied with an **double** value and will return a String representation of the Object which is most closely associated with it in the array.

In the earlier example, the ChoiceFormat instance called *finalFormatter* is constructed from the array *limits* declared on line 0013 and the array *finalPhrases* of Strings declared on lines 0021 to 0023. When its format() method is called with the value 0, it will return the first element from the array (*Überweiungen*); when called with the value 1, the second element of the array (*Überweiung*) and any value greater than or equal to 2 will return the last element from the array (*Überweiungen*).

The packaging of the two ChoiceFormat instances into the *contents* array is essentially identical with the description of the use of ListResourceBundles given earlier. This ResourceBundle is used by the *ChoiceDemo* application, implemented as follows.

```
0001    // Filename ChoiceFormatDemo.java.
0002    // Program to illustrate different formatting of messages.
0003    //
0004    // Written for JI book, Chapter 9 see text.
0005    // Fintan Culwin, v 0.2, August 1997.
0006
0007    import java.text.ChoiceFormat;
0008    import java.util.ResourceBundle;
0009
0010    public class ChoiceFormatDemo extends Object {
0011
```

```
0012        public static void main(String args[]) {
0013
0014        Integer          numberOfTransactions;
0015        ResourceBundle   resources;
0016        ChoiceFormat     initialPhrase;
0017        ChoiceFormat     finalPhrase;
0018
0019          System.out.println( "\n\t Choice Format Demo\n");
0020
0021          resources     = ResourceBundle.getBundle( "ChoiceDemoResources");
0022          initialPhrase = ((ChoiceFormat) resources.getObject(
                                                    "initialFormatter"));
0023          finalPhrase   = ((ChoiceFormat) resources.getObject(
                                                    "finalFormatter"));
0024
0025          numberOfTransactions = new Integer( 0);
0026          System.out.println( initialPhrase.format( numberOfTransactions) +
0027                      numberOfTransactions                      +
0028                      finalPhrase.format( numberOfTransactions) + ".");
0029
0030          numberOfTransactions = new Integer( 1);
0031          System.out.println( initialPhrase.format( numberOfTransactions) +
0032                      numberOfTransactions                      +
0033                      finalPhrase.format( numberOfTransactions) + ".");
0034
0035          numberOfTransactions = new Integer( 1000);
0036          System.out.println( initialPhrase.format( numberOfTransactions) +
0037                      numberOfTransactions                      +
0038                      finalPhrase.format( numberOfTransactions) + ".");
0039        } // End main.
0040    } // End ChoiceFormatDemo.
```

In this example, the two ChoiceFormat instances are retrieved from the *resources* ResourceBundle on lines 0022 and 0023. Each is then used three times on lines 0025 to 0038, illustrating how the initial and final phrases can be retrieved from the corresponding ChoiceFormat instance to produce the German language phrases given. However, the third line of output produced by the program was as follows.

```
Gab es 1000 Überweiungen.
```

This shows that the locale-specific formatting of numeric values has not been applied. In order to accommodate this requirement, the most complex class in the Format hierarchy–the MessageFormat class–will have to be used. This class not only allows a number of Format instances to be associated with a single message phrase, but also allows for the order in which the various formatted phrases are to appear in the message to be varied between locales. For example, the English language form of a message which might form part of a transaction processing system may appear as follows.

```
There were  1,234  transactions totalling £1,234.56
at 09:15:00 on Saturday, 1 January 2000.
```

However, to be linguistically correct in German the data and time information must appear at the start of the message. The equivalent phrase would be as follows.

```
Am 10:15:00 on Samstag, 1. Januar 2000
gab es 1.234  Überweiungen totaliert DM 1.234,56.
```

A MessageFormat instance contains a *generator* String containing place holders (identified as *{n}*), where the corresponding n^{th} element from an array of Objects, supplied as an argument, will be substituted when format() method is called. For example, to produce the message illustrated there are three Objects required: *theDate*, the *numberOfTransactions,* and the total *amountTaken.* If they are stored in this sequence in an array, then every occurrence of *{0}* in the *generator* will be replaced with *theDate,* every occurrence of *{1}* with *numberOfTransactions,* and every occurrence of *{2}* with *amountTaken.*

However, before the substitution takes place the values are formatted using a formatter from an array of Format instances also contained within the MessageFormat instance. The formatters are applied strictly in the sequence in which they appear in the Format array, to the corresponding occurrence from the *generator* String. Using the English language message shown earlier as an example, the *generator* String is as follows.

```
"{1} {1} {1} totalling {2}\n at {0} on {0}.")
```

The first place holder is *{1},* and its corresponding formatter is the *initalFormatter* ChoiceFormat instance. Thus, the first *{1}* will be substituted by the phrase "*There was*" or "*There were*" depending upon the value of the *NumberOfTransactions* Integer instance in the first array location. The second and third place holders are also *{1},* so the *NumberOfTransactions* will be used again with a general NumerFormat instance to produce the numeric value and the *finalFormatter* ChoiceFormat instance to produce the phrase "*transaction*" or "*transactions.*"

The *{2}* identifies the *amountTaken* Double instance in the Object array and is formatted with a CurrencyFormat instance to produce the currency value at the end of the first line of output. The final two place holders are both *{0}*;identifying *theDate* and the last two Format instances are a TimeInstance and a DateInstance respectively which, when applied and substituted, produce the second line of output. The Message-Format *generator* and the *formatters* Format array are prepared in a ListResource-Bundle, called *MessageDemoResources*, as follows.

```
0001   // Filename MessageDemoResources.java.
0002   // English (UK) resources for the MessageFormatDemo program.
0003   //
0004   // Written for JI book, Chapter 9 see text.
0005   // Fintan Culwin, v 0.2, August 1997.
0006
```

```
0007  import java.util.ListResourceBundle;
0008  import java.text.*;
0009
0010  public class MessageDemoResources extends ListResourceBundle {
0011
0012  static final double[]      limits           = {0.0, 0.1, 0.2};
0013
0014  static final String        initialPhrases[] = {"There were ",
0015                                                  "There was ",
0016                                                  "There were "};
0017  static final ChoiceFormat initialFormatter  =
0018                      new ChoiceFormat( limits, initialPhrases);
0019
0020  static final String        finalPhrases[]  = {" transactions",
0021                                                  " transaction",
0022                                                  " transactions"};
0023  static final ChoiceFormat finalFormatter   =
0024                      new ChoiceFormat( limits, finalPhrases);
0025
0026  static final Format formatters[] = { initialFormatter,
0027                                        NumberFormat.getInstance(),
0028                                        finalFormatter,
0029                                        NumberFormat.getCurrency
                                            Instance(),
0030                                        DateFormat.getTimeInstance(
0031                                            DateFormat. MEDIUM),
0032                                        DateFormat.getDateInstance(
0033                                            DateFormat. FULL)
0034                                      };
0035
0036  static final MessageFormat generator = new MessageFormat(
0037                "{1} {1} {1} totalling {2}\nat {0} on {0}.");
0038
0039     static final Object[][] contents = {
0040         { "formatters", formatters },
0041         { "generator",  generator }
0042     }; // End contents.
0043
0044     public Object[][] getContents() {
0045        return contents;
0046     } // End getContents.
0047  } // End class MessageDemoResources.
```

Lines 0012 to 0024 prepare the two ChoiceFormat instances, *inititialFormatter* and *finalFormatter*, which were described earlier. Lines 0026 to 0034 then declare the array *formatters* containing the six required Format instances. The *generator* String is declared on lines 0036 and 0037 containing six place holders and referencing, via the place holder numbers, the three Objects which it will use to produce the output. The remainder of the class declaration makes the *formatters* array and the *generator* String available to its client, using the same techniques as before. The implementation of the *MessageFormatDemo* application is as follows.

```
0001    // Filename MessageFormatDemo.java.
0002    // Program to illustrate different formatting of messages.
0003    //
0004    // Written for JI book, Chapter 9 see text.
0005    // Fintan Culwin, v 0.2, August 1997.
0006
0007    import java.text.*;
0008    import java.util.*;
0009
0010    public class MessageFormatDemo extends Object {
0011
0012        public static void main(String args[]) {
0013
0014        Integer numberOfTransactions = new Integer( 1234);
0015        Date     theDate             = new GregorianCalendar(
0016                                        2000, 0, 1, 9, 15).getTime();
0017        Double  amountTaken          = new Double( 1234.56);
0018        Object  arguments[] = { theDate,
0019                                numberOfTransactions,
0020                                amountTaken
0021                              };
0022
0023        ResourceBundle resources     = ResourceBundle.getBundle(
0024                                        "MessageDemo Resources");
0025        MessageFormat  generator     = ((MessageFormat) resources.
0026                                        getObject( "generator"));
0027        Format         formatters[]  = ((Format[]) resources.
0028                                        getObject( "formatters"));
0029
0030          generator.setFormats( formatters);
0031          System.out.println( generator.format( arguments));
0032        } // End main.
0033    } // Endf MessageFormatDemo.
```

Lines 0014 to 0017 of the *main*() method construct the three Objects which will be formatted, and lines 0018 to 0021 store them in an array called *arguments*. Lines 0023 to 0028 then open the *ResourceBundle* and retrieve the Format array, *formatters*, and the MessageFormat instance called *generator* containing the *generator* String. It was not possible for the *formatters* to be associated with the *generator* in the *ResourceBundle* as it can only contain declarations and not methods. Accordingly, on line 0030 the *set-Formats()* method of the **MessageFormat** generator instance is called to associate the *formatters* with the *generator*. Having done this, the *format()* method of the *generator* instance can be called. This will substitute the *arguments* into the generator string, having first formatted them as described, producing the English language output shown.

The German language output was produced from the same application, temporarily specifying a German linguistic environment, causing it to reference the *MessageDemoResources_de* ResourceBundle, implemented as follows.

```
0001  // Filename MessageDemoResources.java.
0002  // German language resources for the MessageFormatDemo program.
0003  //
0004  // Written for JI book, Chapter 9 see text.
0005  // Fintan Culwin, v 0.2, August 1997.
0006
0007  import java.util.ListResourceBundle;
0008  import java.text.*;
0009
0010  public class MessageDemoResources_de extends ListResourceBundle {
0011
0012  static final double[]  limits = {0,1,2};
0013
0014
0015  static final String       finalPhrases[]  = {" Überweiungen",
0016                                                " Überweiung",
0017                                                " Überweiungen"};
0018  static final ChoiceFormat finalFormatter  =
0019                    new ChoiceFormat( limits, finalPhrases);
0020
0021  static final Format formatters[] = { DateFormat.getTimeInstance(
0022                                              DateFormat.MEDIUM),
0023                                        DateFormat.getDateInstance(
0024                                              DateFormat.FULL),
0025                                        NumberFormat.getInstance(),
0026                                        finalFormatter,
0027                                        NumberFormat.getCurrencyInstance()
0028                                     };
0029
0030  static final MessageFormat generator = new MessageFormat(
0031              "Am {0} on {0} \ngab es {1} {1} totaliert {2}.");
0032
0033      static final Object[][] contents = {
0034          { "formatters", formatters },
0035          { "generator",  generator }
0036      }; // End contents.
0037
```

```
0038        public Object[][] getContents() {
0039           return contents;
0040        } // End getContents.
0041    } // End class MessageDemoResources_de.
```

This is comparable to the English language resources already described in detail. The *generator* string changes the position of the date and time by referencing the zeroth place holder at the start of the string and only requires five formatters, omitting the *initialFormatter* whose German output does not differ according to the number of transactions.

This has necessarily been only an introduction to the Java localization and internationalization capabilities. However, it has demonstrated the basic mechanisms and reinforces the design advice that an artifact should be designed for use in multiple locales from the outset, rather than having to be retrofitted with the capability after construction.

Chapter Summary

- *Customization* allows the user to configure an artifact to their own individual requirements and also allows the artifact to configure itself to its hardware and operating system.

- *Localization* (*L12n*) allows an artifact to configure itself to the user's language, *internationalization* (*I18n*) allows it to configure itself to national conventions.

- Java has very advanced facilities for localization and customization, due to its role for use on the Web.

- The *system properties list* can inform an artifact about the hardware, operating system, and user's preferences.

- Customization of an applet involves using the <PARAM> tag within the <APPLET> tag.

- Customization of an application involves passing information via the command line.

- The *ResourceBundle* hierarchy supplies the facilities for localization and internationalization.

- An extended *ListResourceBundle* supplies the default phrases, and other resources, for an interface. Other extensions, using a systematic naming convention, supply resources for different linguistic locales.

- The Format hierarchy supplies resources for the formatting (according to the locale) of dates, times, currency values, and general numeric values.

- The MessageFormat class supplies the most sophisticated, and complex, resources for the generation of locale-specific messages.

Exercises

9.1 Obtain the *ExitDialog* source code, as extended in this chapter, and demonstrate the customization of the interface both as an applet and as an application.

9.2 Prepare and demonstrate additional linguistic locales for the *ExitDialog* and *DatePanel*.

9.3 Extend the customization of the *ExitDialog* by allowing the user to specify different fonts for the message and for the button labels.

9.4 Using the techniques in the *ExitDialogDemonstration* class, revisit the *DatePanelDemonstation* class and *PostIt* note class from Chapter 3 to allow them to be customized. Demonstrate that the customization is effective and then produce a template for all demonstration classes which support the facility.

9.5 Extend the *PostIt* note class so that the command line can specify the message to be displayed, as well as the font and colors, resulting in a single *PostItNote* instance containing the message being posted.

9.6 Revisit the *open* and *save* interfaces from Chapter 8, adapting them for different linguistic locales.

9.7 Extend the MessageFormatDemo application to make it suitable for use in other locales.

APPENDIX A

Other Resources

For novices starting software development for the first time, and for more experienced developers who want a very rigorous introduction to Java, I would recommend:

Fintan Culwin
Java: An Object First Approach
Prentice Hall, Europe, 1998, ISBN 0-13-858457-5

A very useful book, containing little more than an overview guide to Java and a reprint of the API documentation, is:

David Flanagan
Java in a Nutshell, 2nd edition.
O'Reilly & Associates, 1997, ISBN 1-56592-262-X

A more comprehensive and detailed reference for the AWT is contained within:

John Zukowski
Java AWT Reference
O'Reilly & Associates, 1997, ISBN 1-56592-240-9

However, the information which is most useful from these two books is also available, free of charge, in HTML format, from SunSoft at:

http://www.javasoft.com/products/jdk

This is also where a free-of-charge Java Developers Kit (JDK) can be obtained for Windows NT &'95, Sun Unix, and Macintosh platforms. (This site also contains a Java Beans Development Kit (BDK), which is what this book would continue with if it were longer.)

Details of a Linux port of the JDK can be obtained from:

http://www.blackdown.org/java-linux.html

A version in the Java API documentation in Windows help file format, called godfather, is available from:

http://www.schlenzig.de/sfs

The most definitive reference material is Sun's official series of books, the most interesting of which is co-authored by James Gosling who is credited with the development of Java:

Ken Arnold & James Gosling
The Java Programming Language
Addison Wesley, 1996, ISBN 0-201-63455-4

SunSoft has also commissioned an official series of books, the most useful of which is:

Gary Cornell & Cay S. Horstmann
Core Java, 2nd edition
Prentice Hall, 1997, ISBN 0-12-518405-0

The list of ISO 3166 country codes, and the list of ISO 639:1998 language codes, from Chapter 9 can be found at:

http://www.chemie.fu-berlin.de/diverse/doc/ISO_3166.html
http://www.chemie.fu-berlin.de/diverse/doc/ISO_639.html

The most useful Java Web site is undoubtedly Gamelan, which maintains lists of all other Java resources available on the Web and can be found at:

http://java.developer.com/

The list of heuristics, and much more information about how to ensure that interfaces with a high degree of usability are produced, can be found in:

Jakob Nielsen
Usability Engineering
Academic Press, 1993, ISBN 0-12-518405-0

Finally, a summary of details of the Unified Modeling Language (UML) design notation, as used throughout the book, is given in Appendix C. The full specification of the notation is available from:

http://www.rational.com/

APPENDIX B

Source Code Omitted from the Chapters

Chapter 1—The *ClickCounter* Class

```
0001  // Filename ClickCounter.java.
0002  // Provides the ClickCounter application class.
0003  // Written for the Java Interface book Chapter 1.
0004  //
0005  // Fintan Culwin, v 0.2, August 1997.
0006
0007
0008  public class ClickCounter extends Object {
0009
0010
0011  private static final int DEFAULT_MAXIMUM = 999;
0012  private static final int DEFAULT_MINIMUM = 0;
0013  private static final int STRING_WIDTH    = 3;
0014
0015  private int  minimumCount;
0016  private int  maximumCount;
0017  private int  clicksCounted;
0018
0019     public ClickCounter(){
0020        this( DEFAULT_MINIMUM, DEFAULT_MAXIMUM);
0021     } // End default constructor.
0022
0023     public ClickCounter( int minimum){
0024        this( DEFAULT_MINIMUM, maximum);
0025     } // End alternative constructor.
0026
```

```
0027        public ClickCounter( int minimum, int maximum){
0028           super();
0029           minimumCount  = minimum;
0030           maximumCount  = maximum;
0031           clicksCounted = minimum;
0032        } // End principal constructor.
0033
0034
0035        public boolean isAtMinimum(){
0036           return clicksCounted == minimumCount;
0037        } // End isAtMinimum.
0038
0039        public boolean isAtMaximum(){
0040           return clicksCounted == maximumCount;
0041        } // End isAtMaximum.
0042
0043
0044        public void count() {
0045           if ( ! this.isAtMaximum()) {
0046              clicksCounted++;
0047           } // End if.
0048        } // End count.
0049
0050
0051        public void unCount() {
0052           if ( ! this.isAtMinimum()) {
0053              clicksCounted—;
0054           } // End if.
0055        } // End unCount.
0056
0057
0058        public void reset() {
0059           clicksCounted = minimumCount;
0060        } // End reset.
0061
0062
0063        public int countIs() {
0064           return clicksCounted;
0065        } // End countIs.
0066
0067        public String countIsAsString() {
0068
0069        StringBuffer buffer;
0070
0071           buffer = new StringBuffer( Long.toString(
0072                                          this.countIs(), 10));
0073           while ( buffer.length() < STRING_WIDTH) {
0074              buffer.insert( 0, 0);
0075           } // End while.
0076           return buffer.toString();
0077        } // End countIsAsString.
```

```
0078
0079   } // End ClickCounter;
```

Chapter 3—The *DateUtility* Class

```
0001   // Filename DateUtility.java.
0002   // Utility class containing static methods to return
0003   // the number of days in a month and the day of the week.
0004   //
0005   // Written for JI book chapter 3.
0006   // Fintan Culwin, v 0.2, August 1997.
0007
0008   package DatePanel;
0009
0010
0011   import java.util.Calendar;
0012   import java.util.GregorianCalendar;
0013
0014
0015   final class DateUtility extends Object {
0016
0017      // Return the number of days in the month supplied.
0018      public static int daysThisMonthIs( int thisYear, int thisMonth) {
0019
0020      int localDays;
0021
0022         switch ( thisMonth) {
0023            case 4:
0024            case 6:
0025            case 9:
0026            case 11:
0027              localDays = 30;
0028              break;
0029            case 2:
0030              if ( isLeapYear( thisYear)) {
0031                 localDays = 29;
0032              } else {
0033                 localDays = 28;
0034              } // End if
0035              break;
0036         default:
0037              localDays = 31;
0038         } // End switch
0039         return localDays;
0040      } // End daysPerMonthIs.
0041
0042
0043      private static boolean isLeapYear( int thisYear) {
0044         return ( ((thisYear % 4) == 0) && (thisYear != 1900));
```

```
0045      } // End isLeapYear.
0046
0047
0048      // Return the day of the week for the first day of the date
0049      // given, with 0 indicating Sunday, using Zeller's congruence.
0050      public static int dayOfWeekIs( int thisYear,
0051                                     int thisMonth,
0052                                     int thisDay) {
0053
0054      int thisCentury;
0055      int zellers;
0056
0057         if ( thisMonth < 3) {
0058            thisYear-;
0059            thisMonth += 10;
0060         } else {
0061            thisMonth -= 2;
0062         } // End if.
0063         thisCentury  =  thisYear /100;
0064         thisYear     %= 100;
0065
0066         zellers = (( (26 * thisMonth -2)/10  + thisDay +
0067                       thisYear + thisYear/4 +
0068                       thisCentury /4 - 2*thisCentury )%7);
0069         if ( zellers < 0) {
0070            zellers += 7;
0071         } // End if.
0072         return  zellers %7;
0073      } // End dayOfWeekIs.
0074
0075
0076      public static int firstDayOfMonthIs( int thisYear,
0077                                           int thisMonth) {
0078         return dayOfWeekIs( thisYear, thisMonth, 1);
0079      } // End firstDayOfMonthIs.
0080
0081
0082      public static int yearIs(){
0083         return new GregorianCalendar().get( Calendar.YEAR);
0084      } // End yearIs.
0085
0086      public static int monthIs(){
0087         return new GregorianCalendar().get( Calendar.MONTH) +1;
0088      } // End monthIs.
0089
0090      public static int dayOfMonthIs() {
0091         return new GregorianCalendar().get( Calendar.DATE);
0092      } // End dayOfMonthIs.
0093
0094  } // End class DateUtility.
```

Chapter 4—The *Tuttle* Class

There is a possible bug in the *forward()* method of the *Tuttle* class as presented in Chapter 4. It shows itself when the tuttle is not pointing in one of the cardinal directions and is asked to move forward a small number of steps; when the integer approximation of the floating point calculation is made, this may result in the tuttle not moving. For example, if the tuttle is pointing 40° and is asked to move forward 1 step it does not move at all. This may or may not be regarded as an error, depending upon the application. For situations where it is erroneous the following fragment will correct for this be ensuring that, so long as the tuttle is not asked to move 0 steps, it will always move at least 1 step in some direction. The new code is in lines 0144 to 0166, with the old line 0144 renumbered as 0168.

```
0139        possibleNewX = xLocation +
0140               (int) (Math.cos( radians) * (double) steps);
0141        possibleNewY = yLocation +
0142               (int) (Math.sin( radians) * (double) steps);
0143
0144        // Ensure that if steps is non-zero then the tuttle moves at
0145        // least one unit in some direction!!
0146        if ( (steps != 0)                    &&
0147            ( possibleNewX == xLocation ) &&
0148            ( possibleNewY == yLocation ) ){
0149
0150            double deltaX = (Math.cos( radians) * (double) steps);
0151            double deltaY = (Math.sin( radians) * (double) steps);;
0152
0153            if ( Math.abs( deltaX) > Math.abs( deltaY) ){
0154                if ( deltaX > 0.0) {
0155                    possibleNewX++;
0156                } else {
0157                    possibleNewX−;
0158                } // End if.
0159            } else {
0160                if ( deltaY > 0.0) {
0161                    possibleNewY++;
0162                } else {
0163                    possibleNewY−;
0164                } // End if
0165            } // End if.
0166        } // End if.
0167
0168        if ( (possibleNewX >= -SCREEN_STEPS) &&
0169            (possibleNewX <= SCREEN_STEPS) &&
0170            (possibleNewY >= -SCREEN_STEPS) &&
0171            (possibleNewY <= SCREEN_STEPS) ) {
```

Chapter 6—The *VersionDialog* Class

```
0001   // Filename VersionDialog.java.
0002   // Supplies a Dialog containing showing the
0003   // version information for an applet.
0004   //
0005   // Written for Java Interface book chapter 6.
0006   // Fintan Culwin, v 0.2, August 1997.
0007
0008   package MenuBarTuttle;
0009
0010   import java.awt.*;
0011   import java.awt.event.*;
0012
0013   import MessageCanvas;
0014
0015
0016   class VersionDialog extends    Dialog
0017                       implements ActionListener {
0018
0019   private MessageCanvas  versionMessage;
0020   private Panel          buttonPanel;
0021   private Button         dismiss;
0022   private Window         itsParentWindow;
0023
0024
0025     protected VersionDialog( Frame  itsParentFrame,
0026                              String itsMessage){
0027
0028       super( itsParentFrame, "Version", false);
0029       itsParentWindow = (Window) itsParentFrame;
0030       this.setFont( itsParentFrame.getFont());
0031
0032       versionMessage = new MessageCanvas( itsMessage);
0033       versionMessage.setBackground( Color.white);
0034
0035       buttonPanel = new Panel();
0036       buttonPanel.setBackground( Color.white);
0037
0038       dismiss = new Button( "OK");
0039       dismiss.addActionListener( this);
0040       buttonPanel.add( dismiss);
0041
0042       this.add( versionMessage, "Center");
0043       this.add( buttonPanel, "South");
0044       this.pack();
0045     } // End VersionDialog constructor.
0047
0048
0049     public void setVisible( boolean showIt) {
0050
```

```
0051      Point          itsParentsLocation;
0052      Dimension      itsParentsSize;
0053      Point          itsLocation;
0054      Dimension      itsSize;
0055
0056        if ( showIt) {
0057           itsParentsLocation = itsParentWindow.getLocationOnScreen();
0058           itsParentsSize     = itsParentWindow.getSize();
0059           itsSize            = this.getSize();
0060           itsLocation        = new Point();
0061
0062           itsLocation.x = itsParentsLocation.x +
0063                           itsParentsSize.width/2 -
0064                           itsSize.width/2;
0065           itsLocation.y = itsParentsLocation.y +
0066                           itsParentsSize.height/2 -
0067                           itsSize.height/2;
0068          this.setLocation( itsLocation);
0069        } // End if.
0070        super.setVisible( showIt);
0071      } // End setVisible.
0072
0073      public void actionPerformed( ActionEvent event) {
0074         this.setVisible( false);
0075      } // End actionPerformed.
0076 } // End VersionDialog.
```

Chapter 8—The *TuttleSaveDialog* Class

```
0001  // Filename TuttleSaveDialog.java.
0002  // Supplies a dialog containing an exit/ yes/ no
0003  // question and sends ActionEvent if yes replied.
0004  //
0005  // Written for Java Interface book chapter 8.
0006  // Fintan Culwin, v 0.2, August 1997.
0007
0008  package MenuBarTuttle;
0009
0010  import java.awt.*;
0011  import java.awt.event.*;
0012
0013  class TuttleSaveDialog extends FileDialog {
0014
0015  private String          saveFilename = null;
0016  private String          saveDirname  = null;
0017  private Frame           itsParentFrame;
0018  private ActionListener  itsListener;
0019
```

```
0020    protected TuttleSaveDialog( Frame           parentFrame,
0021                                 ActionListener listener) {
0022       super( parentFrame, "Tuttle Save", FileDialog.SAVE);
0023       itsParentFrame = parentFrame;
0024       itsListener = listener;
0025    } // End TuttleSaveDialog constructor.
0026
0027
0028    public void setVisible( boolean showIt) {
0029
0030    String     tempDirname;
0031    String     tempFilename;
0032    Point      itsParentsLocation;
0033    Dimension itsParentsSize;
0034    Point      itsLocation;
0035    Dimension itsSize;
0036
0037       if ( showIt) {
0038          itsParentsLocation = itsParentFrame.getLocationOnScreen();
0039          itsParentsSize     = itsParentFrame.getSize();
0040          itsSize            = this.getSize();
0041          itsLocation        = new Point();
0042
0043          itsLocation.x = itsParentsLocation.x +
0044                          itsParentsSize.width/2 -
0045                          itsSize.width/2;
0046          itsLocation.y = itsParentsLocation.y +
0047                          itsParentsSize.height/2 -
0048                          itsSize.height/2;
0049          this.setLocation( itsLocation);
0050          this.setDirectory( "");
0051          this.setFile( "*.tutt");
0052
0053          saveFilename = null;
0054          saveDirname  = null;
0055
0056          super.setVisible( true);
0057
0058          tempFilename = this.getFile();
0059          tempDirname  = this.getDirectory();
0060          if ( ( tempDirname != null)) {
0061             saveDirname  = new String( tempDirname);
0062          } // End if.
0063          if ( ( tempFilename != null)) {
0064             saveFilename = new String( tempFilename);
0065             itsListener.actionPerformed( new ActionEvent( this,
0066                                          ActionEvent.ACTION_PERFORMED,
0067                                          "saveit"));
0068          } // End if.
0069       } else {
0070          super.setVisible( true);
```

```
0071              } // End setVisible.
0072
0073
0074     protected void setFullFilename( String filename,
0075                                     String dirname) {
0076          saveFilename = new String( filename);
0077          saveDirname  = new String(  dirname);
0078          itsParentFrame.setTitle( "Menu Bar Tuttle [" +
0079                                  saveDirname + saveFilename + "]");
0080      } // End setFullFilename.
0081
0082     protected void clearFullFilename() {
0083          saveFilename = null;
0084          saveDirname  = null;
0085          itsParentFrame.setTitle( "Menu Bar Tuttle ");
0086      } // End clearFullFilename.
0087
0088     protected boolean isFilenameAvailable() {
0089          return ( saveFilename != null);
0090      } // End isFilenameAvailable.
0091
0092     protected String filenameIs(){
0093          return new String( saveFilename);
0094      } // End filenameIs.
0095
0096     protected String fullFilenameIs() {
0097          return new String( saveDirname + saveFilename);
0098      } // End fullFilenameIs.
0099
0100     protected String dirnameIs() {
0101          return new String( saveDirname);
0102      } // End dirnameIs.
0103 } // End TuttleSaveDialog.
```

Chapter 8––The *TimeStamp* Class

```
0001  // Filename TimeStamp.java.
0002  // Providing a very minimal TimeStamp class.
0003  //
0004  // Written for JI Book Chapter 8.
0005  // Fintan Culwin, v 0.2, August 1997.
0006
0007
0008  import java.util.GregorianCalendar;
0009
0010  public class TimeStamp extends Object {
0011
0012  private static final int SECONDS_PER_MIN  = 60;
```

```
0013    private static final int SECONDS_PER_HOUR = SECONDS_PER_MIN * 60;
0014    private static final int INVALID_TIME    = -1;
0015    private int               theStamp       = INVALID_TIME;
0016
0017       public TimeStamp() {
0018          super();
0019          this.stamp();
0020       } // End TimeStamp constructor.
0021
0022       public TimeStamp( boolean toStampNow) {
0023          super();
0024          if ( toStampNow) {
0025             this.stamp();
0026          } // End if.
0027       } // End TimeStamp alternative constructor.
0028
0029
0030       public void stamp() {
0031
0032       GregorianCalendar now = new GregorianCalendar();
0033
0034          theStamp = ( now.get( GregorianCalendar.HOUROFDAY) *
                                                    SECONDS_PER_HOUR) +
0035                     ( now.get( GregorianCalendar.MINUTE)    *
                                                    SECONDS_PER_MIN)  +
0036                        now.get( GregorianCalendar.SECOND);
0037       } // End stamp.
0038
0039
0040       public int elapsed( TimeStamp anotherStamp) {
0041          if ( (anotherStamp.theStamp == INVALID_TIME ) ||
0042             (this.theStamp        == INVALID_TIME ) ){
0043            return INVALID_TIME;
0044          } else {
0045            return anotherStamp.theStamp - this.theStamp;
0046          } // End if.
0047       } // End elapsed.
0048
0049
0050       public String toString() {
0051
0052       StringBuffer theTime = new StringBuffer( "");
0053
0054          if ( theStamp != INVALID_TIME) {
0055
0056          int hours;
0057          int mins;
0058          int secs;
0059          StringBuffer theHours = new StringBuffer( "");
0060          StringBuffer theMins  = new StringBuffer( "");
0061          StringBuffer theSecs  = new StringBuffer( "");
```

```
0062                hours =  theStamp / SECONDS_PER_HOUR;
0063                theHours.append( hours);
0064                if ( theHours.length() == 1) {
0065                    theHours.insert( 0, "0");
0066                } // End if.
0067                secs  = theStamp % SECONDS_PER_MIN;
0068                theSecs.append( secs);
0069                if ( theSecs.length() == 1) {
0070                    theSecs.insert( 0, "0");
0071                } // End if.
0072                mins  = (theStamp - ( hours * SECONDS_PER_HOUR)) /
                                                        SECONDS_PER_MIN;
0073                theMins.append( mins);
0074                if ( theMins.length() == 1) {
0075                    theMins.insert( 0, "0");
0076                } // End if.
0077                theTime.append( theHours + ":" + theMins + ":" + theSecs);
0078            } else {
0079                theTime.append( "**:**:**");
0080            } // End if.
0081            return theTime.toString();
0082        } // End toString;
0083    } // End TimeStamp.
```

Terminology and Design Notations

Terminology

Object Oriented Design (OOD) and Object Oriented Programming (OOP) are interpreted by different developers, and different environments, in significantly different ways. For example, C++ implements a mechanism called *multiple inheritance* where a class can inherit resources from more than one parent class. Most other environments, including Java, regard this as potentially very confusing and only allow a class to inherit directly from a single parent class (*single inheritance*). In such environments some other mechanism, in Java the *interface* mechanism, is supplied to provide the benefits of *multiple inheritance* without any of the disadvantages.

This divergence between environments is compounded by differences in terminology. For example a *method* in Java and C++ is referred to as an *operation* in Unified Modeling Language (UML) and an *action* in Ada '95. Many of the terms used to describe Java are taken directly from C++ and have existing non-OOP connotations which are seen (by the author of this book) as potentially confusing and dangerous.

For example: the term *field* is used in C++ and Java to describe what is referred to in UML (and this book) as a *data attribute*. The term *field* is also used in non-OOP languages to denote a component part of a non-homogenous iterative structure known as a *record* (in C and C++ implemented as a `struct`). In these environments, there are no mechanisms which allow the component parts of a record to be hidden, and hence to only be made available outside the scope of the record by defined operations. Thus, a part of a program which can see the record can always see, and manipulate, all of its fields. This leads to the possibility of the component parts having their individual values changed in such a way as to make the aggregate value of the record inconsistent and so invalid.

One distinct advantage of OOP is to prevent this from happening. By encapsulating all data attributes within an object and only allowing them to be manipulated by defined operations, it can be guaranteed that the aggregate value of all data fields will always be valid.

A novice OOP developer who has already had experience of non-OOP programming will thus have a cognitive model of *fields* and *records*. By using the term *field* in an OOP environment, it implies directly that an *object* is in some way comparable to a *record*. This can, and does, lead to designs and implementations where *data attributes* are declared public by default; causing the encapsulation mechanism to be avoided and the advantages of information hiding lost.

To avoid problems of this nature, to facilitate communication between OO developers using different environments, and to allow an individual to transfer their knowledge and skills between environments a single set of agreed terms should be used. The most language-independent terms are those used in UML. The terminology used in this book is a combination of UML and that used in the 'Java White Paper', which is published by Sun to describe the Java language. Table C1 presents the terms used in this book where the Java and/or UML equivalents are significantly different

Design Notations

The design notations used in this book are UML (Unified Modeling Language) compliant. The highest level is a *class hierarchy* diagram, which shows the parent/ child relationships between a collection of classes. Figure C1 illustrates the general form of a class hierarchy diagram.

If the classes are collected together in a **package,** then the name of the package should be given at the top left of the diagram. An abstract class is shown with dotted lines and a generic class has the names of its generic parameters shown in a dashed lined box intercepting it at the top right. (There are no generic classes in this book.) Because the diagram may be used to illustrate the contents of a package any associated classes, or associated class hierarchies, can also be shown in the diagram.

As Used	Java White Paper	UML
resources	members	attributes
method	method	operation
data attribute	field	data attribute
manifest value	constant field	constant
instance attribute	variable field	instance attribute
class-wide attribute	class attribute	class-wide attribute

TABLE C1   Significant Differences in Terminology between this book, the Java White Paper, and UML

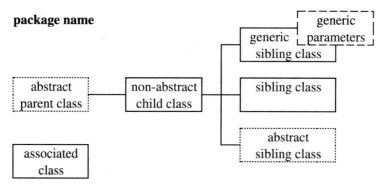

FIGURE C1 Class Hierarchy Diagram Summary

Each of the boxes in a class hierarchy diagram can be thought of as a scaled-down representation of its *class diagram*, the general form of which is shown in Figure C2.

At the top of the diagram, the parent/ child relationship is shown—if the parent is missing, then it is assumed that the class is extended from the Java Object class. If the parent's name is given in bold, then it indicates that a standard Java class is being extended. The child box contains the name of the class as its first line and may be accompanied by other lines, below it in a smaller font, giving other relevant information. The two most common pieces of information given are the **package** to which the class belongs and the **interface**s which it implements.

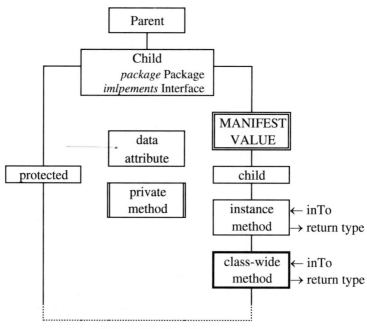

FIGURE C2 Class diagram summary.

Below it details of the class are given, any details crossing the right-hand side of the diagram are fully **public**, and those on the left have a restricted visibility. In this book this is always **protected** but Java also allows **private protected** attributes, which have a more restricted visibility. Anything shown inside the class diagram is **private**. It is expected that the class diagram will indicate all of its **public** and **protected** attributes, but need not show all of its **private** attributes. If a class diagram does not show all of its visible attributes, the bottom of the class diagram should be shown with dotted lines to indicate this.

Manifest values, with any visibility, are shown with a double lined box; all other **public** or **protected** attributes are assumed to be methods and are shown with single lined boxes. Any method with the same name as the class is a constructor. The full data flow *inTo* method, and its *return type* if not **void**, should always be shown and should not be considered optional. Class-wide, as opposed to instance, methods are shown in a heavy box. The **private** attributes can be data attributes or methods and their name should usually indicate which; however, to make it explicit, **private** methods are shown with doubled vertical lines on their boxes.

It is possible, though not shown in this book, for a class to contain one or more **private** classes. This would be implemented by the class source code file containing the additional class declarations without the visibility modifier **public**, following the public class declaration. These would be indicated as shown in Figure C3.

Full details of the contained class, such as its parent or its methods, need not be shown on this diagram as it only shows the containment relationship but should be given in the contained class's own class diagram.

Instance diagrams are used to illustrate the actual instances of the classes which are required for a particular artifact and also the relationships between them. The instances are shown in hexagonal boxes and will contain the name of the instance, if any, and its class. Each instance can have an *instance of* relationship shown, which links it to a class box and can be thought of as a scaled-down representation of its full class diagram. This is illustrated in Figure C4.

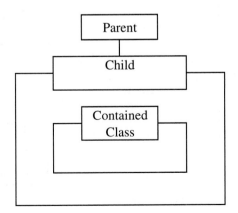

FIGURE C3   Class containment in a class diagram.

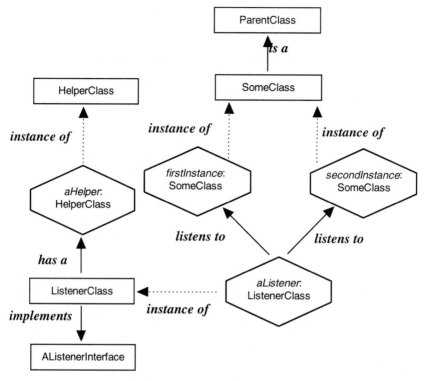

FIGURE C4   Instance diagram summary.

The diagram shows two instances of *SomeClass* called *firstInstance* and *secondInstance,* both of which are being listened to by an instance of the *ListenerClass* called *aListener. SomeClass* is shown as a child class of its *ParentClass*, as indicated by the *is a* relationship. The *ListenerClass* is shown as implementing the *AListenerInterface* and as containing (*has a*) an instance of the *HelperClass* called *aHelper.* The labels shown on the connecting relationships between class instances are arbitrary, and are intended to allow the full complexity of the inter-relationships to be expressed.

The final style of notation used in this book is a *State Transition Diagram* (STD) and is used to model the behavior of an interface over time as the user interacts with it and as the application responds to the interactions. The general form of a STD is shown in Figure C5.

The diagram shows a transition, labeled 1, from the initial state, shown as a solid circle, to *state1*. From this state: transition 6 will lead to a terminal state, shown as a bulls-eyed circle, or transition 2 will lead to *state2*. From *state2,* transition 3 leads to *state3* and transition 4 leads back from *state3* to *state2.* When transition 4 is taken, the dashed arrow leaving the diagram indicates that an event is generated from this interface. The rounded box bounding *state2* and *state3* indicates that from either of these states transition 5 can be taken, which will lead back to *state1*.

The double-lined transition (transition 7) from *state 3* to *state 4* indicates that multiple instances of *state 4* can occur within the same artifact, all of which exist con-

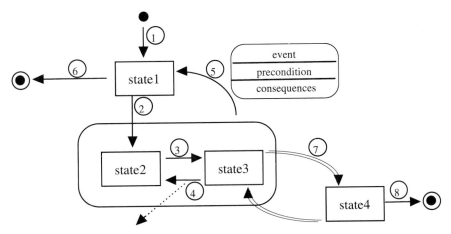

FIGURE C5   State Transition Diagram summary.

currently and all of which have their own transition (transition 8) to a terminal state. The unlabeled transition from *state 4* back to *state 3* is taken after each instance of *state 4* is created.

A transition is accompanied by an *event*, a *precondition,* and its *consequences.* In order for a transition to be taken, the *event* has to occur. The event can be generated by the user interacting with the interface, by the receipt of an event generated by another part of the interface, or by the application. When the *event* occurs, the *precondition* is tested and, if evaluates true, the transition is followed. As the transition is taken, any *consequences* including visible changes to the interface, the calling of methods in the application layer, or the dispatching of events are affected.

The *events, preconditions,* and *consequences* can be given alongside the transition, as shown with transition 6, or can be given in an associated table keyed by their transition numbers. The representation of the states can be nominal named representations or can be illustrations of how the interface will appear when it is in that state. A state in a user interface is defined as a location in the behavioral space of the interface that is functionally and visually distinct.

Index

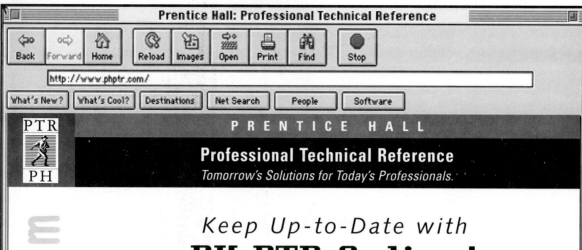